RADICAL PATHWAYS

RADICAL PATHWAYS

UNDERSTANDING MUSLIM RADICALIZATION IN INDONESIA

Kumar Ramakrishna

PRAEGER SECURITY INTERNATIONAL
Westport, Connecticut • London

Library of Congress Cataloging-in-Publication Data

Ramakrishna, Kumar.
  Radical pathways : understanding Muslim radicalization in Indonesia /
Kumar Ramakrishna.
    p.   cm.
  Includes bibliographical references and index.
  ISBN 978-0-313-37219-3 (alk. paper)
  1. Islamic fundamentalism–Indonesia–History.   2. Jihad.
  3. Islam–Indonesia.   4. Terrorism–Indonesia–Bali Island.   I. Title.
  BP63.I5.R29   2009
  320.5′5709598–dc22   2008047794

British Library Cataloguing in Publication Data is available.

Library of Congress Catalog Card Number: 2008047794
ISBN: 978–0–313–37219–3

First published in 2009

Praeger Security International, 88 Post Road West, Westport, CT 06881
An imprint of Greenwood Publishing Group, Inc.
www.praeger.com

Printed in the United States of America

The paper used in this book complies with the
Permanent Paper Standard issued by the National
Information Standards Organization (Z39.48–1984).

10 9 8 7 6 5 4 3 2 1

For Foo Kim Boon, who taught me that faith and reason can coexist

and

Ong Chit Chung, who showed me how to make this balance
real in our lives

Contents

Contents

Preface

At 12:15 A.M., Indonesian time, on November 9, 2008, three Javanese men, Imam Samudra, Mukhlas, and Amrozi, members of a clandestine Indonesian-based but transnational terrorist network called Jemaah Islamiyah (JI), were shot dead by firing squad on the prison island of Nusakambangan. The three had been on death row since 2003 for their roles in the horrific Bali nightclub attacks of October 12, 2002, that killed 202 people—mainly young Australians. The 2002 Bali attacks had demonstrated the determination of JI to wreak havoc against Western governments and their Southeast Asian allies—and seemingly reinforced the notion that Southeast Asia was the "Second Front" in the George W. Bush administration's Global War on Terror. To be sure, the Bali attacks compelled a previously complacent Indonesian government to take the threat of terrorism far more seriously. Since Bali, therefore, Jakarta, in concert with concerned regional governments, has devoted much attention and resources to neutralizing the JI network in Indonesia. Nevertheless, more than half a decade after that fateful evening in October 2002, it is clear that although JI in the Indonesian archipelago has been very much disrupted by concerted law enforcement activity, it is by no means finished. JI struck Jakarta in 2003 and 2004 and even hit Bali again in October 2005. Since then there has been a series of near-misses, with a much-improved Indonesian security apparatus thus far—as this book was going to press—proving adept at isolating and breaking up terror cells before they mount fresh attacks. The fact is that although the JI network in Indonesia has become heavily factionalized, it remains very much a significant threat because of one compelling factor: its ability to regenerate through the continuing radicalization of new recruits to the radical Islamist cause.

Hence the major purpose of the current volume is to lay bare this regeneration-through-radicalization process that has enabled an otherwise weakened JI to replenish its ranks and sustain an essential organic coherence despite intensified security force pressure. The key to this enterprise, in specific terms, is to better understand the various paths—the "Radical Pathways," so to speak—undertaken by more or less unremarkable men—like Imam Samudra, Amrozi, and Mukhlas—toward various degrees of violent radicalization in the Indonesian context. The volume does so by closely examining the diverse backgrounds and militant careers of several Javanese Muslims who have been associated with the JI movement—and who played some sort of direct or indirect role in the Bali atrocity of October 2002. In addition to the three executed militants identified earlier, we will also be studying in detail the lives and backgrounds of JI's putative spiritual leader Abu Bakar Ba'asyir; the senior operational leader Hambali; the Bali Cell foot soldier Ali Imron; and finally one of the two Bali suicide bombers, Arnasan.

A secondary purpose of the volume is to reinvigorate Southeast Asian terrorism scholarship in the face of a stream of criticism from Southeast Asian country specialists in particular. To be fair, these area scholars have on occasion been justified in criticizing extant Southeast Asian terrorism scholarship for a lack of detailed understanding of Southeast Asian histories and political cultures in general and the varieties of regional expressions of Islam in particular. It would be utterly mistaken, however, to entirely dismiss the contributions of terrorism specialists working on the region. Done well, terrorism studies can offer a more sophisticated, richer, and nuanced understanding of Southeast Asian militancy than most area scholars are willing to admit. Rather than throwing the baby out with the bathwater, therefore, what is needed is more rigorous and theoretically informed terrorism scholarship on Southeast Asia, including Indonesia. To this end, in uncovering the processes of violent radicalization of the JI militants responsible in various ways for the Bali attacks of October 2002, this volume will adopt a wide-ranging multidisciplinary approach. It will trawl the insights of disciplines ranging from Islamic philosophy, and the history and geopolitics of Islam in Indonesia, to cognitive, social, and evolutionary psychology, and cognitive neuroscience. The book will show how the dangerous and violent *Darul Islamist* ideology of the Bali bombers—as much a legacy of the old Darul Islam militant movement as more recent Global Jihad ideational currents—was certainly an important driver of the violent radicalization of the JI Bali Cell and its leaders. Hence this ideology is examined in detail. However, the book goes well beyond this, as ideological explanations in fact merely scratch the surface of a much more complex phenomenon. The key argument of this book is that the far more basic and primordial fear of identity group extinction was the true driver of the violent radicalization of the JI Bali Cell members and their leadership. The Radical Pathways or RP Framework employed in this work will demonstrate that the idiosyncratic and unique interaction of the three elements of the Framework—Existential Identity, Culture, and the Situated Individual Personality—in the lives of each JI member studied here generated what we may call *Existential Identity Anxiety*. This anxiety or fear of group extinction ultimately lay behind the October 2002 JI Bali attacks. In sum, this book pleads for an end to the current interdisciplinary conflict afflicting the study of Southeast Asian militancy and terrorism. It makes an impassioned call instead for intensified cooperation across the disciplines to generate the kind of integrated knowledge that is needed to counter the increasingly complex challenge of violent Muslim radicalization in Indonesia—and beyond.

I would like to thank the following colleagues, past and present, who have created the excellent, highly collegial, and stimulating intellectual atmosphere within the S. Rajaratnam School of International Studies that has greatly assisted me in shaping this book: Ang Cheng Guan, Rohan Gunaratna, Bernard Loo, Norman Vasu, Adam Dolnik, Beverley Loke, Hoo Tiang Boon, Joey Long, Joseph Liow, Tan See Seng, Ralf Emmers, Adrian Kuah, John Harrison, S. Harish, Ong Wei Chong, Manjeet Pardesi, Luenne Choa, and Leonard Sebastian deserve particular mention. I would also like to express my gratitude to my excellent team within the Centre of Excellence for National Security—Yvonne Lee, Yolanda Chin, Jennifer Yang, Ng Sue Chia, and Greg Dalziel—for all their hard work and support. The students I have taught in the Master of Science in Strategic Studies classes through the years have always been a source of great insight and enthusiasm and I have benefited tremendously from my intellectual exchanges with them. Special thanks go out to Lord John Alderdice, Ilan Mizrahi, Mark Woodward, Muhammad Haniff Hassan, Greg Dalziel, and Khong Yuen Foong for taking the time to read portions or all of the manuscript and for making extremely useful suggestions for improvement. I must go on record to express my personal intellectual debt to Greg Fealy, Tony Bubalo, Tito Karnavian, Noor Huda Ismail, Farish Noor, Al Chaidar, Mohamed Bin Ali, Bruce Hoffman, Andrew Silke, Frank Cilluffo, Greg Saathoff, Jean-Louis Tiernan, Katy Oh Hassig, Bill Durodie, Sally Neighbour, Sidney Jones, Marc Sageman, Bilveer Singh, James Veitch, David Heyman, Arnaud De Borchgrave, Tom Sanderson and Hekmat Karzai, who, in various direct and indirect ways, have inspired me to think through some of the issues discussed in this volume. Any omissions in this work are entirely my responsibility, not theirs. I must also thank the dedicated multinational analysts of the Global Futures Forum, who have done so much important work on the issue of violent radicalization, and whose contributions to policy knowledge on the issue should be acknowledged.

Barry Desker, Dean of the School, as well as Kwa Chong Guan, Sng Seow Lian, Lau Teik Soon, and Edwin Thumboo, have provided much encouragement and support through the years, and I am grateful for it. I must acknowledge as well Peter Ho, Head of the Singapore Civil Service, and Lee Ark Boon, Patrick Nathan, and Yeong Gah Hou of the National Security Coordination Secretariat in the Singapore Prime Minister's Office for being supportive of my research as well as my institutional duties and responsibilities. The President of the Republic of Singapore, SR Nathan, has long been a tremendous personal inspiration for both his commitment to excellence and deep humanity. I am most grateful to Tim Furnish, Mary Therese Church, and Amy Zelle of Greenwood, as well as Peter Katsirubas of Aptara, Inc. for steering this project through to completion with such great professionalism. In Singapore, Ian Pringle was instrumental in helping me—once again—get a book project off the ground, and I benefited much from conversations with Paul Kratoska on academic publishing for the policy community. I am grateful to my family and friends—particularly Koh Ho Kiat, Helena Koh, and Simon Wan—for their companionship and support through many years. To my wife Rosemary and children Joshua Luke, Jonathan, and Jordan Ling, I could never have done this without you. Last but not least, thanks be to God, who has always kept me steadfast in times of trial.

Kumar Ramakrishna

December 2008

Abbreviations

ARNO	Arakan Rohingya Nationalist Organization
ASEM	Asia-Europe Meeting
BRN	Barisan Revolusi Nasional (National Revolutionary Front, Southern Thailand)
DDII	Dewan Dakwah Islamiyah Indonesia (Islamic Propagation Council)
EIG	Egyptian Islamic Group
EIJ	Egyptian Islamic Jihad
FPI	Front Pembela Islam (Islamic Defenders Front)
GAM	Gerakan Aceh Merdeka (Free Aceh Movement)
GMIP	Gerakan Mujahidin Islam Pattani (Pattani Mujahidin Movement, southern Thailand)
GWOT	Global War on Terror
HTI	Hizbut Tahrir Indonesia (Indonesian Party of Liberation)
IAIN	*Institut Agama Islam Negeri* (National Academies for Islamic Studies)
ICG	International Crisis Group
ITB	Institut Teknologi Bandung (Bandung Institute of Technology)
JMA	Jemaah Mujahidin Anshorullah
KAMMI	Indonesian Muslim Student Action Union
KMM	Kumpulan Militan Malaysia/Kumpulan Mujahidin Malaysia (Malaysian Militant Group/Malaysian Mujahidin Group)

LIPIA	Institute for the Study of Islam and Arabic
LJ	Laskar Jihad
MILF	Moro Islamic Liberation Front (Mindanao, southern Philippines)
MMI	Majelis Mujahidin Indonesia (Indonesian Mujahidin Council)
NII	Negara Islam Indonesia (Islamic State of Indonesia)
NU	Nahdlatul Ulama (Renaissance of Islamic Scholars)
PK	Partai Keadilan (Justice Party)
PKI	Partai Komunis Indonesia (Indonesian Communist Party)
PKS	Partai Keadilan Sejahtera (Prosperity and Justice Party)
PSII	Partai Sarekat Islam Indonesia (Indonesian Islamic Party)
PULO	Pattani United Liberation Organization (PULO)
RM	Rabitatul Mujahidin (Mujahidin League)
RSO	Rohingya Solidarity Organization
STAIN	Sekolah Tinggi Agama Islam (State Islamic College)
TII	Tentara Islam Indonesia (Indonesian Islamic Army)
UI	University of Indonesia
UIN	National Islamic University
UTM	Universiti Teknologi Malaysia (University of Technology, Malaysia)

Prologue

Jalan Legian, Kuta District, Bali, October 12, 2002

The white Mitsubishi L-300 minivan ambled out of the garage of the house along Jalan Pulau Menjangan in Tabanan district in the popular Indonesian island resort of Bali. It was about 10:20 P.M. on October 12, 2002. Turning south, the L-300 headed at 40 kilometers an hour toward the tourist belt along the world-famous Kuta beach. Seated in the minivan were three young men from the island of Java; Ali Imron, from Lamongan, East Java, was driving the vehicle. Next to him was Arnasan, from Malimping, West Java, and furthest from Imron, next to the left door, was Feri, from Central Java. These three young men would have seemed altogether unremarkable to onlookers who cared to glance in their direction. The truth was far more sinister. These young Javanese—of whom Arnasan and Feri were poised to become suicide bombers within the hour—were part of a Cell comprising members of a clandestine terrorist network called Jemaah Islamiyah or JI. JI, whose alleged spiritual leader or *amir* at that time was a bespectacled, controversial cleric called Abu Bakar Ba'asyir, believed that the Islamic world was at war with a powerful, godless coalition of countries led by Israel and the United States, which stood accused of brutally oppressing Muslims in places such as Afghanistan, Chechnya, and Palestine. Committed to armed struggle or *jihad* against this putatively wicked "Jewish-Crusader alliance," JI sought the violent overthrow of pro–United States governments in Indonesia and Southeast Asia—and their replacement by a pan-regional Islamic caliphate. Tonight the JI Cell intended to strike back in spectacular fashion at Jewish, American, and other Western "infidels," for the L-300 was packed with more than a ton of explosives intended to kill and maim as many Westerners as possible. These explosives, comprising a highly combustible mixture of potassium chlorate, sulfur, and aluminum powder, as well as the L-300 vehicle itself, had earlier been purchased by Ali Imron's older brother, the vehicle mechanic Amrozi.[1] The explosives had been packed into twelve plastic filing cabinets in the back of the minivan and were set to be detonated later by Arnasan, who held a circuit board for this purpose, while next to him Feri held onto a specially constructed suicide vest packed with TNT and RDX.[2]

The targets had already been selected by Cell leader Imam Samudra, of Banten, West Java: the Sari Club and Paddy's Irish Bar, both sited diagonally across from each other along Jalan Legian in Kuta district. The hugely popular Sari Club had a large, covered dance floor flanked by thatched-roof bars, welcomed only foreign tourists, and that night was packed full of boozy young Westerners, mainly Australians, dancing the night away and flirting with equally inebriated young female tourists. Over at Paddy's Bar, a similar crowd of drunk and bare-chested young male tourists pranced to the loud dance music while enjoying the company of both foreign and local women. This latter point had earlier infuriated Samudra, who complained later that Bali was a place where "whiteys" engaged in "immoral acts" aimed at destroying "the virtue of Indonesian women."[3] Although he was the JI Bali Cell leader, Samudra was not actually acting on his own volition. The origins of the imminent Bali operation could be traced back to a February meeting that same year in Bangkok that had been hastily called following the thwarting by Singaporean authorities of a JI plot to attack American and Western diplomatic missions and commercial interests in that country in December 2001.[4] The Bangkok rendezvous had represented the JI leadership's first serious planning meeting in the wake of the attacks by the affiliated Al Qaeda network on New York and Washington, D.C. on September 11, 2001. In Bangkok, the charismatic Hambali, JI's chief strategist from Cianjur, West Java, discussed the difficulties of attacking heavily fortified U.S., Australian, and British embassies and agreed that seeking softer targets in Indonesia offered better prospects for success. Among other possibilities, the meeting, which also included the senior Malaysian JI operatives Dr. Azahari Husin, Noordin M. Top, and Wan Min Wan Mat—as well as Ali Imron's older brother, the hardened senior operative Mukhlas—fingered Bali nightspots as potential soft targets.[5] Samudra, as noted, later pinpointed Bali's Sari Club and Paddy's Bar as the sites that fulfilled the broad operational mandate Hambali laid down in February 2002.[6]

As the L-300 minivan turned into Jalan Legian on that fateful night of October 12, a nervous Ali Imron, who had been compelled to drive the vehicle, as both would-be suicide bombers Arnasan and Feri—country bumpkins from rural Java after all—could not drive, briefed the two silent young men on the final preparations for setting off the planned blasts. Imron then got out of the vehicle, and Arnasan, who could maneuver only in a straight line, slowly inched the minivan along the road packed with bumper-to-bumper traffic toward the Sari Club. According to some sources, Arnasan stopped the vehicle once he was abreast of the Sari Club, and Feri, who had by now donned his suicide bomb vest, got out, crossed the road, and entered Paddy's Bar, where by some accounts he quickly got into a heated exchange with a bargirl.[7] An American tourist who survived the blasts, David Greecy, was in Paddy's that night and recalled seeing Feri being accosted by young Australian male partygoers as well.[8] At any rate, just after 11:07 P.M., Feri detonated his bomb. There was a "split second, a flash and a roar, then the crashing of brick and wood and glass, flames and people screaming."[9] The shock of the blast in Paddy's compelled revelers in the Sari Club and other nearby bars to rush out to the street—as the JI Cell had hoped and where Arnasan sat silently in the L-300 minivan, cradling the active circuit board. At 11:08 and 23 seconds, Arnasan detonated the bigger vehicle bomb, and it seemed that "the whole world had exploded."[10] The bomb that obliterated the L-300 minivan and its occupant produced utter, hellish devastation all around as well. One local Balinese man who rushed to the scene later recounted:

> Everywhere I looked in the Sari Club, there were bodies. Some had been blown against the north wall and most were in a horrible condition....I carried some away, a person's head in one arm and an arm in the other....I will always remember this white lady. She had been cut by a piece of glass....I could see her heart beating through her chest....Then I saw her heart stop beating and she died in my arms. I closed her eyes with my hand and cried.[11]

Paddy's Bar survivor David Greecy suffered burns to 70 percent of his body in the blasts and described the resulting inferno as "like walking through the middle of the sun." Everywhere one could hear the sounds of *Beer Bintang* bottles popping from the intense heat. Broken glass and flames posed a constant threat to would-be rescuers and traumatized survivors alike. One eighteen-year old Balinese Muslim called Jafar, who was among the scores of locals who rushed to help the victims, spoke later of the smells of burnt flesh, wood, and plastics that mixed and mingled to awful effect. Jafar could not at first bring himself to carry out the mangled, blackened bodies and body parts and held a torchlight as other, braver souls did so. Eventually, the sheer scale of the task forced him to overcome his fears and assist in picking up dead victims and miscellaneous body parts. Horrifyingly, Jafar soon realized that one of the luckless victims—whose head had been sheared off by flying glass—had in fact been a relative. The scale of the carnage overwhelmed the local Balinese emergency services. Over at the local hospital, one survivor, Nigel Davenport, recounted that there was "no floor left, only blood." Due to the paralysis of the medical services, shocked rescuers were forced to carry victims to nearby hotels where the latter could immerse their hideously burned, charred bodies in the swimming pools to alleviate the intense pain. The horribly burned were the luckier ones. So badly obliterated were the remains of those who perished that next-of-kin had to rely on dental records for identification of deceased loved ones. Distraught parents—many of them Australian—who caught the first flights out from Australia to Bali found that they could not find their children among the piled-up bodies in the several makeshift morgues that had been hastily set up. Someone later described the scene at these morgues as akin to a "meat market." Even those blast victims who made it through that night relatively physically unscathed were not left unscarred psychologically. Some young Australians who returned home remained severely traumatized for six to eight weeks afterward; they could not stop their hands from shaking or muster the courage to step outside their homes.[12]

The sheer power of the Bali vehicle bomb created a crater 60 centimeters deep and four meters in diameter. Eyewitnesses spoke of seeing a big mushroom cloud, experiencing "strong air pressure from the source of the explosion," and of being able to hear the blast "within a radius of 25 kilometers,"[13] while pieces of the L-300 minivan were later found 500 meters away as well.[14] Moreover, blast fires scorched structures 100 to 200 meters away, while "ruined buildings" could be found as far as 400 meters from ground zero.[15] This is not to suggest, however, that the JI Bali Cell had achieved textbook technical success. As it turned out, only a third of the precursor chemicals in the L-300 minivan had exploded and the rest burned in a huge fireball. However, "in a sick twist," as Ken Conboy observes grimly, the physical configuration of the blast zone perversely *completed* the handiwork of the Cell. First, at the point of detonation of the L-300, the rapidly expanding blast waves hit the back wall of a partially constructed bank building across Jalan Legian from the Sari Club, as well as the big concrete walls at the back and sides of the Club's open dance floor. The net effect was that the blast waves were "contained, concentrated and reversed by the rear walls of the bank and the Sari Club in a deadly echo effect."[16] Worse, as the blast waves reverberated back from the back wall of the Club, its weak thatched roof collapsed on the packed dance floor, the thatch ignited, and patrons—already concussed and severely injured from the blast itself and resultant flying debris—were both trapped and burned alive. Witnesses told later of "howling, burning people with missing ears, missing limbs, missing skin, trapped behind walls of fire, unable to escape as they burned to death."[17] The compact area between the uncompleted bank and the Sari Club had been, in a sense, the perfect killing zone.[18] In the end, 202 people were confirmed killed, including 88 Australians. Three hundred and fifty others were wounded. In addition, 58 buildings were damaged and 19 cars and 32 motorcycles were destroyed.[19] Four years later, the pain of those affected by the Bali attacks remained palpable. One Australian girl who lost her brother in Bali posed a question during a television interview that was both harrowingly simple in conception and yet utterly vexing to answer: "Who do you blame? Governments? Culture? Individuals? Religion? Countries?"[20]

This volume represents one attempt to come to grips with this question. It seeks to unearth the forces—geopolitical, cultural, political, historical, psychological, and ideological, as the case may be—that combined to radicalize more or less ordinary Javanese Indonesians to such an extent that they were able to engage in the mass murder of people they had not even known personally. We intend to identify and trace, as much as possible given the available evidence, what we may call the *Radical Pathways* that led men from the simple, rural hinterlands of Java—such as suicide bomber Arnasan—to the fiery inferno that decimated Jalan Legian that hellish October night in Bali.

1

The Radical Pathways Framework

It should not be imagined that the JI attack in Bali on October 12, 2002, was an aberration. JI struck in Bali again three years later, on October 1, 2005, although this time the casualty count was relatively lower: nearly two dozen dead and more than one hundred wounded.[1] Almost seven years after the first Bali strikes and eight years after the September 11, 2001, Al Qaeda attacks in New York and Washington, DC, that killed about three thousand people, Southeast Asia remains widely regarded as the so-called Second Front in the Global War on Terror (GWOT).[2] There are reasons for the currency of this dubious appellation. Part of the planning by Al Qaeda elements for anti-American strikes, including the September 11 attack, was carried out by Al Qaeda elements in Kajang, Selangor State, Malaysia, in January 2000 with the assistance of elements of the JI Malaysian Cell.[3] JI itself, between the two Bali bombings of October 2002 and October 2005, executed attacks against the Jakarta Marriott in August 2003[4] and outside the Australian embassy in the same city in September 2004.[5] Although JI poses a serious transnational threat to Southeast Asian security, unfortunately it is by no means the only danger. A comprehensive survey of Southeast Asian militancy and terrorism also would have to include, *inter alia*, the Moro Islamic Liberation Front and the diabolical Abu Sayyaf Group in the southern Philippines; the Laskar Jihad, the Islamic Defenders Front (FPI), the Free Aceh Movement (GAM), and other assorted radical Islamist militant networks in Indonesia; the Kumpulan Mujahidin Malaysia (KMM) group that was linked to JI; and since January 2004, a host of resurgent Thai Muslim separatist groups, such as the Barisan Revolusi Nasional (BRN), Pattani Mujahidin Movement (GMIP), and Pattani United Liberation Organization (PULO) in the embattled Thai South.[6] The Al Qaeda- and JI-linked Abu Sayyaf Group, for example, together with the Rajah Solaiman Movement, demonstrated that it shared JI's ruthlessness when it bombed Superferry 14 in Manila Bay in February 2004, killing 116 people.[7] Southeast Asia's problem with militancy and terrorism is a real one, and policy makers in Washington, London, and elsewhere remain keenly aware that sea lines of communication vital to the health of global trade and the energy supply routes of major powers and key Western partners, such as Japan and South Korea, must traverse the archipelago. Hence instability, conflict, and loss of confidence engendered or exacerbated by a steadily worsening terrorism and militancy problem would have not merely local but global repercussions. The effects of terrorism and militancy in Southeast Asia in general, and of what JI can do to the biggest Southeast Asian country, Indonesia, in particular, matter—a great deal.[8]

MAKING SENSE OF SOUTHEAST ASIAN MILITANCY AND TERRORISM I: CONCEPTUAL, MORAL AND METHODOLOGICAL CHALLENGES

Conceptual Issues

For conceptual, moral, and methodological reasons, the study of Southeast Asian terrorism and militancy is not a straightforward task. Conceptually, it is well known that the term "terrorism" is both emotively charged and highly contested, and satisfactory, universally acceptable definitions of the phenomenon remain elusive. In 1937, the old League of Nations sought to forge an international consensus on the term "terrorism" to mean "all criminal acts directed against a State and intended or calculated to create a state of terror in the minds of particular persons or groups of persons or the general public." This attempt, however, was stillborn.[9] Its successor, the United Nations (UN), similarly has yet to agree on a universal definition of terrorism that would be the basis for the much-sought-after "comprehensive convention of terrorism which some countries favor in place of the present 12 piecemeal conventions and protocols."[10] In fact, the respected terrorism scholar Walter Laqueur warns that the UN may well not attain agreement on a single universal definition of terrorism.[11] There are good reasons for his pessimism. First of all, terrorism is an old and highly mutable phenomenon, and its nature and character have been changing across time and space. David Rapoport has argued that the world has in fact experienced four waves of terrorism in the modern era. The first wave, which lasted from the 1880s to the 1920s, saw groups employing violence to force civil and political reforms within autocratic political systems such as Czarist Russia. The long second wave, Rapoport observes, overlapped with the first, encompassed the 1920s to the 1960s, and was characterized by organizations such as Irgun in Palestine and the Irish Republican Army, which engaged in anticolonial violence in pursuit of national self-determination. The third wave, arising from the preceding nationalist surge and developing impetus in the 1970s before trailing off at the end of the 1980s, featured in the main left-wing revolutionary groups such as the Red Brigades and the Japanese Red Army Faction, which mounted violent attacks against the agents and supporters of Western market-capitalist governments, putatively on behalf of impoverished Third World masses regarded as entrapped in a world imperialist economic system of exploitation. The current wave, according to Rapoport, began really with the fall of the Shah of Iran in 1979, gathered momentum with the Soviet defeat in Afghanistan a decade later, and seemed to suggest that "religion now provided more hope than the prevailing revolutionary ethos did."[12] The respected American terrorism analysts Steven Simon and Daniel Benjamin concur, stating that the contemporary mode of terrorism is largely "religiously motivated."[13] Laqueur thus is on firm ground when he contends that modern definitions of terrorism may not be quite comprehensive enough to describe terrorist activity in 1850 or 1930— "just as a definition of democracy in ancient Greece would be of little help with regard to democracy in the modern world."[14]

The evolving, changing nature of terrorism is precisely why Laqueur argues that relatively common and seemingly unproblematic definitions such as that provided by Title 22 of the U.S. Code of Federal Regulations, which describes terrorism as "premeditated, politically motivated violence perpetrated against noncombatant targets by subnational groups or clandestine agents, usually intended to influence an audience," remain, on closer analysis, sadly lacking. First, terrorist violence may no longer be only politically motivated, but may be driven, as the current UN "academic consensus definition" derived from the work of the Dutch terrorism expert Alex P. Schmid suggests, by "idiosyncratic" or "criminal" motives as well.[15] Second, terrorist groups today attack not only "noncombatants" but also the military and police. Merely confining the victims of terrorism to the singular category of noncombatant civilians "may not be very helpful in the real world."[16] For instance, if terrorism does not include attacks on combatants, then the bomb attack that killed nineteen U.S. soldiers who not only were *not at war*, but were merely *sleeping* in a military housing complex in Dhahran, Saudi Arabia, in June 1996 would not be seen as an act of terrorism—and this assertion would be contested by many observers.[17] Third, the suggestion in the U.S. Code that terrorism is carried out only by "subnational groups or clandestine agents" also is problematic. This is where the old sophism "one man's terrorist is another man's freedom fighter" comes into play. On one hand, the Organization of the Islamic Conference (OIC), at the end of its summit in Kuala Lumpur in April 2002, declared that the definition of terrorism should not include "resistance to foreign aggression and the struggle of peoples under colonial or alien domination and foreign occupation for national liberation and self-determination."[18] This line of thinking thus would regard subnational groups and clandestine agents engaged in, for example, suicide attacks against foreign U.S. or British troops occupying Iraq to be freedom fighters engaged in national liberation and not terrorists—a stance that both Washington and London would contest. Alternately, one also could make the argument that not only clandestine actors and non-state groups engage in terrorism; governments are equally capable of doing so. After all, Edward Peck, a former Deputy Director of the White House Terrorism Task Force during the Reagan Administration, candidly concedes that if by "international terrorism" one means activities that "appear to be intended to affect the conduct of a government by mass destruction, assassination or kidnapping," then certainly "a number of countries" were "involved in such activities," including both the United States and Israel. This prompted him to admit that "the terrorist, of course, is in the eye of the beholder."[19]

Finally, the evolving nature of terrorism has required modern analysts to reconsider the famous aphorism by Brian Michael Jenkins that "terrorists want a lot of people watching, not a lot of people dead."[20] In previous waves of terrorism, militant organizations did indeed seek to employ frequently extreme acts of violence to influence an audience—a very old idea that animated the ranks of nineteenth-century Russian and European anarchists and social revolutionaries. For instance, the Italian anarchist Carlo Pisacane argued that "intellectual propaganda" is an "empty gesture" and great ideas always emanate from "deeds."[21] Agreeing, the Russian Prince and anarchist Peter Kropotkin held that "deeds that attract general attention" could do far "more propagandizing in a few days than do thousands of leaflets."[22] These intellectual currents played a part in compelling the French radical Paule Brousse to coin the famous phrase "propaganda of the deed."[23] However, the current wave of religiously motivated, mass-casualty terrorism exemplified by the September 11 attacks suggests that terrorism today no longer should be seen merely as propaganda of the deed, deliberately calibrated to influence an audience to behave in ways the terrorists desire. The so-called "new terrorism" seems intended not so much to influence but rather to *punish* "godless" governments and civilian populations deemed apostate and deserving of divinely sanctioned mass destruction. Simon and Benjamin capture this succinctly in their assessment of Al Qaeda's motivations for perpetrating the September 11, 2001, atrocity:

> [T]he motivation for the attack was neither political calculation, strategic advantage, nor wanton bloodlust. It was to humiliate and slaughter those who defied the hegemony of God; it was to please Him by reasserting His primacy. It was an act of cosmic war. What appears as senseless violence

actually made a great deal of sense to the terrorists and their sympathizers, for whom this mass killing was an act of redemption.[24]

In short, when one considers the fourth wave of modern, religiously motivated terrorism, it would seem that the terrorists want a lot of people dead *and* lots of people watching as well. The new terrorism fundamentally remains, as Bruce Hoffman notes, a form of "psychological warfare" designed to inflict "unbridled fear, dark insecurity and reverberating panic."[25] What is novel, however, about the current fourth wave is that the levels of lethality and destructiveness that the new, religiously driven terrorists are prepared to inflict are simply unprecedented.[26] The grisly, mass-casualty Bali attacks of October 2002 fit squarely into this mold.

There are thus significant conceptual dilemmas associated with the constantly mutating phenomenon of "terrorism": whether it should encapsulate violence committed for political reasons only; if it should include violence committed against combatants as well as noncombatants; and whether certain violent acts undertaken by states could also be considered "terrorist." Finally, there is a steadily closing conceptual gap between "acts of terrorism" and "acts of war"[27] arising from the increasing lethality of the new, apocalyptic, religiously motivated terrorism—the threat of chemical, biological, radioactive, or nuclear (CBRN) terrorism would be a primary example.[28] This suggests that perhaps a search for an all-encompassing, one-size-fits-all definition of terrorism that would be universally and legally applicable across time and space is ultimately self-defeating. This should not, however, prevent us from bluntly and honestly acknowledging that the JI attack on Bali was indeed a "terrorist" act and the individuals who composed the Bali Cell "terrorists." It is a basic and irreducible fact that *violence was committed for instrumental purposes against defenseless innocents that fateful evening.*

Nevertheless, it is important to avoid being drawn into fruitless quests to pin down a universal definition of terrorism, as such attempts only constitute a huge red herring. Jenkins remains utterly correct that people "reasonably familiar with the terrorist phenomenon will agree 90 percent of the time about what terrorism is, just as they will agree on democracy or nationalism," simply because, as Laqueur adds, despite the futility of pinning down a "scientific, all-comprehensive definition," terrorism "is an unmistakable phenomenon."[29] The key is to bypass arid, universalizing definitional debates and instead analyze the mutable terrorism phenomenon in its *temporally limited as well as geographically and culturally localized manifestations.* Jonathan Drummond concurs, recommending a "culturally contextualized" approach to the study of terrorism.[30] Similarly, Michael Stevens observes that because "terrorism and terrorists are found in a wide array of cultures," it is incumbent on analysts to "place manifestations and perpetrations of terrorism within specific cultural contexts" to "minimize stereotyped representations."[31] Accordingly, rather than split hairs over whether to call the JI Bali Cell "terrorists" or "militants," we will focus on identifying *what motivated them* to participate, in varying degrees of directness, in the Bali atrocity in the first place. From this perspective, employing the terms "terrorism" and "militancy" interchangeably becomes less controversial and no longer detracts from the key object of our enterprise—to contextualize, as suggested by Drummond and Stevens. Hence this study seeks to embark on a systematic, theoretically informed, "bottom-up" or contextualized analysis of the processes by which key individuals who emerged from the Javanese sociocultural milieu ultimately formed the JI Cell that perpetrated the October 2002 Bali attacks.

Moral and Methodological Issues

A second set of issues that has confounded the systematic study of Southeast Asian terrorism and militancy has been moral and methodological. The moral issue is a particularly problematic one. A common concern among many observers is that seeking to understand and explain the terrorism phenomenon is tantamount to excusing it at some level. This anxiety is not unfounded. In experiments designed to "explore the exonerating effects of explanations," American social psychologists have found that "a variety of cognitive and affective processes" work to "produce a relatively condoning attitude toward perpetrators as a result of explaining their actions."[32] These studies suggest that academic work in the form of social psychological analysis runs "the risk of reducing the perceived intentionality and responsibility attributed to perpetrators."[33] Little wonder that some studies of terrorism motivations tend to be extremely self-conscious. Drummond, for instance, makes it a point to remind readers that they "should not mistake empathy or an intense attempt to understand" why terrorists committed a particular atrocity "with sympathy or excusal."[34] Similarly, psychiatrist John E. Mack spills a fair bit of ink pointing out that in seeking to understand the causes of terrorism, he is "not excusing or lending legitimacy whatsoever to aggression."[35] The author of this volume personally experienced this tendency to conflate explanations of terrorism with excusal. At a May 2004 seminar in Bangkok for journalists covering conflict zones, held, significantly, two months after the Madrid train bombings,[36] the author found himself severely chastised by a Spanish journalist for appearing to condone terrorism in the process of seeking to explain it. There is no need, however, to believe that perpetrators of atrocities should be morally exculpated simply because their behavior can be explained. Social psychologist James Waller argues in this connection that perpetrators are never "just the hapless victims of human nature or their social context," and retain "full moral and legal accountability for the atrocities they committed."[37] In analyzing the various pressures and forces that led the JI Bali Cell to commit the atrocity of October 12, 2002, it would be crucial to heed Waller's injunction to understand that evil without at the same time condoning it. In fact, the notion that to "understand is not to forgive" is not new and has been addressed by philosophers such as Kant, Hume and Sartre, among others.[38]

The moral issues overlay significant questions of methodology as well. In essence, seeking an understanding of what made certain members of the JI network engage in the terrorist atrocity at Bali requires answers to two key questions: first, what made these individuals decide to join the network in the first place? Second, what forces enabled some in the Bali Cell to subsequently kill their victims—and in the case of the suicide bombers, themselves at the same time? The first major roadblock one encounters is the inability to actually get to the militants themselves, as not all of them are readily available for interviews by researchers. This is a genuine problem. Andrew Silke, a leading forensic psychologist and terrorism researcher, has expressed concern that analysts who have had "extensive, personal contact" with terrorists tend to arrive at different assessments of the motivations of such individuals than do other researchers who do not have similar access and instead have to rely on "secondary sources" such as "newspapers and magazines."[39] In fact, Silke hints that "any explanation not backed by direct examination of terrorists" amounts to "little more than idle speculation."[40] This position assumes, of course, that "up-close-and-personal," face-to-face contact is possible with militants, which unfortunately is not the case. Often the researcher "has to work without access to much important information."[41] Within the JI milieu, for example, although spiritual leader Abu Bakar Ba'asyir has been relatively accessible to researchers and made numerous public pronouncements to publicize his prognostications,[42] JI militants similar to Hambali and Imam Samudra may not be available to talk until they are captured—and then only if the authorities give researchers access to them. This is not always possible because of operational security reasons. Hambali, for instance, was not permitted to talk to Indonesian security officials let alone to other researchers following his capture in August 2003 and his rendition into U.S. custody.[43]

On the other hand, security agencies may well *agree* to grant researchers restricted and conditional access to detained militants, but this creates different sorts of problems. In particular, researchers who appear to have cultivated a good relationship with security agencies may then be vilified in some quarters as being overly identified with and promoting a specific agenda associated with "major funding bodies, governmental agencies, and other centers of state power."[44] Such researchers, Natasha Hamilton-Hart warns, are vulnerable to the schemes of nefarious "officials to disseminate information that is either less than complete or outright disinformation."[45] In like vein, David Martin Jones and Michael L. R. Smith charge—not very fairly—that academic scholarship in Singapore and other Southeast Asian states has been "de-intellectualized by the pervasive influence of the authoritarian Southeast Asian developmental state which blurred the distinction between scholarship and bureaucracy."[46] To put it mildly, the task of the Southeast Asian terrorism analyst is particularly challenging. Compounding matters further is that it may not always be even *legal* to approach active militants who are willing to talk. The well-known Australian sociologist Riaz Hassan, who received an Australian Research Council grant for a study on suicide terrorism worldwide, had planned to interview elements of the leadership and rank and file of Hezbollah in Lebanon, Hamas in the Palestinian territories, the Egyptian Islamic Jihad, Lashkar-e-Toiba in Pakistan, the Tamil Tigers in Sri Lanka, and—not least—JI in Indonesia. He was compelled to significantly modify his research plans, however, after being warned by Canberra's attorney general in September 2006 that he may be in breach of antiterror laws governing consorting with people belonging to these groups or their "military wings" who happen to be considered "terrorist organizations by the federal government."[47] The point is that although Silke does have a valid observation concerning the utility of face-to-face interviews with militants, this may not always be possible for even the most eager researchers. Cognizant of these difficulties, this study takes to heart Hamilton-Hart's comment that information gleaned from "official sources is not necessarily inaccurate but does demand interpretation and cautious handling."[48] Accordingly, this work employs biographical information on the backgrounds of key individuals and militants associated with JI and its Bali Cell, compiled from a combination of sources that have been cross-checked in attempt to ensure factual accuracy as much as possible. These sources range from authoritative secondary works such as the International Crisis Group Jakarta office reports; works by journalists with excellent access to Indonesian police records and contacts, such as Sally Neighbour and Ken Conboy; Indonesian police interrogation and other reports on JI and the Bali bombing obtained by the author himself; and personal interviews with qualified Muslim scholars and other Indonesian analysts who are very familiar with the JI network and its key leaders.[49]

The thorny issues associated with gaining access to militants and their statements represent only one conundrum facing the Southeast Asian terrorism researcher. Even if access and other relevant information are made available, can the combination of factors that prompted the individual to play some part in a terrorist atrocity ever be accurately and exhaustively pinpointed? In Harper Lee's classic novel *To Kill a Mockingbird*, Atticus Finch observes, "You never know the person until you jump into their skin and walk around in it."[50] This pithy observation applies with full force to any study of terrorism motivations. Yet to jump into the skin of a terrorist and walk around in it is an exceedingly difficult enterprise, compelling historians, political scientists, and sociologists to look beyond their disciplinary silos to engage the assistance of psychologists and social psychologists. As eminent terrorism scholar Martha Crenshaw assures us, "It is difficult to understand terrorism without psychological theory, because explaining terrorism must begin with analyzing the intentions of the terrorist actor."[51] While this volume readily accepts the necessity of a psychological approach to the study of terrorism motivations, it does not go as far as do some observers to suggest that such a study best be left to professional psychologists and/or social psychologists. Political economist Hamilton-Hart, for instance, appears to dismiss the work of non-psychologists in attempting to address the issue of terrorism motivations, taking as a given that "amateur psychologists" really "cannot" possess "anything like the kind of data criminologists rely on to develop models of deviant behavior."[52] She overstates her case, frankly. It is not unknown for historians, for instance, to draw upon social psychology in their own studies of past events. The historian Christopher R. Browning drew upon the work of social psychologists Stanley Milgram and Philip Zimbardo in his well-known examination of the mass killing activities of the Nazi Reserve Police Battalion 101 in World War Two in Poland.[53] On the other hand, social psychologists like Neil J. Kressel, psychologists like Alan C. Elms, and psychiatrists such as Willard Gaylin have drawn extensively upon historical episodes and/or personalities to illustrate key psychological processes.[54] Elms, for his part, does not appear to endorse Hamilton-Hart's apparent myopic preference for hermetically sealed-off disciplinary boundaries. He concedes that good "psychobiographies" have been composed by "psychoanalytically inspired political scientists, historians, and literary scholars" and suggests that the "personal qualities" needed to become "a decent psychobiographer" can be discovered "in any field": in particular, "a controlled empathy for the subject and a devotion to collecting solid biographical data."[55] In a similar vein, the historian Browning eschews disciplinary parochialism, urging instead the importance of "multicausal interpretations based on multidisciplinary scholarship" in the study of genocide and mass killing, a broad rubric that of course includes terrorism.[56] There is also the pragmatic reality, according to the eminent Harvard sociobiologist E. O. Wilson, that most "of the issues that vex humanity daily—ethnic conflict, arms escalation, overpopulation, abortion, environment, and endemic poverty," simply "cannot be solved without integrating knowledge from the natural sciences with that of the social sciences and humanities."[57] The multidimensional challenge of religiously motivated militancy and terrorism would fit easily into Wilson's partial list. Wilson argues persuasively that only "fluency across the boundaries will provide a clear view of the world as it really is, not as seen through the lens of ideologies and religious dogmas or commanded by myopic response to immediate need."[58] Wilson thus calls for an interdisciplinary approach to the study of pressing global problems, resulting in—to use a word coined by nineteenth-century philosopher William Whewell—"consilience" or a "jumping together of knowledge."[59] The current study thus remains on extremely, and quite unapologetically, firm ground in seeking a multicausal analysis, based on multidisciplinary scholarship, of the Radical Pathways (RP) that led the JI militants from rural West Java to Bali.

MAKING SENSE OF SOUTHEAST ASIAN MILITANCY AND TERRORISM II: THE EXTANT LITERATURE CRITIQUED

This volume is merely the latest of a series of attempts to make sense of the broad issue of Southeast Asian militancy and terrorism. One helpful, regional overview of the problem was generated by the Rand analyst Peter Chalk, who identifies "insensitivity to local concerns, regional neglect, military repression and the contemporary force of militant Islam" as the prime reasons for the rise of "ethno-religious unrest" and "separatism" in southern Thailand, southern Philippines, and Aceh.[60] Another broad survey positing that Muslim militancy in Southeast Asia is less a product of "primordialist" religious identity factors and more the result of "situationalist" pressures arising from "economic deprivations, unequal patterns of development and fragile democratic institutions" has been provided by the political scientist Syed Serajul Islam.[61] In recent years, useful edited volumes providing insight into the complex, multifaceted threat of terrorism to regional stability have become available.[62] Specifically, the transnational JI network itself has received much attention: analysts such as Rohan Gunaratna, Zachary Abuza, Maria Ressa, Bilveer Singh, and particularly the well-respected Sidney Jones of the Jakarta office of the International Crisis Group (ICG) have produced useful works that trace the origins and nature of the wide-ranging personal, logistical, financial, and ideological connections between JI militants in Indonesia and other groups in Malaysia, Singapore, and the Philippines, as well as underscore the catalytic impact of both the Afghanistan war in the 1980s and the historic Darul Islam movement in Indonesia.[63] Solid journalistic accounts by Ken Conboy, Sally Neighbour, Mike Millard, and Tracy Dahlby have also appeared that, *inter alia*, provide much useful detail on key JI and for that matter other figures—ranging from liberal Muslims to radical Islamists—not just in Indonesia but elsewhere in the region.[64] For their part, area studies scholars such as Greg Fealy, Greg Barton, and Anthony Bubalo have produced excellent studies of the evolution of JI's own ideological outlook against the wider backdrop of political Islam in the Indonesian archipelago and the extent to which the outlook of senior JI leaders was shaped by local Darul Islam traditions, as well as by later intellectual currents from the Middle East.[65] More recently, the theoretically informed area studies scholar John T. Sidel has produced a commendable study that, among other things, attempts to situate the JI phenomenon within a wider theoretical framework that seeks to explain religious violence in Indonesia as the product of an existential fear of a loss of religious identity.[66] Sidel argues for a macro-level analysis that eschews "actor-centered" explanations of religious violence, including terrorism, in Indonesia in favor of the "powerfully determining effects of historical and sociological context."[67] The macro-level contributions of area studies scholars are certainly helpful. Carl Thayer is right in asserting that through "their knowledge of regional languages," the "country studies" scholars can provide "deeper insights into the history, politics, culture, religious values, and societies they are studying," enabling critical distinctions to be made between "al-Qaeda affiliates and autonomous local groups" and avoiding the disadvantageous lumping together in the "same analytical basket" of these entities.[68]

Nevertheless, although the area studies scholarship is essential to our understanding of Southeast Asian militancy and terrorism, it would be folly to imagine that scholars with "regional expertise," who are able to "provide a counterbalance to the studies that have focused narrowly on terrorist links and activities,"[69] also can provide the final word on the issue of terrorism *motivations*. They simply cannot, precisely because of the macro-level analyses that they tend to adopt in the main. Although Sidel, for instance, is correct to draw attention to the "powerfully determining effects of historical and sociological context," the fact remains that not everyone exposed to such forces becomes a terrorist. The reasons why some did and others did not compel us to return to the *micro-level of the actor and his or her immediate social group*. Even if the historical and sociological contexts create "certain shared goals and orientations," observes terrorism scholar Walter Reich, "individual terrorists, the groups to which they belong, and ultimately the communities from which those groups arise, are not necessarily alike in their psychological characteristics."[70] This is another reason why a bottom-up analysis of the motivational profiles of the JI Bali Cell and its leaders will be preferred in our current study. The aim here must be to "take special care to identify the individuals and groups whose behaviors" are being studied, "limit" explanations "to those individuals and groups," and avoid "over-generalization."[71] In sum, this volume maintains that the best way to generate an adequate understanding of Southeast Asian militancy and terrorism is through a detailed, bottom-up analysis—employing a multidisciplinary, multicausal approach—of a particular Southeast Asian terrorist network that has significant cross-border operational potential, and whose ideological leanings legitimize mass-casualty terrorism. This is why this volume opts to study the Indonesian JI, which has demonstrated both the attributes of a transnational agenda and a mass-casualty outlook.

This focus on JI is important for other reasons. Despite repeated arrests or elimination of its top leaders and rank and file—such as the June 2007 twin arrests of JI's senior military commander Abu Dujana and new *amir* Zarkasih, a big blow to the network, no doubt—JI retains the ability to radicalize fresh cohorts of young Indonesian Muslims. The capacity of JI to regenerate itself cannot be underestimated. Sidney Jones, perhaps the most authoritative commentator on JI today, argued soon after the arrests of Dujana and Zarkasih that it was "important to look beyond the leaders" and to "look at the base" of the network,[72] and two months later she reiterated that JI's "ideology now has deep roots in the region and you can't say the danger is over."[73] Jones' comments legitimize a major argument of this book: although *counter-terrorist* strategies privileging "hard" law enforcement measures, such as killing or capturing terrorists, cutting terror financing, imposing tighter border and immigration controls, harnessing technological solutions, and disrupting flows of arms and explosives material, are important for *mitigating* the real-time physical threat of terrorism, they do nothing to *neutralize* the underlying conditions that give rise to the threat in the first place. In short, the short-term, here-and-now focus of counter-terrorist strategies is necessary but incomplete. These badly need complementing by broader, much more creative *counter-terrorism* approaches that seek to *undercut, disrupt, and even reverse the radicalization processes* by which relatively ordinary people become transformed into fully indoctrinated militants, committed to using violence to further their aims.[74] This is where this current volume comes into the picture. It will seek to explain the complex radicalization processes—the Radical Pathways—within a terrorist network driven by a religiously inspired ideology—in this case, JI. To this end, the remainder of this chapter will focus on constructing a framework for understanding such radicalization processes. The basic elements of the framework will then be systematically applied in succeeding chapters to draw out the important motivational factors driving key JI militants and leaders who were involved directly or indirectly in the Bali attacks. At this juncture, it may be worth setting out the central organizing idea that this volume shall adopt and defend: that ultimately, religiously inspired and legitimated terrorist violence is the product of an *amplified sense of Existential Identity Anxiety.*

THE EMERGING IMPORTANCE (TO TERRORISM STUDIES) OF GEERT HOFSTEDE

We begin our analysis, perhaps counterintuitively, with an examination of the ideas of a researcher who is not usually associated with the study of terrorism: the Dutch social psychologist Geert Hofstede. Hofstede has been extremely influential in the development of the relatively young field of cross-cultural psychology.[75] In the late 1960s and early 1970s, Hofstede was part of a team of researchers employed by the U.S. information technology giant IBM to conduct morale and value surveys of the company's employees in more than 70 countries worldwide. This massive research project resulted in the accumulation of 116,000 responses, enabling Hofstede to conduct "extensive analyses of these data," which he eventually published in 1980 in his classic text *Culture's Consequences.*[76] Hofstede's study proved very interesting. Because these multinational IBM employees worked in "almost perfectly matched" jobs in their respective national domains, "the effect of nationality differences in their answers" to the value survey questions stood out "unusually clearly."[77] Hofstede found that that there was in fact considerable empirical backing for the classic 1954 finding of two U.S. researchers, the sociologist Alex Inkeles and psychologist Daniel Levinson, that *all* societies faced the four following challenges:[78]

- social inequality, including the relationship with authority;
- the relationship between the individual and the group;
- concepts of masculinity and femininity: the social and emotional implications of having been born as a boy or a girl; and
- ways of dealing with uncertainty and ambiguity, linked somewhat to the control of aggression and emotional expression.

Very importantly, the national cultural differences identified in Hofstede's original IBM research findings were generally replicated by surveys done by other researchers working with non-IBM staff as well. The Israeli psychologist Shalom H. Schwartz compiled a list of 56 putatively universal values based on a cross-national survey of the available relevant literature. He then surveyed the attitudes of college students in fifty-four countries and elementary school teachers in fifty-six countries regarding these values and in a 1994 publication reported that cross-national comparisons could be made according to seven dimensions: "conservatism, hierarchy, mastery, affective autonomy, intellectual autonomy, egalitarian commitment, and harmony." There were "significant correlations" between Schwartz's country scores and Hofstede's IBM scores.[79] Another well-known multinational survey by U.S. political scientist Ronald Inglehart, the World Values Survey, commenced in Europe in the 1980s and today spans the world. It comprises a set of coordinated opinion surveys repeated every few years and draws upon "representative national populations."[80] Inglehart identified "two dimensions of variation across nations,"[81] namely, well-being versus survival and secular-rational versus traditional authority.[82] The World Values Survey correlated well with Hofstede's IBM results, particularly those that highlighted national differences in popular attitudes toward social inequality and the place of the individual in the wider society.[83]

Another 1987 study, by Michael Bond in Hong Kong, should be mentioned, as it was a conscious attempt to see to what extent Hofstede's research had been biased by its "Western origins." Bond asked a group of Chinese scholars to identify values that were important in Chinese society and then used these values as a basis for a survey that was administered to university students in twenty-three countries. Bond generated nation-level scores for each country and found correlations with the Hofstede dimensions that emphasized national polarities in popular attitudes toward social inequality as well as the status of the individual in relation to the wider society.[84] Yet another 1996 study of the values of organizational employees in forty-three countries by Dutch business consultant Fon Trompenaars and the British psychologists Peter Smith and Shaun Dugan found support for "two principal dimensions of variation," the first comparing "individuals whose involvement in their organization was based on loyalty and those whose involvement was more utilitarian." The second dimension of polarity compared conservative with more egalitarian values. Again, these findings suggested general support for Hofstede's research conclusions.[85] The recognition, validated by cross-cultural research involving both IBM and other databases, that all societies, whether Western, Asian, African, Arab, or other, had to cope with common basic problems compelled Hofstede to fine-tune and develop several dimensions of national culture over time. In order to do justice to the Hofstede formulation and in the process elucidate its relevance to our task in this book, it is well worth carefully unpacking his understanding of "culture":

> Every person carries within him- or herself patterns of thinking, feeling and potential acting that were learned throughout their lifetime. Much of it has been acquired in early childhood, because at that time a person is most susceptible to learning and assimilating.... Using the analogy of the way computers are programmed [we can] call such patterns of thinking, feeling and acting *mental programs*.... The sources of one's mental programs lie within the social environments in which one grew up and collected one's life experiences. The programming starts within the family; it continues within the neighborhood, at school, in youth groups, at the workplace, and in the living community.[86]

Hofstede goes on to define "culture" as the "collective programming of the mind that distinguishes the members of one group or category of people from others."[87] He adds that the idea of culture as "mental software" is the understanding preferred by sociologists and anthropologists.[88] Other researchers concur, pointing out that rather than focus on a single individual's "values, beliefs, or other attributes," it is analytically more useful to study the extent to which "nations can be characterized by sets of shared beliefs, meanings or mentalities."[89]

It should be noted that culture exists for a good reason: it represents an *evolutionary* adaptation of a people to their environment. Gelfand, Nishii, Raver, and Lim have in recent years explained that, at the structural, systemic level:

> Certain ecocultural and historical factors create an increased need for predictability and coordinated social action within cultures. For example, factors such as high population density, lack of natural resources, extreme temperatures, and/or a history of external threat are associated with the

need to create social structures, to facilitate order and coordinated action with the social environment.[90]

Accordingly, these ecological, systemic factors strongly shape the *structure of situations* that comprise the cultural context of a geographical locality. Some ecological constraints create so-called "strong situations," while other environments foster "weak situations." Gelfand and colleagues again:

> Strong situations create order and coordinated social action by having many clearly defined norms wherein there are a limited number of behavioral patterns that are acceptable, and by increasing the propensity for censuring inappropriate (deviant) behavior. By contrast, weak situations have few clearly defined norms, permit a wide range of acceptable behavior, and afford much latitude for individuals' behavioral choices.[91]

The point of all this is simple: individuals in cultural systems are "socialized to develop social psychological characteristics" that are necessary to enable them to "function effectively within the typical situations that characterize their cultural group."[92] Hence individuals within societies facing "high situational constraint" would be socialized from youth to have several key characteristics: first, "a greater need for structure, greater impulse control and conscientiousness, and a greater concern for sanctioning of inappropriate behavior as compared to individuals in societies with low situational constraint." Second, high-constraint societies tend to produce individuals focused on what they *ought* to be doing and what *should not* be done, while individuals in low-constraint societies generally feel socially unencumbered in the pursuit of their own subjectively defined wants, goals, and desires. A third difference is that cognitive styles—or "preferred ways of gathering, processing and evaluating information"[93]—would also differ: individuals in high-constraint societies would have conservative, risk-averse "*adaptor* cognitive styles," while counterparts in low-constraint societies would have relatively more risk-taking, proactive, "*innovator* cognitive styles."[94] Finally, in high-constraint societies that place a heavy emphasis on social harmony, there would be higher levels of "socially shared cognition" than in low-constraint societies.[95]

The upshot of the preceding discussion is that culture inescapably remains a product of a particular ecological context. There can be no such thing as an undifferentiated universal culture common to all localities. Different natural environments—such as a cool climate versus a tropical one—give rise to differing sets of ecological challenges that in turn require "different cultural solutions" to ensure "survival."[96] Precisely because culture represents an ancient social adaptation to the natural environment of a particular geographic locality, the collective programming that constitutes that culture tends to reproduce itself from generation to generation to ensure that the social-psychological mechanisms for group survival in that particular context persist.[97] Hence culture remains relatively resistant to change, and transgenerational, collectively shared patterns of feeling, thinking, and acting are so deeply ingrained that it is very difficult for individuals born into the culture to unlearn them later in life.[98] Hofstede knows what he is talking about. The controversial Dutch-Somali parliamentarian and women's activist Ayaan Hirsi Ali, a Muslim-turned-atheist, observes in her trenchant memoir *The Caged Virgin*:

> I now see how important upbringing is.... Psychological conditioning is very powerful, and it takes great energy and force of mind and will to break out of it. Muslim girls are brought up...to live subserviently and submissively. It is very difficult for them to liberate themselves from this cage when they are older.[99]

Of profound interest to us is the way the "social environments in which one grew up" have profound impacts on attitudes towards other ethnic, religious, or national groups. Ayaan again:

> As a child I used to hear nothing but negative comments about Jews. My earliest memory dates from the time we lived in Saudi Arabia in the mid-seventies. Sometimes we had no running water. I remember hearing my mother wholeheartedly agreeing with our neighbor that the Jews had been pernicious again. Those Jews hate Muslims so much that they'll do anything to dehydrate us. "Jew" is the worst term of abuse in both Somali and Arabic. Later, when I was a teenager and living in Somalia and Kenya, from the mid-eighties onward, every prayer we said contained a request for the extermination of the Jews. Just imagine that: five times a day. *We were passionately praying for their destruction but had never actually met one* [italics added].[100]

Ayaan Hirsi Ali's recollections of the sheer power of collective cultural programming in shaping popular attitudes toward out-groups like the Jews is not at all unique. Brigitte Gabriel, a Lebanese-born American Christian journalist, remembers that, as a child growing up in southern Lebanon, the fault lines between that country's diverse identity groups were continually sustained by a cultural milieu supercharged by "ancient and persistent hatreds and rivalries."[101] She recalls:

> Sunni and Shiite Muslims were taught to hate each other because of a theological disagreement more than twelve centuries old. Muslims in general hated the Christians over a theological disagreement even older, and the Christians hated the Muslims in return. The Christian clans mistrusted and feuded with one another, and the Druze were the odd people out. But

everybody had one thing in common: we were all taught to hate Israel and the Jews.... All I heard was "Israel is the devil, the Jews are demons, they are the source of all the problems in the Middle East, and the only time we will have peace is when we drive all the Jews into the sea."[102]

Like Ayaan's, Gabriel's mental software taught her to hate and fear Jews from the time she was "a little girl" who had "never met a Jewish person or even knew that they even lived in Lebanon."[103]

The preceding discussion suggests that any analysis of the Muslim radicalization process in modern-day Indonesia should not neglect the cultural milieu—the shared, learned ways of thinking, feeling, and potential acting.[104] In particular, any explanatory framework must seek to unearth how cultural factors may well play a role in generating the deeply ingrained, simmering visceral resentment toward non-Muslim out-groups that resides at the core of Muslim radicalism. If culture matters, what then are those dimensions of national culture that are relevant to our study of JI in Indonesia? This is where the research of Hofstede is particularly applicable.[105] Following his lead, we could identify three dimensions of national culture in particular that are especially relevant to the current volume: "*power distance* (from small to large), *collectivism versus individualism*, and uncertainty avoidance (from weak to strong)."[106] These dimensions require elaboration:

- *Power distance*—the extent to which the less powerful members of social collectivities within a society "expect and accept that power is distributed unequally."[107]
- *Collectivism*—the organizing principle of societies in which "people from birth onward are integrated into strong, cohesive in-groups, which throughout people's lifetimes continue to protect them in exchange for unquestioning loyalty."[108]
- *Uncertainty avoidance*—"the extent to which the members of a culture feel threatened by ambiguous or unknown situations."[109]

To elucidate further, in large power-distance societies, both lowly and highly educated people tend to display "authoritarian values." That is, the lower classes rely on the power elites to preserve social security, harmony, and public order. Parents teach children obedience; respect for parents and older relatives is a lifelong basic virtue; and teachers are respected as "gurus who transfer personal wisdom" who actively shape students' "intellectual paths." Hofstede observes that in large power-distance societies, there "is a pattern of dependence on seniors that pervades all human contacts, and the mental software that people carry contains a strong *need* for such dependence."[110] Calculating a power distance index (PDI) based on the IBM survey scores for seventy-four countries, Hofstede found that Arab countries and Southeast Asian countries like Malaysia, Singapore, the Philippines, and Indonesia scored highly on the PDI. That is, their societies were characterized by large power distances. Countries that scored low on the PDI, suggesting that their societies were generally characterized by more egalitarian, smaller power-distance relationships, included, *inter alia*, Austria, Germany, the Nordic countries, the United States, the United Kingdom, and Israel.[111]

Societies can be considered collectivist in orientation if their children grow up learning to conceive of themselves as part of a "we" group—that is, a "relationship that is not voluntary but is given by nature." Hofstede adds:

> The "we" group is distinct from other people in society who belong to the "they groups," of which there are many. The "we" group (or in-group) is the major source of one's identity and the only protection one has against the hardships of life.... Between the person and the in-group a mutual dependence relationship develops that is both practical and psychological.[112]

In collectivist societies, the individual grows up deeply enmeshed within social networks built around respected elders who provide cues in terms of appropriate attitudes, beliefs, and values and who insist on the preservation of harmony. In the collectivist society, personal opinions "do not exist—they are predetermined by the group."[113] In fact, the collectivist individual seeks from youth to learn the skill and attitude sets that would enable him or her to win the acceptance of the group. The need for group acceptance is why collectivist societies are also *shame* cultures—as opposed to individualist societies that are *guilt* cultures. In an individualist society, a person who breaks a social rule may feel guilt based on an individually developed moral conscience. On the other hand, the collectivist person breaking a social rule would feel not guilt but rather shame—derived from a sense of personal failure in meeting a widely perceived collective obligation. This explains why a particularly important concept in collectivist societies is that of "face"—a sense of self-esteem derived from perceiving oneself as having a correct relationship with the social environment. Hofstede makes the important point that the "importance of face is a consequence of living in a society very conscious of social contexts"—that is, in a highly collectivist culture.[114] Hofstede's IBM country data showed that the United States, Australia, the United Kingdom, and Canada were the most individualist and hence least collectivist countries. Some Arab countries appeared more collectivist than others (Saudis more so than Lebanese and Egyptians, for example). Among Southeast Asian countries, the Philippines appeared less collectivist than Malaysia, Singapore, and Thailand. Interestingly, Indonesia was found to be the most collectivist Southeast Asian country.[115] Hofstede adds the important observation that in collectivist societies, "people are *usually* also dependent on power figures."[116] In other words, collectivist societies tend also to be large power-distance ones.

The third dimension of Hofstede's framework, which is of considerable importance for our purposes, is uncertainty avoidance. Hofstede accepts that all human societies have to cope with uncertainty, but his crucial insight is that there are significant national differences in coping with the ambiguous and the unknown. These differences are expressed across all social spheres. For example, in *weak* uncertainty-avoidance societies—that is, societies that are relatively comfortable with uncertainty and ambiguity—there are lenient rules for children regarding what is dirty and taboo; at school, students are comfortable with open-ended learning situations and concerned with good discussions, while teachers may admit "I don't know" without feeling that they have failed in their duty of imparting knowledge. In the workplace, ambiguity and chaos are tolerated, and there is a belief in generalists and common sense. Society tends to rely on relatively few rules, general laws, or unwritten codes. By contrast, in *strong* uncertainty-avoidance societies—that is, societies in which ambiguity and uncertainty are disliked—children are socialized into firm rules of what is dirty and taboo; at school, students prefer structured learning situations and seek "the right answers," which teachers are expected to have. In the workplace, there is an emphasis on precision and formalization as well as on experts and technical solutions. Society as a whole prefers numerous, precise rules for regulating social behavior. In fact, as Hofstede observes tellingly, in these strong uncertainty-avoidance societies, there "is an emotional need for rules, even if these will not work."[117] Of particular interest to our enterprise in this work is the notion that strong uncertainty-avoidance cultures tend to display higher levels of *ethnic intolerance*. Hofstede again:

> Dirt and danger are not limited to matter. Feelings of dirt and danger can also be held about people. Racism is bred in families. Children learn that persons from a particular category are dirty and dangerous. They learn to avoid children from other social, ethnic, religious, or political out-groups as playmates.[118]

The experience of childhood racism and social discrimination certainly was part of the life experience of the so-called twentieth hijacker in the 9/11 attacks, Zacarias Moussaoui. His brother Abd Samad recounts an incident that occurred when both he and Zacarias were immigrant Moroccan children of eight and ten, respectively, in Mulhouse, France. A white French child with whom the two brothers had been playing marbles for months suddenly refused to play with them any further. When the Moussaoui brothers asked him to explain the sudden change in behavior, the child told them that his parents had said that the Moussaoui children were "niggers, and they don't want me to play with niggers."[119] A close study of Abd Samad Moussaoui's book suggests that an enduring, influential element in the long pathway toward Zacarias Moussaoui's eventual radicalization within the ranks of Al Qaeda was precisely his lifelong struggle with racism and social and economic discrimination. This is one important element among the mix of factors common to many similar young Muslim male second- and third-generation immigrants finding themselves torn between the cultures of the Western countries in which their parents had settled and the religious traditions of their homelands. In these cases, radical Islamism often fills up the emotional and religious-ideological void within such unhappy, resentful young men.[120]

Yet another telling feature of a strong uncertainty-avoidance outlook is its intolerance for differing *ideas*, which also could be seen as "dirty and dangerous."[121] Hofstede expresses it succinctly:

> Children in their families learn that some ideas are good and others taboo. In some cultures the distinction between good and evil ideas is sharp. There is a concern about Truth with a capital T. Ideas that differ from this Truth are dangerous and polluting. Little room is left for doubt or relativism.[122]

As a consequence of these deeply ingrained, intolerant orientations toward difference, strong uncertainty-avoidance cultures tend to display xenophobic tendencies, greater levels of ethnic prejudice, the conviction that in "religion, there is only one Truth and we have it," and that this Truth should be imposed on others.[123] While in weak uncertainty-avoidance cultures, it is held that if "commandments cannot be respected, they should be changed," in strong uncertainty-avoidance ones, it is felt that if "commandments cannot be respected we are sinners and should repent."[124] This is precisely why it is the strong uncertainty-avoidance cultures that disproportionately produce "religious, political, and ideological intolerance and fundamentalisms" seeking to remake entire societies according to some preferred vision of a just moral, social, political, and economic order.[125] Hofstede's research further suggests that countries that are home to diverse "ethnic, linguistic, or religious groups" whose respective outlooks are characterized by both collectivism and strong uncertainty avoidance tend to be prone to "violent intergroup strife."[126] He adds that Serbia, Turkey, and the Arab countries are well within this category, while the African countries and, tellingly, Indonesia are not far off as well.[127]

CULTURE IS IMPORTANT—BUT SO IS HUMAN NATURE

While Hofstede spends a great deal of time explicating the various dimensions of national culture, he is by no means a simplistic cultural determinist. In other words, he recognizes that human behavior is a product not just of culture but also of at least two other factors—human nature and the individual's personality. Hofstede regards human nature as the "universal level in one's mental software" and the "operating system" that determines a human being's ability to "feel fear, anger, love, joy, sadness" and "shame."[128] In other words, human nature is what all human beings, regardless of cultural background, have in common because of their shared evolved, biological heritage. While human nature represents the universal, inherited traits of all individuals anywhere in the world, culture is "learned, not innate" and "specific to group or category."[129] Finally, the personality of an individual is "her or his unique set of mental programs that needn't be shared with any other human being."[130] One's individual personality is based on traits that are "partly inherited within the individual's unique set of genes and partly learned"—"learned" in this case meaning "modified by the influence of collective programming" or culture as well as "by unique personal experiences."[131] Hofstede's analysis in fact serves as the conceptual launching pad for evolving a more specialized explanatory framework for understanding the radicalization process of the JI militants we will be studying in this volume. We could call our version the Radical Pathways Framework or RP Framework for short.

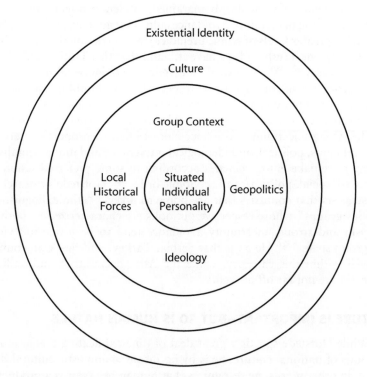

Figure 1.1: The Radical Pathways (RP) Framework.

In the RP Framework, Hofstede's three original elements of Human Nature, Culture, and Individual Personality have been modified somewhat. The outer ring of the RP Framework represents what we may call Existential Identity—an element of Human Nature that is essential in understanding the radicalization process and merits further elaboration in the following section.[132] The second ring retains the Culture variable, and the inner core of the Framework contains what we may call the Situated Individual Personality. In essence, the RP Framework suggests that the primal human drive at the core of the radicalization process—what we may call *Existential Identity Anxiety*—is a product of the interaction between Existential Identity, Culture, and a complex set of Individual Personality variables interacting with structural factors such as geopolitical developments, local historical forces, ideology, and the small group context that *in toto* comprise the environmental "Situation" of that Individual Personality. Basically, the RP Framework shows that the idiosyncratic and unique interaction of the elements of Existential Identity, Culture, and the Situated Individual Personality in the lives of each JI militant generated an Existential Identity Anxiety. This Anxiety was refracted through the prism of each individual's personal life histories and circumstances, culminating in varying degrees of individual radicalization. Ultimately, these various individual trajectories of radicalization—the Radical Pathways—of the JI militants converged in the form of the Cell that carried out the October 2002 Bali attacks. In a sense, although socioeconomic, historical, political, ideological, and other factors were not insignificant, ultimately an *amplified Existential Identity Anxiety* was perhaps the single most critical "root cause" of radicalization in the case of the JI militants we shall be studying. To understand why requires unpacking further the notion of Human Nature.

American social psychologist James Waller's recent interdisciplinary work in this area is very helpful. He argues that there exists a "universal, evolved psychological architecture that we all share by virtue of being humans—*a* human nature."[133] Put another way, Human Nature refers to "an endowment of cognitive and emotional faculties that is universal to healthy members of *Homo sapiens*."[134] Evolutionary psychology informs us that Human Nature is driven by a "set of *universal reasoning circuits* that were *designed by natural selection* to solve *adaptive problems* faced by our *hunter-gatherer ancestors*."[135] This requires elaboration. All human beings carry in their heads thousands of neural circuits that are designed to "generate behavior that is appropriate to our environmental circumstances."[136] Such universal reasoning circuits in the "wet computer" that is the human brain have been designed by Darwinian natural selection to ensure that human beings are able to produce the necessary "adaptations" in attitudes, thinking, and behavior that would increase the chances of "survival and reproduction" in a particular environment.[137] The adaptations produced by our universal reasoning circuits include the "way we interpret our experiences," the "recurrent concepts and motivations" that characterize our mental life, and the "universal frames of meaning that allow us to interpret the actions and intentions of others."[138] The reality is, as anthropologist John Tooby and psychologist Leda Cosmides point out, that the human brain is a "naturally constructed computational system whose function is to solve adaptive information-processing problems."[139] These universal reasoning circuits or "instincts" are "inherited mechanisms" and a legacy of the human past, as they had "increased the likelihood of survival and reproduction among our ancestors." Human instincts, however, should not be regarded as immutable "behavior patterns that are inevitably expressed and impenetrable to environmental, social and cultural influences"; instead they continually adapt so as to preserve "functional relationships to aspects of the environment of any particular organism."[140] There exists in fact a complex relationship between Human Nature and Culture. E. O. Wilson again:

> Culture is created by the communal mind, and each mind in turn is the product of the genetically structured human brain. Genes and culture are therefore inseverably linked. . . . Genes prescribe epigenetic rules, which are the neural pathways and regularities in cognitive development by which the individual mind assembles itself. The mind grows from birth to death by absorbing parts of the existing culture available to it, *with selections guided through epigenetic rules inherited by the individual brain* [italics added].[141]

The epigenetic rules common to all human beings result in "prepared learning of social behavior"—that is, "humans are innately prepared to learn certain behaviors, while being counter-prepared against—that is, predisposed to avoid—others."[142] This prepared learning in all human beings from childhood onward is inescapably "adaptive," geared toward conferring "Darwinian fitness" on human beings and enhancing their capacity for "survival and reproduction."[143] It is important to reiterate that basic human instincts first evolved in response to the environmental challenges confronting our common hunter-gatherer ancestors.[144] This is a very significant fact, as "well over 99 percent of our species' evolutionary history" has comprised life as "foragers in small nomadic bands."[145] Waller explains:

> In their lifelong camping trip, our Pleistocene ancestors faced some daunting adaptive problems. Among others, these included problems like detecting and avoiding predators and other dangerous animals, gathering and eating the right foods, forming friendships, developing alliances to defend against aggression, helping children and other kin, communicating with other people, and selecting mates—all, ultimately, having an impact on the survival and reproduction of our species over time.[146]

Waller adds that because natural selection is a slow, glacial process, there is always an extremely long time lag between the appearance of a new adaptive problem and the evolution of an instinct and associated behavior to deal with it. If we consider that fewer than 10,000 generations separate the global human community of today from the small group of our common hunter-gatherer ancestors—a duration that, as Waller notes, is but a blip in evolutionary terms—then it becomes readily apparent that there simply has not been enough time for natural selection to generate *new* universal reasoning circuits that are well adapted to every aspect of our modern environment. This is why Cosmides and Tooby assert that "Our modern skulls house a stone age mind," because "our brains are better at solving the kinds of problems our ancestors faced on the African savannahs than they are at solving the more familiar tasks we face in a college classroom or a modern city."[147] Human beings today are *not perfectly adapted* to the challenges of the modern environment. This is pregnant with significance for any study of the radicalization process. Waller aptly explains:

> Human behavior in the *present* is generated by universal reasoning circuits that exist because they solved adaptive problems in the past. As a result these past-oriented circuits will not always necessarily generate adaptive behavior in the present. In some cases, what the circuits were designed to accomplish in the hunter-gatherer context can even lead to maladaptive behavior in response to contemporary environmental contexts.[148]

Waller goes on to note that, since the days of our common hunter-gatherer ancestors, human beings—in their quest for survival and reproduction— have evolved as part of small social groups locked in competition for scarce resources with other groups.[149] This has given rise to three evolutionary adaptations that persist today. First, it is human instinct to at some level seek the shelter provided by a social group. After all, adaptation to "group living promoted individual survival," especially in "settings where collective action facilitated defense or the acquisition of food."[150] Second, precisely because individual survival presupposed group survival, human beings have evolved genuinely altruistic motives and behavior—what the anthropologist Robert L. Trivers calls reciprocal altruism[151]—so as to maximize group "fitness" vis-à-vis competing groups. Third, such an intensely intimate individual-group dynamic tends to produce "within-group niceness and between-group nastiness."[152] The implication, as Waller suggests, is that "every human in every culture comes endowed with psychological mechanisms that leave us capable of committing extraordinary evil" on behalf of the group "when activated by appropriate cues."[153] Waller identifies three such "psychological mechanisms," which he describes as "innate," "animal," "underlying," and "distant." These are "social capacities lying at the core of human nature" that "studies worldwide" have shown are "universal in people" and "start in infancy": ethnocentrism, xenophobia, and the desire for social dominance.[154]

Ethnocentrism, xenophobia, and the desire for social dominance are rooted in a prior, more basic but powerful psychological mechanism—the innate human tendency to engage in *social categorization*. The French anthropologist Claude Levi-Strauss termed this the "binary instinct," which E. O. Wilson explains as "the innate tendency" to "use two-part classifications in treating socially important arrays."[155] The human mind needs to use a "quick and easy mental algorithm"[156] that, as social psychologist Neil J. Kressel observes, "groups people, as well as objects, into categories," which helps "simplify the present and predict the future more effectively."[157] Henri Tajfel and Joseph P. Forgas agree, adding that such a process of "social categorization" reduces environmental complexity, enhancing the efficiency of human information-processing.[158] Concurring, Waller asserts that social categorization "simplifies an incredibly complex world by filtering the amount of data we must actively process," and is a phenomenon that is "universal and pervasive across humankind."[159]

The effect of social categorization is to effectively divide the social world into "us" and "them," or, in the words of the well-known American sociologist William Graham Sumner, the "we-group, or in-group, and everybody else, of the others-group, out-groups."[160] This "intuitive" mental classification process tends to have some major consequences. First, we tend to think that other in-group members are "more similar to us than to out-group members" across a "wide range of thoughts, feelings and behaviors"—the "assumed similarity effect."[161] Second, as a result of the "out-group homogeneity effect," we tend to assume that all out-group members are alike. This causes us to persuade ourselves that "if we know something about one out-group member," we "feel that we know something about all of them."[162] The out-group homogeneity effect explains why humans tend to *stereotype* members of an out-group.[163] Third, social categorization also produces the "accentuation effect," in which we, as members of the in-group, tend to magnify and play up differences between "us" and "them," thereby leaving us "biased toward information that enhances the differences" between the groups and "less attentive to information about similarities between members of social categories."[164] Interestingly, long ago the legendary psychoanalyst Sigmund Freud referred to this tendency of closely interacting and related social groups to deliberately emphasize their differences and underplay their commonalities as the "narcissism of minor differences."[165]

Waller argues that although social categorization is widespread and normal, it is not without implications. This is because the "mere act of dividing people into groups" cannot but set up "a bias in group members in favor of the in-group and against the out-group."[166] We "generally like people we think are similar to us," Waller asserts, "and dislike those we perceive as different."[167] Kressel concurs, adding that it is a "small step from categorization to stereotyping and favoritism for one's own group."[168] Favoritism for one's own group brings us to the phenomenon of *ethnocentrism*. Ethnocentrism is a term coined by the early American sociologist Sumner, encountered earlier, who in a 1906 book, *Folkways,* defined it to mean "this view of things in which one's own group is the center of everything, and all others are scaled in reference to it."[169] Ethnocentrism is a useful evolutionary adaptation, found in virtually every society on the planet[170] and providing an "advantageous reinforcement of communal identity and we-ness" that promotes the survivability of the group and, *ipso facto*, of the individuals within it.[171] In fact, ethnocentric tendencies are apparent from infancy, and by the age of six or seven, children have been known to show a strong preference for their own nationality well before the concept has been fully understood. As Waller explains, all humans have an "evolved capacity to see our group as superior to all others and even to be reluctant to recognize members of other groups as deserving of equal respect."[172] Recent social psychological research has shown that the very concepts "us" and "them" carry "positive emotional significance that is activated automatically and unconsciously."[173]

However, ethnocentrism, while widespread,[174] tends to be accompanied by a somewhat darker evolutionary adaptation: a "complementary tendency to fear outsiders or strangers," or xenophobia.[175] This is why Waller goes so far as to suggest that in "forming bonds" we simultaneously "deepen fissures"; in short, the "evolution of sociability, altruism, and cooperation" is accompanied by the "evolution of animosity to outsiders." There can be no "us" without "them."[176] Such "binary oppositions," the eminent Oxford natural scientist and theologian Alister E. McGrath states, define the realm of human experience, whether religious, ethnic, or cultural origin; language; social class; age and sexual orientation; and so.[177]

THE ANATOMY OF EXISTENTIAL IDENTITY ANXIETY: THE PRIMAL FORCE DRIVING RADICALIZATION

Our evolved tendency to "seek proximity to familiar faces because what is unfamiliar is probably dangerous and should be avoided" very much sets the scene for another key feature of Human Nature, or to use the more precise term of our RP Framework—*Existential Identity*: the desire for a positive group identity and social prestige—a drive rooted in the far deeper human need for individual self-esteem.[178] The group is important to human beings not merely because the former helps ensure the latter's physical survival and reproduction. The wider group is needed to shore up individual human self-esteem as well. The individual need for "self-esteem" is "the major underlying motive for in-group bias" because intergroup comparisons "indirectly contribute to individual self-esteem."[179] The intimate nexus between individual esteem and the group's collective dignity brings us to the issue of *identity*—a subjective and persistent sense of "sameness."[180] Fathali M. Moghaddam elaborates that when a human being reflects on (what we term) his or her Existential Identity, he or she asks two basic questions: "What sort of person am I? How am I seen and valued by others?"[181] Moghaddam argues that for human beings to enjoy an "authentic identity" that satisfies their deep esteem needs, three conditions must be met. First, an authentic *individual* identity presupposes an authentic *group* identity. In other words, "individual authenticity arises from collective authenticity."[182] If one belongs to a group that is stigmatized, it is unlikely that one can enjoy a positive individual identity. Individuals want to belong to groups that have "prestige and value," because this indirectly enhances their own individual self-worth and a "distinct and positive identity."[183] Second, Moghaddam makes the extremely important observation that an authentic group identity also presupposes that the sources of that collective identity are *internal* to the group and not located externally. This is, however, easier said than done. Moghaddam explains:

> [T]his requirement for attaining authentic identity is difficult to achieve for many minority groups. This is because in many situations, *the main sources of identity for minority groups are majority out-groups....* The main determinant of the sources of identity is *group power: groups that enjoy power superiority can shape the identity of groups with less power* [italics added].[184]

This is no surprise: the American political scientist Joseph Nye has argued that American "soft power" has long been an extremely pervasive influence on other societies—at least until the 2003 Iraq invasion.[185] It is no accident that historically, many educated young people in Islamic countries have been heavily influenced by Western identity ideals. Moghaddam again:

> The West is the main source of the music, films, clothing, books and magazines, video games, electronic communications, and "culture" broadly, which influences youth in Islamic societies. This has created the problem of "imported ideals" and a lack of authenticity in Islamic communities.[186]

The third and final requirement for an authentic group identity is *distinctiveness*. Moghaddam affirms that individuals want to belong to groups that are considered high-prestige and "positively evaluated" by others. This is one reason why many Muslim immigrants in Europe have all but abandoned their "heritage cultures and identities," assimilated into Western culture to gain positive evaluation," and lost the "characteristics that set them apart."[187] However, not every Muslim immigrant in a Western context, or Muslims in countries such as Indonesia and Malaysia, is comfortable psychologically with such a loss of distinctiveness. Mogaddham correctly states:

> [In] the global context, minority groups, such as Islamic communities, are confronted by the threat of being overwhelmed by imported cultural systems and identities. True, minority groups are concerned about being evaluated positively, *but an even higher priority challenge is for them to retain or manufacture a distinct, different identity* ... distinctiveness has become even more difficult and more essential to achieve than positiveness [italics added].[188]

This primal drive to carve out and preserve a distinct and high-status religious, nationalistic, or ethnic "group tent"—this *Existential Identity Anxiety*—can precipitate violent behavior, even mass murder, if thwarted. The respected psychoanalyst Vamik Volkan has explained the distinction and relationship between an individual identity and an overarching group identity:

> We all wear, from childhood on, two layers of clothing. The first garment, which belongs just to the individual who is wearing it, fits snugly and represents personal identity. The second set of looser outer clothes is made from the fabric of the large group's ethnic (or religious or ideological) tent. Each member of the large group is cloaked by a piece of the same cloth, and it protects the person like a parent or caregiver. The canvas of the tent thereby shelters thousands or millions of individuals under it as though it were a gigantic single piece, and represents the large-group identity.[189]

Volkan, assuring us that "human psychology, whether of individuals or large groups, has not changed," makes the crucial observation that when the "shared identity" of members of large ethnic or religious groups is "threatened," and the "canvas of the tent is shaken or torn" during periods of "shared helplessness and humiliation caused by 'others'," ethnic or religious group members would quite willingly "humiliate, cripple, burn, and kill 'others'" in response, "even when our own physical survival is not threatened."[190] In like vein, Michael J. Stevens argues that during times of intergroup conflict, "social components of self-concept become more prominent than individual components," and concern with "the in-group replaces self-interest."[191] Lord Alderdice, the psychiatrist and psychotherapist who played a role in the Northern Ireland peace process and was subsequently speaker in the Northern Ireland Assembly, elaborates, explaining that perceived threats to the Group Tent can create situations in which ordinary human beings, who are neither "poor, ignorant, lonely, psychologically disturbed or criminal," may nevertheless undergo what to all intents and purposes is a *radicalization process* in which "the individual self becomes conflated with" the "group," and "identification" with "fellow group members" becomes predominant.[192] *In fact, individual regression to a primitive state of mind in which the individual self is subsumed into the collective self, or an "us"—while various out-group selves are simultaneously collapsed into a single overarching "them"—represents the cognitive essence of radicalization.* In conflict zones, individual regression into primitive forms of us-versus-them cognition moreover is often complemented and accompanied by wider *group or community regression* into easily manipulable "primitive states of mind"[193] that downplay individual identities in favor of the larger overarching group identity.[194] The Croat writer Slavenka Drakulic captures this "identity simplification dynamic"[195] that a radicalization process at the group level produces extremely well:

> Along with millions of other Croats, I was pinned to the wall of nationhood—not only by outside pressure from Serbia and the Federal Army but by national homogenization within Croatia itself. *That is what the war is doing to us, reducing us to one dimension: the Nation.* The trouble with this nationhood, however, is that whereas before, I was defined by my education, my job, my ideas, my character—and yes, my nationality too—now I feel stripped of all that [italics added].[196]

As in the case of individual radicalization, if one aspect of radicalization at the group level involves identity simplification within the in-group, this is also accompanied by an intensification of the assumed out-group homogeneity and accentuation effects alluded to earlier. In other words, in group radicalization, the multiple identities in a community are reduced to a single overarching in-group, "us," while similarly the multiple affiliations and self-identifications in the other community are reduced to a single, overarching, adversarial "them," the out-group. Alderdice alluded to this in describing how, during the troubles in Northern Ireland,

> *The community had regressed* from a myriad of individual differences maintained in a broad mosaic of relationships, to *a narrower frame of reference* where the single difference between Protestant Unionist and Catholic Nationalist assumed pre-eminence [italics added].[197]

Furthermore, the point at which the Existential Identity Anxiety processes driving the group radicalization process described above degenerates into violence, including terrorism, is when members of the in-group perceive that they are on the *verge of extinction as a separate, distinctive identity group.*[198] This is precisely why the eminent French literary theorist Rene Girard has asserted that it is not so much intergroup differences per se but rather the "loss of them that gives rise to violence."[199] Girard, incidentally, has pointed to another potent driver of the Existential Identity Anxiety at the heart of intergroup violence: mimetic desire. He argues that human beings "desire things because others have them."[200] Human beings, in other words, possess the inborn capacity to learn their desires from observing others as well as the concomitant drive to possess what others possess. This socially learned desire, and the drive to possess the object of that desire, together constitute mimetic desire. The objects of mimetic desire may be material, such as economic wealth, or metaphysical, such as social status and power.[201] The point is that "their possession by others gives them value in our eyes."[202] In situations in which the objects of group desire are perceived as *unjustly unattainable*, frustration resulting in conflict may result.[203]

Unpacking and elaborating on the Existential Identity and Culture elements of the RP Framework sets the stage for explaining the third and final element of the Framework, the Situated Individual Personality. This is an extremely complex and multifaceted variable that can best be explicated through direct application to the very different lives of the JI militants we will be examining in the coming chapters, particularly Chapters Three and Four. It suffices at this juncture to say that the Situated Individual Personality element of the RP Framework will show how the Existential Identity Anxiety of the JI militants—originating in their common Human Nature and mediated by immersion in certain subcultural milieus—was further refracted by the unique and idiosyncratic combinations of *situational* and *dispositional* factors in order to generate radicalization. Such factors, as we shall see, include the presence and content of a virulent, religiously motivated, dehumanizing ideology exploiting the inchoate prejudices of the wider subcultural milieu; the particular nature of the individual's locus of control of reinforcement; the impact of an antisocial, ambient personality; the power of situational pressures on individual volition and capacity for critical, independent thought; and "primitive" mental states facilitating us-them stereotyping and delusional beliefs. We shall see, in short, that there were not one but several Radical Pathways to Bali.

OUTLINING THE "BOTANY" OF RADICALIZATION: OF GARDENS, BOUQUETS, AND FLOWERS . . .

The foregoing discussion has critically surveyed the state of scholarship on terrorism in general as well as analytical coverage of the phenomenon in Southeast Asia in particular. We have argued that effective analysis of the so-called fourth wave of religiously inspired terrorism in the Southeast Asian context should be bottom-up in order to capture key localized nuances, focused less on interminable, dead-end debates about the suitability of terminology such as "terrorism" or "militancy" and more on the factors driving the religious radicalization process. To this end, the study has opted to examine the radicalization processes that transformed several more or less ordinary Javanese Muslims into the JI Cell that perpetrated the traumatic Bali bombings of October 12, 2002. The current chapter, building on the important work of the Dutch social psychologist Geert Hofstede and other scholars, has described what it calls the Radical Pathways or RP Framework, consisting of three elements, Existential Identity, Culture, and the Situated Individual Personality. The RP Framework will be employed to understand and explain how selected key JI militants involved to varying degrees in the Bali attacks underwent radicalization. We also can make use of Hofstede's work in another way to aid in our task. He has asserted:

> Societies, organizations and individuals represent the *gardens, bouquets and flowers of social science*... the three are related and [are] part of the same social reality. To understand our social environment, we cannot have ourselves fenced in to one level only: we should be prepared to count with all three [italics added].[204]

Hofstede holds that while anthropologists or political scientists study the "garden" (or societies as a whole), organizational sociologists examine the "bouquet" (or organization), while the individual "flowers" are really the preserve of "personality research in individual psychology."[205] Hence achieving a thorough understanding of the radicalization processes undergone by the JI Bali Cell members and their putative leaders requires engagement with the available data at all three levels of analysis: "garden," "bouquet," and "flowers."

Accordingly, this pithy botanical metaphor suggested by Hofstede will be used to organize the rest of the chapters. Thus the next chapter seeks to understand the wider historical and cultural "Garden" within which JI has its deep roots. Of particular interest to us would be the emergence of the three "Trees" of Indonesian Islam and the theological cross-exchanges between them: Javanese traditionalism, Javanese modernism, and what may be called Arabized modernism. In Chapter Three we will study the emergence of one result of the cross-fertilization of the ideational pollen emanating from these Trees within the Garden of Indonesian Islam: the "Bouquet" of Darul Islam. We shall see how the deeply prejudiced if inchoate Darul *Islamic* subculture was later crystallized into the somewhat better-defined, politicized Darul *Islamist* ideology that deeply influenced the worldviews of key JI figures such as Abu Bakar Ba'asyir, Mukhlas, and Imam Samudra. In Chapter Four we will see how the Situated Individual Personality element of the RP Framework helps us understand how individualized dispositional and situational factors interacted in unique ways to radicalize the extremely different JI personalities Hambali, Amrozi, Ali Imron, and the suicide bomber Arnasan. Chapter Five attempts to tie the analysis together and suggests that blocking Radical Pathways of the type that the members of the JI Bali Cell traversed requires not so much winning but rather *denying* Indonesian Muslim hearts and minds to JI ideologues. The precise details of such a denial—or what we have termed a "cognitive immunization" strategy—can be meaningfully explicated only after our Radical Pathways Framework has been employed to make sense of the available evidence. It is this task that this analysis must now undertake.

2

Inside the "Garden" of Indonesian Islam

To comprehend the inner dynamics of the JI network, it is crucial to appreciate that it has always been much more than merely the Southeast Asian arm of Osama bin Laden's Al Qaeda movement.[1] Although JI certainly reflects a strong Middle Eastern imprint, it equally has very old roots in historic Indonesian Islam, particularly the Islam of West and Central Java. Hence to understand JI it is will be necessary to analyze its deep cultural background. Accordingly, this chapter seeks to study more closely the wider "Garden"—employing Hofstede's metaphor—within which today's JI network is inextricably rooted. The underlying aim of this chapter is to demonstrate how the Garden of historic Islam in Indonesia has impacted the *collective mental programming* of today's JI militants and their immediate support network. The chapter will trace and analyze the emergence of Javanese Islam in particular[2] and how, over the centuries, Javanese Muslims have evolved three broadly distinct interpretations, and consequently subcultures, of Islam: traditionalism, modernism, and what we may call Arabized modernism. To further develop the Hofstede metaphor, we could even say that these three subcultural variants—each growing up around its own educational and associational networks—today represent large "Trees" within the Garden of Indonesian Islam. The analysis in this chapter, in sum, represents an attempt to illuminate the Culture element in the RP Framework developed in the previous chapter. The current chapter will set the stage for us to examine, in Chapter Three, how the historic interaction between the three subcultural Trees of Indonesian Islam, in conjunction with other structural forces in twentieth-century Indonesian political history, interacted with one another to pave the way for the emergence of the subcultural "Bouquet"—to borrow and adapt another Hofstede metaphor—of Darul Islam. The latter was the true wellspring from which the militant Cell that executed the Bali attacks of October 12, 2002, was to ultimately arise.

THE ARRIVAL AND SPREAD OF ISLAM

Although Arab traders had known about the Southeast Asian archipelago and its trading and commercial opportunities for "generations," Southeast Asian area scholars suggest that Islam began to find local adherents only from the thirteenth century onward, although at that time the faith was confined to the "scattered ports and coastal trading routes."[3] In addition, although "Muslim teacher-traders probably came from various parts of the then Islamic world," a number of historians point to southern Indian Muslim traders as influential early purveyors of Muslim ideas in early Southeast Asia.[4] What made southern Indian Islam attractive to the indigenous Javanese and other Southeast Asian coastal peoples at this stage were its sheer richness, diversity, and hence adaptability to local conditions. Of particular importance, the religion proved itself flexible and robust enough to lubricate rather than impede commercial exchanges between Muslim merchants and their various indigenous partners. Southern Indian Islam—characterized by both "adaptability and tolerance"[5]—proved to be a faith that grew out of and was very suited to a busy, bustling "commercial urban environment."[6] Eventually, it was the mainstream Sunni branch of Islam, and in particular its Shafi'i school of jurisprudence or *fiqh* (adhered to by most southern Indian Muslims), that took hold in the Indonesian islands and the rest of the archipelago—although it was adapted to local realities, giving "Southeast Asian Islam a distinctive character which it has retained to the present day."[7] Although the Islamic faith appeared to have established its earliest beachheads in north Sumatra and eastern Java,[8] it was the conversion of the rulers of the powerful ancient Malay trading port of Melaka on the western coast of the Malay peninsula in the fifteenth century that marked a "milestone in the history of Islam's expansion into Southeast Asia."[9] Successive Melaka rulers were aware of the commercial power of the transnational Muslim traders' network that stretched from "Europe to Maluku" and included key ports such as Bengal, Aden, and Hormuz—as well as the geopolitical emergence of the Ottoman Turks with the fall of Constantinople in 1453. The rulers were thus keen to emphasize their Islamic credentials. To this end, Melaka's power elites assiduously courted Muslim traders from India and the Arab world, offering them commercial concessions, building mosques and homes, and granting them audiences in the royal court.[10] Melaka also made efforts to build itself up, like Ottoman Istanbul (formerly Constantinople), as a center of regional Islamic scholarship and culture. Even more significantly, Melaka tried to promote Islam in neighboring states, "persuading" or even "compelling" their rulers to embrace the faith.[11]

The Islamization of Melaka was to have profound and enduring implications for the Malay archipelago. Because Malay was the language of trade, and Malay-speaking Melaka the focal point of regional trade and commercial networks, Islam, as it gradually percolated outward along long-established trade routes, became, over time, closely enmeshed with Malay culture. So strong and enduring was this process that the phrase *masuk melayu*, or to become a Malay, ultimately came to imply the adoption of Islam as one's faith as well.[12] This is how Islam gradually came to constitute an integral aspect of a pan–Southeast Asian Malay identity throughout the archipelago.[13] It was along the expanding trade routes between Melaka and the Spice Islands of eastern Indonesia that the northern coastal ports of Java—initially exposed to earlier waves of Hindu and Buddhist influences— now experienced Islamic teachings for the first time.[14] By the seventeenth century, Javanese traditions were suggesting that Islam had arrived through the efforts of nine Sufi *walis* or saints, some of whom were traders who had studied or lived in Melaka as well.[15] It is said that Gresik and Surabaya were among the first Javanese ports to deeply embrace Islam.[16] Islam's expansion did not stop there. From Ternate in northern Maluku (part of the Spice Islands), Muslim missionaries began to spread Islam to the southern Philippines as well.[17] The subsequent expansion of European Christian colonial power into the region resulted, *inter alia*, in the fall of Melaka to the Portuguese in 1511, but this development merely accelerated the spread of Islam rather than retard it. By closing off Melaka to Muslim commerce, Muslim traders and merchants were forced to look elsewhere within the region. As a consequence, Aceh, a kingdom on Sumatra's northern tip that had adopted Islam in the mid-fourteenth century, grew far more important as a Muslim regional trading center after Melaka's eclipse. Aceh's rulers became renowned for their Islamic fervor and military prowess and helped propagate the faith down both Sumatran coastlines. Brunei, located in northwest Borneo, also soon acquired a stronger Islamic hue and began proselytizing efforts in the Philippine archipelago. Well before the Spanish arrived in the Filipino archipelago in 1565, Muslim rulers were in control of Sulu and Maguindanao.[18]

Another development that facilitated Islam's growing hold in Java was the defeat of the Majapahits by a coalition of northern Islamic Javanese states led by the sultanate of Demak in 1527. Demak's formerly Hindu ruler had taken the Ottoman-like title of Sultan three years earlier, and with the decline of Majapahit, Demak consolidated its politico-military control throughout West and East Java. In fact, under Demak's influence, Banten in West Java became an important Islamic center, and the Bantenese began in turn to influence Lampung in Sumatra.[19] By this time, Islam had developed an almost irresistible momentum. Even after Demak's decline in the 1550s, the faith continued to spread through the missionary work of other Javanese kingdoms such as Gresik. In this way, Islam penetrated far-flung areas like Lampung, Lombok, Maluku, and, of no small importance, the militarily powerful kingdom of Makassar in South Sulawesi in the East. Following the conversion of Makassar's rulers in 1605, within forty years, most of its surrounding neighbors in the eastern archipelago had become Muslim.[20] It also should be noted that by the sixteenth and seventeenth centuries, Islam was on the ascendant worldwide, and this would not have been lost on Muslim ruling circles in Java and elsewhere in the Indies, thanks in part to growing links with the Middle East and the arrival of teachers from key nodes of Islamic learning, such as Mecca, Egypt, and Istanbul. Muslim rulers in Java and elsewhere would have heard of the continuing success of the Ottomans, who were by then controlling Mecca, Medina, and Jerusalem, and following the subjugation of the Balkans, had turned "the Mediterranean into a Muslim lake."[21] Similarly, Turkish mercenaries skilled in the use of muskets and large-siege cannons were incorporated into Acehnese armies attacking Christian Portuguese Melaka in the sixteenth century, as Ottoman and Acehnese ruling classes were actively discussing the possibility of a joint "counter-crusade" against Melaka.[22] The success of the Muslim Mughals in the Indian subcontinent in the sixteenth century also seemed to demonstrate the apparent all-conquering power of Islam. Especially under the rule of Akbar (1556–1605), the Mughals dominated all of India, and his exploits inspired the Acehnese ruler Iskandar Muda (1607–1636) to style himself after his Mughal exemplar.[23] By the time the Dutch East India Company set up its headquarters in Batavia or Jayakarta in 1619 and inaugurated three centuries of Dutch colonial domination, "Islam was clearly the rising faith in island Southeast Asia."[24]

INTERLUDE: THE DEEP ARAB ROOTS OF ISLAM

Islam was able to achieve such success in island Southeast Asia in general, and Java especially, by the seventeenth century only partly because of geopolitical and commercial factors. Another very important reason was that its source was southern India and not Arabia. This meant that the Islam that arrived on Java's shores was almost surely deeply shaped by Sufism.[25] The content and significance of Sufism for the Javanese milieu, however, cannot be adequately appreciated without taking several steps further back and appreciating—in some detail—what organized Sufism has traditionally *reacted* to: the historic, strident early Islam of the Bedouin Arabs. Not insignificantly, Islam emerged in the seventh century amid the desert wastelands of Arabia. Very much in line with our previous discussion on how ecological factors have shaped cultural systems, the British scholar and acute observer of Arab history and culture Anthony Nutting asserts that the "Arabs' social life, like their religion, was related to the demands of a harsh and often dangerous existence." As such, "the rules and customs of the tribes" were "specifically designed to overcome the dangers and hardships of desert life."[26] The cultural anthropologist Raphael Patai agrees, stating that the harsh desert environment of Arabia directly shaped the "special social form that grew up" among the "desert people, the nomads."[27] Nutting provides a glimpse into the average Bedouin Arab lifestyle in the time of the Prophet Mohammad—many aspects of which survive today as external identity markers of Arabized Islam:

> According to a cycle of life unchanged and unchangeable since pre-Islamic times, the nomadic Bedouin of fifteen hundred years ago lived, ate, slept, traveled and traded exactly as his descendants do today. Then, as now, his staple diet consisted of dates, flour and camel's or goat's milk—water he usually reserved for the camels, goats and sheep; his clothes were, and still are, a shirt stretching to his knees over which a robe fell to his ankles, and a shawl held by a cord covered his head and was wound round his neck and face to protect him against the sun and to keep the dust out of his nose and mouth.[28]

The nomadic Bedouin Arabs at the time of Mohammad lived in a rough fashion, in tents made from goat or camel skin. They survived by rearing sheep, goats, camels, and at times horses, which were bartered for food and other necessities. At times, when trade and peaceful means of barter or exchange were not possible, various Bedouin tribes engaged in raids against each other to steal what they needed. The Bedouin also considered the settled town or village Arabs, known as *al-Hadhar*, fair game. The *al-Hadhar*, who engaged in agriculture, trade, or craftsmanship in towns such as Hejaz, Palmyra, or Petra, lived in houses of stone or mud and were despised by the hardy Bedouin, who saw themselves in contrast as "altogether more manly, noble and superior."[29] In fact, popular myths of Bedouin martial prowess and moral codes endure in the Arab world, providing "powerful influences on value systems and behavior patterns alike."[30] At any rate, precisely because seventeenth-century Arabia was wracked by internecine tribal warfare over scarce resources, the importance of the tribe could not be overstated.[31] Bedouin Arabs were strongly governed by the code of *asabiyya*, or tribal solidarity, something that demanded their utmost "life and loyalty."[32] In other words, the desert Arabs were *extremely collectivist*. As Nutting notes:

> For the tribe was the basis of Bedouin society. To the desert Arab, it was his family, his trade union, his club—indeed his entire social circle. It gave him protection and employment, social standing and subsistence. Without it he was an outlaw with every man's hand against him. Within it he could lead as full and safe a life as his desert surroundings permitted.[33]

As suggested in the previous chapter, collectivist societies also tend to reveal large power-distance orientations. We find this to be equally true of the Bedouin Arab tribes. The tribal sheikh, although having to first prove to his followers that he possessed in abundance the necessary qualities of "courage, powers of leadership," and not least, "good luck," was nevertheless, once chosen, readily accepted as the "father of his people."[34] However, this elite status brought huge responsibilities. In line with Hofstede's observation that in large power-distance societies, the mental software people carry contains a strong need for dependence on "seniors," in the large power-distance society of the Bedouin Arabs, the sheikh was expected to "dispense hospitality, including occasional feasts for his hungry tribesmen"; be intimately familiar with the family problems of his followers; settle disputes; and make judgments in criminal cases. "His word was law," Nutting observes, and he quite literally "wielded a power of life and death over his tribesmen."[35] That the religion of Islam itself remained deeply influenced by the collectivist, large power-distance cultural imprint of the Bedouins was attested to by no less a figure than the Prophet Mohammad himself, who recognized that even the revolutionary message of Islam was never quite "enough to transform permanently an Arab way of life that had persisted for thousands of years."[36]

However, although the Arab Islam that the Prophet founded retained the collectivist and large power-distance orientations inherent to Bedouin desert life, there was one crucial discontinuity with the past. Pre-Islamic Arabia—despite being home to remnant monotheistic Abrahamic sects such as the Hanifiyya—was on the whole characterized by widespread idol worship and great diversity in pagan beliefs and lifestyles.[37] In contrast to the Persians of the time, who were sun worshippers, Arabs generally worshipped the moon. The moon, pre-Islamic Arabs reckoned, brought the cooling dews and darkness after "the torturing heat and blinding light of the day."[38] In fact, the huge black stone known as the Kaaba in Mecca, the chief city of Hejaz, which was seen as a sacred site long before the advent of Islam, was "held by pagan legend to have been dropped from the sky by Hobal, the moon-god."[39] Other Arab tribes, desiring fertility and shade, worshipped caves, trees, and wells (the Zamzam well near Mecca was especially famous, as it was said to have saved Ishmael and Hagar from dying of thirst in the wilderness).[40] By the late sixth century C.E., the Kaaba boasted as many as 300 idols "catering to every taste."[41] Immoral activities were also par for the course—the annual poet's fair at Ukaz in Hejaz, for instance, was well-known to local tourists of the time for drunkenness and orgies involving pilgrims and caravan drivers plying their trade along the land route from southern Arabia.[42] It was into such a milieu that Mohammad was born in 571 C.E. He was part of the Hashim clan, in turn an offshoot of the dominant Quraysh tribe.[43] In fact, as a young boy, Mohammad formed an abiding "abhorrence for the idolatrous and vicious way of life prevalent in Mecca."[44] Obviously seeking to impose some sort of order on the freewheeling moral and religious chaos he had observed in Mecca—a condition later termed as *jahiliyya*[45]—Mohammad became concerned "with the need for one God and for someone to arise and proclaim himself His prophet."[46] In 610, Mohammad began receiving the first of his revelations from the angel Gabriel and two years later began his prophetic career:

> So, calling his faith after the Arabic word for submission (to God)—Islam— and his followers Moslems, from the word for one who submits, he proclaimed to the citizens of Mecca that God was one, the all-powerful creator of the universe, that a Judgment Day would come when idolators would perish in Hell's fires and the faithful would enjoy eternal Paradise.[47]

In other words, the Prophet, in his desire to rid Mecca, and later on all Arabia, of various stripes of pagan worship, excess, and idolatry, displayed *strong uncertainty avoidance*: that is, in place of the *jahili* chaos into which he had been born, he sought above all to inject the *structure and certainty* of a new "spiritual discipline"[48] into Arab society by introducing a new Islamic order and morality. This structure and certainty was not merely morally, but also politically and strategically necessary, because the Prophet and his small band of early followers were under threat of at best domination and at worst elimination by powerful, hostile enemies. Following the *hijrah* (flight) from the Mecca of the unfriendly Quraysh tribe to the more agreeable political milieu of Yathrib (later renamed Medina) in 622, the Prophet, behaving like the classic tribal sheikh of Arab culture, proceeded to lay down rules and codes of conduct for the members of the fledgling Muslim community, governing their relationships with one another and with non-Muslims.[49] It was from the secure "base area" of Medina that the Prophet was eventually able to expand his influence and ultimately subdue Mecca in 630.[50]

It has to be said that the Prophet, very much a product of, and responding to, his historic cultural, moral, political, and strategic environments, founded an Islamic faith that could not help but evince signs of *adaptation to such a milieu*. In truth, Mohammad was more than just a spiritual leader. He was also simultaneously both "head of state and commander-in-chief" of the Arab Muslim bands. Nutting is persuasive when he asserts:

> For within his spiritual message there was a call to social revolution every bit as clear as the writings of Karl Marx or the speeches of Gamel Abdul Nasser. . . . Thus, unlike the message which Christ's followers had spread around the Mediterranean basin six centuries earlier, the faith of the Prophet was used more as a political instrument than as a purely spiritual appeal, and in the great Arab conquests that followed the Prophet's death, Islam became more a device to unite the conquerors than a call to convert the conquered.[51]

THE SUFI REACTION AND IMPACT ON EARLY JAVANESE ISLAM

That Mohammad had bequeathed an enduring legacy was well illustrated by the fact that within twenty years of his death in 632, the "Muslims had laid hold of large parts of the Roman Empire and had wholly absorbed the Persian."[52] By any standard, the military record of the Arab Muslims was mightily impressive: Damascus had fallen to Muslim raiding parties in 635, a mere three years after Mohammad's demise; Jerusalem was wrested from the Eastern Roman armies in 638; Alexandria in Egypt capitulated in 642 and Tripoli further west in 643; and by 698 the entire northern African coast had come under Arab Muslim rule, despite determined Berber opposition. Spain was invaded in 711 and the entire Iberian Peninsula was under Muslim dominion within seven years.[53] This record of conquest, however, was not without significant psychic costs. One former scholar at Al Azhar University in Cairo suggests that "the constant warring damaged the heart and soul of Muslims," and that by Islam's second century, many Muslims longed for "reconciliation with others and reconciliation within themselves."[54] Another impetus for this generalized soul-searching among Arab Muslims was that during the conquests they had come into contact with non-Arabs such as Christian monks, who lived ascetic lives and sought a closer relationship with their Creator. This deep spirituality created a lasting impression.[55] These factors set the stage for Sufi ideas to thrive and gain a wider following. Sufism was a mystical folk tradition that had developed among some of the earliest Arab Muslim communities, emphasizing "spiritual values, ecstatic and direct perception of God, and the heart of the believer and his or her love for God."[56] Sufis were and still are known for their colorful rituals called *zikr*, involving "chanting, singing, and swaying as a way to achieve an ecstatic state thought to bring adherents closer to God."[57] In reaction to the widespread soul-searching created by the Arab Muslim conquests, Sufi reformers emerged, such as Al-Hasan al-Basri (642–728 C.E.) who made a name for himself in the Basra mosque in what is today southern Iraq. Another well-known early Sufi mystic was a woman, Rabi'a al-Adawiya (717–801 C.E.), who lived in present-day Iraq and argued that Muslims "should focus on the love of Allah, not the fear of Allah."[58]

In fact, by the time of the rise of the Mongols in the thirteenth century—at about the same time southern Indian Muslim traders were bringing Islam to Southeast Asia—Sufism was at its peak and, to some observers, was in a position to dominate the future development of the Islamic faith thereafter.[59] Sufi orders or *tariqa* were, and still are, built around central charismatic sheikhs whose religious interpretations are considered authoritative and who are accorded both affection and prestige as respected, parent-like figures.[60] This latter point demonstrates why Sufism had earlier taken root in the villages of southern India, where a long tradition of veneration for holy men existed. Three Sufi orders in particular, the Qadariyya, Shattariyya, and

Naqshabandiyya, proved very influential in the villages of southern India, and it was these three Sufi *tariqa* who "also became the most popular in Southeast Asia."[61] Sufi-mediated Islam took root in Java for a few key reasons. First, Sufism, which emphasized various methods of seeking an ecstatic union with the Divine through means such as dancing, singing, music, drumming, meditation, and the chanting of Qu'ranic passages, was "similar to the religious practices" of pre-Islamic Javanese, who, prior to Islam's arrival, had conceived of life as a constant interaction between the world of men and the world of spirits.[62] Also, and importantly, Sufism, with its "willingness in certain forms and traditions to accommodate existing beliefs," enabled Javanese to see "Islamic beliefs not as imported but as an integral part of their own culture."[63] In other words, in Hofstedian terms, what enabled Sufi Islam to take root in the Javanese milieu was its relatively open, flexible, *weak* uncertainty-avoidance orientation. In addition, precisely because Sufism tended to be organized in extended *collectivist, large power-distance* social networks (*tariqa*) of believers held together through the teachings of charismatic sheikhs, it was easier for Islam to be enmeshed with local social structures that predated its arrival.[64]

At the core of these pre-Islamic Javanese social structures were "individuals powerful in their own right yet outside the sociopolitical order."[65] Such individuals were usually hermits and sages or the *adjar*, who resided in remote mountain caves. The *adjar*—not entirely unlike the Christian monks of Syria and Egypt chanced upon by Arab conquerors during the early years of Islam's rapid outward expansion—sought to lead ascetic lives so as to "penetrate the secrets of the universe" and "call attention to the state of decay of a kingdom." For this reason, the *adjar* were respected and regarded with some anxiety by Java's then-Hindu/Buddhist elites. At times of social crisis, the *adjar* were seen by the local rural folk as natural leaders and prophets pointing to "messianic ideas, such as the appearance of a *ratu adil* (just king)."[66] When Islam appeared on the Javanese scene, the independent, at times antiestablishment roles played by the pre-Islamic *adjar* were continued by new, independent Islamic counter-elites in the form of the *kyai*, who provided alternative loci of mass allegiance in counterpoint to the Javanese aristocratic and later Dutch colonial order. In the words of the authoritative *Cambridge History of Southeast Asia*:

> The *kyai* (venerated teacher of Islam) established reputations and followings in *pesantren*, or schools, often located in remote villages beyond the administrative control of the state. There were also the gurus or masters of Sufi...*tarekat*, which mushroomed in Java and parts of Sumatra in the nineteenth century.[67]

In times of upheaval, these Islamic teachers, together with some of their pupils, "would emerge from their isolated *pesantren* and *tarekat*" to help ease the transition from an old order to a new dispensation.[68] The Javanese *kyai*'s popularity in rural circles was only partly due to his formal credentials as representative of the Islamic faith. In a Javanese religious milieu characterized by a syncretism involving a curious mix of Hindu and Islamic concepts and ideas, the *kyai* tended to assume, in the eyes of their followers, "immense potency" as "healers and prophets," whose teachings often heralded the imminent arrival of the *ratu adil*, who would bring an end to oppression and suffering and institute a new order of justice and plenty.[69] This zeitgeist reinforced the large power-distance orientation found within *kyai*-dominated social networks in Java.

"TOLERANT" JAVANESE ISLAM TODAY

While the harsh desert environment of Arabia shaped the early Islam of the Prophet and his followers, creating an Arab Muslim culture that possessed collectivist, large power-distance, and strong uncertainty-avoidance outlooks, the Javanese Islam that had developed by the nineteenth century was not entirely similar. One factor that was common to both the Arab and Javanese contexts was an inclement climate. While the pre-Islamic Bedouin Arabs had had to cope with the desert, the pre-Islamic Javanese had to deal with the challenges of a tropical climate. To be sure, the fertile volcanic soil regions of Java, together with the frequent monsoons, promoted agricultural productivity,[70] particularly centered on widespread wet rice cultivation,[71] but Javanese peasants had to cope with the constant threat of infectious diseases such as malaria, a far more potent problem in the tropics than in temperate zones further north.[72] Furthermore, although the climate is relatively lush in tropical zones compared with temperate, colder ones, the Javanese, while generally not too worried about the state of the soil, nevertheless had to be warier of conflict with other human "predators" for the products of that same soil and other resources.[73] As communities grew larger and more complex, the intricacies of food production, involving, *inter alia*, "clearing woods, planting, weeding, harvesting, cooking, feeding pigs and chickens, and fishing," eventually gave rise to both a horizontal division of labor among Javanese peasants as well as a vertical stratification between them and local chiefs and religious elites.[74] Hence Javanese communities gradually evolved a collective mental software suited to their unique environment, one that predisposed them to accept implicitly that "better chances for survival" existed for them if they "organized themselves hierarchically and in dependence on one central authority" that kept "order and balance."[75] Over time, this gave rise to the highly *collectivist* and *large power-distance* outlook of Javanese culture and Javanese Islam. The key point is that although Bedouin Arab and Javanese Islam share these first two dimensions of culture, it is on the third dimension that they part ways dramatically: *Javanese Islam was, and remains, characterized by a*

*weak uncertainty-avoidance orientation, while Arab Islam has always pos-
sessed a strong uncertainty-avoidance outlook.* To reiterate, one reason for
this difference was very practical: as merchants and traders, the Javanese
needed a faith that would lubricate and not hamper operations in the highly
cosmopolitan, competitive, commercial environment of maritime Southeast
Asia. After all, at the height of their power in the fourteenth century, the
Javanese Majapahits oversaw a thriving, cosmopolitan maritime empire in
which Javanese merchants did business with traders from India, China, and
the mainland Southeast Asian kingdoms.[76] The second, far more important reason was, as noted, the deep impact Sufism had in shaping Javanese
Islam. Sufism, built around social networks or *tariqa* centered on charismatic
sheikhs, promoted the rise of a "traditionalist" Javanese Islam equipped with
a collective mental software featuring the key elements of collectivism, large
power-distance, and crucially, weak uncertainty avoidance. This was, and is,
the "tolerant, smiling" Javanese and Indonesian Islam that is world famous
to this day.[77]

The rapid industrialization and urbanization brought about by the bu-
reaucratic/military technocrats steering President Soeharto's New Order
regime (1966–1998) produced demographic and socioeconomic changes
that somewhat reduced intra-Javanese religious heterogeneity by the
1980s.[78] Nevertheless, Javanese Islam today still can be analytically teased
apart into two relatively distinct strains: the *abangan* and *santri*.[79] *Abangan*
Javanese Muslims range from nominal, not particularly observant Muslims
to those who lead "rich but highly syncretic religious lives, in which Islam
is blended with other religious or spiritual observances" such as folk beliefs or Hindu/Buddhist elements.[80] In fact, the term *"abangan,"* although
originally applied to the Javanese, the biggest ethnic group in Indonesia, has
increasingly been applied to nominal non-Javanese Indonesian Muslims as
well.[81] It should be recognized, moreover, that some estimates suggest that
abangan Muslims today comprise 50 to 70 percent of the Indonesian population as a whole.[82] By contrast with their Javanese *abangan* counterparts,
Javanese *santri* Muslims take Islamic orthodoxy and praxis more seriously.
They pray, fast, go on the pilgrimage (*haj*) to Mecca, and generally are "concerned about making Islam an important part of their lives."[83] However,
Javanese *santris* are not all alike. They historically have been divided into
two main *aliran* (theological streams): traditionalist and modernist. Traditionalist *santris* seek to preserve the authority of medieval Islamic scholarship. They adhere strictly to the Shafi'i school, especially the assumption
that the classical scholars "possessed an erudition unrivalled in subsequent
centuries and that their teachings offer the most authoritative interpretation of how Islam should be practiced."[84] Traditionalists, in other words,
hold that there exists an authoritative and verifiable transmission of Islamic
scholarship linking the present all the way back across the generations to the

time of the Prophet, a process known in Arabic as *talaqqi*.[85] Moreover and importantly, Javanese *santri* traditionalists display their weak uncertainty-avoidance orientation with their willingness to "combine local mystical and spiritual practices with the more orthodox elements of Islam."[86] Hence devout Javanese *santri* traditionalists see no problem with offering prayers at the tombs of saints, believing in spirits and miracles, using amulets, and incorporating Sufi rituals into their worship.[87]

A second key characteristic of Javanese traditionalists, again arising from their weak uncertainty-avoidance orientation, is their strong sense of tolerance for other faiths and persuasions. They display little tendencies toward "fundamentalism or militancy" and in fact stand out for their "moderation and inclusiveness" as well as openness to "interfaith dialogue and cooperation."[88] In this regard, Abdurrahman Wahid (or Gus Dur, as he is affectionately known among his millions of followers), the former president of Indonesia, leading scholar of the Sunni Shafi'i school of jurisprudence, and former leader of the 40-million-strong traditionalist mass organization Nahdlatul Ulama (NU), presents an excellent modern example of a Javanese traditionalist. As a committed *santri*, he is extremely pious, observes the various Islamic rituals, and performs extra prayers at night. At the same time, Gus Dur recites *zikr* as Sufis do and employs numerous references to the Qu'ran and the Hadith in his speeches. He is also known to visit the tombs of the saints, including that of his late father.[89] Gus Dur is especially famous for his commitment to a religiously tolerant, multifaith, democratic Indonesia, rather than a theocratic state dominated by Islam.[90] The essence of the *santri* traditionalist position—that Islam must not be diluted, but rather contextualized to meet Javanese realities—is captured in the following extract from one of Gus Dur's many writings, in which his obvious disdain for an uncritical imitation of Arab religious practices shines through:

> The danger of the process of Arabization or the process of identifying oneself with Middle Eastern cultures is that it takes us away from our own cultural roots. More than that, it is not certain that Arabization is appropriate for our needs. Indigenization is not an attempt to avoid resistance from the forces of local culture but rather [to avoid] the disappearance of that culture.... Islam must retain its characteristics. The Qur'an must remain in Arabic, particularly in the prayers, because these things constitute the norms [of Islam]. Translations of the Qur'an are intended only to facilitate understanding, not to replace the Qur'an itself. The indigenization of Islam is not "Javanization" or syncretism, because the indigenization of Islam only takes local needs into account in formulating religious laws, without changing the laws themselves.... Indigenization of Islam is part of the history of Islam, both in its place of origin and elsewhere, including Indonesia.[91]

In sum, like many *santri* traditionalist scholars, Gus Dur has called for an *Indonesianized* Islam that does no violence to indigenous cultural characteristics. This is also why Gus Dur has gone on record to argue that the concept of the Islamic State is an Arab construct, not applicable to the Indonesian case.[92]

ENTER THE MODERNISTS

Although *santri* traditionalism represents one very significant subcultural Tree in the Garden of Indonesian Islam, its chief tenets are counterbalanced somewhat by a second important Tree: *santri* modernism. Islamic modernism was not invented in Indonesia but rather in the Middle East, particularly Cairo, where in the late nineteenth century reformists like Muhammad Abduh (1849–1905) and his protégé Rashid Rida (1865–1935) were its chief advocates. Seeking to revitalize Islamic civilization in the face of "Western gains in education, technology, and other fields," Abduh and Rida argued for a pristine Islam purified of all doctrinal accretions since the time of the Prophet and the first four Rightly Guided Caliphs.[93] They insisted instead on a return to the Qur'an and the Traditions as the main sources of Islamic thought and praxis. Precisely for this reason, reformist thinkers like Abduh and Rida were originally known as *Salafis*—after *salaf*, or the Companions of the Prophet. The leading moderate scholar Khaled Abou El Fadl elaborates:

> The founders of Salafism maintained that on all issues, Muslims ought to return to the original textual sources of the Qur'an and the Sunna (precedent) of the prophet. In doing so, Muslims ought to reinterpret the original sources in light of modern needs and demands without being slavishly bound to the interpretive precedents of earlier Muslim generations.[94]

This set the Salafis or modernists apart from traditionalists, who placed great stock on what preceding scholars had to say. El Fadl again:

> Furthermore, by rejecting juristic precedents and undervaluing tradition as a source of authoritativeness, Salafism adopted a form of egalitarianism that deconstructed traditional notions of established authority in Islam. According to Salafism, effectively anyone was considered qualified to return to the original sources and speak for God. The very logic and premise of Salafism was that any commoner or layperson could read the Qur'an and the books containing the traditions of the Prophet and his Companions and then issue legal judgments.[95]

The fact that Salafi modernism promoted a more egalitarian approach to the issue of interpretation of Islamic sources was one key difference with traditionalism. The other lay in the relatively more pronounced, if very human, *ethnocentric* impulse of the modernists to upgrade the great civilizational "in-group" of Islam in order to ultimately overhaul the West.[96] Hence Abduh "admired Europe" for its "strength," "technology," and "ideals of freedom, justice and equality" and sought to emulate these achievements by developing an authentically Islamic basis for "educational, legal, political and social reform." It bears recognizing that the *underlying impulse* of modernists like Abduh and Rida was always a restoration of the Islamic world's "past power and glory."[97] Importantly, modernists welcomed Western science and technology but not Western culture. Indeed the latter was dismissed as "secularist, materialist, nationalist and racist."[98] Modernist ideas spread throughout the rest of the Muslim world in the early decades of the twentieth century, including the areas that today comprise modern Indonesia, probably because they met the desire of many Muslims for material progress, but not at the cost of the authenticity and distinctiveness of core Islamic identities—a point discussed in the previous chapter.

In what precise ways did modernist ideas find their way to Indonesia? As noted earlier, since the sixteenth century, Islamic teachers from the Middle East had resided on the Indonesian islands. Moreover, from the eighteenth century onward, not just Javanese, but also Muslims from Sumatra, South Sulawesi, and Kalimantan began spending long periods of time studying with renowned religious teachers in the Middle East. When these students returned to the archipelago, they formed their own social networks and passed on the "mainstream" Islam they had learned abroad. In this way, Islamic thinking from centers such as Mecca, Medina, Syria, the Yemen, and India "flowed in vernacular form to Indonesian Muslims."[99] Beginning in the late nineteenth century, however, it was the Egyptian Abduh's "universalistic Islamic 'modernism'," rather than the ideas associated with the religious scholars of the Hejaz, that was the key Arabic intellectual influence on the "growing numbers of Muslim scholars in the modern Malay world."[100] By the early twentieth century, new generations of students from the Malay archipelago, including Muslims from peninsular Malaya, the Straits Settlements (Singapore, Melaka, Penang), southern Siam, and particularly Sumatra, soon outnumbered Javanese students in the ideological epicenter of Islamic modernism, Cairo. These modernist students, on their return to the archipelago, came to be called *kaum muda* (young generation) as opposed to the older generation (*kaum tua*) of traditionalist scholars and *ulama* "whose orientation was to Mecca rather than Cairo."[101] Like their ideological counterparts in the Middle East, moreover, the *kaum muda* were driven by deeper ethnocentric—and mimetic—impulses manifested overtly in the form of strident anticolonial sentiments. Of special importance to the spread of modernist ideas in the Javanese and wider Malay worlds were two ethnic communities: the Minangkabaus (or Minangs), the primary ethnic group of west Sumatra, and the Hadrami Arab immigrant community.

Because of improved communications and shipping between Southeast Asia and the Islamic heartlands in the course of the eighteenth century, increasing numbers of Hadrami Arabs from the "arid coastal strip of the Yemen" began settling in Sumatra, including Minangkabau.[102] These Arab "Sayid" migrants were "received with honor" because of their presumed descent from the Prophet, their command of Arabic, and their "assumed expertise in all things Islamic."[103] Influential Hadrami Arab communities soon developed in the port towns of Java and Sumatra and proceeded to exert a "considerable effect on the development of Indonesian Islam."[104] Certainly, it would seem that by the 1780s, "Islamic schools in Minangkabau were giving increased emphasis to the teaching of Muslim law and its application to daily life."[105] Little wonder then that by the early twentieth century, west Sumatra had become an important source of Islamic intellectuals, writers, artists, and teachers, and that Minang men were especially known for their "ability, competence," and importantly, "Islamic piety."[106]

The extent of such piety was amply demonstrated by the Padri Wars of the early nineteenth century. Three Minang pilgrims on an extended visit to the Holy Land encountered the Wahhabi Arab sect, founded by the extremely puritanical Muhammad ibn Abd al-Wahhab (1703–1787). The sheer impact of the al-Wahhab sect on the evolution of Islam in general and the three Minang visitors in particular is so important that it bears closer scrutiny. Al-Wahhab considered the Ottoman Turks, who at the time were exercising dominion over large tracts of the Middle East, including Mecca and Medina, to be "blasphemers for their constant infractions" of the Qur'an, such as "wine-drinking, gambling, fornication and idolatry."[107] Much as the Prophet had done centuries earlier, al-Wahhab and his acolytes, or "Wahhabis," responded to the excesses of the prevailing *jahili* society in severe fashion: they destroyed shrines, tombs, and sacred objects that they considered "idolatrous."[108] Even relatively observant Arab Muslims were not spared from al-Wahhab's wrath: as long as they did not embrace his extremely rigid, absolute monotheistic interpretation of the faith, he condemned them as guilty of *shirk* or apostasy—implying that corrective violence could legitimately be employed against them—and it was.[109] In this way, al-Wahhab—who proceeded to forge a religio-political alliance with the powerful tribal sheikh Muhammad bin Saud, an axis that was ultimately to result in the founding of the future Saudi kingdom—successfully spread his ideas throughout the Arabian peninsula from the middle of the eighteenth century.[110] In essence, al-Wahhab sought—by force if necessary—to ensure that Muslims remain on what he considered the true path of Islam and steer clear of "corruptions" such as "mysticism, the doctrine of intercession, rationalism, and Shi'ism."[111] In essence, al-Wahhab sought to respond to the challenges of early modernity, with its "overpowering moral and social insecurities," by "running for shelter" in the form of "clinging onto particular

Islamic texts for a sense of certitude of comfort."[112] To El Fadl, al-Wahhab and his followers were in essence *radical synchronizers*:

> The Wahhabis tended to treat everything that did not come out of Arabia proper to be inherently suspect, and they believed that un-Islamic influences came from nations such as Persia, Turkey, and Greece. For example, Wahhabis believed that Sufism was a Persian import; belief in the intercession of saints and the veneration of gravesites, a Turkish import; and rationalism and philosophy, a Greek import. These Wahhabi claims are overly simplistic and inaccurate, but there is no question that *Wahhabis have always equated the austere cultural practices of Bedouin life with the one and only true Islam* [italics added].[113]

At any rate, the severely reductionistic piety of the Wahhabis—the product of a *strong uncertainty-avoidance outlook*, aptly summed up by Hofstede's pithy comment that "what is different is dangerous"[114]—made a deep impression on the three Minang pilgrims. On their return to west Sumatra in 1803, they promptly attempted to "Wahhabize" their communities, precipitating a thirty-year civil war in west Sumatra. Significantly, the Minang reformers, who came to be called the "Padris," were quite willing to resort to forceful methods, including *jihad*, to compel fellow Muslims to return to the so-called "fundamentals" of Islam. To this end, the Padris sought to eradicate gambling, cockfighting, opium- and tobacco-smoking, alcohol and betel-nut consumption, and even the wearing of gold ornaments.[115] This was a significant development in Southeast Asian Islam at the time. For all intents and purposes, the Padris were the west Sumatran Wahhabis,[116] and their impact on Minang Muslims, in particular, proved enduring.

The Padri conflict called into sharp relief the issue that has occupied Indonesian Islam since that time: what the proper relationship between Arab "metropolitan" Islam and the "little" Islams mixed with local customs on the periphery should be.[117] For their part, Minang religious teachers were keen to ensure that Muslim teaching and behavior in the Indies was "upgraded" to be more in line with that found in the Middle East. Thus Minang scholars were very open to the incipient puritanism implicit in modernist ideas and were very critical of the Sufi-inspired saint worship, mystical practice, and the use of amulets, spells, and charms associated with Javanese *abangan* and *santri* traditionalists.[118] Minang scholars based in Singapore, such as Tahir Jalal al-Din al-Azhari (d. 1957) and Sayyid Shaykh Al-Hadi (d. 1934), as well as the well-known Haji Rasul of west Sumatra, took the doctrinal fight to the Javanese traditionalists, arguing, *inter alia*, that the traditionalist fixation on medieval and early modern Islamic scholarship only bred stagnation and atrophy.[119] This, they argued, was precisely why the global Muslim *ummah* had exchanged the glories of an earlier era with Western colonial domination by the nineteenth century.[120] Another important reason for the harsh, uncompromising tone of the pronouncements of Minang modernists, especially in the first decades of the twentieth century, was that the highly influential Rashid Rida, Abduh's protégé and "caretaker of the Cairene tradition" after Abduh's demise, was "also more 'Wahabist' than his teacher." Hence later cohorts of "Malay and Minangkabau students in Cairo" were exposed to "a version of Islamic modernism far less tolerant of local tradition and of the West."[121] As it turned out, the "harsh arguments of the Minang modernists" were "downplayed" and moderated by the leading Javanese modernist Ahmad Dahlan (or Dachlan), who sought "practical changes" to embed Islamic modernism in "the Javanese environment."[122] To this end, in 1912 in Yogyakarta, Java, Dahlan founded Muhammadiyah, an Islamic organization whose "earliest members were mainly religious officials, religious teachers and merchant traders."[123] The foundation of Muhammadiyah was to set a pattern for the organized propagation of Islam in Indonesia, an important subject to be explored in the next section.

THE "PILLARIZATION" OF INDONESIAN ISLAM

The founding of Muhammadiyah draws attention to perhaps the most profound legacy of Dutch colonial rule: the system of "pillarized" (*verzuiling*) educational and associational networks that have cleaved modern Indonesian Islam. These were based on the so-called Protestant and Catholic "pillars" of late nineteenth-century Dutch society, otherwise known as the *verzuiling* system. In the metropolitan Netherlands, the latter comprised "dense webs of educational and associational activity divided along religious lines."[124] As Albert Schrauwers explains:

> These deep religious cleavages resulted in the development of separate religious school systems, religious political parties, and a host of religiously oriented service agencies such as housing developments, unions, newspapers, radio stations, and hospitals, which elsewhere in the West were sponsored by a secular state. Earlier in this century, typical pillarized Dutch working-class citizens would, for example, rent a house in a Protestant church-sponsored housing development, send their children to a church-sponsored school, read protestant newspapers, and vote for the Anti-Revolutionary Party (the Orthodox Calvinist Party).[125]

In the Dutch East Indies, Muhammadiyah gradually began erecting a Javanese modernist "pillar" as well: it started an urban-based network of modern religious schools or *madrasah*, which offered a wide range of general subjects taught in Western schools along with religious topics.[126] Dahlan did not stop at educational institutions, however. Over time Muhammadiyah also opened clinics, hospitals, and libraries.[127] By 1938 Muhammadiyah had spread throughout Indonesia and boasted a membership one quarter of a million strong.[128] The emergence and success of the modernist Muhammadiyah were bound to have an impact on the Javanese traditionalists, and in 1926 they responded with an educational and associational pillar of their own—the rural-based network known as Nahdlatul Ulama (NU), founded by Gus Dur's grandfather, Muhammad Hasyim Ash'ari.[129] NU members were largely rural religious boarding school (*pesantren*) graduates themselves; a number had studied in Mecca, had little contact with Western education, and preferred "Arabic customs, clothing styles, and religious beliefs."[130] Nevertheless, NU members, while certainly theologically conservative, remained "socially and politically liberal."[131] NU's formation represented a traditionalist defense of the old system of rural Islamic boarding schools on Java and elsewhere.[132] These boarding schools or *pesantren* were characterized by a method of learning built around "an oral tradition of scholasticism" in which venerated *kyai* "led instruction in the vocalization and interpretation of the Qur'an and other key Islamic texts in classical Arabic."[133] The Dutch scholar of Indonesian Islam Martin van Bruinessen observes:

> The *pesantren* tradition is pervaded by a highly devotional and mystical attitude . . . many *kyai* are moreover affiliated with a mystical order (*tariqa*) and teach their followers its specific devotions and mystical exercises. Visits to the graves of local saints and great *kyai* are an essential part of the annual cycle; most Javanese *pesantren* hold annual celebrations on the anniversaries of their founding *kyai*.[134]

The NU educational and associational network of *pesantren* was a closed one, with intimate personal ties among the "owner-operator-teachers" of the schools.[135] Hence the *pesantren* network did more than serve an educational role. It was in fact a "milieu within which *santri* remained immersed, circulated, and accumulated cultural, intellectual, and social capital."[136]

While the NU and Muhammadiyah networks generally reproduced Javanese *santri* of either traditionalist or modernist persuasions, respectively, the key point is that graduates within these two *aliran* were Muslims who above all were generally tolerant; i.e., they possessed a relatively *weak* uncertainty-avoidance orientation. This was perhaps true more so of NU, with its intrinsic openness to Sufi and other syncretic Javanese practices, but even the Yogyakarta-based Muhammadiyah displayed significant sensitivity in embedding modernist ideas in a Javanese context. The late Nurcholish Madjid (1939–2005), a leading Javanese modernist intellectual, clearly demonstrated the relatively weak uncertainty-avoidance outlook of Javanese Islamic modernism in comments made about the need for respecting religious pluralism in Indonesia. To Cak Nur, as he was fondly called by his followers, what was different was *not* necessarily dangerous:

The Islamic community is . . . commanded to stress always that all of us, the followers of different scriptures, together worship the One Almighty God, and together surrender ourselves unto Him. In fact, even if we think we know for certain that other people are praying to an object that is not the One Almighty God, we are still forbidden from behaving improperly towards those people. . . . The Words [of the Qur'an] apply here: "For you, your religion, for me, my religion. . . . " This quotation is not a question of lack of concern for other faiths, let alone a loss of hope; rather it is driven by an awareness that religion cannot be coerced, and that each person, regardless of their faith, must be respected as a fellow creature of the One Almighty God.[137]

For his part, Ahmad Shafii Maarif, a professor at the State Islamic University of Yogyakarta, who himself was national chairman of Muhammadiyah from 2000 to 2004, when asked if Indonesia should make *shariah* or Islamic Law the basis of the law of the land, replied:

Certainly we are the nation with the largest Muslim majority in the world. Yet it should be remembered that historically, Islam entered Indonesia mainly through a process of acculturation with local cultures. . . . As you know, the actual number of those who are syncretic and nominal Muslims is quite high. You can imagine what would happen if sharia were actually to be implemented as state law. Dissension would occur not only between Muslims and non-Muslims, but also within the Muslim community itself. This would clearly be dangerous.[138]

THE ENDURING IMPACT OF ARABIZED MODERNIST ISLAM

There were other Islamic modernist persuasions in Indonesia, however, that clearly displayed far higher levels of intolerance. Significantly, these were spearheaded not by the relatively open Javanese but rather by the Minang and Hadrami Arab immigrants, who evinced a harder-edged modernism defined by stridently anti-Western, antisecular, and anti-Sufi sentiments. The tendency toward harder-edged scriptural orthodoxy in Southeast Asia possessed relatively established roots in the "intense religio-intellectual contacts and connections since at least the sixteenth century between Malay-Indonesian students and their co-religionists and *ulama* in the Middle East, particularly in the *Haramayn* (Mecca and Medina)." Also, "returning students or scholars implanted a more *shariah*-oriented Islam in the Malay-Indonesian archipelago, which forced the so-called "pantheistic" (or "*wu-judiyyah mulhid*") Sufism to cede ground."[139] This portended the rise of a more scriptural orthodoxy and literalism in Southeast Asian Islam.[140] By the early decades of the twentieth century, two organizations had emerged that evinced a hard-line, literalist scripturalism in the Indies: the Persatuan Islam

(Islamic Association or Persis, founded in 1923) and Jam'yyat al-Islah wal-Irsyad (Union for Reformation and Guidance, or simply Al-Irsyad, founded in 1913). Persis was an educational and associational network founded by Muslims of Hadrami Arab descent and "by others influenced by the teachings of modernist Islamic scholars in the Middle East."[141] Persis is still described today as by far the most "puritan" of Indonesian reform movements.[142] The schools of both Persis and Al-Irsyad were, quite simply, crucibles for the development of a *highly Arabized* or *Wahhabi* outlook. As John Sidel observes:

> From their inception, Al-Irsyad and Persis schools placed great emphasis on the study of Arabic and, far more than the more Westernized *madrasah* of Muhammadiyah, prepared their students for higher education in centres of Islamic learning far from the Indonesian archipelago.[143]

Sidel goes on to illuminate the ways in which educational practices within this particular "pillar" of Indonesian Islam fostered a *strong uncertainty-avoidance* outlook:

> In their religious teachings and practices, Al-Irsyad and Persis were also more openly and stridently antagonistic toward the influence of Christianity in the archipelago and toward the accretions of local customs, the worship of saints and shrines, and the mysticism of Sufis and Javanists alike.[144]

The bottom line was that Persis and Al-Irsyad promoted among its Hadrami Arab immigrants, and later local Javanese, Minang, and other students, both a "sense of separateness" from Javanese Islam and "an outward orientation, back to the Middle East." Tellingly, Persis and Al-Irsyad graduates came out feeling intuitively an emotional fealty not to the Indies, but rather "'there,' in the heartland of the Arab world."[145] The Persis/Al-Irsyad educational networks, in short, were largely responsible for the production of puritanical Wahhabism. Using our Garden of Indonesian Islam metaphor, we can think of Wahhabism as constituting one "Branch" of the Tree of Arabized modernism. The historic Persis/Al-Irsyad "pillar" has without question profoundly influenced Indonesian Islam down through the decades. One important historic figure emerging from the Persis *aliran* was Mohammad Natsir (d. 1993), a west Sumatran Minang who served for a short while as Indonesian prime minister in the early 1950s. As a young man, Natsir, after attending Dutch-style schools, moved to Bandung, Java, and was an "advanced student" at the Persis school there.[146] In the interwar years, Natsir, in response to the comments of secular nationalist leaders such as Soekarno and Soetomo that Muslims needed to downplay overt religiosity and focus more on the practical requirements of building a modern society, countered instead that "piety was important," and only a genuinely strong Islamic society and state would ensure national success. Displaying a strong anti-Western bent, Natsir insisted that "imitating the Dutch and adopting Dutch institutions as the nationalists suggested" was to be avoided.[147] Later on, during the run-up to the first national elections in independent Indonesia's Liberal Democracy era in 1955, Natsir again called for Islam to be instituted as the state religion and rejected the Western systems of capitalism, socialism, and communism.[148]

Another product of the Persis *aliran* was M. Isa Anshary, like Natsir a west Sumatran Minang who had also studied at the Persis school in Bandung and become a "leading ideologue" in Persis circles.[149] During the 1955 national debates, Anshary called for the adoption of the so-called Jakarta Charter. This referred to a constitutional statement that had been devised by Muslim leaders ten years earlier in the months leading up to Indonesia's declaration of independence in August 1945. The Charter contained a seven-word clause that obliged Muslims to implement Islamic law. The Charter also called for the Islamizing of the constitution as well as for the president to always be a Muslim. The Charter was never adopted by the secular nationalist leaders of the independent Indonesian republic.[150] Instead, Soekarno opted for the Sanskrit phrase *Pancasila* or Five Principles, which included a "Belief in God the Only One," felt to be more widely acceptable.[151] In 1955, Anshary, unconvinced of the capacity of the *Pancasila* formulation "to give the state moral substance," let alone "substantive meaning," once more called for the Jakarta Charter to be adopted. After all, Anshary insisted, "Indonesian society should reflect Islamic characteristics because most of its people were Muslims."[152] Yet another key figure in the history of Arabized modernist Islam in Indonesia was a highly devout Tamil Muslim, born and educated in a Singapore Muslim family, called Ahmad Hassan (d. 1957). Hassan played a key role in shaping the doctrinal trajectory of Persis. Between 1926 and 1941, Hassan advised Persis ideologues on a range of issues pertaining to the application of modernist ideas to Islamic thought and practice in Java and the wider archipelago. Among other things, Hassan warned Muslims against overly identifying with nationalist symbols and sentiments at the expense of their devotion to God. Thus he severely criticized the "use of flags, anthems, and statues to heroes" as akin to "polytheism"—a serious offense in the sight of God. Considerd by Federspiel to be "the most strident and uncompromising" of Indonesian reformers, Hassan was a big intellectual influence on later modernist leaders such as Anshary.[153]

Both the Persis activists Mohammad Natsir and Ahmad Hassan were to play leading roles in the important postwar modernist political party Masjumi (Majelis Syuro Muslimin Indonesia, or Indonesian Muslim Consultative Council). In fact, Persis formed the "backbone" of Masjumi throughout its existence.[154] Throughout the era of Liberal Democracy until the late 1950s, when Soekarno set up a more authoritarian Guided Democracy structure expressly based on Javanese political and cultural hegemony, Masjumi leaders clashed not only with the secular nationalist Soekarno but also with the Indonesian Communist Party (PKI) over the issue of making Islamic Law or *shariah* the basis of the Republic's constitution. Soekarno finally banned Masjumi at the end of the 1950s following the latter's support of a short-lived Muslim separatist revolt in west Sumatra and South Sulawesi.[155] The Masjumi/Persis ethos did not disappear, however. It persisted in the form of the Dewan Dakwah Islamiyah Indonesia (DDII or Islamic Propagation Council). The DDII was set up in February 1967 by a Masjumi/Persis clique of activists led by Natsir. Rather than seek political power outright like Masjumi, DDII switched strategies: Natsir apparently declared: "Before we used politics as a way to preach, now we use preaching as a way to engage in politics."[156] To this end, DDII, very much an offshoot of the Persis pillar, developed a pillar in its own right that comprised a network of mosques, preachers, and publications. In this way, Natsir sought to target *pesantren* and university campuses.[157] In a sense, the formation of DDII represented recognition by the harder-edged Arabized modernists that, following the failures of Muslim politicians to enshrine the Jakarta Charter in the Indonesian constitutional debates of the 1940s and 1950s, a more gradual, bottom-up approach to religious proselytization (or *dakwah*) was a better way of Islamizing society.[158] Significantly, like its Persis/Al-Irsyad doctrinal forebears, DDII was characterized especially by a fear of Christian missionary efforts.[159]

The DDII subsequently—and unsurprisingly—established close ties with the Saudi-based World Islamic League (Rabitat al-'Alam al-Islami).[160] Natsir himself "long formally served as a prominent member" of the Rabitat."[161] In this way, the DDII became the "main channel in Indonesia for distributing scholarships" from the Rabitat for study in the Middle East.[162] In fact, "young, talented Muslim preachers" sponsored by DDII for study in the Middle East have been "expected to spearhead the expansion of *da'wa* activities to reach remote areas" on their return in the "hinterlands of Java and other Indonesian islands."[163] In addition, through Natsir's influence, the Institute for the Study of Islam and Arabic (LIPIA) was set up in 1980 with Saudi funding. LIPIA was from the start a branch of the Imam Muhammad bin Saud University in Riyadh, and its faculty were mainly Saudi scholars who taught a curriculum modelled on the parent university. All tuition at LIPIA is conducted in Arabic, and admission standards were, and still are, high. Once accepted, however, tuition was free and students were provided with a generous stipend, by Indonesian standards.[164] LIPIA graduates have gone on to become preachers on many Indonesian university campuses, as well as publishers, teachers, and *ulama*.[165] LIPIA graduates also have established Arabized modernist *pesantren* with Saudi funding, and these have provided a "mechanism" for spreading Arabized modernist Islam through outreach activities and through training local "teachers and propagators."[166] Consequently, the permeation throughout society of the particularly harder-edged Saudi Wahhabi interpretations of Islamic modernism has been ensured.[167] Fealy and Bubalo go so far as to aver that "no single institution seems to have done more than LIPIA to propagate contemporary forms of *salafism* in Indonesia."[168]

THE WAHHABI CO-OPTATION OF SALAFISM AND THE IMPACT ON INDONESIAN ISLAM

The observant reader would have noted the apparent conflation of the terms Wahhabism and Salafism in the previous section in relation to the spread of Arabized modernist Islam in Indonesia. Certainly, in the nineteenth century, Salafism and Wahhabism would never have been equated. Unlike Wahhabis, early Salafis like Abduh were relatively tolerant and not hostile to Sufism or mysticism.[169] By way of elaboration, as noted, the early Salafis were driven by the ethnocentric impulse to catch up with the West, as its founders "strove to project contemporary institutions such as democracy, constitutionalism, or socialism onto the foundational texts" and to "justify the paradigm of the modern nation-state within Islam."[170] In essence, as El Fadl argues, ultimately early Salafism was opportunistic at its core:

> Its proponents tended to be more interested in the end results than in maintaining the integrity or coherence of the juristic method. Salafism was marked by an anxiety to reach results that would render Islam compatible with modernity, far more than a desire to critically understand either modernity or the Islamic tradition itself.[171]

The resultant intellectual weaknesses at the core of Salafi modernism compelled its adherents, by the middle of the twentieth century, to "transform Islam into a politically reactive force engaged in a mundane struggle for identity and self-determination."[172] Salafis responded to the challenges of the modern world by "adopting pietistic fictions about the presumed perfection of Islam"—asserting, for example, that Islam was responsible for promoting democracy, pluralism, and women's rights well before the West did. Rather than seeking to critically engage with Islamic traditions themselves, the Salafis—clearly driven by ethnocentric and mimetic in-group impulses—raised these issues "primarily as a means of affirming self-worth and attaining a measure of emotional empowerment."[173] According to the Salafis, all that a society needed to do in order to fully enjoy the "benefits of democracy, human rights, economic development, or women's rights was to give full expression to the real and genuine Islam."[174] Thus by the middle of the twentieth century the term "Salafism," because of its "intellectual carelessness" and dearth of "systematic and rigorous analysis," had developed a "flexible and malleable meaning."[175] The word "Salafi" enjoyed a "natural appeal" because it "connotes authenticity and legitimacy";[176]

thus it eventually was *co-opted and absorbed* by Saudi Wahhabism. El Fadl again:

> By the late 1970s, Wahhabism had co-opted the Salafi creed to the point that Salafism had become a code word for antiliberal values. The puritanism that resulted from this co-optation was invariably intolerant, supremacist, oppressive toward women, opposed to rationalism, hostile towards most forms of artistic expression, and rigidly literalistic.[177]

The above discussion helps us appreciate why this current work shall, accordingly, henceforth employ the term "Salafism"—in its modern *Wahhabized* sense—to denote one Branch of the Tree of Arabized Islamic modernism in Indonesia. The space devoted here to the etymology of latter-day Salafism is warranted because its impact on Javanese Islam has been felt in profound ways. First and foremost has been the propagation of the idea that true Muslims must rid Islam of any cultural "contamination" or "innovation" (*bida*). This immediately has put Salafis at odds, as we saw earlier, with traditionalists, whose Islam is both heavily influenced by reliance on a long line of scholarship dating back to the time of the Prophet and infused with Sufi and Javanese mystical elements, including saint worship. This *radical synchronizing* tendency of the latter-day Salafis is in essence an attempt to transform modern Javanese and Indonesian Islam into facsimiles of seventh-century Arabian Islam. It is worth reiterating that this motivation was in fact what drove the founder of Wahhabism himself. El Fadl again:

> Effectively, 'Abd al-Wahhab was declaring the particulars of Bedouin culture to be the one and only true Islam and then universalizing these particulars by making them obligatory upon all Muslims.[178]

This is precisely why the teaching curriculum at LIPIA, for example, was seen by ex-students such as the liberal Indonesian Muslim activist Ulil Abshar Abdalla, who studied there from 1988 to 1993, as "hostile to the local Indonesian culture and Muslim practices."[179] In addition to having Arabized modernist educational backgrounds, many Indonesian Salafi leaders today also happen to be of Hadrami Arab descent and retain strong emotional connections not to Java but rather to the Middle East. For example, Habib Rizieq Shihab, leader of the Front Pembela Islam or Islamic Defenders Front, a militia notorious for attempting to "cleanse" Indonesian society by "smashing up Jakarta nightclubs, bars, and pool halls it considered dens of vice," remains very proud of the Hadrami Arab lineage that he openly proclaims he shares with Al Qaeda leader Osama bin Laden, whose own father had been born in Yemen and migrated to Saudi Arabia.[180] Furthermore, in his Jakarta home, Shihab not only has a large color portrait of bin Laden, but also "a framed poster with dozens of portraits of Muslim holy men who were responsible for spreading the teachings of Islam centuries ago in far-off Yemen."[181] Shihab is unequivocal in proclaiming the superiority of Arabs to the Javanese in terms of being the "most aggressive protectors of Muslim interests and partisans of strict Islamic rule."[182]

Another Salafi militant leader, Jafar Umar Thalib, leader of the Laskar Jihad militia that took part in sectarian fighting in the Maluku conflict in eastern Indonesia in 2000, is also of Hadrami Arab descent and a DDII scholarship recipient who studied in Saudi Arabia.[183] The leading Indonesian moderate scholar Azyumardi Azra echoes El Fadl when he asserts that in Indonesia, many Arabized modernist leaders of the Salafi bent "believe that the Islam they adhere to and their interpretation of Islam is more accurate than the indigenous brand."[184] This is reinforced by a generalized "core-periphery dynamic" in Indonesian and for that matter Southeast Asian Islam that creates an "infantile religiosity" among Southeast Asian Muslims and creates a collective mindset that tends to consider a "brilliant but nevertheless non-theologically trained, non-Arabic speaking Muslim leader" as less "credible" than someone who has "the credentials of speaking and reading Arabic, being educated in the Middle East," and who "exemplifies piety with his robe, cap and beard."[185] It is the very pronounced ethnocentric, Arab-Islam-is-superior impulse that prompted Habib Rizieq Shihab to inform the American journalist Tracy Dahlby that Indonesia would resolve its multiple moral, economic, and social crises only when the government adopted *shariah* Islam and stopped being deluded that Western culture was "good, superb."[186] It is worth recognizing that what is happening to Javanese Islam today is not at all unique. A colorful but telling description of the strident worldwide modern Salafi drive to promote scriptural literalism over traditional scholarship and *synchronize* all expressions of Islam with the ostensibly correct and superior Bedouin Arab interpretation is provided by one keen Muslim observer in the United Kingdom:

> [The Saudi-trained preachers] spoke passionately about the idea of one God, *tawheed* in Arabic, and ceaselessly warned against *shirk*, or polytheism.... Most impressively, they always referred directly to the Koran or the Prophet Mohammed's wisdom, bypassing fourteen centuries of commentary and scholarship on Islam's primary sources.... They had huge bushy beards and their trousers were very short, just below their knees. They looked like people from another era, austere in their ways, harsh in their conduct, and constantly reprimanding us for our own.[187]

The eminent French scholar of Islam Olivier Roy similarly has observed that the Saudi-sponsored global Salafi movement represents a "disembedding and asceticising" project, as it has long sought the "purification of religious practice of all elements of social and cultural context."[188] Essentially, Salafi Islam is a "de-territorialized Islam," bereft of "national or cultural identities, traditions and histories"—save for the Bedouin Arab culture at its core—and reduced to an "abstract faith and moral code."[189]

ENTER THE ISLAMISTS

To be sure, Salafism and its rigid emphasis on "correct" Islam has not been the only way in which Arabized modernist Islam has cast a looming shadow over indigenous Javanese variants. Beginning in the late 1970s and continuing into the 1980s, DDII played a key role in translating key texts of the Egyptian Muslim Brotherhood, the other major Middle Eastern modernist movement that has profoundly impacted Indonesian Islam.[190] The Brotherhood had been formed by schoolteacher Hassan al-Banna in 1928. Inspired by the original reformist Salafis such as Abduh and Rida, al-Banna was likewise concerned with Islam's relative decline vis-à-vis the West, a fact driven home by the dissolution of the once-powerful Ottoman caliphate in 1924 and the carving up of its empire by Western powers. Like Abduh and other early Salafis, al-Banna felt that to reverse the slide, the Muslim world had to return to the fundamentals of Islam.[191] Unlike the early Salafis, however, who "sought to revive Islam essentially through the force of their ideas and individual activism," al-Banna established a *movement* designed to restore Islam to its past glories.[192] Al-Banna reckoned that a return to Islam necessitated the establishment of an Islamic State based on the *shariah* or Islamic Law. Political parties would be banned, administrative posts would be given to those with a religious background, and government would closely regulate private morals. Al-Banna advocated a gradualist, bottom-up strategy of Islamization of society as a prelude to the setting up of an Islamic State. Hence Brotherhood activists were engaged in grassroots work ranging from education and social welfare activities to setting up medical clinics, factories, and athletic clubs for youths.[193] The idea was to spark a "spiritual awakening" from below to slowly build the foundations of a genuine Islamic State.[194] The Brotherhood, moreover, as part of its drive to transform society, could not ignore the need for political activity. In fact, throughout the Brotherhood's existence the internal debate concerning the relative merits of spiritual and social strategies for Islamizing society as opposed to more overtly political modalities has never quite been satisfactorily resolved. Thus in the late 1940s, Brotherhood members, social welfare work aside, also pushed for the reform of Egypt's constitution, agitated against official corruption, and participated in the Arab-Israeli war in 1948; they launched strikes and even engaged in acts of terror and political assassination. The Brotherhood's violent confrontation with Cairo led to al-Banna's assassination in 1949.[195] Al-Banna's demise paved the way for the rise of another Brotherhood activist with decidedly more revolutionary and violent views on the need for Islamizing society: Sayyid Qutb, whose impact will be scrutinized more closely in the next chapter.

Muslim Brotherhood ideas came to be circulated in the Indonesian context through, as noted, DDII translations into Bahasa but also, importantly through LIPIA. Many LIPIA faculty members have Muslim Brotherhood backgrounds.[196] To elaborate: given the shared desire to return to the pristine fundamentals of the Prophet's Islam of seventh-century Arabia, there were sufficient commonalities in faith and doctrine between the Saudi Salafis and the Egyptian Brotherhood activists.[197] In the 1950s and 1960s, therefore, King Faisal of Saudi Arabia, anxious about the secularist threat posed by Gamal Abdul Nasser's pan-Arab nationalist ideology, had discreetly supported Muslim Brotherhood subversive activity within Egypt. However, Nasser cracked down on the Brotherhood, imprisoning many members, including Qutb, who himself was executed in 1966. Following this, the Saudis welcomed persecuted Brotherhood cadres into the Kingdom, and many of the latter were employed in teaching positions on the proviso that they not propagate the more politically activist aspects of their philosophy.[198] This was because the Saudi Salafis saw themselves as religious activists above all else and regarded "most forms of political organization and political activity as an unacceptable diversion from the focus on faith."[199] At any rate, in Indonesia, perhaps because of the residual Brotherhood influences at LIPIA, throughout the 1980s and into the 1990s, some observers noted that LIPIA graduates at times evinced a Salafi puritanism combined with a Brotherhood-like politically activist outlook.[200]

Muslim Brotherhood ideas also found expression in the Indonesian milieu through the Campus Islam movement that sprouted in the 1980s in response to the New Order regime's banning of political activity in universities.[201] The largest campus-based movement was Gerakan Tarbiyah, whose student members were greatly attracted to the Brotherhood model of forming small, tight-knit cells or *usroh* within which emphasis was placed on strict observance of ritual obligations, mutual support, acquisition of Islamic knowledge, and social welfare activities.[202] One informant for this book, Al Chaidar, originally from the traditionally conservative Islamic city of Aceh in Sumatra, began to feel alienated while studying at the University of Indonesia in Jakarta as he found that, being "a local remote area person from Aceh," he could not quite fit in with his peers, who were, in his words, "very Jakarta-style minded" or liberal. This is why he gravitated towards Gerakan Tarbiyah, whose members actively engaged in "reciting Qur'an or reading and discussing the religious thing."[203] He provided this author with an insight into the very practical way in which the Tarbiyah activists worked to win recruits to the *usroh* cells:

> [They] gave me a kind of true solidarity. I never found it before. I feel that this is a *true kind of brotherhood in the religion* and they really help me in any kind of way of my troubles . . . in times of staying away from my hometown in Aceh. So I feel myself like there is some, my own brother who

will try to, what say, look after me and try to provide some help if I need [italics added].[204]

Tarbiyah members saw themselves as a vanguard tasked with bringing genuine Islamic values to Indonesian society. Like al-Banna, whose works were widely read, Tarbiyah activists believed that while Islam and the State were inseparable, a genuine Islamization of society had to come before the successful setting up of an Islamic State.[205] When the Asian Financial Crisis struck and Soeharto's by-then unpopular and corrupt New Order regime began to teeter in May 1998, the originally apolitical Tarbiyah members began to engage in direct political activity, forming in April 1998 an anti-Soeharto student organization, KAMMI (Indonesian Muslim Student Action Union), which helped to bring the regime down in the following month. In August of the same year, Tarbiyah activists formed Partai Keadilan (PK or Justice Party) and proceeded to win 1.9 percent of the vote in the 1999 elections and seven seats in the national parliament. Encouraged, the party rebranded itself in time for the 2004 elections as the newly reorganized but essentially the same Partai Keadilan Sejahtera (PKS or Prosperity and Justice Party). It won 7.3 percent of the votes and 45 seats in the new 550-member parliament.[206] The interesting fact about PKS is that it does not wear its Islam on its party sleeves. In the 1999 and 2004 elections, PK and subsequently PKS campaigned not so much for an Islamic State, but rather for secular (if still Islamically relevant) issues such as fighting corruption, socioeconomic equality, and political reform. However, PKS leaders betray residual Muslim Brotherhood influences in admitting that a genuinely Islamic State is still "an aspiration," but that "if the substance sufficiently represents the name (i.e., 'Islamic state'), the name does not need to reflect the substance."[207] Other important Campus Islam movements include Hizbut Tahrir Indonesia (HTI or the Indonesian Party of Liberation) and Jemaah Tabligh (Preaching Community).[208]

To return to our Garden of Indonesian Islam metaphor, what the Muslim Brotherhood–inspired PKS activists of today represent is the *second* Branch of the Tree of Arabized modernism: Islamism. If the Salafi Branch stridently seeks to propagate and regulate the "correct" interpretation of Islam, the Islamist Branch seeks to secure political power in order to enforce that correct interpretation. In other words, while Salafism represents a puritan outlook, Islamism represents a *political ideology*. Salafis promote above all the idea that a good Muslim must strictly observe *shariah*-derived standards of worship, ritual, dress, and overall behavioral standards. They want to encourage Indonesians to be "total Muslims," applying Islam in all aspects of their lives.[209] The majority of Salafis, in fact, may possess "neither a systematic ideology" nor "global political agenda."[210] Islamism, on the other hand, "turns the traditional religion of Islam into a twentieth-century-style ideology."[211] Daniel Pipes states aptly that Islamists seek to "build the just society by regimenting people according to a preconceived plan, only this time with an Islamic orientation."[212] Despite national variations, Islamists worldwide share the common belief that seeking political power in order to Islamize whole societies is the only way Islam as a faith can revitalize itself—and recapture the former preeminent position it enjoyed vis-à-vis the West. Modern Islamist movements thus include the Egyptian Muslim Brotherhood, the Jama'at-I Islami in the Indian subcontinent, and the Iranian ideological forces behind the 1979 Revolution that brought down the Shah. These Islamists have sought to construct "ideological systems" and "models" for "distinctive polities that challenged what they saw to be the alternative systems: nationalism, capitalism and Marxism."[213] However, it is important to understand that the *same ethnocentric, mimetic impulse* to restore Islam's past glories underlie both the Salafi ambition to closely police individual Muslim conduct to ensure that the "proper" Arabized interpretation of Islam is preserved, as well as the Islamist quest for political power to ensure Islam's societal ascendancy. Salafism and Islamism are related in the sense that they are both Branches of the same Tree of Arabized modernist Islam, but they are analytically distinguishable. While Salafis are genuinely pious if extremely dogmatic in their proselytizing zeal, Islamists, in relentlessly pursuing power, may lose touch with the ethical core of the very faith they are seeking to preserve and champion.[214] This process of ethical or moral disengagement is one powerful reason why a slide into a violent mindset supportive of militancy and terrorism is possible, as we shall see shortly.

CONCLUSION

In this chapter we have sketched out the key features of the Garden of Indonesian Islam from which the JI network has ultimately emerged. We have seen that the picture is somewhat complex. For one thing, the Islam that was transplanted from the thirteenth century onward in Java and elsewhere in the Indonesian islands, in particular its Sunni/Shafi'i theological basis, has been shaped by Javanese ecology and strongly suffused with mystical, soft, Sufi-influenced southern Indian elements. This means that the Islam of Java was traditionally built on cultural foundations characterized, in Hofstedian terms, by collectivism, large power-distance sentiments and, importantly, a weak uncertainty-avoidance outlook. In fact, despite social, economic, and demographic changes in Javanese Islam since the 1960s, the collectivist and large power-distance dimensions still hold true across the board. It is, however, possible to make one broad distinction between competing Javanese Muslim subcultures on the all-important dimension of uncertainty avoidance. It is possible to distinguish, for analytical purposes, three key subcultures—or Trees, as we have euphemistically termed them—within the Garden of Indonesian Islam. The first is the large, dominant Tree of *abangan* and *santri* traditionalist Islam that has grown up around the core of the NU educational and associational pillar. This Javanese Muslim subculture has long remained defined by a relatively weak uncertainty-avoidance outlook. The second, smaller Tree represents the Javanese *santri* modernists, built around the Muhammadiyah pillar, characterized by a more conservative outlook but nevertheless still marked by relatively weak uncertainty-avoidance levels. Third, and of great significance, the smallest Tree represents the heavily Arabized modernist Muslim community, coalesced around the Middle East–oriented educational and associational pillar with organizations such as Persis, Al-Irsyad, DDII, and LIPIA at its core. We saw that the Tree of Arabized modernist Islam in Indonesia has grown two "Branches": Salafism, which seeks to radically synchronize all expressions of Islam in the archipelago with "the particulars of Bedouin culture"; and Islamism, which seeks political power in order to effect such a radical synchronization from above. What both Branches of Arabized modernism have in common, in a Hofstedian sense, is *a very strong uncertainty-avoidance outlook*. For both the Salafis and the Islamists in the Indonesian milieu, in other words, *what is different is most definitely dangerous*. As we shall now see, these three Trees, which have long dominated the Garden of Indonesian Islam, have interacted with one another as well as with twentieth-century Indonesian geopolitical and political developments to produce a specific "Bouquet" of Javanese Islamic radicalism: the subculture of Darul Islam. This was the crucial next step along the Radical Pathway to the formation of the JI network, and it is to this that we must now turn.

3

The "Bouquet" of Darul Islam

In the previous chapter, we sketched out the key features of the theological landscape of Indonesian, particularly Javanese Islam today, which we euphemistically termed the Garden. Broadly speaking, we saw that three metaphorical "Trees," each signifying a distinct Muslim subculture, can be distinguished analytically. While the Tree of Javanese traditionalism grew up around the core of NU educational and associational "pillars" at its theological epicenter, the Tree of Javanese modernism arose from the various linked institutional nodes of the Muhammadiyah pillar. Finally, the Persis/Al-Irsyad/DDII/LIPIA educational and associational pillar gave rise to a third Tree, the subculture of Arabized modernism. In the current chapter we shall narrow our analytical focus even further, zooming in on one particular "Bouquet" that has flowered at the point where Branches from these Trees have grown into and "entwined" around one another. We shall call the ensuing emergent subcultural Bouquet Darul Islam—after the armed revolt of the so-called Darul Islam movement against the secular Indonesian Republic from 1948 to 1965. We shall see that it was the rather inchoate elements of what we may call *Darul Islamic* subculture that gave rise in turn to the more pronounced *political ideology* of what we may term *Darul Islamism*. Understanding how and why the Bali tragedy of October 2002 occurred requires comprehension of how elements of the Darul Islamic subculture of the rural hinterlands of Java was transmuted, first, into the virulent Darul Islamist ideology of the historic Negara Islam Indonesia

(NII—also called the Darul Islam or DI) movement; and thereafter, following the Afghan *jihad* against the Soviet military in the 1980s, into the even more radical paradigm driving the NII's later mutation, JI.

As a discrete historical episode, the Darul Islam/NII revolt certainly constituted a massive trauma for the secular Indonesian Republic, costing the lives, by some estimates, of 15,000 to 20,000 people and resulting in one million refugees. The damage done to Indonesian society and economy by the DI rebellion dwarfs by far anything modern terror networks like JI have been able to inflict: bridges, railway lines, roads, government offices, and other communications infrastructure were destroyed, "with severe disruption to agriculture and industry."[1] Throughout the seventeen years of the DI revolt, there were five main affected provinces: West Java (violence broke out in late 1948), Central Java (late April 1949), South Sulawesi (August 1953), Aceh (September 1953), and South Kalimantan (late 1954). Of these, "West Java was by far the most important." As Greg Fealy suggests:

> It was not only the base of [DI leader] Kartosoewirjo and "seat" of the Indonesian Islamic State, it was also the province which presented the most severe security challenge to the central government and its military forces. More lives and property were lost there than in any other region of the DI rebellion.[2]

Although DI ultimately failed to attain its political goal of an Indonesian Islamic State, it nevertheless "inspired subsequent generations of radical Muslims with its commitment to a *shari'a*-based state and its heavy sacrifices in the cause of *jihad*."[3] It was ultimately from the specific Bouquet of Darul Islam that today's JI network "flowered." To understand the profound and continuing impact of Darul Islam on and its ongoing intimate links with, JI requires an in-depth look at the iconic founder of DI, the charismatic Javanese Sekarmadji Maridjan Kartosoewirjo. Against the backdrop of the highly collectivist, large power-distance milieu of Javanese culture and society, Kartosoewirjo remains the "primary political inspiration for Abu Bakar Ba'asyir, his associates and thousands of others" who continue to press for the fullest application of Islamic law in the Indonesian Republic.[4]

Kartosoewirjo had two major formative ideational experiences within the Sarekat Islam organization, the first national-level mass Muslim interest association in Indonesian history. First, political life in the intellectually variegated Sarekat environment, with its aggressively competitive, sometimes cross-cutting Islamic, nationalist, socialist, and communist elements—precariously united only by a common opposition to Dutch colonial domination—greatly sharpened Kartosoewirjo's very human, ethnocentric tendency toward *categorical, us-them thinking*, despite the deeply ingrained Javanese cultural capacity for tolerating difference (a.k.a. weak uncertainty avoidance). Second, the Sarekat interlude also impressed upon

Kartosoewirjo the importance of promoting a muscular Islam—very much in the vein of the outward-looking, aggressive, revolutionary desert Islam that the Prophet himself developed in the inclement, *jahili* political milieu of seventh-century Arabia—that actively sought a restructuring of Indonesian society around a corpus of Islamic values by whatever means possible, including *jihad*. The experience of World War Two and its immediate aftermath, with the political victory of the secular Republican forces over the advocates of an Islamic Indonesian state, sharpened both Kartosoewirjo's us-versus-them mental template and reinforced an underlying xenophobia that fuelled his belief in armed *jihad* as not merely an obligation, but a necessity, to ensure the success of Islam in the Indonesian context. Following this examination of Kartosoewirjo's background, we will then isolate and examine the key premises of Darul Islamic subculture and its ideological by-product of Darul Islamism and study the varying ways in which three key players in the future JI network, *viz.* JI spiritual leader Abu Bakar Ba'asyir and the operational leaders Mukhlas and Imam Samudra, were shaped by their early socialization into both subcultural and ideological milieus. In sum, this chapter will show that the collective worldview of these three JI activists, while undoubtedly influenced by more recent so-called "Salafi Jihadist" thinking originating in the Middle East, was nevertheless even more profoundly shaped by learned ways of thinking, feeling, and acting derived from their immersion in the subcultural Bouquet of Darul Islam.

THE GARDENER TENDING THE BOUQUET: S. M. KARTOSOEWIRJO, FATHER OF THE DARUL ISLAM MOVEMENT

Kartosoewirjo was by far, as the Dutch scholar Cornelis van Dijk observes, "the outstanding leader" of the Darul Islam movement, both a "skillful organizer" and "capable of attracting a large following among the rural population."[5] Kartosoewirjo was born near Cepu, a small, quiet town on the border between Central and East Java in early February 1905. He came from a relatively well-off middle-class family that was not particularly religious. His father was a civil servant in the Dutch colonial administration, and the young Kartosoewirjo, a highly precocious boy, was sent for his education to the best schools: at age six, he was sent to the Native School of the Second Grade for his four-year elementary education. The Native Schools were of a higher quality than the People's Schools, which were intended to provide the mass of the population with a rudimentary education. Kartosoewirjo first attended the Dutch Native School and at fourteen enrolled in the European Primary School, both elite institutions in which the colonial language Dutch was taught. Knowledge of Dutch was the key to upward mobility in the socio-political order constructed by the colonizers.[6] Kartosoewirjo thus received a relatively good education for a non-Dutch colonial subject and he exploited it, displaying great energy and ambition, while coming of age politically in the first quarter of the twentieth century—just as the first stirrings of Indonesian nationalism and restiveness with Dutch colonial rule were increasingly pronounced. In fact, in 1927, at twenty-two years of age, while studying at the prestigious Netherlands Indies Medical School in Surabaya, Kartosoewirjo found himself expelled for engaging in far too overt political activities.[7] Kartosoewirjo was hardly unique in this sense. He was part of a growing movement of newly educated Indonesian elites, essentially products of Dutch schools, some of whom had learned about nationalism and Marxist ideas in Europe.[8] Spearheading this anticolonial movement in the first decades of the twentieth century was the Sarekat Islam (Islamic Association), a mass organization that was founded in 1912 and began as an economic association meant to "promote Javan merchant interests to offset competition with Chinese traders active throughout the Southeast Asian region."[9] The Sarekat Islam had grown out of an association formed three years earlier, the Sarekat Dagang Islamiyah (Islamic Commercial Union), which had not been very successful.[10] The Sarekat Islam quickly took on a political hue as an umbrella organization for a variety of groups, individuals, and factions who saw the advantage of cooperating with one another. Although the organization initially had Islam in its name, this was in truth a bit of a misnomer, as this "did not discourage people from joining it who were only nominal Muslims or had no relationship with Islam at all."[11] In fact, as Federspiel notes, Sarekat Islam

> became a mass organization without regard for religion, ethnicity, or ideology, allowing those with Muslim, secularist, and communist agendas to work within a common framework in which the greater goal, usually left unsaid, was removing the Dutch from power.[12]

This innate flexibility enabled the Sarekat Islam to become the first national-level, "genuinely mass-based Islamic-nationalist organization."[13] Sarekat Islam leaders came from Java, but the membership was more diverse. Javanese and Minangs were the two most prominent groups, but there were other ethnic groups from across the Indonesian islands as well. At the height of the Sarekat's popularity between 1912 and 1919, its membership numbered between two to three million.[14] The educational backgrounds of Sarekat leaders at this time were fairly eclectic; some had Islamic backgrounds, some Javanese, and many had been exposed to a Western education.[15] The first years of the Sarekat were not actually seized with the issue of uplifting the status of Islam in the archipelago. Anticolonial nationalism proved to be the main motivation, and already by 1915, the Sarekat was split between moderate nationalists, who wished to work with the Dutch toward gradual disengagement, and communist-inspired militants, who actively called for direct confrontation with the colonial government.[16] Things came to a head in 1926, when the Dutch, in response to the call for a general strike in the public sector, arrested scores of activists. Significantly, collateral damage was inflicted in the form of severe restrictions on associational freedoms that so severely enfeebled the Sarekat that membership levels fell precipitously thereafter.[17] Nevertheless, the ability of the Sarekat to survive for some fifteen years as an unmolested legal entity prior to the 1926 crackdown was due to the skill of key leaders, particularly the charismatic Javanese Raden Umar Sayed Tjokroaminoto (1882–1934), who, not insignificantly, counted the young rising star Kartosoewirjo as a protégé.[18] As a matter of fact, Kartosoewirjo, shortly after his expulsion from the Netherlands Indies Medical School, went to live with Tjokroaminoto, working as his private secretary from 1927 to 1929.[19] It is interesting that Tjokroaminoto was at different times a political mentor not just to Kartosoewirjo but also to future Indonesian president Soekarno and even to future communist leaders such as Alimin and Musso. Tjokroaminoto was a gifted man who was said to possess a "very flexible mind capable of absorbing a combination of Islamic, nationalist and socialist ideas," and whose house was the "centre of the anti-Dutch movement" in politically restive Surabaya.[20]

Although Tjokroaminoto was a committed nationalist, the degree to which he was genuinely committed to Islamic ideals can be questioned. A highly intelligent graduate of the Dutch Native School system, Tjokroaminoto, like his protégé Kartosoewirjo, was a shrewd politician who boosted the early mass appeal of Sarekat Islam—as well as his own personal standing—by exploiting the messianic aspects of Javanese culture. In fact, the Javanese masses—culturally predisposed toward a large power-distance outlook—were well-versed in the so-called "Djayabaya prophecy" concerning a Javanese liberator who would come after a period of "distress and oppression" and came to regard Tjokroaminoto as Prabu Hery Tjokro, the long-awaited *ratu adil* or just king.[21] Tjokroaminoto's opportunistic exploitation of Javanese cultural beliefs prompted criticism from strongly *santri* Sarekat leaders such as the modernist Agus Salim, who helped impart a more grounded Islamic modernist character to the Sarekat.[22] In fact, Kartosoewirjo joined forces with Tjokroaminoto only after the 1926 crackdown, when the Sarekat was already declining in political influence. While the organization was shorn of its communist wing through a combination of expulsions and Dutch repression, Soekarno, Tjokroaminto's other well-known protégé, began building up a strong mass secular nationalist movement in Bandung that soon assumed the leading role in the anticolonial movement. Worse, by the late 1920s, Muhammadiyah and NU had begun to attract even urban and rural Muslim support away from the Sarekat. The upshot of all this was that by 1927, Tjokroaminoto's personal political capital had been diminished and the Sarekat reduced to the status of a "minor Islamic party."[23] Perhaps it was the need to consolidate the position of the enfeebled Sarekat within the Muslim constituency that compelled Tjokroaminoto to adopt harder-edged Islamic modernist convictions by this time. For instance, although he agreed with the avowed goal of the communists to achieve social justice for the masses, he now maintained more explicitly that the secular, atheistic outlook of communism was anathema to Muslims. Tjokroaminoto argued instead that while Islam also promoted the themes of egalitarianism and social justice espoused by the communists, "the tithe, the poor tax, and other Islamic institutions" were the superior Islamic solutions to meet society's welfare needs.[24]

Tjokroaminoto also changed the name of the organization to Partai Sarekat Islam Indonesia (PSII) by 1930, emphasizing its move away from "its earlier international pan-Islamitic ideals" to a focus on uplifting the status of Islam in the East Indies itself.[25] The more strongly modernist character of the Sarekat of the late 1920s and narrowing worldview of Tjokroaminoto appeared to mirror Kartosoewirjo's own political and ideological evolution. Kartosoewirjo's first taste of political activism had been in the Surabaya branch of the Jong Java or Young Java youth movement in 1923.[26] However, because the Jong Java stressed traditional Javanese values and culture and did not seem sufficiently Islamic, Kartosoewirjo eventually defected to the harder-edged Jong Islamieten Bond (Young Muslim League), a self-consciously modernist movement formed in 1925 by disaffected Muslim Jong Java activists and led by the modernist Sarekat leader Agus Salim, mentioned earlier. The Jong Islamieten Bond shared with the Sarekat of the late 1920s the stock modernist perspective that "Western domination could only be combated by stripping Indonesian Islam of its heretical components and adopting those achievements of Western civilization that had given the West its technical superiority."[27] Kartosoewirjo became a Jong Islamieten Bond leader, and it was because of his activities as part of the movement that he was expelled from the Netherlands Indies Medical School in 1927.[28]

After 1930, the Sarekat/PSII's transformation into a strongly modernist Muslim party with a smaller and leaner membership than in its heyday continued apace. This was because the second-echelon leaders who had assumed leading roles following the leftist purge had been educated in Islamic schools, in contrast with the pre-1926 Sarekat leadership cohort, and, significantly, "had not been much exposed to Western learning."[29] Meanwhile, Tjokroaminoto passed away in 1934, precipitating a leadership struggle.[30] At issue was whether a policy of cooperation with, or active resistance against, the Dutch offered a superior prospect for ultimately evicting the latter from the Indies. In 1935, a year after Tjokroaminoto's demise, Agus Salim, now the PSII chairman, argued that the party should review its long-standing policy of noncooperation or *hijrah*, a "total disregard of the Dutch for the sake of building up an independent Indonesian, Muslim-inspired society." Salim reckoned that the confrontational *hijrah* policy would only invite reprisals, weakening the party further given the increasingly repressive attitudes of the Dutch colonial government.[31] Opposing Salim was Abikusno Tjokrosujoso (d. circa 1960), the brother of the late Tjokroaminoto, who insisted on preserving the *hijrah* posture. In July 1936, Tjokrosujoso's faction won control of the party at the twenty-second PSII congress. Significantly, Tjokrosujoso's victory was aided in no small measure by the strong support of the increasingly powerful Kartosoewirjo; together both men were able to command the support of younger party members. Tjokrosujoso wasted little time in doing two things: first, he moved to marginalize Agus Salim and his associates (they were expelled from the PSII the following year). Second, Tjokrosujoso made Kartosoewirjo vice-chairman of the party.[32] As vice-chairman, Kartosoewirjo was then tasked to flesh out the *hijrah* policy to codify the congress's endorsement of the concept. This assignment Kartosoewirjo eagerly accepted, proceeding to construct an argument explaining the Prophet's exercise of *hijrah* and its relationship to *jihad* and transposing it to the prevailing colonial context.[33] According to Kartosoewirjo, *hijrah* or withdrawal enabled the Indonesian Muslim community to engage in the great *jihad* of internal purification and strengthening to "assert itself as an instrument of God's will."[34] Kartosoewirjo, given the somewhat inclement political context, was astute enough to avoid "too aggressive an interpretation" of either concept, commenting that *jihad* should be understood as a genuine effort to follow "the path of God, the path of Truth, the path of Reality" and not be regarded simply as "war in the sense in which it is often understood by Western or Westernized people."[35] Nevertheless, implicit in Kartosoewirjo's arguments was the moral necessity for committed Muslims at the same time to remain ready to engage in the "small *jihad*," or "the application of force towards the enemy that threatened the Islamic community."[36]

Kartosoewirjo's political and ideological alliance with Tjokrosujoso did not last, however. By 1939, another bitter struggle broke out within the PSII's ranks, again over the issue of the appropriate political posture to be adopted vis-à-vis the Dutch. By this time, even Tjokrosujoso had changed his position and appeared to move closer to the position of his earlier rival Agus Salim—that perhaps a more conciliatory attitude in the face of steadily intensifying colonial Dutch repression would yield better dividends for the PSII and the wider Muslim community. This immediately enraged Kartosoewirjo, precipitating a bitter quarrel that ended with the latter's expulsion from the PSII, together with several like-minded associates, in particular Kyai Jusuf Tauziri and Kamran, then the PSII youth leader. Both men would in time become principal lieutenants in Kartosoewirjo's subsequent creation of the Darul Islam militant movement.[37] Kartosoewirjo proceeded to set up another party in March 1940, also calling it PSII, to make the point that the old PSII under Tjokrosujoso had betrayed the "true struggle of the Islamic community" and was no longer deserving of the name Partai Sarekat Islam Indonesia.[38] Kartosoewirjo inaugurated this "Second PSII" in Malangbong, a small town near Garut and Tasikmalaya in West Java from which he had operated as the PSII provincial representative since 1929. It was decided at the meeting inaugurating the rival PSII that "the *hijrah* policy should not only be continued, but should even be carried through in a more radical way."[39] The success of the Second PSII was very much limited, however, to the West Java region, partly because the nervous Dutch colonial government imposed martial law on May 10, immediately banning public political meetings, after the German assault on the Netherlands in May 1940 and the emergence of a Japanese threat in the Southeast Asian region. Hence Kartosoewirjo was able to attract support for the Second PSII from only six old PSII branches: Cirebon, Cibadak, Sukabumi, Pasanggrahan, Wanaraja, and of course, Malangbong.[40] Still, the short-lived Second PSII initiative did pave the way for the future DI movement because one outcome was the decision to set up an Islamic school for the education of a new leadership to "train propagandists in the new ideology" Kartosoewirjo was very keen to propagate.[41] Accordingly, in the same month when the Second PSII was established, Kartosoewirjo also set up the Suffah Institute, "a commune equipped with a modern *pesantren* at Bojong, Malangbong."[42] In this context, "Suffah" alluded to an institution organized by the Prophet himself to personally train young men to engage in the propagation of the faith.[43]

Kartosoewirjo, who sought to emulate somewhat literally the actual *hijrah* of the Prophet in physically relocating to Medina in 622 C.E., instructed his followers to pool their wealth and move to the Suffah commune, where they were expected to lead a simple, egalitarian lifestyle, enduring both the hardships of an agrarian existence and less–than-ideal medical facilities. The Suffah commune was not uniformly successful, as some of Kartosoewirjo's followers who were wealthy landlords could not quite stomach the transition. Nevertheless, the Suffah Institute did attract *santri* from not just West Java but from beyond as well. Kyai Jusuf himself sent two sons and a nephew to join Kartosoewirjo as trainers and trainees.[44] Of no small importance, apart from regular, religious classes, astrology, and Dutch, the Suffah *pesantren* also propagated "militant Islamic doctrine."[45] In particular, Kartosoewirjo, who taught at the Suffah *pesantren* personally,[46] evinced the "dualistic view of humankind" that an underlying strong uncertainty-avoidance outlook generates when he emphasized the classical division between the Darul Islam and the Darul Harb and promised that the Darul Islam was bound to triumph over Islam's enemies in the Darul Harb.[47] Van Djik offers a useful description of the modus operandi of the Suffah Institute in the interval before the arrival of the Japanese:

> It formed a closed community, the student-members of which worked the institute fields, thus making it to a large extent self-supporting, where it was possible for strong personal ties to develop between students and teachers.[48]

In a pattern to be repeated much later in the case of the *pesantren* set up by JI leaders, it seems that Kartosoewirjo implicitly understood the value of *deliberate isolation* in facilitating personalized ideological programming of a small community of believers.

As it turned out, Kartosoewirjo did not have long to wait to put his abstract militant ideas into action. The Japanese invasion of the Dutch East Indies resulted in the banning of the Second PSII as well as the formal discontinuation of the Suffah Institute. However, precisely because the Suffah Institute was situated "at some distance from the centres of politics and administration," and was supposedly an educational institution, the Japanese left it alone for quite a while. This enabled Kartosoewirjo to surreptitiously build up a "militant rural base in West Java" by providing paramilitary training at the commune.[49] Kartosoewirjo thus was able to create a core cadre of trained fighters who formed, first, the "two principal post-war Islamic guerrilla organizations, *Hizbu'llah* and *Sabili'llah*," and later the "Islamic Army in West Java"—the Darul Islam militia.[50] As the tide of the war inexorably turned against Tokyo, Kartosoewirjo was inducted into the Hizbullah militia set up by the Japanese and was appointed head of the Malangbong Hizbullah branch. He also played a supervisory role in the Japanese-sponsored and secular nationalist-dominated *Java Hokokai* mass movement in neighboring Banten.[51] It was not long, however, before Kartosoewirjo's supporters turned against the Japanese and then the Dutch.[52] Following several aborted attempts to found an Islamic State in West Java in 1945, by February 1948, Kartosoewirjo, aided by Muslim militia from Sabilillah and Hizbullah, was actively setting up the administrative framework for an Islamic State in West Java (Negara Islam Indonesia or NII) along with an Indonesian Islamic Army (Tentara Islam Indonesia or TII). Later that year an Islamic constitution was drafted, and by late 1948, the Muslim forces engaged against both Republican and Dutch troops were calling themselves Darul Islam or TII.[53] Then, on August 7, 1949, Kartosoewirjo formally proclaimed the Negara Islam Indonesia (NII) in the village of Cisampak in Tasikmalaya. He had appointed himself DI Imam on May 5 the year before.[54] By the end of the 1940s the NII bureaucratic and security apparatus comprised a TII force of 12,000 men, complete with its own police and tax collectors, and covered most of rural West Java.[55] In attempting to pacify Kartosoewirjo, Soekarno had offered him the Defense Minister portfolio of the fledgling secular Indonesian Republic, but the newly self-declared DI Imam was having none of it. Kartosoewirjo's parting shot was that by "turning its back on Islam, the new government had made itself "as evil an enemy as the Dutch."[56]

THE ROOTS OF DARUL ISLAMIST VIOLENCE

It may reasonably be asked how Kartosoewirjo's DI, quite unusually for a Javanese-based movement, came to be characterized by a strong uncertainty-avoidance outlook. This is where our previously developed RP

Framework can be helpful, as it suggests that an individual's attitudes and behavior, while profoundly shaped by Culture, is at the same time affected by other elements, such as his or her level of Existential Identity Anxiety, Individual Personality attributes, and the group context in which the Individual finds himself situated.[57] First, it should be noted that Kartosoewirjo did not actually come from a *santri* family background, and although his education was excellent, it took place in secular and not Islamic schools. This curious fact does not escape the notice of Van Dijk:

> [Kartosoewirjo] attended the best schools that were open to "natives," where only the children of the "native" well-to-do and aristocracy were admitted. It is paradoxical for a man who for many years was to be leader of an Islamic rebellion that his formal education was essentially secular in nature. There are no indications that Kartosurwirjo visited any of the many Islamic schools.[58]

To be sure, as a young man he made an attempt to study the Qur'an and Islam but could do so only through Dutch sources, as he did not know Arabic. Moreover, Kartosoewirjo never ventured to the Middle East to deepen his knowledge of the faith in "Arab centres of Islam and Islamic modernism."[59] So how did Kartosoewirjo eventually become a violent Islamist? The most important element is clearly that from youth Kartosoewirjo could be said to have possessed a strong *internal* locus of control. First developed by J. B. Rotter in 1966, this social psychological construct, known more technically as "belief in internal locus of control of reinforcement," refers to the idea that "individuals are responsible for what happens to them, rather than other people, fate, chance, and so on."[60] In other words, people with this attribute believe that they can, through their own efforts, actively shape their environment and destiny. By contrast, individuals with an *external* locus of control believe that external factors, circumstances, and individuals are decisive in shaping their lives.[61] Although it is true that Kartosoewirjo was born into a large power-distance, collectivist Javanese culture that emphasized "harmony, obedience, and avoidance of conflict,"[62] the RP Framework informs us that Culture, while potent, is not necessarily decisive in shaping Individual Personality. Hence as an "internal," Kartosoewirjo, a very intelligent, well-educated individual who went to the top schools in the Dutch colonial order, did not passively accept his lot and that of his community, but felt instead that he could make a difference as a sociopolitical reformer, which is precisely why he joined the anticolonial movement and linked up with Tjokroaminoto. "People," the Canadian journalist Stewart Bell observes, "who think they can do anything in the world can just as easily be caught up in the quest for a radically better future, for extreme change, as those who have nothing. Perhaps even more so."[63] Bell may just as well have been talking about Kartosoewirjo.[64] That sociopolitical reform was needed in West Java, in any case, would have been obvious to Kartosoewirjo, who had firsthand experience, especially in the 1930s while he was based in Bojong, Malangbong, West Java, of the "contrast between the deprived rural villagers and the Dutch estate managers."[65]

This powerful inner drive to actively shape rather than be shaped by the environment suggests something else about Kartosoewirjo's psychological disposition. Social psychologists such as Leon Festinger and sociologists like Peter Berger have pointed out that human beings seek "cognitive consistency and a concomitant desire to avoid the experience of dissonance," because dissonance tends to produce "profound psychic stress and discomfort."[66] Religious individuals undergoing cognitive dissonance thus seek to cope in one of three ways. Either they "surrender" or reject those aspects of their belief systems that do not square with the existing social reality; they reinterpret their beliefs in light of the real-world evidence so that dissonance is somewhat reduced; or "rather than compromise their beliefs they seek to remake reality to fit their religious cognitions and expectations."[67] In short, as the sociologist Charles Selengut argues, the latter group seeks to "engage in militant transformation to force all others to accept their religious beliefs and demand that society be based on their religious views." The modalities of transformation may range from political activity and employment of propaganda to, ultimately, "religious violence."[68] The desire to reduce cognitive dissonance by reshaping and simplifying the myriad complexities and nuances of the surrounding sociopolitical order in accordance with one's preferred religious vision is the chief dispositional characteristic of the *religious fundamentalist*. As Moojan Momen explains, a key personality attribute of the fundamentalist is his overwhelming desire for "certainty." The fundamentalist individual tolerates "no ambiguities, no equivocations," and "no reservations."[69] Ambiguity, Momen adds, is "deeply unsatisfactory to the fundamentalist psyche."[70] Some psychologists like J. Harold Ellens go so far as to suggest that fundamentalism may be a form of "psychopathology":

> An essential component of this psychology is a rigid structuralist approach that has an obsessive-compulsive flavor to it. It is the mark of those who have *a very limited ability to live with the ambiguity inherent to healthy human life*. . . . Fundamentalism is a psychopathology that drives its proponents to the construction of orthodoxies. . . . [italics added].[71]

Although his internal drive to make a difference compelled Kartosoewirjo to join the Jong Java movement in Surabaya in 1923, the organization's lukewarm embrace of Islamic tenets and toleration of Javanese cultural accretions meant that the eclectic, cultural Islam it promoted probably grated on Kartosoewirjo's black-and-white fundamentalist disposition, prompting him to defect to the harder-edged and more unambiguously modernist Jong Islamieten Bond. Several factors reveal the "come-out-and-be-separate" tendency of what critical theorist Stuart Sim terms the "fundamentalist mentality": Kartosoewirjo's later, uncompromising insistence on maintaining the PSII's *hijrah* policy of noncooperation with Dutch colonial authorities in the 1930s; his setting up—in his mind—of a "purer," "undefiled" Second PSII; and most tellingly, his literalistic reading of the Prophet's *hijrah* in 622 to Medina, leading to the establishment of the geographically isolated Suffah commune in Malangbong in 1940. As Sim suggests, not only do fundamentalists seek the "desire for certainty," they equally seek "the power to enforce that certainty over others."[72] Sim argues that in the final analysis, the theological or ideological content of "religious fundamentalism" aside, fundamentalism of any kind as a *psychological, dispositional characteristic* has "more to do with power than spiritual matters." In other words, "power is a political rather than a spiritual issue." In essence, by disposition, the fundamentalist seeks "control, control, control."[73] Kartosoewirjo's powerful internal locus of control, combined with an innate, black-and-white fundamentalist disposition, represented important stepping stones toward his ultimate radicalization.

Another milestone on Kartosoewirjo's personal Radical Pathway was his "born-again" Muslim experience, so to speak, while at Malangbong, West Java, after 1929. As noted, prior to that time he had very little Islamic education and "never attended a pesantren," let alone ventured to the Middle East to learn Arabic and Islam from well-known Arab Muslim teachers.[74] It was instead the "rural Islamic leaders of West Java," such as Kyai Jusuf Tauziri and Kyai Ardiwisastra, Kartosoewirjo's father-in-law, who imparted to him a traditionalist/Sufi rather than a modernist understanding of Islam.[75] Kartosoewirjo became, in the words of Horikoshi, a "dedicated Sufist" who lived simply and "spent many hours in self-discipline and communication with the supernatural."[76] In essence, by the 1930s Kartosoewirjo had become a genuinely committed Muslim, perhaps more so than his political mentor Tjokroaminoto had ever been. Nevertheless, the political apprenticeship at the side of the illustrious Tjokroaminoto did result in Kartosoewirjo's "considerable intellect" gaining in "sophistication."[77] Thus like Tjokroaminoto before him, Kartosoewirjo consciously exploited the mysticism of the Javanese cultural milieu by taking pains to cultivate an image of himself among his DI followers as the "Just King (Ratu Adil) and Divinely Guided Leader (Imam Mahdi)."[78] Horikoshi paints a colorful picture of Kartosoewirjo's impact on the "poor and unsophisticated peasants" of rural West Java:

> His sharp mind, eloquent tongue, and above all striking personality over-shadowed his weak voice and small, unprepossessing figure. His speeches tended to be uncompromising and *berat* (heavy), often appealing to his audience's conscience. He evidently possessed the invaluable quality, typical among Java's *jago* ("champions"), of being *gagah* (translated in a colloquial

sense as "having guts") . . . men who are *gagah* fear nothing but God, and are strongly convinced of their cause. . . . Such a charismatic man inspires awe (*segan*) in his followers, who are themselves prevented from acting by fear of possible threats to their lives.[79]

Furthermore, from the time of the establishment of the Suffah Institute, Kartosoewirjo's supporters addressed him as Imam, and in fact he deliberately propagated the message that he had been instructed by God to become Imam of the World Caliphate. Moreover, the DI leadership consciously shielded him from the majority of the DI rank and file, and his photograph was never taken. Kartosoewirjo also wore two "magical swords, Ki Dongkol and Ki Rompang," which, according to popular folklore, when wielded in unison "would bring prosperity to the land and victory in battle" to the person who did so.[80] Eventually many unsophisticated DI militants throughout the 1950s actually believed that Kartosoewirjo was capable "of vanishing with the speed of light," "remaining immortal," causing "generals to fly into the air before followers," and invoking potent curses on followers who dared to defect to the government side.[81] In a Javanese cultural milieu deeply inflected with large power-distance and collectivist elements, such overt myth making by the DI Imam was nothing short of a political masterstroke of the highest order and helped sustain the DI insurgency for years.

The final milestone in Kartosoewirjo's radicalization was his immersion in the inclement political environment of the pre–World War Two Dutch-dominated Indies and his experiences during the Japanese Occupation. Certainly by the 1930s, Kartosoewirjo's transformation into a "dedicated Sufist" provided him with a *distinct Islamic Group Tent* that he sought to preserve against marginalization and possibly extinction in the face of the political onslaught by the Dutch on one side and the secular nationalists and communists on the other. Kartosoewirjo's Existential Identity Anxiety was certainly heightened considerably by the events at the end of the Occupation that led to the abandonment of the so-called Jakarta Charter. Between May and August 1945, a Japanese-initiated Study Committee for the Preparation of Independence, comprising 62 prominent Indonesian leaders of every stripe, met to discuss the political trajectory of postwar Indonesia. Kartosoewirjo was not part of the Muslim component of the Committee, though Abikusno Tjrokosujoso, who in contrast with Kartosoewirjo had been politically and publicly active during the Occupation, was.[82] Soekarno used the Committee hearings to expound on the five principles or pillars of *Pancasila* as the ideological basis for a secular, multifaith postwar Indonesian State. These five pillars were Belief in God, Humanity, Democracy, Social Justice, and Nationalism.[83] Soekarno was supported by Mohammad Hatta, independent Indonesia's future vice-president. Essentially, both men, especially Soekarno, who "had the situation in Java" in mind, argued that although "a large majority of the Indonesian population" was Muslim, in

reality, "a considerable proportion" was "fairly lax in the discharge of its religious duties" and would prefer a "secular" over an "Islamic state."[84] The
Muslim leaders on the Study Committee, predictably, did not accept this
position. Accordingly, the Study Committee agreed to establish a smaller
nine-man subcommittee to study the status of Islam in Indonesia after the
war. The subcommittee deliberations resulted in a compromise that later
came to be known as the Jakarta Charter. This called for a reformulation of
Soekarno's *Pancasila* formula to require that over and above Belief in God,
Muslims in Indonesia would be obligated to "practise Islamic law."[85] Subsequently, the full Study Committee also agreed after much debate that the
president of Indonesia should be a Muslim.[86] However, the sudden capitu-
lation of the Japanese government in Tokyo on August 14, 1945, following
the U.S. atomic bombings of Hiroshima and Nagasaki, and Soekarno's hasty
proclamation of Indonesian independence three days later, transformed the
situation completely. The secular members of the twenty-one-man Preparatory Committee for Indonesian Independence, set up by the Japanese to
complete the work of the original Study Committee, took full advantage of
the confused situation as well as the fact that many heavyweight Muslim
leaders from the original Study Committee were absent (the Preparatory
Committee was intended to reflect not religious/ideological but rather regional diversity). It decided on August 18 to drop both the Jakarta Charter
as well as the stipulation that the president should always be a Muslim.
Soekarno and Hatta were elected president and vice-president, respectively,
of the new Indonesian Republic as well. The argument advanced by Hatta in
particular was that given the historic opportunity afforded by the Japanese
surrender and Indonesian independence, only a "'secular' constitution stood
a chance of being accepted by the majority of the population."[87]

All of these Machiavellian machinations were not lost for a moment
on Kartosoewirjo, who now considered the emergent secular Republic of
Indonesia an abomination and an existential threat every bit as evil as that
posed by the returning Dutch. As noted, by 1948, a "three-cornered contest" for control of West Java was ensuing between the Republic, DI, and
the Dutch. Dutch forces controlled the urban fringes and the towns by day,
while DI commanded the villages, hills, and rural areas by night. Such was
the strength of the DI insurgency that Republican forces tended to avoid
West Java after 1948, while Dutch troops showed DI more respect than
they did the Republican forces.[88] By the time the Dutch transferred formal
sovereignty to the Republic on December 27, 1949, DI dominated most of
the mountainous areas of southwest Java from Banten to Priangan.[89] The
sheer intensity of the struggle for survival of the Islamic Group Tent in
West Java compelled Kartosoewirjo and his associates to *regress* to a highly
ethnocentric, xenophobic mode of existence. The DI Imam and his acolytes
thought in terms of us-versus-them and adopted a highly categorical, "narrow and absolutist definition of the boundaries of the Islamic community."[90]

To put it another way, Kartosoewirjo by this point had become truly *radicalized*, seeing the world through an exclusively binary worldview. As Fealy explains:

> DI leaders...saw the world as starkly divided into two realms: that of Islam (*darul islam*) and that of Islam's enemies (*darul harbi* or "abode of war"). They argued that it was only within *darul Islam* that the Shari'ah could be fully implemented and Muslims would be able to live piously. For DI leaders, Muslims in Indonesia had a choice: they could join the DI struggle and live according to God's law, or they could live in *darul harbi* (the Republic) which, in effect, meant siding with Islam's foes living outside Islam.[91]

From the outset, DI managed to win the support of many West Java towns and villages, particularly those that traditionally had been known for their strong Islamic piety, such as Tasikmalaya, Cianjur, and Banten. These all were quickly incorporated into the NII. Kartosoewirjo's judgment, on the other hand, of those Javanese Muslims who opted to remain within Republican areas was violently harsh. He considered them "apostate" and declared that their "lives and possessions could be taken as part of *jihad fi sabilillah*."[92] The practical implications of what amounted to a black-and-white labeling exercise were horrific: throughout the 1950s, entire villages that refused to join the DI movement were pronounced "infidel" and assaulted. Crops and buildings were burned, valuables stolen, and villagers killed, at times with great brutality, such as by having their throats slit. Throughout all of this mayhem, Kartosoewirjo steadfastly maintained the essential justness of his all-or-nothing campaign to not only defend and expand but also purify the moral community of the NII against the evil, dirty encroachments of the secular Republic. As he declared in the thoroughly absolutist language of the convinced religious fundamentalist:

> It seems not yet enough filth of the world has been eliminated and chased away in the 1st and 2nd World Wars....In short, God's justice in the form of God's Kingdom does not yet exist on earth with peace, security and calm. [Each person has one choice]: eliminate all infidels and atheism until annihilated and the God-Granted State exists firmly in Indonesia, or die as martyrs in a Holy War.[93]

Much as American Founding Father Thomas Jefferson once declared in quite another context that "the tree of liberty must be nourished by the blood of martyrs,"[94] Kartosoewirjo ordered DI commanders to "bring the Islamic community of the Indonesian people towards the place of God's Mercy (*Mardlotillah*). If need be by force."[95] Within Kartosoewirjo's *binary worldview*, in other words, establishing the ideal society built on Islamic law was the overriding consideration, and to this end both *hijrah* and *jihad*—literally apprehended in the case of the former and violently articulated if need be in the case of the latter—were morally justified and fully religiously legitimated. Such attitudes, as we shall see, would be carried over to the future JI leadership.

FROM SUBCULTURE TO POLITICAL IDEOLOGY: THE ELEMENTS OF DARUL ISLAM AND DARUL ISLAMISM

Because of tactical innovations by the Indonesian army,[96] by the early 1960s the DI was on the back foot, and in 1962, with the capture and execution of Kartosoewirjo, the movement all but collapsed.[97] While many DI commanders surrendered, others went underground and continued the struggle, albeit at a lower level of intensity. From the late 1960s, DI elements began to revive the movement secretly, but this effort was badly hampered by factional splits. Worse, the Indonesian New Order regime set up by Soekarno's successor Soeharto, who, somewhat like Kartosoewirjo, was "devoted to the intense inner mysticism of rural Java" rather than to Islamic "legalism,"[98] was consequently deeply suspicious and hostile to organized political Islamic movements, especially clearly revisionist and violent ones like Darul Islam. Spearheaded by the key Soeharto lieutenant General Ali Moertopo and his all-powerful BAKIN intelligence agency, the New Order government intervened in these internal DI factional disputes, manipulating the various groups against one another, and this resulted in "rival factions killing their opponents."[99] To this day the Darul Islam movement continues to exist, with a membership in the thousands, but it remains heavily factionalized, with no central leadership.[100] One January 2006 estimate put the number of DI factions at eighteen.[101] Incidentally, in 1991, DI elements affiliated with Kartosoewirjo disciple Ajengan Masduki and active on the campus of the University of Indonesia in Jakarta persuaded Al Chaidar—whom we encountered earlier—to leave the Gerakan Tarbiyah, as it was deemed not sufficiently committed to developing a political strategy for replacing the secular Indonesian government with an Islamic State. Chaidar subsequently became deeply immersed in the DI movement and became a spokesperson for seven DI factions.[102]

Kartosoewirjo's Darul Islam struggle has left a subcultural and even ideological legacy whose effects are enduring. As a *subculture*, or according to Hofstede, as a "learned way of thinking, feeling and acting," the Darul Islam movement inaugurated by Kartosoewirjo was always defined by five core elements. First and foremost, it was driven by an intense sense of Existential Identity Anxiety. Its adherents have tended to be gripped by the fear of extinction as a religious identity group in the face of Westernization, secularism, nationalism, or other generalized cultural threats. This visceral anxiety underlay Kartosoewirjo's literalistic reading of the Prophet's *hijrah* in 622 to Medina as well as his own establishment of the geographically isolated Suffah commune in Malangbong. The same anxiety later impelled him to advocate violent *jihad* to defend the NII against its secular enemies, whether Dutch or Republican. This Existential Identity Anxiety—in essence this fear of extinction—has been carried over to the JI leadership today in similar ways. In contrast to Kartosoewirjo, though, who was very Sufi-oriented, the Existential Identity Anxiety of the modern JI leaders—shaped by modernist influences—manifests itself in the desire to de-emphasize Javanese and Sufi influences and practices while promoting Arabized authenticity, distinctiveness, and difference. Chaidar, the Darul Islam movement spokesperson who has had much interaction with JI militants, explains that the average JI militant is much more "hard-line" than his DI counterpart, and one way this harder-edged stance is expressed is through attitudes toward dressing. While DI members today are relatively relaxed about wearing Western-style jeans, for example, considering this relatively unimportant, their JI counterparts would consider any such dressing as strongly indicative of a *kuffar* mindset.[103]

Second and related to the previous point, Kartosoewirjo's committed acolytes tended to display an almost pathological propensity for black-and-white, categorical thinking. They were and remain religious fundamentalists by disposition, possessing a very limited ability to live with ambiguity and preferring rather the psychological comforts of totalizing orthodoxies. Little wonder that this ossified mindset has readily supplemented a strong uncertainty-avoidance cultural outlook that in turn generated a "narrow and absolutist definition of the boundaries of the Islamic community." Colonel Tito Karnavian, a senior Indonesian police officer and informant who has interacted very closely with many captured JI militants, notes that the latter trust only "insiders" and consider non-Muslims and even other Muslims possessing a less strict interpretation of the faith as "outsiders" and "infidels" whose "blood " is "*halal*"—that is, who may be legitimately targeted.[104] A third distinctive element of the Darul Islamic subculture that has grown up around Kartosoewirjo and continues to be manifest in the attitudes of his successors in the modern JI movement is a strong sense of moral entitlement, derived in part from their self-image as a pious community divinely appointed to further social justice in the land and in part by an acute sense—a product of their innate Existential Identity Anxiety—of having been historically victimized and humiliated by powerful enemies. As a corollary, the notion that armed *jihad* is a morally legitimate method of striking back, of exacting revenge on the enemy, and of victimizing the erstwhile victimizers themselves has a certain visceral appeal even beyond the narrow circle of active JI militants. Fourth, rural Javanese Islam left a lingering imprint not only on Kartosoewirjo but also on senior JI spiritual leaders such as the late Abdullah Sungkar and Abu Bakar Ba'asyir. This is because as a subcultural system, Darul Islam reflects the large power-distance orientations

ingrained in Javanese traditionalism, evinced by both the emphasis on personalized transfer of knowledge from *kyai* to student within the closed *pesantren* environment and the web of intimate, kin- and alumni-based closed
social networks that tend to arise around these *kyai*.[105] After all, as Tim
Behrend states, many traditional *pesantren* in rural Java and in some cities
are run as the "social and intellectual fiefdoms of charismatic *syeikh*" who
play a highly personal role in "constructing the religious psyche" of *pesantren* students.[106] Such personalized dynamics certainly have been evident
in the way some graduates of the Al-Mukmin *pesantren* set up by Sungkar
and Ba'asyir had their psyches "constructed" by elders in that institution.
In like vein, Karnavian also points out the strategic role that "respect" for
"seniors" plays within the JI movement—no surprise, of course, given the
large power-distance, collectivist Javanese cultural context.[107]

Fifth, while Darul Islam as a subculture bears distinct Javanese traditionalist imprints, it shows unmistakable evidence of stock modernist ones as
well. This is most evident in the atavistic desire of not merely Kartosoewirjo
but also, as we shall see, his successors in the JI leadership to purify the
Islamic community so as to empower Muslims to the point where they
could successfully wrest power from the infidel godless enemies of God,
erect the longed-for Islamic State, and thereby establish the "natural order"
of things. This *mimetic* impulse to wrest away the power, status, and prestige
that the infidels are perceived to possess and claim these attributes for the
Muslims instead complements the concomitant strong fear of group extinction. It is this curious, dangerous mixture of envy and fear that lies at the
core of both the older Darul Islam and current JI radicalism. In truth, these
five core—if somewhat amorphous—elements of Darul Islamic *subculture*
have represented free-floating prejudices, notions, practices, and sentiments
that Kartosoewrijo and his successors in both today's DI and JI movements
more systematically developed into a *political ideology*. Ervin Staub captures the distinction between culture and ideology elegantly when he advises
readers to:

> Distinguish between the *existing culture*, which consists of beliefs, mean-
> ings, values, valuation, symbols, myths, and perspectives that are shared
> largely without awareness, and *ideology*, which I [Staub] define as a pri-
> marily consciously held set of beliefs and values.[108]

Hence the JI Cell that attacked Bali in October 2002 was driven by a "consciously held set of beliefs" that identified the United States, Israel, and
the allied Western coalition as the so-called "far enemy" and considered
the wanton targeting of civilians as morally and religiously justified. The
members of the Cell had become proponents of a systematically articulated political ideology that drew attention to the global political repression
that Muslims everywhere were perceived to be chafing under, identified the

enemy responsible for the situation, and suggested the strategy for rectifying the situation: Global Salafi *Jihad*. Although the adoption of the Global
Salafi *Jihad* perspective was due to the impact of the participation of some
senior JI figures such as Mukhlas in the Afghan *jihad* against the Soviets in
the late 1980s, this was in fact merely an ideological overlay; it does not
diminish the reality that these JI militants had been far more profoundly
influenced by a common *Darul Islamic* subcultural heritage whose five elements have been sketched out above. Al Chaidar informed this author
that, in his estimation, "about 90 percent" of the DI and JI interpretation
of *jihad* is similar.[109] The differences between JI and the older DI movement are significant but not so fundamental as to drastically reduce the
porosity of the ideological boundaries between both entities: for instance,
JI militants who were formerly DI cadre prefer to follow Al Qaeda leader
Osama bin Laden's *fatwas* rather than those of DI Imams; DI believes that
efforts to establish an Islamic State should be confined to Indonesia, whereas
JI—at least prior to the 2002 Bali strikes—felt that such efforts could legitimately be mounted in countries with sizeable ethnic Malay communities,
such as Thailand, Malaysia, Singapore, Brunei, and "certain parts of the
Philippines."[110]

More precisely, the JI militants today, including the ones we shall be
looking at in this study, rather than representing a stand-alone phenomenon,
are in truth more accurately described as self-conciously politically driven
Darul Islamists, setting out to take the fight to the infidels—whether secular Indonesian government or the United States, Israel, and the Western
coalition—as part of the perceived cosmic war between Darkness and Light.
Essentially, the Javanese villages and towns that experienced the full impact
of government repression of the Darul Islam revolt in the 1950s became
home to more or less regressed, radicalized social networks and communities
that have since comprised the *Darul Islamic subculture*—Kartosoewirjo's
Bouquet, if you like. Darul Islamic subculture has become the wellspring of
the various factions of the politicized, ideologically mobilized Darul Islam
militant movement that has survived Kartosoewirjo's martyrdom. The JI
network of today remains very much an integral, if relatively more virulent,
part of this movement. Moreover, the Darul Islamic subculture of Java represents a potential *strategic reserve* on which the militants of both DI and
JI can draw to sustain and nourish their ranks.[111] This is possible precisely
because the amorphous, free-floating prejudices of the wider Darul Islamic
subculture can be actively and deliberately "intensified and focused"[112] into
the more consciously held Darul Islamist political ideology—the life-blood
of the Darul Islam militant movement—and to reiterate, of which the JI
network remains a part. The ways in which the elements of Darul Islamic
subculture have been consciously intensified and focused into Darul Islamist
ideology can be illustrated in the backgrounds and pronouncements of three
senior JI leaders whom we shall now examine.

ABU BAKAR BA'ASYIR

Abu Bakar Ba'asyir was born in Jombang, East Java, in 1938. He came from a deeply devout family descended from Hadrami Arabs and was named after the Prophet's trusted aide Abu Bakar.[113] Ba'asyir's deep piety came not only from his family. He grew up in an environment that further reinforced his strong Islamic self-identity. After all, Jombang was known as the "city of 1,000 pesantrens" and was a center of NU-style traditionalist Islam.[114] However, this did not mean that Ba'asyir was an unreconstructed *santri* traditionalist. Throughout his formative years he had ample exposure to modernist ideas. It could be said that early in life he imbibed the innate modernist mimetic impulse to empower Islam to recapture lost glories. While still in high school, Ba'asyir was caught up in the modernist wave that swept through Java and the rest of the Indies in the first half of the twentieth century. He joined the village branch of the Masjumi-linked student organization Gerakan Pemuda Islam Indonesia (GPII), which was "dominated by modernists."[115] By 1959, moreover, as Soekarno was eviscerating Masjumi politically in the process of putting in place the authoritarian system known as Guided Democracy, the young Ba'asyir enrolled in the well-known modernist Islamic boarding school at Gontor in East Java and spent four years there. The late modernist intellectual Nurcholish Madjid or Cak Nur was in Gontor at the same time and recalled Ba'asyir as "so puritanical, so uncompromising."[116] By this time, Ba'asyir had, like Kartosoewirjo in his Sarekat Islam days, developed the zeal of the committed activist. Subsequently, Ba'asyir moved to Solo, Central Java, and enrolled in the Universitas Al-Irsyad, a "leading hub for Indonesian modernists of Arab descent."[117] Ba'asyir apparently was so deeply involved in student activism that he never actually completed his *dakwah* course. It was in Solo in 1963 that he met Abdullah Sungkar, a like-minded soul one year younger than Ba'asyir and also of Hadrami Arab descent who later would co-found JI with him.[118] As Ba'asyir was coming of age politically in the Indonesia of the 1950s, the Darul Islam revolt was at its height, and Kartosoewirjo's single-minded struggle against the secular Republic captured the imagination of Ba'asyir and thousands of other like-minded Javanese Muslims. Kartosoewirjo became Ba'asyir's "hero."[119] Like his role model, Ba'asyir developed a tendency toward categorical thinking as well as the deeply held moral superiority of those who believe themselves to be unjustly victimized. As he later wrote about the uphill Darul Islam struggle against first the Dutch and Japanese and then the secular Indonesian republic:

> Under the colonisation of the Dutch and the Japanese, the Islamic community of Indonesia saw their rights oppressed and misappropriated in a most brutal fashion . . . with the help of Allah, the Muslims successfully drove the

[*kuffar*] Dutch and Japanese from their soil. At that time Muslims had the perfect opportunity to implement their rights—namely to apply the laws of Islam. However that golden opportunity soon elapsed and instead a new disaster replaced that of before.[120]

The capture and execution of Kartosoewirjo in 1962 and the collapse of the NII had a "profoundly galvanising" effect on Ba'asyir and other activists.[121] Kartosoewirjo's demise, in the words of the noted psychoanalyst Vamik Volkan, represented a "chosen trauma" for Ba'asyir and other Darul Islam supporters and militants, a defining moment that over time became a collective "identity marker" for the Darul Islam—and later JI—forces arrayed against the regime.[122] It could be asserted that Kartosoewirjo's martyrdom sharply increased Ba'asyir's Existential Identity Anxiety and intensified his determination to carry on Kartosoewirjo's struggle to build an Indonesian Islamic State. Following the October 1965 coup, Soekarno was deposed, and in his stead emerged the arch-secularist Soeharto and the New Order government, a bureaucratic-authoritarian regime, that came to be dominated by Catholic and Protestant military, administrative, and Chinese business elites.[123] Ba'asyir and Sungkar, reckoning that Soeharto's highly repressive New Order regime was "a disaster worse than and more terrifying than what had happened before," began campaigning openly for an Islamic state in Indonesia.[124] To this end they set up a clandestine radio station, Radio Dakwah Islamiyah Surakarta, in Solo in 1967. Radio Dakwah openly broadcast calls for *jihad* in Central Java and was eventually shut down in 1975.[125] The Radio Dakwah broadcasts of Ba'asyir and Sungkar propounded a common theme: the need for small, vanguard *jemaah isla-miyah* (Islamic communities) under strict Islamic law to pave the way for the formation of an Islamic State. In this goal both Ba'asyir and Sungkar were inspired by the second Caliph Umar bin Khattab, who had apparently observed: "No Islam without *jamaah*, no *jamaah* without leadership and no leadership without compliance."[126] Both men maintained this strong conviction, even after Radio Dakwah was shut down by the New Order government, by proceeding to organize their small but growing number of followers into *jemaah islamiyah*. While all of this was happening, Ba'asyir and Sungkar oversaw the establishment of the Pondok Pesantren Al-Mukmin on March 10, 1972, in Jalan Gading Kidul in downtown Surakarta, Central Java. This moved to the village (*desa*) of Ngruki in central Surakarta two years later.[127] Although Al-Mukmin was to become a center of symbolic resistance to the New Order regime, its true significance lay elsewhere: as a socializing mechanism for Darul Islamism—a point to which we shall soon return.

Significantly, seeing themselves very much as inheritors of the martyred Kartosoewirjo's original vision, Ba'asyir and Sungkar decided to affiliate the early JI network of *jemaah islamiyah* with the already existing DI.

Consequently, the Ba'asyir-Sungkar *jemaah islamiyah* officially became part of the Central Java DI in Solo in 1976. Both Sungkar and Ba'asyir swore an oath of allegiance to the DI Central Java leader Haji Ismail Pranoto, better known as Hispran.[128] This institutional affiliation with DI and contact with veterans of the DI revolt may have played a part in further radicalizing Ba'asyir and Sungkar in the sense of nudging them intellectually closer to the acceptance of violence in pursuit of the Islamic State. Hence in February 1977, both men set up the clandestine Jemaah Mujahidin Anshorullah (JMA), which some analysts believe to be the precursor organization to today's militant JI network.[129] Ba'asyir and Sungkar also became involved in the activities of a violent underground movement called Komando Jihad, which sought to set up an Islamic state in Indonesia and perpetrated the bombings of nightclubs, churches, and cinemas. Incidentally, Komando Jihad was to a large extent a creation of Indonesian intelligence and was set up to discredit political Islam in Indonesia and legitimize the New Order's subsequent crackdown on "less radical and non-violent Muslim politicians."[130] In 1978, both Sungkar and Ba'asyir were arrested and sentenced to nine years in jail for their involvement in the Komando Jihad. They were released in 1982, but it was obvious that prison life had had a further radicalizing effect, reinforcing their sharp categorical thinking and intensifying their hatred of secular, "godless" regimes. Hence on his release, Ba'asyir began gathering all his followers who had been persecuted or detained and started a monthly religious study group at Al-Mukmin. Seeking to further intensify a siege-like solidarity amongst his *jemaah*, Ba'asyir now demanded that people who wished to join his flock must swear an oath of loyalty or *ba'iah*.[131] Following that, he ordered his followers to return to their towns and villages to set up individual groups or *usroh* (family), an idea he appears to have borrowed from the Egyptian Muslim Brotherhood. By the 1980s, Ba'asyir would have come across Brotherhood publications, as these had by then been translated and were in circulation in Indonesia.[132] These mingled and fused with the individual experiential and ideational trajectories of Sungkar and Ba'asyir. Hence the injunctions of Brotherhood founder Hassan al-Banna to set up a "vanguard" community to serve as the "dynamic nucleus for true Islamic reformation within the broader society"[133] would have struck an immediate chord with both men.

In the Brotherhood conception, the struggle toward the realization of an Islamic State depended on several steps: first, moral self-improvement; second, becoming part of a family of like-minded individuals, or *usroh*, who would be committed to "guide, help and control" one another and thus stay on the right path; third, coalescing the various *usroh* to form a wider *jemaah islamiyah*; and finally, coalescing the various *jemaah islamiyah* into an Islamic State. It should be noted that this idea of the *usroh* would readily have been meshed with the extant Javanese traditionalist concept of the closed social network of kin and *pesantren* alumni built around venerated *kyai* such as B'aasyir. By the mid-1980s, Ba'asyir and Sungkar had established a network of committed young Muslims, "some of them quietist, some of them militants, all of them opposed to the Soeharto regime, organised in 'families,' that together were to constitute a true community of committed Muslims, a *Jama'ah Islamiyah*."[134] As it turned out, Ba'asyir and Sungkar were soon wanted men again. Al-Mukmin had already drawn attention to itself for steadfastly refusing to fly the Indonesian flag or display presidential icons. Then in 1984, Soeharto decreed that *Pancasila* must be the underlying foundational principle (*asas tunggal*) for all social organizations, including Muslim entities. Naturally, Ba'asyir and Sungkar refused to comply.[135] They were hardly alone. Many Muslim groups across the spectrum in Indonesia were equally outraged. In September of that year, the anger boiled over as a prayer meeting in "the poor, overpopulated" harbor district of Tanjung Priok in Jakarta transformed itself into a protest. In retaliation, Indonesian security forces opened fire, killing dozens.[136] This was followed up by more security force heavy-handedness, with the result that 200 more people were killed.[137] The "Tanjung Priok Incident," or as Javanese Muslims called it, *Peristewa Tanjung Priok*, "came to signify the marginalization and abuse of Indonesia's poor Islamic majority at the hands of an oppressive—and ostensibly Christian-led—regime.[138] For Ba'asyir and Sungkar, moreover, the "bloody events of Tanjung Priok," like the execution of DI Imam Kartosoewirjo twenty-two years before, constituted yet another defining moment, a chosen trauma, that further "hardened the pair's resolve"—as well as deeply reinforced their xenophobic fear and hatred of the secular New Order regime.[139] Then in February 1985, the Indonesian Supreme Court ruled that both men should be incarcerated again to complete the remaining five of their original nine-year jail terms. This prompted Ba'asyir, Sungkar, and several of their followers to decamp to Malaysia in April 1985.[140]

THE *HIJRAH* TO MALAYSIA AND THE IMPACT OF GLOBAL SALAFI *JIHAD* IDEOLOGY

Ba'asyir and Sungkar later likened this escape to Malaysia as akin to the Prophet's own *hijrah* to Medina fourteen centuries before, as "strategic evasion" in an attempt to elude their enemies, rebuild, and strike back later.[141] According to one account, both men arrived illegally in Malaysia without proper documentation, settled in Kuala Pilah, about 250 kilometers southeast of Kuala Lumpur, and stayed at the home of a Malaysian cleric for about a year. While in Malaysia, Ba'asyir adopted the pseudonym Abdus Samad and Sungkar took on the *nom de guerre* Abdul Halim.[142] During the next several years, both men, through the financial support base generated by their effective preaching activities, were able to buy property of their own in other parts of the country. Wherever they went, they set up

Qur'an reading groups and were invited to preach in small-group settings in both Malaysia and even in Singapore. In 1992 they set up the Luqmanul Hakiem *pesantren* in Ulu Tiram in the southernmost Malaysian State of Johore. Luqmanul Hakiem was a clone of Al-Mukmin back in Solo. Ba'asyir later told the Indonesian magazine *Tempo* that in Malaysia he had set up "As-Sunnah, a community of Muslims."[143] The Malaysian interlude from 1985 to 1999 was very important, because it was during these years that Ba'asyir and Sungkar began to edge even further away from a *dakwah*-oriented approach to societal Islamization to a harder-edged, *jihadi*-driven one. Both Ba'asyir and Sungkar, it should be noted, never downplayed the importance of *dakwah*; Sungkar after all had been the chairman of the DDII Central Java branch, and Ba'asyir had majored in *dakwah* at Universitas Al-Irsyad in Solo.[144] This belief in *dakwah* also had led them to set up Pondok Pesantren Al-Mukmin in Solo in 1972 as well as the numerous *jemaah islamiyah* later. At the same time, however, they were long-term DI sympathizers who embraced at some level the Kartosoewirjo argument that Islamizing the polity by force was the only feasible approach. They even affiliated the nascent JI movement with Hispran's DI and were involved in the Komando Jihad. It would seem that the period of incarceration from 1978 and subsequent targeting by the New Order regime—necessitating their flight across the Melaka Strait to Malaysia—may have been the "tipping point" in terms of bringing them to the final insight that *dakwah* in the absence of *jihad* would be utterly inefficacious. Little wonder that the Indonesian journalist Blontank Poer observes that the *jihadi* emphasis in the overall strategy of Sungkar and Ba'asyir became more developed after the shift to Malaysia in 1985.[145]

The Ba'asyir-Sungkar radicalization experience mirrors that of the Egyptian Muslim Brotherhood's Sayyid Qutb. Qutb had in fact been a highly educated and widely read moderate Muslim for most of his life, someone who considered himself a Salafi in its original liberal reformist sense, familiar with not only the works of ideologues like al-Wahhab but also Western philosophers. He had thus written well-regarded studies on the Qur'an and literary criticism. It was the experience of being arrested and tortured by the Nasser regime that transformed him into an "extremist," whereupon he composed his most famous revolutionary tract, *Milestones on the Road*.[146] Qutb, who was never a "trained jurist,"[147] duly transformed "the ideology of [Muslim Brotherhood founder Hassan] al-Banna and [Jama'at-I Islami founder Mawlana] Mawdudi into a rejectionist revolutionary call to arms."[148] Given the combined effect of the experiences of Ba'asyir and Sungkar at the hands of the repressive New Order regime, as well as the knowledge of the life and fate of their political hero Kartosoewirjo, both men by the mid-1980s in Malaysia would have viscerally embraced the radicalized Qutb's absolutist, polarized view of the world:

There is only one place on earth which can be called the home of Islam (Dar-ul-Islam), and it is that place where the Islamic state is established and the Shariah is the authority and God's limits are observed and where all Muslims administer the affairs of the state with mutual consultation. The rest of the world is the home of hostility (Dar-ul-Harb).[149]

By the 1980s, moreover, within international Islamist circles, the issue of the proper balance between *dakwah* and *jihad* had been given detailed treatment by yet another Egyptian radical: Mohammad al-Faraj, executed by Cairo in 1982 for his role in the assassination of President Anwar Sadat in 1981.[150] Faraj, himself influenced by the works of al-Banna, Mawdudi, and Qutb, unequivocally rejected the efficacy of *dakwah* as a means of Islamizing *jahili* society.[151] Faraj argued that the decline of Muslim societies was due to the fact that Muslim leaders had hollowed out the vigorous concept of *jihad*, thereby robbing it of its "true meaning."[152] In his pamphlet *Neglected Obligation*, Faraj argued that the "Qu'ran and the Hadith were fundamentally about warfare" and that the concept of *jihad*, in contrast to the conventional wisdom, was "meant to be taken literally, not allegorically."[153] He argued that *jihad* represented in fact the "sixth pillar of Islam" and that *jihad* calls for "fighting, which meant confrontation and blood."[154] Faraj held that not only infidels but even Muslims who deviated from the moral and social dictates of *shariah* were legitimate targets for *jihad*. Faraj concluded that peaceful means for fighting apostasy in Muslim societies were bound to fail and that ultimately, the true soldier of Islam was justified in using "virtually any means available to achieve a just goal."[155] After their treatment at the hands of the New Order regime, Sungkar and Ba'asyir would not have disagreed with Faraj on the necessity for a literal understanding of *jihad* and would have come to accept his wider argument that *jihad* represented the highest form of devotion to God.[156] This is precisely why, in that crucial year of 1985, when the Saudis sought volunteers for the *jihad* in Afghanistan against the invading Soviets, Sungkar and Ba'asyir willingly raised groups of volunteers from among their followers in Malaysia.[157] The Afghan theater was seen as a useful training ground for a future *jihad* in Indonesia itself.[158]

As it turned out, rather than Afghanistan being seen as a training ground for a *jihad* aimed at setting up an Indonesian Islamic state, that conflict became the source of ideas that modified somewhat the original Indonesia-centric vision of Ba'asyir and Sungkar. Prior to the 1990s, the programmatic element within the overall Darul Islamism of both men could be termed "Salafi Jihad."[159] The original aim of the JI émigré community in Malaysia had been to one day return to wage a *jihad* against the Soeharto regime—in Faraj's terms, the so-called "near enemy"—and set up an Islamic state in Indonesia. However, returning Indonesian veterans of the Afghan *jihad* exposed Sungkar and Ba'asyir to fresh thinking on this issue. In Afghanistan, Indonesian and other Southeast Asian *jihadis* had been inspired to think in global terms by the teachings of the charismatic Palestinian *alim* (singular for *ulama*) Abdullah Azzam. Azzam, a key mentor of Al Qaeda leader Osama bin Laden, had received a doctorate in Islamic jurisprudence from Al-Azhar University in Cairo, had met the family of Sayyid Qutb, and was friendly with Sheikh Omar Abdul Rahman. Sheikh Omar Abdul Rahman—better known as the "Blind Sheikh"—was the spiritual guide of two key Egyptian militant organizations, the Egyptian Islamic Jihad (EIJ) and the Egyptian Islamic Group (EIG)—and later would be implicated in the 1993 World Trade Center bombing in New York. When the Soviets withdrew from Afghanistan in 1989, Azzam, who had played a big part in recruiting non-Afghan foreign *mujahidin* worldwide—including from Southeast Asia—for the anti-Soviet *jihad* in the first place, set his sights further. He argued that the struggle to expel the Soviets from Afghanistan was in fact "the prelude to the liberation of Palestine" and other "lost" territories. He wrote:

> Jihad is now . . . incumbent on all Muslims and will remains [sic] so until the Muslims recapture every spot that was Islamic but later fell into the hands of the *kuffar* [infidels]. Jihad has been a *fard 'ain* [individual obligation] since the fall of al-Andalus [Spain], and will remain so until all other lands that were Muslim are returned to us . . . Palestine, Bukhara, Lebanon, Chad, Eritrea, Somalia, the Philippines, Burma, Southern Yemen, Tashkent and al-Andalus . . . The duty of jihad is one of the most important imposed on us by God. . . . He has made it incumbent on us, just like prayer, fasting and alms [zakat].[160]

However, Azzam, unlike Faraj, did not sanction *jihad* against "apostate" Muslim governments in Egypt, Jordan, and Syria. His understanding of *jihad* was a traditional one in the sense of evicting infidel occupiers from Muslim lands. He did not wish to see Muslim wage *jihad* against Muslim. However, after his death in a car-bomb explosion in Peshawar in November 1989, the Afghan Arab *mujahidin* community, and Osama bin Laden in particular, again accepted the Faraj argument that targeting Muslim governments seen as apostate was perfectly legitimate.[161] Subsequently, at the beginning of the 1990s, once American troops arrived in Saudi Arabia and Somalia, both Muslim territories, "a more global analysis of Islam's problems" occurred. As Sageman concisely explains:

> Local *takfir* Muslim leaders were seen as pawns of a global power, which itself was now considered the main obstacle to establishing a transnational umma from Morocco to the Philippines. This in effect reversed Faraj's strategy and now the priority was jihad against the "far enemy" over the "near enemy."[162]

Sageman observes that this gradual shift in strategic targeting philosophy within what by the early 1990s had become Al Qaeda took place during bin

Laden's Sudanese exile during that decade; in contemporaneous separate but parallel discussions within Islamist circles in New York leading to the 1993 New York World Trade Center attack; and in Algeria and France just before the wave of bombings in those countries.[163]

These shifts in global radical Islamist ideology post-Afghanistan were not at all lost on Sungkar and Ba'asyir. In addition to their discussions with returning Indonesian veterans of the Afghan war, both men also met with international *jihadi* groups in Malaysia. Consequently, by 1994, Sungkar and Ba'asyir were no longer talking about establishing merely an Islamic state in Indonesia, but also a "*khilafah* (world Islamic state)."[164] In this construction, a "world caliphate uniting all Muslim nations under a single, righteous exemplar and ruler" was the ultimate goal.[165] It was no coincidence that at about that time, Sungkar and Ba'asyir reportedly made contact with Egyptian radicals associated with the Blind Sheikh.[166] Subsequently, in the early 1990s, Sungkar and Ba'asyir disassociated themselves from the Central Java DI movement because of serious doctrinal differences with regional DI leader Ajengan Masduki, whose increasingly overt Sufi leanings towards nonviolence and tolerance infuriated both men. Sungkar and Ba'asyir, casting off the overarching DI appellation, rebranded their movement "Jemaah Islamiyah."[167] JI accordingly was officially founded on January 1, 1993, in Malaysia.[168] This is the JI that, infused with the post-Afghanistan ethos of Global Salafi *Jihad*, took it upon itself to wreak "vengeance against perceived Western brutality and exploitation of Muslim communities."[169] Its spiritual leader, Ba'asyir—Sungkar passed away in November 1999—declared publicly that he supported "Osama bin Laden's struggle because his is the true struggle to uphold Islam, not terror— the terrorists are America and Israel."[170] In sum, during the Malaysian *hijrah,* the twin impacts of firsthand experience of New Order repression as well as the global Muslim response to the Soviet intervention in Afghanistan transformed the inchoate Darul Islamic subcultural beliefs of Ba'asyir into the systematically articulated, and by the 1980s, globally conscious political ideology of *Darul Islamism*. One significant result of this was that radical Islamist Middle Eastern writers like Azzam, Qutb, and Faraj began to be featured "prominently on JI reading lists."[171] Al Chaidar, the DI spokesman, also confirmed in a January 2006 interview that although Qutb continued to have a profound impact on DI members, "Abdullah Azzam is more popular amongst JI" militants.[172]

PONDOK PESANTREN AL-MUKMIN: SOCIALIZATION MECHANISM FOR DARUL ISLAMISM

Against the backdrop of the gradual transmutation of the Darul Islamic subcultural belief systems of Ba'asyir and Sungkar into the systematic political ideology of Darul Islamism, the Pesantren Al-Mukmin continued to function, churning out alumni some of whom would later be drawn into JI's clandestine activities. A closer look at the *pesantren* is therefore warranted. To be sure, Al-Mukmin is part of a number of Islamic educational institutions that are run by the *Yayasan Pendidikan Islam dan Asuhan Yatim Miskin Ngruki* (Ngruki Foundation for Islamic Education and the Care of Orphans and the Poor, YPIA). In addition to Al-Mukmin, the YPIA runs four *sekolah tadika* or kindergartens in the Surakarta area for children aged four to six; one primary school (*Sekolah Dasar Ngruki*, SDM) in Ngruki village itself for children aged between six and twelve; one middle-level school (*Sekolah Menengah Umum al-Islam Ngruki*, SMU) for students aged between fifteen and eighteen, as well as the Islamic Academy (*Ma'ahad Aly*), also in Ngruki village, which offers courses for students aged between eighteen and twenty-four years leading to national university–type "BA degrees" designed for "graduates of the *pondok pesantren*, the *sekolah menengah*, and non-Ngruki students as well."[173] Pondok Pesantren Al-Mukmin itself is "the only school offering board and lodging to full-time students between four and nineteen."[174] Al-Mukmin students remain because many of them come from different parts of the country and have no other accommodation in the city of Surakarta.[175] In common with other Javanese *pesantren*, Al-Mukmin thus functions "as a community with a compound, mosque and boarding system where students and teachers eat, sleep, learn and generally interact throughout the day."[176] As alluded to earlier, the profound and enduring impact of a highly insular, personalized *pesantren* education on its students cannot be overstated. The large power-distance dimension of highly collectivist Javanese culture ensures that elders, particularly the *alim* or *kyai* or *ustad* who run the *pesantren*, play a critical personal role in "constructing the religious psyche" of *pesantren* students.[177] Although Al-Mukmin is organized according to traditionalist Javanese Muslim precepts, its curriculum bears modernist imprints and has sought to combine the best aspects of two well-known modernist institutions, Gontor in East Java (where, as we saw, Ba'asyir studied), with its excellent Arabic training, and the harder-edged, Arabized modernist Persis school in Bangil, East Java, which remains noted for its teaching of *shariah*.[178]

Within the "closed compound of the *pondok pesantren*" Al-Mukmin itself are several institutions: one *sekolah tadika* or kindergarten for children aged four to six; the *Madrasah Sanawiyah* (primary level), open to boys and girls aged between twelve and fifteen; the *Madrasah Aliyah* MAAM (senior level), open to both boys and girls between fifteen and eighteen; and the *Kulliyatul Muallimin/Muallimat* KMI (teachers' college) for male and female students aged between fifteen and nineteen years. The KMI offers degrees on par with the *Sekolah Perguruan Guru Agama* or SPG (Religious Teachers Training College) degree offered by SPG-type institutions run by the Department of Religious Affairs of the Indonesian government. Al-Mukmin also offers intensive one-year courses for *takhosus* students from outside the *pesantren* itself in special cases.[179] Al-Mukmin usually draws students from West Java, Sumatra, Lombok, Central Java, West Irian, Sulawesi, Kalimantan, Singapore, Malaysia, and even Australia.[180] In 2007, Al-Mukmin enrolled about 1,500 students of both sexes.[181] The curriculum in the *pesantren* emphasizes both secular and religious subjects. Secular subjects include mathematics, physics, Bahasa Indonesia, English, business skills, social sciences, biology (though not Darwinism), national citizenship (a compulsory course since the New Order era), and computers. Religious subjects taught include *fiqh* (Islamic jurisprudence), Arabic, and *aqidah* or faith. Arabic, Bahasa Indonesia, and English are spoken in Al-Mukmin, but most students speak Arabic. The school day is a long one, lasting from 3:00 A.M. to 10:00 P.M. During this time, students pray, read the Qur'an, attend classes, and take part in sports or physical activity such as martial arts, soccer, badminton, mountaineering, and even long marches.[182] Importantly, the "curriculum of the *pondok pesantren* is set by the director of the *pondok* and members of the YPIA," in accordance, since the 1980s, with the "standards set by the Departemen Agama (Religious Affairs Department) of the Indonesian government.[183] Moreover, some of the textbooks used at Al-Mukmin are similar to those used in other traditional *pesantren*.[184] The Malaysian analyst Farish A. Noor, who visited Al-Mukmin in May and June 2007, and who is generally keen to avoid drawing a direct connection between what is taught at the *pesantren* and the religious militancy of some of its graduates, concedes, however, that "many books are drawn from Salafi sources and, as such, Ngruki offers a form of Islamic education that cannot be compared to many of the more traditional *pesantrens* and *madrasahs* of the country."[185] He adds that in general, Al-Mukmin's overall approach is to inculcate in its students the two Islamic doctrines of *Da'wa wal-Jihad* (missionary activity and struggle) and *al-Wala wal-Bara* (the "doctrine of solidarity between Muslims of the same persuasion and the avoidance of non-Muslims as well as Muslims of different sects or schools of thought")— all of which, he observes, "points to the exclusive approach of Islam taught at the place."[186]

Moreover, precisely because the twin doctrines of *Da'wa wal-Jihad* and *al-Wala' wal-Bara* are "deliberately left vague and undefined," their specific content is very much shaped by the "distinct profiles and personalities" of individual teachers.[187] This is not even a complete picture of how at least some of the teachers at Al-Mukmin educate their charges. Complementing the relatively innocuous formal curriculum is the somewhat more telling semiformal "general culture" of the institution.[188] According to Al-Mukmin alumni, the stay-in, boarding-school nature of the *pesantren* expedites virtual "24-hour monitoring" of students by teachers and senior students in all spheres of activity: lessons, language, sports, cleaning, et cetera. This close contact ensures that the "emotional bond between teachers and students is very strong."[189] For instance, journalist Noor Huda Ismail, who attended

Al-Mukmin from 1984 to 1990, between the ages of twelve and seventeen, used to share a "dingy student dormitory together with twenty other students and a volunteer resident assistant named Fadlullah Hasan" who was three years his senior and had "a perpetual blue bruise on his forehead from bowing his head to the floor as the result of his five prayers per day." After daily morning prayers at the adjacent mosque, Hasan would lead the boys in reading the Qur'an and urge them to "study and proselytize Islam," and Hasan and Ismail eventually developed a "tight bond."[190] Ismail added that Qur'an reading classes, moreover, were conducted in groups of twenty students aged twelve to thirteen who were taught the putatively "correct" interpretation of passages by a senior student, usually sixteen years old himself, who himself had been taught in the same way.[191] Such close personal ties between teachers, seniors, and younger students within a collectivist, large power-distance milieu are, as noted, very important, particularly in socializing young people into the prevailing ideological ethos. The *Darul Islamist* content of this ethos—which is the key point—has been evidenced by the fact that Al-Mukmin has organized frequent public-speaking sessions on Thursday nights, and the "most popular topic," according to Ismail, was "the threats facing Islam," such as "Global Jewish power and Indonesia's Christian-controlled economy"[192] as well as "jihad."[193] That such topics promote and reinforce categorical thinking and a good-versus-evil, us-versus-them outlook should be apparent.

Other semiformal ways in which Al-Mukmin students have been immersed in Darul Islamism are through *halaqah* or small-group discussions involving students and specific teachers as well as with one-way lectures or *tausiyah* conducted by such teachers. The Indonesian journalist Ismail also recounted how, during *halaqah* sessions, the *ustaz* would ask students what they intended to do after graduation, and when the latter replied that they may go into business, the *ustaz* would subtly plant the idea that perhaps participating in *jihad* to defend their oppressed Muslim brethren would be a better option. Other subtle indoctrination measures have been used as well: during arduous six-day marches from Solo to Surabaya and martial arts training, the students would be urged by teachers to "be strong" and overcome fear and weakness, as Islam needed to be defended from its enemies.[194] Additional insidious elements subtly programmed into the general culture of Al-Mukmin also helped reinforce Darul Islamist categorical thinking and Existential Identity Anxiety. These included the regular playing of martial music called *nasyid* glorifying *jihad*[195] as well as posters and signs proclaiming messages like "Jihad, Why Not?" and "No Prestige without Jihad" pasted ubiquitously "on walls, lockers, and walkways leading to classrooms."[196] Other graffiti scrawled around Al-Mukmin and spotted by journalists visiting in 2004—evincing the incorporation of Global Salafi *Jihadi* elements into Darul Islamist ideology—revealed the simmering anti-Western radicalism being bred within the school. These included messages such as "Bush and Sharon, if you like dead, come to here" and somewhat less elegantly, "Bush is f*cked."[197] Visiting American journalist Tracy Dahlby inadvertently shed more light on the highly xenophobic environment of the *pesantren* simply by nonchalantly glancing down at students' *sandals*:

> When we reached the front steps of the school and I bent down to remove my shoes as custom required, I couldn't help but notice that the dozens or so pairs of cheap plastic sandals scattered around the base of the stairs all had interesting little pictures or symbols of some kind etched in ballpoint pen on their insteps. When I took a closer look, however, my heart gave a thump—the little symbols were in fact crude renditions of the Holy Cross and the Star of David.[198]

Seeing Dahlby's shocked expression, his guide explained matter-of-factly: "So students can always step on them."[199] Significantly, perhaps due to extensive international media speculation about the alleged links between JI and Al-Mukmin, by the time the Malaysian analyst Farish Noor visited the *pesantren* in May and June 2007, overt signs of Darul Islamist ideology had been deliberately muted. Thus banners about *jihad* as well as "posters depicting the suffering of the people of Palestine, which were adorned with images of Kalashnikovs and jihadis in battle dress," were taken down.[200] However, even then Farish Noor was moved to acknowledge the possibility that despite the fact that a large number of educationists work in Al-Mukmin, and it certainly cannot be assumed that all of them accept the JI worldview, nevertheless "a pattern of close-knit cells or circles of students and teachers" engaged in "discussions, meetings and possibly even plotting" could well be "carried out outside the ambit of the pondok's regular activities."[201]

THE REAL PROBLEM WITH BA'ASYIR—AND AL-MUKMIN

To be sure, Ba'asyir, who, since his release from prison in June 2006 for his involvement in the 2002 Bali attacks, and who has resumed teaching at Pondok Pesantren Al-Mukmin, is in no position to shape the formal curriculum of the institution.[202] It also should be noted that Ba'asyir himself does not publicly advocate violence against the Indonesian state, and through his Muslim Mujahidin Council (MMI), an umbrella association formed on August 7, 2000—significantly, the fifty-first anniversary of Kartosoewirjo's proclamation of the NII—he and other like-minded Indonesian Islamists have sought to agitate for an Islamic State through ostensibly peaceful *dakwah*.[203] Nevertheless, it is not so much the modality chosen by Ba'asyir and his fellow ideologues to realize their Islamic State vision that is at issue but rather the *vision* itself. Ba'asyir's worldview—like that of his role model Kartosoewirjo—remains sharply polarized. It is in essence a *binary worldview*. John E. Mack defines a worldview as "an organizing principle or philosophy" that is similar to an ideology, but "broader in scope" and a sort of "mental template into which we try to fit events."[204] Ba'asyir's binary, all-or-nothing worldview was clearly articulated during a sermon at an open-air mosque:

> God has divided humanity into two parts, namely the followers of God and those who follow Satan. . . . God's group are those who follow Islam, those who are prepared to follow his laws and struggle for the implementation of *shariah* [Islamic] law. . . . Meanwhile what is meant by Satan's group are those people who oppose God's law, who . . . throw obstacles in the path of the implementation of God's law.[205]

Ba'asyir was emphatic in declaring that there was no hope of conciliation between true Muslims who believed in the complete implementation of Islamic law and those who opposed this:

> We would rather die than follow that which you worship. We reject all of your beliefs, we reject all of your ideologies, we reject all of your teachings on social issues, economics or beliefs. Between you and us there will forever be a ravine of hate and we will be enemies until you follow God's law.[206]

In Ba'asyir's vision, Christians would have to accept the status of a minority *dhimmi* community with protected but restricted rights in an Indonesian Islamic State.[207] Muslims would tolerate but not embrace Christians and would "not seek to mingle with them."[208] In like vein, Farish Noor, who interviewed Ba'asyir at Al-Mukmin in 2007, has observed that in Ba'asyir's harder-edged interpretation, "Ngruki's doctrine of *al-Wala' wal-Bara*" has taken on a "decidedly conservative and exclusive tone, prompting students of Ba'asyir to exclude themselves from the wider circles of Indonesia's plural multireligious society."[209] It is noteworthy that even as sympathetic an observer as the Indonesian country specialist Tim Behrend concedes that Ba'asyir's message is "not simply anti-Zionist or anti-Israeli, but very deeply and personally anti-Jewish."[210] In essence, according to Noor, Ba'asyir has formulated a "maximalist" interpretation of Islam that "is couched in terms of an oppositional dialectic that juxtaposes Islam against everything else that is deemed un-Islamic or anti-Islamic [such as] secularism, Western culture and values, democracy, worldly politics," and "other religions" and "all man-made secular ideologies."[211] The ideology of Darul Islamism as articulated by Ba'asyir represents a heavily politicized and ideologized interpretation of Islam. As Noor expresses it:

> Baasyir sets out to provide a form of Islamic scholarship that posits the view of Islam as a comprehensive, totalising, hermetically-sealed discursive economy that has its own cosmology, worldview, value system, guideline (both epistemic and moral), political economy and ideology.[212]

In short, Baa'syir, very much like his hero Kartosoewirjo, can be regarded as a religious fundamentalist seeking to radically restructure the social order in accordance with Islamic dictates. It also is highly likely that, again like Kartosoewirjo, Ba'asyir is a fundamentalist not merely by inner conviction but also by psychological disposition. In short, Ba'asyir simply cannot accept environmental ambiguity and seeks the psychic comforts of a "totalizing, hermetically-sealed discursive economy," as Noor puts it. Evidence of this can be deduced from the fact that Ba'asyir seems curiously unaffected by his education at the famous modernist Gontor institution, which, *inter alia*, promoted respect for all four Islamic schools of jurisprudence and avoided doctrinal rigidity; encouraged the innovative critical study of traditional religious texts; and fostered debates on religious issues among students and between students and teachers. Although Gontor was credited with helping sharpen the critical reasoning powers of fellow students of Ba'asyir, such as the late eminent modernist scholar Nurcholish Madjid, the latter recalled that B'asyir came across then as "so puritanical, so uncompromising."[213]

Despite Ba'asyir's frankly unhealthy intellectual and doctrinal rigidity, he enjoys a strong personal standing and wide influence as the only living founding member of Al-Mukmin, a not insignificant fact within the highly collectivist, large power-distance Javanese milieu.[214] Ba'asyir's sheer mass appeal among his followers both within and outside Al-Mukmin—and consequently his ability to shape popular opinion on the ground—is evident in the following atmospheric description of his first public appearance at a mass rally held in Solo, Central Java, in 2006, following his release from prison on terrorism charges:

> The voice on the speakers quavers: *"Dan masa sudah tiba, kita sambut ketibaan bapa kita, Ustaz kita, pemimpin kita, guru kita, Ustaz Abu Bakar Bashiiiiiiiir..."* (The time has come to welcome our father, our religious teacher, our leader, our teacher, Ustaz Abu Bakar Bashiiiir).... Then before we know it, there he is, the man himself, towering before us on the stage.... In the searing light, he seems angry and beautiful, perhaps beatific.[215]

Ba'asyir's shrewd exploitation of his stature to push the stock Darul Islamist message of a global Islamic community oppressed by a nefarious Jewish-Crusader Axis is further captured by the observer:

> He launches into a bitter tirade against the injustices that the world has meted out upon Muslims, and the crowd grows angrier with every word. The interminable litany of atrocities: Afghanistan, Bosnia, Kashmir, Iraq, Palestine, Chechnya, Mindanao, Aceh, Lebanon.....The sheer timeliness of the last reference triggers the reaction that is long awaited. Out come

the kerosene and lighters, and the flags of Israel and America go up in smoke; stomping feet; crushed effigies... booming speakers; angry shouts; fists punching the air above. Surakarta's legion of radical movements has come out to welcome their hero. Ustaz Abu is home, the city his again.[216]

Ba'asyir's mass appeal ensures that his virulent interpretation of Islam resonates strongly within the confined spaces of Pondok Pesantren Al-Mukmin.[217] To be sure, while the respected International Crisis Group is right to assert that to "have gone to a JI-linked pesantren does not make one a terrorist,"[218] and the noted scholar Greg Fealy is similarly justified in reminding us that not all JI members "are engaged in terrorism, and the network also has groups conducting peaceful religious education and welfare functions,"[219] all of this actually is beside the point. The issue is that precisely because of the intensity of the indoctrination—there really is no other word for it—to which Al-Mukmin alumni have been subjected, almost surely *some among their number* remain in truth "walking time-bombs." An explanation is warranted here: as we saw in an earlier chapter, ethnocentrism and xenophobia are part of being human, and this tendency manifests itself in the form of overt prejudice toward various out-groups. Analysts like J. Harold Ellens lament that "prejudice is a devastating force in our political and social order" that emerges from "a very sick psychology at the center of our souls."[220] In general, the prejudiced individual is dismissive of and indifferent to the sensibilities and sufferings of the out-group.[221] It does not stop there, however. Among the wider group of prejudiced individuals there is a smaller number, whom the psychoanalyst Willard Gaylin considers *bigots*, who are "strongly partial to one's own group, religion, race, or politics." Rather than being passively indifferent, bigots are *actively* "intolerant of those who differ."[222] The bigot, Gaylin informs us, would "support legislation and social conditions that deprive the minority of its autonomy and its right to be respected."[223] Finally, it is from the smaller pool of bigots that the *haters* emerge. Whereas a "bigot may feel malevolence whenever he thinks of the despised group," he "is not obsessively preoccupied with them."[224] On the other hand, hatred "requires both passion and a preoccupation with the hated group."[225] In this vein Aristotle once pointed out that whereas the "angry man wants the object of his anger to suffer in return; hatred wishes its object not to exist."[226] Gaylin notes that there could be "significant slippage" between the bigots and the haters.[227] However, he is forthright in condemning not just hatred but also the *preceding transition points* to this end-state:

Prejudice and bigotry also facilitate the agendas of a hating population. They take advantage of the passivity of the larger community of bigots, a passivity that is essential for that minority who truly hate to carry out their malicious destruction.[228]

Gaylin hits the nail on the head when he draws attention to the fact that deep-seated prejudice, bigotry, and for that matter full-blown hatred, especially when systematically promoted, are never harmless:

> As recently as the summer of 2002 the *New York Times* reported an interview in which a professor of Islamic law explained to a visiting reporter: "Well of course I hate you because you are Christian, but that doesn't mean I want to kill you." Well, the professor may not wish to kill the reporter, but the students he instills with his theological justifications of hatred may have different ideas about the proper expressions of hatred.[229]

It is in the "culture of hatred" that "monstrous evil can be unleashed," and when "everyday bias is supported and legitimated by religion," the "passions of ordinary malcontents will be intensified and focused."[230] This is precisely the problem with Al-Mukmin: although it may well be informal, the Darul Islamist–inspired general culture within its environs nevertheless *religiously legitimates the social death of nonbelievers*. Social death in this context refers, *inter alia*, to "excommunication from the legitimate social or moral community and relegation to a perpetual state of dishonor."[231] This may not seem to constitute a serious, immediate problem on the surface, but it is mighty cause for concern. Consigning unbelieving outsiders to the state of social death facilitates the creeping, subtle mental dehumanization that renders killing them later far easier—a point that will be elaborated on shortly.

Contributing to the effective propagation of the informal Darul Islamist curriculum within Al-Mukmin is the relative regimentation of contact with the wider society. Al-Mukmin is physically located in a "culturally and religiously plural area" of Surakarta, Central Java, "with as many mosques as there are churches."[232] Nevertheless, Al-Mukmin alumnus Noor Huda Ismail observes that students generally are required to obey their teachers at all times and are not permitted direct personal contact with the outside world. Television, radio, magazines, and the Internet are all off-limits, as they are seen as vehicles of Westernization. In like vein, smoking, alcohol, jeans, baseball caps, and contact with females are all prohibited. Infractions of these rules could result in the offending student having his hair shaven and having to express regret for his act publicly.[233] Singaporean journalists corroborated Ismail's comments when they discovered that Al-Mukmin students were warned not to talk to strangers and were punished if they did.[234] As late as mid-2007, Al-Mukmin students were not permitted to own headphones and could not leave the premises without the permission of teachers or unless they were on holiday leave. At all other times, students wishing to leave the *pesantren* during the day needed an exit permit from the institution, to be carried at all times outside and returned when they came back to the *pesantren*.[235] In a sense, one could argue that through such practices, Al-Mukmin is doing nothing new and is merely replicating the Javanese traditionalist concept of closed *pesantren*-centred social networks. On the other hand, as the well-known scholar of comparative religion Charles Kimball has warned, problems arise within a religious constituency when "charismatic leadership" and an "unwavering commitment to compelling ideas and teachings" intersect with the "impulse to withdraw from society."[236] Such physical withdrawal, Jonathan Drummond adds, enables religious leaders to promote "alternative news sources" and "closed religious/ritual systems" to "pull one away from competing social networks and constructions of reality."[237] Interestingly enough, following the August 2003 J. W. Marriott JI attack in Jakarta, a pamphlet titled "Marriott Conspiracy Theory" that blamed "Israeli and U.S. intelligence agents" for the incident, was circulated among the Al-Mukmin fraternity.[238] It is hard to avoid concluding that Pondok Pesantren Al-Mukmin, by informally propagating Darul Islamism within its closed compound, appears to be fostering the construction of an alternate reality among its charges, one in which a deep and abiding hatred for Islam's putative enemies, especially so-called Western "infidels," is a central theme.

Of course, some may argue, as did Tracy Dahlby's Al-Mukmin interlocutor, that in the final analysis, the *pesantren*'s students are merely "radicals in their heads, but not in action."[239] Ba'asyir himself once told an Indonesian intelligence official that as a preacher he likened himself to a "craftsman" who sells "knives" but cannot be held responsible for what happens to them.[240] Yet Al-Mukmin students, through continuous immersion in the general culture of Darul Islamism, are systematically being *conditioned* to deny the humanity of non-Muslims, especially Westerners. One may argue that in a myriad of informal ways, elements within Al-Mukmin subject its students to *Skinnerian operant conditioning*, in which the capacity to kill the Hated Other is subtly cultivated at a deeper subliminal level. Although overstated, there is a kernel of truth in the eminent behavioral scientist B. F. Skinner's observation that any "child is a tabula rasa, a 'blank slate' who could be turned into anything" as long as "sufficient control of the child's environment is instituted at an early enough age."[241] In other words, the net effect of Al-Mukmin's type of informal, environmental socialization into the Darul Islamist ideology is to render students, particular those who come from very insular, parochially pious backgrounds and with little contact with alternative sources of information, highly susceptible to what the military psychologist and historian David Grossman calls "acquired deficiency" in the "violence immune system" that exists in their minds. As Grossman puts it:

A hundred things can convince your forebrain to put a gun in your hand and go to a certain point: poverty, drugs, gangs, leaders, politics and the social learning of violence in the media—which is magnified when you are from a broken home and are searching for a role model.[242]

Nevertheless, physically killing other human beings, even in armed combat, is an extremely traumatic experience and, despite media depictions to the contrary, is not that straightforward a task for ordinary people.[243] Regardless, what the social psychologist Albert Bandura calls the socially learned moral "self sanctions" against killing other humans[244] can deliberately and systematically be weakened. Grossman again:

But if you are *conditioned* to overcome these . . . inhibitions, then you are a walking time bomb, a pseudosociopath, just waiting for the random factors of *social interaction* and forebrain rationalization to put you at the wrong place at the wrong time [italics added].[245]

Hence, long after graduation from Al-Mukmin, any Virtual Violent Radical may well act out his fantasies and transmute himself into a Real-Time Violent Radical—given the right kind of immediate small-group context, within which the individual could be subjected to the mutually reinforcing pressures of peer pressure, continued ideological indoctrination, and propaganda relating to certain chosen traumas impacting the Muslim community. This is why evolutionary biologist David Sloan Wilson cautions against "pushing the wrong psychological buttons" that can activate the "facultative sociopathy" of a group already indoctrinated to think in "us" and "them" terms.[246] The former radical Islamist Ed Husain alludes to this *latent capacity for violence* that exists within large numbers of otherwise quiescent Muslims who have at some point in their lives been profoundly immersed in absolutist, deeply polarized, radical Islamist ideological milieus:

Today, across the world, I believe there are tens of thousands of people . . . [who] harbour a confrontational worldview, but are not actively involved in the world of the Islamist movement. However, a cataclysmic event would bring these people, along with new recruits, back to the organizational front line.[247]

THE DARUL ISLAMIST "CHARISMATIC GROUP"

Tellingly, Ba'asyir, in a revealing speech in 2000, showed that he had no qualms defending the organization of Pondok Pesantren Al-Mukmin. He has always reiterated the strategic importance of *pesantren* in strengthening the capacity of the *ummah* to defend itself against the "enemies of Islam." He asserted that "religious boarding schools are the bulwarks of

Islam" and that "graduates of pesantren" must "truly become preachers and mujahideen." Harking back to the "learned men in the early days of Islam," Ba'asyir opined that in addition to "acting as scholars, missionaries and moral teachers, they were also mujahideen who were always prepared to go to war and didn't just sit back in their mosques or schools giving lessons."[248] Since 1971, more than 3,000 alumni have passed through the Al-Mukmin *pesantren* in Solo.[249] These, along with the alumni of spin-off JI "Ivy League" *pesantren* such as Al-Islam in East Java; Al-Muttaqien and Dar us-Syahadah in Central Java; and the now-defunct Luqmanul Hakiem in Ulu Tiram, Malaysia, have formed social networks of relatively like-minded, if geographically dispersed, *jemaah islamiyah*.[250] Furthermore, a 2004 study discovered that more than one hundred marriages involving JI leaders and members exist, integrating—and potentially indoctrinating—entire families in Malaysia, Indonesia, and to some extent the southern Philippines.[251] It appears that a related network of *pesantren* centered on Pesantren Hidayat-ullah in Balikpapan, East Kalimantan, is also sympathetic to the JI cause.[252] In essence, these social networks of JI-linked *pesantren* alumni and families, together with the older networks in Java that actively mobilized in support of Kartosoewirjo in the 1950s, represent the "in-group" of Darul Islamism today. In more technical language, an "in-group" consciously espousing Darul Islamist ideology (or Darul Islamism) would be akin to what the psychiatrist Marc Galanter calls the "charismatic group." According to Galanter, the charismatic group could consist of "a dozen or more members, even hundreds and thousands."[253] The charismatic group is defined by four elements:

> [M]embers (1) have a *shared belief system*, (2) sustain a high level of *social cohesiveness*, (3) are strongly influenced by the group's *behavioral norms*, and (4) impute *charismatic* (or sometimes *divine*) power to the group or its leadership.[254]

This Darul Islamist charismatic group did not arise in a cultural vacuum but rather represents a politicized, ideological offshoot of the even wider, more nebulous "Bouquet" of Darul Islamic subculture that has flowered in Java, as noted. To be sure, the Darul Islamist charismatic group, of which the JI terrorist network is a part, is heavily factionalized, but despite ideological differences between the various factions, the five consciously held core elements of Darul Islamism discussed in the previous chapter combine to give the Darul Islamist charismatic group an overarching unity and common identity. Again, these are the existential fear of group extinction; categorical, us-them thinking; a strong sense of moral entitlement and historic victimization; a focus on personalized socialization of new recruits; and ultimately the driving mimetic desire to ensure the dominance of Islam. That the political ideology of Darul Islamism has been a major Radical

Pathway toward the Bali attacks of October 2002 is clearly evinced by studying the worldviews of two senior JI activists involved in the bombings: Mukhlas and Imam Samudra.

MUKHLAS

It has long been known that intense religiosity tends to generate ethnocentric, prejudiced, discriminatory, and antidemocratic attitudes. Freud understood this very well:

> A religion, even if it calls itself the religion of love, must be hard and unloving to those who do not belong to it. Fundamentally indeed every religion is in the same way a religion of love for all those whom it embraces; while cruelty and intolerance towards those who do not belong to it are natural to every religion.[255]

The discussion in the previous section suggests that such deep religious prejudice can, under certain circumstances—such as within the closed socializing milieus provided by certain student-teacher circles within Pondok Pesantren Al-Mukmin—be exploited as a pathway toward radicalization. This becomes clear on examination of the background of Mukhlas, who was head of JI's Mantiqi (or Region) 1, covering Singapore and Malaysia.[256] Muhklas, also known as Ali Ghufron bin Nurhasyim, was born in Tenggulun village in Solokuru subdistrict, Lamongan regency, East Java, a "very religious region of Indonesia,"[257] on February 2, 1960.[258] He was one of thirteen children of the former village secretary Nur Hasyim, a "respected leader and strict disciplinarian."[259] Mukhlas grew up in a home that socialized him into a strict, Arabized modernist (read Wahhabi or Salafi) code. In fact, Mukhlas's maternal grandfather, Kyai Haji Sulaiman, who had built Tenggulun's very first *pesantren*, wore ankle-length robes, very much like those of the Prophet in seventh-century Arabia.[260] Kyai Haji Sulaiman went on the *haj* to Mecca seven times, remaining for one year each time and "bringing back the latest teachings from Saudi Arabia on his return."[261] Moreover, Mukhlas was educated in Islamic schools, receiving his primary education in Solokuru subdistrict and his religious teachers' education at Payaman, Solukuru, before proceeding to Pondok Pesantren Al-Mukmin, where he attended KMI or teachers' college.[262] The *strong uncertainty-avoidance outlook* fostered by Mukhlas's relatively insular upbringing in a Salafi milieu was intensified by the fact that his father Nurhasyim, regarded by Mukhlas himself as "fanatical in his beliefs," pointedly told his sons that "Javanese customs such as grave worship were heresy under Islam and must be eradicated."[263] Significantly, Nurhasyim, according to Mukhlas's brother Amrozi, also "wanted his children to be warriors not just to defend Islam" but to "champion Islam, to glorify Islam."[264] Little wonder then that Mukhlas was also immersed in the folklore of Darul Islamic subculture: Nurhasyim had fought against the Dutch forces during Indonesia's independence struggle, and Mukhlas's uncle had been killed in an engagement with Dutch troops not far from Tenggu-lun. Mukhlas candidly recounted: "It was these kinds of stories that inspired me and my younger brothers to be mujahideen."[265] Lord Alderdice noted a similar phenomenon in the Northern Ireland conflict, where "most peo-ple who became involved in terrorism" came from "communities where the tradition of using force to address political problems had been maintained for generations," and they "admired fathers and grandfathers honored for their participation in a historic struggle."[266]

Mukhlas arrived at Pondok Pesantren Al-Mukmin in 1979 and re-mained as an apprentice teacher after graduating in 1982. He was there when Ba'asyir and Sungkar returned after their release from prison in 1982.[267] Mukhlas soon fell under the influence of these two men.[268] After they de-camped on their *hijrah* to Malaysia in April 1985, Mukhlas followed suit one year later via Medan, then spent time in Penang before linking up again with his mentors.[269] At the start of 1986, Mukhlas joined the early Indone-sian volunteers on their way to Afghanistan to join in the *jihad* against the Soviets.[270] He remained there from 1986 to 1989 and claimed to have met Osama bin Laden during the Soviet assault on Joji in 1987. He recalled that he had stood his ground together with the *mujahidin* "from all over the world" against the ferocious Soviet attack.[271] The impact of the experience of the Joji battle on the development of Mukhlas' *jihadi* outlook cannot be underestimated. It represented an example of what the psychoanalyst Vamik Volkan calls "chosen glories"—those past triumphs that promote a sense of group cohesion and identity.[272] In Mukhlas' own words:

> It is the sort of pleasure that can't be described, let alone understood by those who have never experienced it. I have had a wife, I have had my first night—but the pleasure is nothing, not even close, compared to the pleasure of war. It was very, very delightful. Especially when we see our friends who bravely died a holy death. They smelled fragrant, they were smiling, and it often made me wonder—why is it not for me to die such a peaceful, contented death?[273]

On his return to Malaysia in the middle of 1989, Mukhlas went to Ulu Tiram, Johore, and spent time working as a laborer as well as teaching Arabic and Islamic law at friends' houses "without asking for payment."[274] Undoubtedly because of his evident deep piety, in mid-1991 Mukhlas was tasked by "Ustad Sungkar" to set up a new religious boarding school in Ulu Tiram, Johore, modeled on Al-Mukmin. Ba'asyir and Sungkar, desirous of propagating their "correct interpretation" of Islam—essentially Darul Islamism—to the next generation, told Mukhlas that "in Malaysia an Islamic boarding school teaching the Quran and Sunna was badly needed, especially by our children, the children of the Indonesians living in Malaysia."[275] Mukhlas proceeded to set up "the Islamic boarding school," which came to be called Luqmanul Hakiem, with funds, land, and building materials donated from "friends."[276] He continued "Islamic preaching at the houses of friends living in Ulu Tiram" until 1998, when these sermons were "stopped by the Malaysian Government."[277] By the early 1990s, Mukhlas had become a senior figure in the JI network, and his personal Radical Pathway toward the 2002 Bali attacks had been well and truly paved.

After his capture by the Indonesian police for his involvement in the Bali attack, in December 2002, Mukhlas was sent to prison. In October 2003 he was sentenced to death by firing squad. While in prison he had time to write a justification for the Bali attacks:

> To us, and our view is based on the axioms of the Qur'an and the Sunnah and the facts on the ground, the enemies of Islam, from past times to the present day, including the Jews, America and their lackeys, do not understand the language of diplomacy. They only understand the language of force... because of that, we communicate with them through bomb explosions so that they hear and pay attention. The aims of a bomb explosion are as follows.... To terrorize, frighten and make tremble the enemies of Islam and Muslims... [and to] avenge their brutal attacks on Muslims.[278]

Some key elements of Darul Islamism come out in Mukhlas' musings: powerful us-them, xenophobic, categorical thinking, tinged with an innate sense of moral superiority (*we* act justly, based on the Qur'an and the Sunnah; by implication, *they*, the nefarious Jews, America, and their lackeys act unjustly); the notion that *jihad* in the form of a horrific bomb explosion was morally justified (they do not understand the language of diplomacy, only force); and the desire to exact revenge for past evils and to transform the infidel victimizers into the victimized (we want to "terrorize, frighten, and make tremble" the enemies of Islam). What is especially striking is that Mukhlas seems to be, in truth, somewhat half-hearted with regard to assessing the tangible strategic effects of the Bali attack in JI's cosmic war against the "Jews, America and their lackeys."

> *Hopefully* God Almighty will put fear into the hearts of the enemies of Islam and Muslims through the Bali Bomb explosions. *If* they are haunted by fear, God willing at least their evil plans and programs, military and non-military, will be hampered, or thank God *if* we can cause their conspiracy and their networks throughout the world, particularly in Indonesia, to fail and break up [italics added].[279]

It appears that the main goal for Mukhlas is to ensure that the erstwhile Western victimizers of Muslims—even if they are represented not by troops

in uniform but by unarmed civilians—*now get a taste of their own medicine.*
Rather than strategic effects, what the Bali blasts really, truly offered to the JI
leadership—whether or not they publicly acknowledged this—was *symbolic empowerment.* As the sociologist Mark Juergensmeyer argues, "religious
activists" engage in "terrorism" because they see themselves as engaged in
a "great struggle," a "cosmic war" in which the true objective is "dehu-
miliation." Terrorism provides "escape from humiliating and impossible
predicaments for those who otherwise would feel immobilized by them."
Hence these religious militants seek "not only to belittle their enemies but
also to provide themselves with a sense of power."[280] This is precisely why
Mukhlas wrote:

> The conclusion is that the pious were commanded by Almighty God to
> become *irhaabi* or terrorists, namely those who can make the enemies of
> Almighty God . . . *tremble, be afraid and be overwhelmed by fear* [italics
> added].[281]

What Mukhlas is saying is very telling. The victimized, humiliated Muslim
victims of Western perfidy would now—through the symbolic effects of the
Bali attacks—become the newly *empowered victimizers* of Western infidels.
In essence, what drove the JI cell and what really motivated key leaders
like Mukhlas to conduct the Bali operation was what some psychologists
call *superego-tripping.* The superego, in Freudian terms, is the individual's
conscience and values. Alan Elms explains:

> [S]uperego-tripping is acting on the assumption that whatever behavior best
> satisfies the demands of one's superego will be most effective in attaining
> one's realistic goals. . . . *[I]f you judge the effectiveness of your overt act in
> terms of whether they make you feel good morally, rather than whether
> they have changed external reality in the ways you had planned, you're
> superego-tripping* [italics added].[282]

IMAM SAMUDRA

The fiery 2002 Bali bomb attack field coordinator Imam Samudra, also
known as Abdul Aziz, presents a slightly different picture. Samudra, the
eighth of eleven children, was born in the village of Lompang near the town
of Serang, Banten province, West Java, on January 14, 1970. Serang is another "very religious region of Indonesia" where DI had been active.[283] The
son of working-class parents in a "shabby part of town,"[284] Samudra's parents had long-term Persis connections, which meant that, like Mukhlas,
Samudra would have been exposed from his youth to Arabized modernist ideas akin to Saudi-style Salafism. Whereas Mukhlas had been thoroughly immersed in formal Islamic education, Samudra's own educational

background had, at least on the surface, a fairly substantial formal secular component. He attended Serang Municipal State Primary School from 1978 and 1984 and attended afternoon classes at Ibtidaiyah Islamic school at the same time. He then attended State Junior High School 4 in Serang until 1987, followed by State Senior High School in Cikulur until 1990. That same year he enrolled in the Special Entry Programme of the State Islamic Institute and was deemed to have passed the course, although he did not quite complete all the requisite modules.[285] Although Samudra attended Islamic school after regular primary school classes, in truth, his interest in Islam did not take off immediately. At first, he was bored with reciting Qur'anic verses during the afternoon religious classes, often skipping them altogether. He much preferred reading whatever he could find in his primary school library. It seems, however, that after attending intensive religious instruction in the ninth grade, Samudra developed an intense religiosity.[286] According to Neighbour:

> He spent hours in the library devouring everything he could find on Islam, from the treatises of the Muslim Brotherhood to the writings of the executed Darul Islam leader Kartosuwiryo, whose short-lived Islamic State of Indonesia had flourished in Samudra's home province [of Banten]. He even read the works of the radical African-American Muslim leader Malcolm X.[287]

Crucially, at the time Samudra was growing up, as was the case with Mukhlas, the myths and stories associated with Darul Islamic subculture were still in circulation. Samudra would have embraced these martial myths for two reasons. First, he was of ethnic Bantenese stock, and it was well-known that the Bantenese tended to see themselves as *pendekar* or warriors. Second, Samudra's great-grandfather, Kyai Wasyid, had fought against the Dutch colonizers with such distinction that the Bantenese provincial capital of Serang put up a monument in his honor.[288] In any case, when Samudra graduated with very good primary school grades and joined the putatively secular but nevertheless "religiously conservative" State Junior High School 4 in Serang,[289] he came under the influence of a former Darul Islam rebel commander, Kyai Saleh As'ad, who had fought under DI Imam Kartosoewirjo. Samudra immersed himself in the "tales of Kartosoewirjo's bravado," which were "the stuff of legend in the schoolyards of West Java"—and he became a "zealous initiate of the Darul Islam cause."[290] It is likely that in high school the young Samudra began to evince both dispositional attributes of the convinced religious fundamentalist: a strong internal locus of control that compelled him to believe that he could shape the environment and not be shaped by it—as well as the tendency to view the world in categorical us-them, good-versus-evil terms—and a tendency to resolve the resulting cognitive dissonance through seeking external transformation rather than introspective self-examination so as to facilitate inner adaptation to "the real world." By the time he was in his late teens, therefore, Samudra had become an "opinionated, domineering young man, with a snappy tongue, a fiery temper and an unswerving belief in the rightness of his cause."[291] Significantly, these were also the years when the great Afghan *jihad* against the Soviet occupation forces was at its height, and it is now known that the teenaged Samudra had devoured Abdullah Azzam's *Allah's Signs in the Afghan Jihad* several times over and developed a burning interest in *jihad*.[292] Moreover, Samudra even then demonstrated his ability to influence young people: he commanded a following at school, conducted *halaqah* or religious study circles, where an oft-discussed topic was *jihad*, and was chosen to lead a provincial association of religious schools.[293] By this time, Samudra's personality would have been a good illustration of the political scientist R. Hrair Dekmejian's description of the *"mutaasib,* or Muslim fundamentalist fanatic,"* as characterized by "rigid beliefs, intolerance toward unbelievers, preoccupation with power," and a "vision of an evil world."[294] The extremely strong, "obsessive-compulsive" nature of Samudra's dispositional fundamentalism went hand in glove with the prevailing strong uncertainty-avoidance orientation of Darul Islamic subculture and Darul Islamist ideology. In Willard Gaylin's terms, Samudra could be regarded as more than just a prejudiced bigot: he had developed into a consummate *hater* of the infidels. So powerful and deeply held was the hate-obsession of Samudra toward the enemies of Islam that, after the Bali blasts, a bemused senior Bali police official was moved to remark on how profoundly Samudra "simply hates Americans."[295]

After graduating, again with excellent grades, from high school, Samudra spent time in Qur'an reading sessions under, tellingly, the auspices of the Arabized modernist DDII, a development that reinforced a deeply anti-Christian worldview.[296] It was then that he met Pondok Pesantren Al-Mukmin alumnus Jabir, who had been long immersed in Darul Islamic subculture and Darul Islamist ideology: Jabir's father had been a DI fighter, and more recently, his brother had been incarcerated for involvement with Komando Jihad.[297] Jabir had been to the Afghanistan training camps, and through his auspices, Samudra proceeded there as well. He remained in Afghanistan from 1991 to 1993, receiving training in the handling of assault rifles and bomb construction. It was in Afghanistan that Samudra had his already pronounced categorical thinking sharpened and intensified, and he internalized the Global Salafi *Jihad* construction of reality—one heavily shaped by both the fourteenth-century Muslim jurist Ibn Taymiyya as well as by the more recent ideologue Abdullah Azzam.[298] The experience of meeting *jihadis*, especially from the Middle East, had a profound influence on him, as it had on Mukhlas. As Samudra himself stated:

> In Afghanistan I met and was exposed to Islamic movements from all sorts of countries. I wasn't stuck with what you could call the parochial

nature of the local Islamic movement, thanks to Allah. I met the Muslim Brotherhood, the Egyptian Islamic Group, the Egyptian Jihad Group, and so on. They were all in Afghanistan.[299]

In 1993 Samudra returned to Serang in Indonesia, got married, and despite public differences on the relative balance between *jihad* and *dakwah* with Sungkar, whom Samudra felt was "too soft," the latter joined the newly formed JI. Samudra proceeded to link up with the Ba'asyir-Sungkar exile community in Sungai Manggis village, south of Kuala Lumpur, Malaysia.[300] It was in Malaysia, at the Mukhlas-founded Luqmanul Hakiem *pesantren* in Ulu Tiram, Johore, that Samudra first met fellow Bali bomber Amrozi in "1997–98."[301] Samudra had met Mukhlas as well in "one of the big mosques in Kuala Lumpur" sometime earlier, "around 1996 or 1997," according to Mukhlas's later police testimony.[302] By the 1990s, then, Samudra not only had become "a leading recruiter in the West Java-Banten region"[303] for JI, but he had already embarked on his own personal Radical Pathway to the Bali blasts of October 2002.

Samudra was arrested for his role in the attacks in November 2002 and later sentenced to death. In prison, like Mukhlas, he wrote extensively and in fact was able to publish a book, *Aku Melawan Teroris* (*I Fight Terrorists*),[304] in 2004, which was "part biography, part manifesto and part practical guide to jihad."[305] In his book, Samudra employs the familiar stock Darul Islamist theme of a moral community (the Muslim "us") being victimized and humiliated by powerful "colonizing" enemies (the Jewish and American "them"). He complains that the "International Jewish and Christian media" have both oppressed and impugned the good name of Muslims everywhere:

> [Muslims] have been called terrorists, hard-line Islam, extremists, radicals and so on, in an effort to create erroneous public opinion around the world. Israel and America have created the image that they [the Muslims] are a race of cruel and sadistic monsters. In fact, in essence it is they themselves who are cruel and sadistic. They are Draculas spawned by monsters.[306]

Samudra, like Mukhlas, is unequivocal in asserting that rectifying the injustices against Muslims meted out by the "Draculas spawned by monsters" requires extreme measures. Thus Samudra argues that although *jihad* refers in general to giving one's best in pursuit of a holy aim, such as to uphold and propagate Islamic law,[307] ultimately, in "terms of sharia, jihad means fighting the infidels who wage war on Islam Muslims."[308] More to the point, citing the Qu'ranic injunction to fight infidels who wage war on Muslims[309] and with reference to the U.S. attack on Taliban-ruled Afghanistan in October 2001, Samudra then argues that the Bali attacks of October 2002 without a doubt constituted "jihad in the path of God."[310] The Darul

Islamist impulse to wage *jihad* to avenge perceived wrongs against the dignity of Muslims is clearly shown:

> Truly, all of the crimes and tyranny of the colonizers cannot just be ignored. Muslims must rise up and oppose them with all their might and in every way. Islamic law decrees that resistance is through jihad. So the Bali bombings were one form of response carried out by a few Muslims who were aware of and understood the meaning of defence and of the dignity of Muslims. The Bali bombing was part of the resistance aimed at the colonizer, America and its allies. The Bali bombing was a jihad which had to be carried out, even if it was only by a few Muslims.[311]

Importantly, Samudra is very insistent that the enemies of Islam—America, Israel, and their allies—be made to feel in equal measure the pain and horror felt by Muslim civilians, the victims of "large scale massacres" in "Afghanistan in the month of Ramadan in 2001" during Operation Enduring Freedom. In other words, Western civilians should be targeted in bombings just as Muslim civilians are targeted by the "blood-sucking monsters," the enemies of Islam.[312] Samudra is well aware that the Qu'ran forbids aggression against civilians such as the elderly, women, and children.[313] However, precisely because, in his view, "the US army of the Cross and its allies" did not adhere to the limitations on war and attacked Muslim civilians, it was only fair that Muslim fighters attack Western civilians in retaliation. Driven by the premise that the "blood of Moslems is expensive and valuable" and cannot be "toyed with and made a target of American terrorists and their allies,"[314] Samudra declares:

> God does not permit His servants to remain in a state of anxiety and degradation. God does not permit His servants to be played foul by the infidels. War will be met with war, blood with blood, lives with lives, and transgressions with the same.... So waging war on civilians ... from the colonizing nations is appropriate for the sake of balance and justice. Blood for blood, lives for lives, and ... civilians for civilians! That is balance.[315]

Again, the overriding conviction that the Western infidel victimizers must become the victimized at the hands of the Muslims is made clear. Samudra wanted the Bali attacks to force the "American terrorists and their allies" to "understand how painful it is to lose" blood relatives such as "mothers, husbands, children, or other family members."[316] Elsewhere, Samudra reiterates that under the leadership of JI, a muscular, powerful Islam will rise to both stop Western infidel aggression against Muslims and mete out punishment in return:

The cries of babies and the screams of the Muslimah [Muslim women] as well as the diplomatic efforts of a small number of Muslims [have] never succeeded in stopping your brutality and it will never succeed. Well here we are the Muslimin [Muslims]!!! . . . We will never let your cruelty on our brothers go unpunished. You will bear the consequences of your actions wherever you are.[317]

Samudra does not stop there. Influenced by his reading of Abdullah Azzam's *Tarbiyah Jihadiyah*, Samudra conceives of the concept of *jihad* as having evolved through four stages in Muslim history. In the first stage, the early Muslims were commanded to remain patient in the face of concerted efforts by the People of the Book—Jews and Christians—as well as the polytheists to compel them to renounce their faith. Instead of fighting back, Muslims instead were commanded by the Prophet to focus on prayer, pay alms, and "forgive the cruelty of the non-believers."[318] To this end, Samudra cites the following verse:

Quite a number of the People of the Book wish they could turn you (people) back to infidelity after ye have believed, from selfish envy, after the Truth hath become manifest unto them: but forgive and overlook, till Allah accomplish His purpose; for Allah hath power over all things (*Sura* 2:109).[319]

After the oppression and violence against the early Muslims intensified and the non-Muslims sought to drive the Muslims out of their homeland, permission to fight was granted, signaling the second stage of *jihad*, Samudra notes. He then draws attention to the following verse:

To those against whom war is made, permission is given (to fight), because they are wronged—and verily, Allah is most powerful for their aid—(They are) those who have been expelled from their homes in defiance of right—(for no cause) except that they say "Our Lord is Allah" (*Sura* 22: 39–40).[320]

However, Samudra points out that the permission to fight given in this verse was not a commandment to engage in general war. Fighting in self-defense was permissible in the second stage but was not an individual obligation.[321] Yet by the third stage of *jihad*, fighting had become an individual obligation or *fardhu ain*. This was, Samudra argues, made clear by *Sura* 2:216:

Fighting is prescribed for you, and ye dislike it. But it is possible that ye dislike a thing which is good for you, and that you love a thing that is bad for you. But Allah knoweth, and ye know not.[322]

According to Samudra, the fourth and final stage of *jihad* was reached when the following verse, among others, was revealed to the Prophet:

> Fight those who believe not in Allah nor the Last Day nor hold that forbidden which hath been forbidden by Allah and His Prophet, nor acknowledge the religion of Truth, (even if they are) of the People of the Book, until they pay the *jizyah* [exemption tax] with willing submission, and feel themselves subdued (*Sura* 9:29).[323]

He added that the above verse, together with *Sura* 8:39, which called on all Muslims to "fight with them on until there is no more tumult or oppression, and there prevail justice and faith in Allah altogether and everywhere," strongly suggests that modern Muslims now have a common obligation: to wage war "until there is no more polytheism and so that the excellent religion of God that is Islam prevails" over other religions.[324] In other words, in Samudra's worldview, Muslims today are in a state of permanent war against all enemies of Islam—both non-Muslims as well as those Muslim apostates who do not share his us-them conception of the world, let alone his interpretation of *jihad*. As is the case for Ba'asyir, for Samudra, the ultimate endgame of *jihad* is the thoroughly mimetic one of ensuring Islamic global dominion. This was the ultimate *putative* aim of the Bali attacks. Nevertheless, a close analysis of the ideological pronouncements of people like Ba'asyir, Mukhlas, and Imam Samudra makes it clear that it would be an error to attempt the distillation of a carefully thought-through, detailed, strategic plan of action for achieving Islamic global domination. What really drove JI leaders to perpetrate the Bali attacks was what essentially drove Kartosoewirjo decades earlier: a deep abiding Existential Identity Anxiety comprising a combustible admixture of fear and envy of Islam's putative enemies. The Bali attacks therefore constituted an example of "devices for symbolic empowerment in wars that cannot be won and for goals that cannot be achieved."[325] From this perspective, however impressive Samudra's *Aku Melawan Teroris* may seem as a meaty ideological tract, it should be seen less as a politico-strategic program than as an unconscious exercise in superego-tripping. Unfortunately, this does not in any way render JI any less dangerous.

CONCLUSION

This chapter has attempted to make the claim that it would not be accurate to consider the JI network simply a transplant of Al Qaeda in Indonesia and for that matter Southeast Asia. We have argued that, on the contrary, JI today is simply the latest manifestation of the historic subculture, or "Bouquet," of Darul Islam. We saw that Darul Islamic subculture and the more consciously held political ideology of Darul Islamism were the product of the interplay of interwar political competition between Muslim and secular political forces, Dutch colonial rule, and the Japanese Occupation, as well as of the interaction between three subcultures—or, to use a metaphor, Trees—in the Garden of Javanese Islam: *santri* traditionalism, modernism, and Arabized modernism. Although the later infusion of Global Salafi *Jihad* tenets into Darul Islamist ideology remains a significant development, this has merely modified some of Darul Islamism's guiding precepts at the *edges*—for instance, in its new *jihad* focus on targeting the interests of Western governments and their civilian populations rather than merely the Indonesian government, security forces, and civilians with Republican sympathies—as during Kartosoewirjo's era. Darul Islamic subculture and the Darul Islamist ideology it begets remain fundamentally unaltered to this day, defined by the core elements of Existential Identity Anxiety—essentially, an intrinsic fear of group extinction; categorical, us-versus-them, good-versus-evil thinking that reinforces the generalized notion that "what is different is dangerous"; a strong sense of moral entitlement and historic victimization that lend themselves to the latter-day moral and religious legitimization of the social death of unbelievers and subtly ease the moral constraints on violence against the latter; a focus on personalized socialization of new recruits rendered vulnerable by the collectivist, large power-distance outlook of Javanese culture within relatively isolated informal ideological spaces if not formal institutions; and ultimately, the mimetic impulse to ensure the dominance of Islam above all comers.

It is in the final analysis Darul Islamist ideology that very much still binds the JI network to its deep roots in the Darul Islamic subculture of Java. It is for good reason that Sidel, for instance, makes the point that "from its inception," JI was "part and parcel" of a "broader Islamist network in Indonesia, one that included the veterans of the Darul Islam rebellion of the 1950s and early 1960s as well as some of their children."[326] Similarly, Fealy notes that "former DI areas have proven a rich source of new members for the JI and are likely to remain so in the future."[327] As late as January 2006, Al Chaidar, the DI spokesman, drew the author's attention to the continuing intimate nexus between DI and JI. In keeping with the botanical metaphor of gardens, bouquets, and flowers adopted in this study, Chaidar observed that both DI and JI militants felt that they were akin to the "branches" of the same "very tall and very strong" tree with "roots" that are "very deep inside of the soil." As long as the root remains, the tree will "always" grow tall "with so many branches."[328] However, it should be noted that immersion in a violent ideology such as Darul Islamism does not *ipso facto* transform an individual into a murderous terrorist. Observers have emphasized that not all alumni of Pondok Pesantren Al-Mukmin are violent militants; many are quietists engaged in peaceful religious education and welfare activities, while others went on to pursue relatively normal if somewhat relatively more religiously devout lives.[329] In the end, as the RP

Framework developed earlier suggests, what transforms an individual into a violent militant depends very much on a complex interaction between individual personality factors and powerful situational pressures emanating from the immediate social context. It is to these factors that we must now turn to better understand how certain "Flowers" within Kartosoewirjo's Darul Islamic Bouquet traversed the climatic Radical Pathways toward their final incarnation as the full-fledged, committed terrorists of Bali.

4

From Haters to Killers—The Final Steps Toward Bali

Understanding what made certain members of the JI network engage in the terrorist atrocity at Bali requires answers to two questions: first, what pressures and forces led these individuals to decide to join the Bali Cell in the first place? Second, what factors ultimately enabled a few of them to take the final few steps from being *haters* of Western civilians to becoming *killers* of those people? These two steps are analytically distinct because, as psychologist John Horgan correctly points out, "pursuing political goals by force requires overcoming significant psychological hurdles"—there is a difference between being a "terrorist" and a "'mere' radical."[1] Of course, attempting to reconstruct what actual combination of psychological factors prompted ordinary people to join terrorist organizations and engage in terrorist activity is a very complex task. Who really knows what goes on inside an individual's head? Yet there is no way to avoid grappling with "psychological theory," because "explaining terrorism must begin with analyzing the intentions of the terrorist actor."[2] Complicating matters is the reality that after almost four decades of research, no single, overarching, one-size-fits-all terrorist profile has been identified,[3] and as Horgan avers, there is simply "no single cause and no set progression" toward radicalization.[4] Furthermore, even when one eschews overarching explanations of terrorist behavior, as Walter Reich advises, and focuses study on a single terrorist organization[5] such as the JI network, the task is still difficult. As highlighted earlier, whereas Andrew Silke argues that truly accurate assessments of terrorist motivations require personal face-to-face contact with them,[6] in reality this task is fraught with difficulties. Journalist Annette Schaefer reminds us that contact with active violent militants can be "extremely dangerous" in addition to demanding "costly and arduous travel."[7] The fate of the *Wall Street Journal* writer Daniel Pearl at the hands of radical Islamist militants in Pakistan is by now a well-known case in point.[8] In another incident in 2006, a local Thai researcher in insurgency-wracked Southern Thailand was shot by still-unknown assailants. The danger is all too real. Furthermore, "researchers who seek to speak with terrorists frequently come to the attention of security forces and the military" and "run the risk of being seen as sympathizers and of being interrogated."[9] The ethical and legal challenges to direct face-to-face interviews, moreover, often are formidable as well. Horgan himself speaks for many terrorism analysts in admitting that it "crosses my own ethical boundaries to get together with people who plant bombs and kill people."[10] Horgan prefers speaking instead with the legal political arms of militant groups as well as with knowledgeable "officials and journalists."[11] Finally, there are at times legal constraints as well: as discussed, in September 2006 the sociologist Riaz Hassan was forced to considerably alter plans to talk to elements of the leadership and rank and file of militant organizations in the Middle East, South Asia, and JI in Indonesia after being warned by Canberra that he could be in breach of antiterror laws governing consorting with people belonging to groups considered "terrorist organizations by the federal government."[12]

The above-mentioned reasons explain why open-source information is perhaps the most important resource for terrorism researchers. Open sources such as published court testimony, journalistic accounts by reporters who have had access to good-quality information on militants, and social scientists and independent Muslim scholars who have had the opportunity to interview and deconstruct the thinking of incarcerated militants are absolutely essential sources of information and analysis to the terrorism researcher. These complement and help validate the official perspectives and documentation the researcher may have been able to gather through his or her own efforts. This chapter will attempt a reconstruction of the individual Radical Pathways of key JI figures involved in the 2002 Bali attacks through reliance on a combination of open-source data as well as official sources of information. It has been helpful that in the six years that have elapsed since the October 2002 Bali strikes, a sufficient amount of credible open-source data on the attacks has gradually become available. Hence some attempt at studying the JI militants behind the atrocity, albeit at a certain analytical distance, is possible, and in accordance with Crenshaw's call for "analyzing the intentions of the terrorist actor" certainly should be attempted. This chapter, accordingly, seeks to unpack the lives and respective Radical Pathways of Hambali, the senior JI strategist; Amrozi, brother of Mukhlas and key link in the logistics chain that supplied the actual perpetrators of the blasts; Ali Imron, another brother of Mukhlas and also a key cog in the logistics support network; and one of the two Bali suicide bombers, Arnasan. The first part of the section on each individual will attempt to tease out those elements that may have compelled the person to join the JI Bali Cell, while the second portion will examine those elements that likely enabled him to engage in actions that led to the actual killing of the people in Paddy's Bar and the Sari Club. Using our recurring botanical metaphor, this chapter addresses the key question of how certain "Flowers" within the Darul Islam subcultural "Bouquet" evolved into the poisonous JI strain.

HAMBALI

Becoming a Hater

No account of the Bali bombings of October 12, 2002, would be complete without reference to the individual known as Hambali, who was, before his arrest in Ayuthya, Thailand, by a joint Thai-CIA team in August 2003, regarded as the JI network's operational strategist. Hambali was born Nurjaman bin Isamuddin in the quiet West Java town of Cianjur in April 1964. Cianjur is situated in the lush volcanic belt of West Java, a region crisscrossed with so many streams and rivers that many villages' names begin with *ci*, meaning water.[13] West Java, moreover, was the seat of the powerful ancient Islamic Sultanate of Demak[14] and much later, as noted, became the heartland of the Darul Islamist charismatic group. Nurjaman, who early on was nicknamed Encep, grew up in a village that was, until Kartosoewirjo's execution in 1962, very much part of the DI Imam's self-proclaimed Negara Islam Indonesia (NII). Legend has it that Demak's feared Islamic warriors would plunge their swords into their bodies without drawing blood, "defying the pain through the strength of their faith"; as journalist Sally Neighbour rightly avers, this was precisely the kind of intergenerational religious "fervour that gave birth to the Darul Islam rebellion" hundreds of years later.[15] The lingering impact of deep Islamic religiosity in Cianjur and its environs has been so strong and deep that as late as 2001, residents elected a local official charged with the mandate of implementing *shariah*-inspired measures, such as banning gambling dens and obliging female students to wear the veil to school.[16] Encep was the second child in a large family of eleven children. His immediate family was very pious. He was in fact part of a line of Islamic scholars: his great-grandfather had founded a local traditionalist *pesantren* and his own father ran a school in Cianjur and was imam at the local mosque. Encep's mother taught religion as well. Perhaps unsurprisingly, as a child, Encep was "educated exclusively in religious schools" in the Cianjur area: these included elementary and junior high schools at a neighborhood *madrasah* founded by a relative followed by three years of senior high school. Along the way, Encep also joined an Islamic youth group.[17]

For the first twenty years of his life, after he completed formal school-ing in 1984, Encep Nurjaman, aka Hambali—very much like Mukhlas and Imam Samudra—had been deeply immersed in the wider subculture—the learned ways of thinking, feeling, and acting—of Darul Islam. The deep, life-shaping impact of early socialization into a highly parochial cultural milieu cannot be overestimated. The British Pakistani ex-radical Ed Husain understood this well. He observed that as late as age sixteen, he had "no white friends" and his "world was entirely Asian, fully Muslim."[18] Such a narrow perspective caused Husain, in the early part of his life, to view the world in highly blinkered us-versus-them terms, and even more so after he was introduced to the polarizing Islamist tracts of South Asian ideologues like Mawlana Mawdudi.[19] The cognitive tendency to interpret the outside world strictly through categorical, black-and-white Darul Islamist ideologi-cal lenses—fueled by a visceral Existential Identity Anxiety—was very much a defining characteristic of Encep's later spiritual leader, Abu Bakar Ba'asyir. It is telling that after Ba'asyir had been incarcerated following the Bali blasts, his own lawyer felt compelled to admit:

> He is, first of all, a very simple man . . . but he is also a very determined man in his own way. . . . *His horizon is very primordial.* Outside of Islam, he is very much ignorant in other matters [italics added].[20]

The twenty-year old Encep would not have been that much different. Having been born into the heart of the Darul Islamic subcultural "Bouquet," he would have grown up deeply concerned about the welfare and sanctity of his Islamic Group Tent. This is likely one major reason why Encep, like Ba'asyir, Sungkar, and countless other Darul Islamists, apparently took deep personal umbrage at the Tanjung Priok massacre in Jakarta in 1984. This collective *chosen trauma* proved to be a key long-term radicalizing factor, filling Encep with "anger over the treatment of Muslims" and transforming him into a "vocal opponent of the Suharto regime."[21]

To be sure, there were other milestones along Encep's personal Radical Pathway to Bali 2002. His childhood had not been particularly memorable. For one thing, Encep was a somewhat rotund, reticent, and introverted child who, although very religious and diligent in studies, did not stand out as especially brilliant. He was no outstanding student, as Imam Samudra had been. What must have been a further significant setback to Encep was his failure to secure a scholarship to study at a leading Islamic school in Malaysia because of insufficiently high grades. His family did not have funds of their own to send him off for further education.[22] Cianjur was a relatively poor area with few job opportunities, and his father's income was barely able to sustain such a large family in their cramped, single-story house.[23] Encep later complained that his family was so poor and the village so waterlogged that they ate only green vegetables, never meat.[24] Having failed to secure the scholarship to Malaysia meant that Encep had to look for a job immediately after graduation from senior high school in 1984. During the next two years, however, he was unsuccessful in this venture as well.[25] Finally, desperate, Encep decided to try his luck in Malaysia, so he set off in a boat to cross the Melaka Strait "with no travel documents, no funds, and no leads."[26] He arrived in the port of Klang in the Malaysian State of Selangor, where a sizeable pool of Indonesian illegal workers resided, looking for work, and soon he started selling chickens at a nearby market each morning. He supplemented this by selling religious books, caps, rugs, and apparently even kebabs at the port in the evenings.[27] Encep managed to eke out a living and eventually was able to send money home as well. To signify a new start, Encep changed his name to Riduan Isamuddin.[28] Riduan managed to share a house in Klang with other Indonesian workers, who unfortunately irritated him greatly by bringing home their girlfriends and generally displaying lax morals. Riduan began feeling homesick and tried to cope by burying himself in the Qu'ran.[29]

Riduan's homesickness soon compelled him to start seeking a surrogate "father figure" in the vicinity.[30] Riduan's behavior at this point is suggestive. As noted, Javanese culture has strong collectivist and large power-distance characteristics, and as a part of that milieu, Riduan would have been programmed from a young age to look to esteemed seniors for guidance for the right direction to take in life. Cultural learning, however, was not the only factor at play in shaping Riduan's thinking, feeling, and acting at this point. Riduan's *Individual Personality*—referencing once again our RP Framework—was another. Matthew Alper has called attention to the reality that there are many instances of individuals who undergo a "sudden cognitive transformation" and in a relatively short time join an "organized cult or religion."[31] Alper's argument is that the reason for such sudden, significant deepening of religiosity is the fragility of the egos of such individuals. Alper explains:

> The human ego is . . . very delicate. . . . If it is not properly nurtured, a person may grow to develop any number of insecurities, neuroses or even psychoses. When a person with a weak sense of self reaches the preliminary stages of adulthood, he or she may not feel ready to take on life's responsibilities.[32]

Riduan came from a very large family in which emotional distances would have been considerable—the age gap between him and his youngest sibling was a massive *twenty-one* years.[33] This hints at the strong possibility that one factor compelling Riduan to seek a father figure in Malaysia was a fragile, underdeveloped "sense of self." According to psychiatrist Arthur Deikman, all human beings have two basic kinds of wishes. They desire a "meaningful life, to serve God or humanity"; and they wish to "be taken care of, to feel protected and secure, to find a home."[34] Deikman calls the latter human impulse the "dependency fantasy," which, he adds, is a "permanent part of the human psyche."[35] As he puts it:

> We do recognize that adults need each other for emotional support, for giving and receiving affection, for validation.... *But underlying such mature interdependency is the longing of the child, a yearning that is never completely outgrown.* This covert dependency—the wish to have parents and the parallel wish to be loved, admired, and sheltered by one's group—continues throughout life in everyone [italics added].[36]

Deikman also points out that people who are vulnerable to following charismatic religious cult leaders also tend to be "dissatisfied, distressed, or at a transition point in their lives"; they desire a "more spiritual life, a community in which to live cooperatively"; and they seek to "become enlightened, to find meaning in serving others, or simply to belong."[37] In short, it is this innate desire for a "powerful, protective parent,"[38] reinforced by "fragile senses of identity and unhealthily developed egos" as a result of generalized parental neglect during childhood, that create the crucial deficits of "inner strength and personal stability" required to endure life's "trials and tribulations."[39] Alper observes that it is when the "crisis reaches a threshold" that a "breakdown occurs in which the suffering individual latches on to some religion to which he will soon convert."[40] It is this cocktail of ego fragility amid a series of personal crises that lies at the root of sudden intensifications of religiosity.

By the time Riduan had arrived in Malaysia, he clearly was experiencing some of these transitional psychic stresses. As noted, he had been unsuccessful in securing either a scholarship or employment and as a result had had to uproot himself from Cianjur and set up a home in the unfamiliar surroundings of Klang port; he had to work very hard day and night to make ends meet; he felt ill at ease with the promiscuity of his relatively socially liberal housemates; and he seemed to long for the structure and certainty of his home community. The combination of these factors soon propelled Riduan into the fold of the Sungkar-Ba'asyir émigré network in Malaysia. Riduan heard about these preachers from his fellow workers and went to hear Sungkar preach in Kuala Pilah in neighboring Negri Sembilan State. Apparently Riduan was hugely impressed with Sungkar, who had earned the telling moniker "Ustad Wahhabi."[41] Riduan, deciding that he had found his father figure, became a regular at Sungkar's "energetic sermons," faithfully making the trip down to Kuala Pilah once a month. Sungkar's sermons proved to be truly marathon affairs, lasting from "sundown to sunrise the following morning."[42] These times of intense religious fellowship facilitated the development of Riduan's networking with other Al Mukmin exiles, as well as his deeper socialization into the explicitly articulated ideology of Darul Islamism. It was also through Sungkar that Riduan was first exposed to the Global Salafi *Jihad*, the theme of the sermons by the fiery Malaysian preacher Abd al-Zukar. By the mid-1980s, the Soviet Occupation of Afghanistan was entrenched, and al-Zukar told his rapt listeners of Asian volunteers streaming to Central Asia to take part in the Afghan *jihad*. This was the Cause that Riduan was looking for, the opportunity to live a "meaningful life, to serve God or humanity." Riduan promptly accosted Sungkar to indicate his willingness to volunteer, and by 1987 he was in the third batch of recruits that arrived in Camp Saddah along the Pakistani-Afghan border.[43]

Camp Saddah was run by the Saudi-financed Afghan warlord Abdul Rasul Sayyaf. Sayyaf, who had been a professor at Kabul University, was leader of the Ittihad Islami faction as well as an acquaintance of both Osama bin Laden and Sungkar, whom he had met while on the *haj* in Mecca.[44] At Saddah, Riduan found that all the Southeast Asians, at the time mainly Indonesians and Malaysians, trained together separately from the Arabs and communicated using a mixture of Malay and English.[45] It was in Saddah that Riduan—symbolically resolving his ego identity issues by submerging his identity within the wider Group Tent of globalized Darul Islamism[46]— changed his name for a second and final time to Hambali, after the first century hard-line Arab jurist who founded the conservative Hanbalite school of jurisprudence that later formed the basis for Wahabbism.[47] As had been the case with both Mukhlas and Imam Samudra, it was probably the experience of rubbing shoulders with *jihadis* from the all over the Muslim world in the crucible of Saddah that further intensified and focused Hambali's Darul Islamist identity and us-them worldview. Hence when he returned to Malaysia in 1989, as soon as he had saved enough money, he moved from Klang, resettling in a ramshackle hut in a kampong located in "a more secluded spot in a village named Sungai Manggis" near Banting in Selangor State.[48] By this time, the fact that Hambali had undergone a personality change was obvious to all. As his landlord noted, while continuing to sell kebabs and traditional medicine, Hambali now "dressed like a cleric, in long white robes and cap."[49] More than that, it seemed that the kampong soon became a haven for Indonesian Arabized modernist (read Salafi/Wahhabi) émigrés as well: all "the men wore white, while the women wore full black burkahs and were forbidden from speaking to men other than relatives."[50] Little wonder that the bemused villagers called them "the Wahhabis."[51] Eventually, Abu Bakar Ba'asyir himself would join Hambali in Sungai Manggis, moving in next door to him. Their adjacent homes would become the epicenter of the Darul Islamist expatriate community in exile, and people from nearby towns and villagers would come to hear the two preach about the necessity for *jihad*.[52] The Darul Islamist émigré commune in Sungai Manggis in West Malaysia was in fact part of a wider Darul Islamist charismatic group that had gone transnational.

The Afghanistan interlude was a very important milestone in Hambali's personal Radical Pathway in other ways. For perhaps the first time in his life, he proved to be a revelation, graduating with top honors in both the military and religious components of the program. He also began developing his international network of *jihadi* contacts, chief of which was the Al Qaeda operations chief, Khalid Sheikh Mohammad, who became a close friend and who later would conceptualize the September 11, 2001, attacks in the United States.[53] It was the Afghan experience that helped sharpen and develop Hambali's *internal locus of control*. As discussed, Hambali undoubtedly was shaped by the common if not always apparent human desire for a parent figure, an element that in his case would also have been reinforced by the highly collectivist, large power-distance outlook of his Javanese upbringing. Nevertheless, he still retained a degree of personal agency. That is, his subsequent thinking and actions were also impacted by aspects of his Individual Personality; in this case his internal locus of control, an innate dispositional quality that led him—probably unconsciously—to assume that "individuals are responsible for what happens to them, rather than other people, fate, chance, and so on."[54] Hambali clearly evinced this quality on his return from Afghanistan. Because Sungkar and Ba'asyir, during the 1990s, provided him with opportunities and avenues to exert his strong internal locus of control orientation, Hambali excelled, developing into an "increasingly powerful figure" in JI and a "brilliant recruiter and strategist."[55] In other words, Hambali's upward mobility within the JI network after 1993 met his (as we have seen) considerable ego needs—and enhanced his self-esteem.[56] Following the death of Sungkar in November 1999, while the relatively *dakwah*-oriented Ba'asyir took over as JI spiritual head, Hambali, as the operations chief, played a bold, decisive role in preparing JI for an overall strategy geared around *jihad*.[57]

Not long after Sungkar's death, Hambali summoned *jihadi* leaders from all over Southeast Asia for a meeting in Kuala Lumpur in late 1999. At this meeting, the Rabitatul Mujahidin (RM) or Mujahidin League was proclaimed. The first RM meeting included, in addition to JI core members, elements from other *jihadi* groups, such as Kumpulan Militan Malaysia (KMM)[58]; Laskar Jundullah and Darul Islam, Free Aceh Movement (GAM), and Republik Islam Aceh from Indonesia; the Moro Islamic Liberation Front (MILF) from the southern Philippines; the Rohingya Solidarity Organization (RSO) and the Arakan Rohingya Nationalist Organization (ARNO) from Myanmar; and the Pattani United Liberation Organization (PULO) from Southern Thailand. The Darul Islam movement activist Al Chaidar, who attended the RM meetings, claims there were a total of four, all held in Malaysia, of which he attended three. According to Chaidar, the gatherings were useful for networking—to enable members of *jihadi* groups in Southeast Asia to get to know one another and exchange ideas and debate issues such as the legitimacy of suicide bombings, as well as attacks on Americans and civilians. However, Chaidar said that RM was "not important" and that Hambali could not use the forum as a mechanism to exercise strategic coordination of all *jihadi* groups in Southeast Asia because not everybody bought into JI's transnational caliphate vision and modus operandi.[59] Nevertheless, although the RM may not have been an effective strategic mechanism, it cannot be discounted totally. Because of the shared experience of *jihad* either in Afghanistan or Ambon in the Maluku archipelago, a sense of "brotherhood" today exists between disparate Southeast Asian *jihadi* groups, and the RM mechanism can, and has, crystallized this commodity for mutual assistance and support. This is why Hambali, after the second RM meeting in Kuala Lumpur in mid-2000—where a resolution "to attack Philippine interests" was passed[60]—consequently planned and oversaw a JI attack on the Philippine ambassador's home in Jakarta in August 2000, apparently in retaliation against Manila's clampdown on the MILF.[61] The point is that by 2000, Hambali had come into his own as JI's key strategist, and it was in this role that he orchestrated the Bali attacks of October 12, 2002.

Becoming a Killer

The above discussion helps shed light on how and why the relatively unremarkable, corpulent Cianjur native Encep Nurjaman eventually evolved into the feared cosmopolitan terrorist Hambali and nailed his colors decisively to the JI mast, but it is not the full story. Joining a terrorist organization is one thing, but actually participating in an operation that is designed to kill people is something else entirely. To understand how Hambali could have played his role in the Bali attacks of October 2002, we need to highlight other factors that defined his personal Radical Pathway. The first would be the sum total of his socialization experiences. He was born into the West Javan subculture of Darul Islam and later became immersed in West Malaysia, in the consciously held Darul Islamist ideology of the Sungkar/Ba'asyir émigré community. Finally, he spent time in Camp Saddah in Afghanistan, where he grafted a globalized perspective onto his Darul Islamist outlook. All of these experiences, quite simply, could not have but drilled into Hambali a strongly held binary worldview in which outsiders such as non-Muslims, and especially Jews, Americans, and other Westerners, would have been categorized as "them." Hambali would have viscerally embraced, for instance, Ba'asyir's declaration that the true Muslims should "reject" all non-Muslim "ideologies" and "teachings on social issues, economics or beliefs," and that between the Muslims and non-Muslims there would "forever be a ravine of hate" until the other group submitted to the dictates of the *shariah*. The key consequence of a binary worldview is that it tends to legitimize the social death of outsiders, excommunicating them "from the legitimate social or moral community" and relegating them "to a perpetual state of dishonor."[62]

This is serious: consigning unbelieving outsiders to the state of social death facilitates the creeping mental dehumanization that is a stepping-stone toward committing atrocities against them later. To understand this dynamic requires probing deeper into a number of elements—integral to the Existential Identity ring of our RP Framework—that make up the underlying psychological structure of such a worldview or mental template. First, people with a binary worldview *display*, *more strongly than usual*, what we noted earlier as the *assumed similarity effect*. That is, they think that all members of the "in-group" are more similar to them than are members of the "out-group." Second, because of the *out-group homogeneity effect*, those with a binary worldview would assume that members of the out-group are all alike. Social psychologist James Waller elaborates:

> So, as cognitive misers, if we know something about one out-group member, we are likely to feel that we know something about all of them. Similarly, since we assume that out-group members are highly similar ... we can use our handy social group stereotype to quickly interpret an individual out-group member's behavior. They are, after all, all alike. Why waste our cognitive energy on attending to potentially distinctive information about a specific individual in the out-group?[63]

Third, because of the *accentuation effect*, people with a binary worldview tend to greatly exaggerate differences between in-group and out-group, thereby biasing themselves toward "information that enhances the differences" between the two groups. They pay little attention to information about *similarities* between members of either group. Finally, people with a binary worldview cannot help but suffer from a pronounced *in-group bias*. They regard "in-group members more positively, credit them for their successes, hold them less accountable for their failures or negative actions," and implicitly trust them more than "out-group members."[64] The rigid us-versus-them mode of categorical thinking at the core of a *binary worldview* is not at all benign. Especially in times of societal stress, when vital group interests are perceived to be at stake, a binary worldview could encourage extreme, black-and-white, good-versus-evil modes of cognition that would prompt violent conduct and conflict. We can surmise that in Hambali's case, regarding the Bali 2002 attacks, his justificatory thought processes probably ran along the following lines:

> Our cause is sacred; theirs is evil. We are righteous; they are wicked. We are innocent; they are guilty. We are the victims; they are the victimizers.[65]

It should be recalled that such sentiments were precisely what drove both Mukhlas and Imam Samudra to take part in the Bali strikes.[66] Hambali would have seen himself as plotting to wreak havoc against the enemy—not *an* enemy or *our* enemy, but *the* enemy—"a usage of the definite article that hints of something fixed and immutable, abstract and evil."[67]

A rigid binary worldview, in short, would have played a role in prompting Hambali to cognitively restructure the flesh-and-blood Western victims of Bali into homogenized, dehumanized, and importantly, thanks to Darul Islamist ideological filters, evil abstractions. Put another way, Hambali's binary worldview would have helped him achieve the necessary *emotional distance* from the victims of Bali. Such emotional distance is necessary to help human beings surmount the inner moral sanctions against killing other human beings.[68] This emotional distance comprises three parts: *cultural* (They are Westerners, unlike us Muslims); *moral* (We are Good, they are Evil); and *mechanical* (I do not actually have to physically kill them myself—others would do it).[69] Certainly mechanical distance facilitates the critical factor of *diffusion of responsibility*. The JI Cell that attacked Bali—of which Hambali was a direct if somewhat physically remote participant—could be seen as akin to a firing squad. When a firing squad shoots at a prisoner, its firers can never know for sure whose bullet it was that killed the victim. In other words, the firing squad confers a sense of anonymity to each of its individual firers, making it psychologically easier for each of them to participate in the exercise. This is why Konrad Lorenz once observed, "Man is not the killer, the group is."[70] Dave Grossman explains:

> Psychologists have long understood that a diffusion of responsibility can be caused by the anonymity created in a crowd.... Groups can provide a diffusion of responsibility that will enable individuals in mobs and soldiers in military units to commit acts that they would never dream of doing as individuals....[71]

Similarly, psychologist M. Scott Peck has spoken of how a group setting contributes to the "fragmentation of conscience" and "compartmentalization of responsibility" that arises from role specialization.[72] Social psychologist Albert Bandura adds that people "act more harshly when responsibility is obfuscated by a collective instrumentality than when they hold themselves personally accountable for what they do."[73] Bandura hits the nail on the head in arguing that when "everyone is responsible, no one is really responsible."[74] Hence, cultural and moral distance aside, Hambali's role as overall JI strategist several steps removed from the actual operation meant that he would have enjoyed a certain sense of "group absolution"[75]—enabling him to play his part in the attacks without facing an immediate personal, moral backlash.

In summary, we have seen that Hambali's religiously parochial upbringing in the midst of poverty in West Java generated considerable ego needs that ultimately led him to seek guidance and solace in the Sungkar-Ba'asyir

Malaysia-based faction of the Darul Islamist charismatic group. In addition, his experiences, especially those in Afghanistan, helped him develop his internal locus of control, and this previously latent drive saw him achieve considerable ego-satisfying and esteem-enhancing upward mobility within the JI network by the 1990s. Furthermore, while his deep immersion in Darul Islamist ideology provided him with a stark, emotionally-driven binary worldview that legitimized the social death of Westerners and non-Muslims, his Darul Islamist desire to not simply ensure the dominance of the Islamic Group Tent but seek revenge for perceived Western victimization of and excesses against the Islamic community led him to be more than just a Hater of the West but a Killer as well. In the latter regard, the psychological mechanisms of emotional distance and diffusion of responsibility were key enabling factors that allowed him to play his part in the Bali attacks. Did a similar set of moral and psychological dynamics facilitate Bali bomber Amrozi's transition to Hater and then to Killer? This is a question we now must address.

AMROZI

Becoming a Hater

Although Amrozi bin Nurhasyim, born on June 5, 1962, in Tenggulun village in Lamongan, East Java, was the younger brother of the senior JI leader Mukhlas, the two could not have been more different.[76] Whereas Mukhlas was in a way the much-admired star of the family, Amrozi, though always his mother's pet and widely regarded as the "cutest boy in the family,"[77] was nevertheless a real rascal. In contrast to his brothers Mukhlas and Ali Imron, Amrozi initially was not very impressed by the family's deep intergenerational religiosity and immersion in Darul Islamic subculture, with its veneration for Kartosoewirjo and historic yearning for the Islamic State in West Java. This is why Amrozi always stuck out like a sore thumb. While Mukhlas was busy memorizing the Qur'an, Amrozi would be "hooning around on his motorbike" or "flirting with the local girls," aided in the latter quest by an easygoing good nature and a "goofy grin."[78] He owned a big KE-250 trail motorcycle of which he was very proud and liked to let his hair grow long and unkempt in order to fool people into thinking that he was younger than he actually was.[79] Not at all the responsible type, at home he would steal items from family members and sell them for cash.[80] His siblings were none too impressed. Younger brother Ali Imron complained that Amrozi was "extremely" difficult to control.[81] In addition to his personal idiosyncratic behavior and family shenanigans, Amrozi got into trouble at school. He was never interested in schoolwork or studying the Qur'an, preferring instead to play pranks on his teachers and fellow students. He surprised no one when he failed to complete senior high school because of his poor attitude.[82] It seemed the only thing Amrozi enjoyed and was good at was using his hands. He immersed himself in figuring out how mechanical things worked and ultimately eked out a living as "the local repairman, fixing everything from cars to mobile phones." Amrozi would become a village icon, traipsing around Tenggulun "with his long hair and oil-stained jeans and his big goofy grin."[83]

Eventually Amrozi got bored and decided to head off—like Mukhlas and Hambali, across the Melaka Strait—to work in Malaysia's construction industry. He landed a job with a road construction firm, blowing up hill-sides to make way for new bitumen roads. It was during this time that he first met foreigners. With the sole exception of his Australian boss, whom he later admitted he considered a friend, he developed a deep dislike for the other Westerners. Significantly, their stories of holidaying in Bali, drinking and "chasing the local women," made "his blood boil," as he interpreted this to be an attempt to "destroy Indonesia," and he "hated them for that."[84] It seems that Amrozi developed into a deeply prejudiced anti-Western bigot from that point onward, convinced that Americans and other Westerners were intent on polluting the minds and "destroying the lives of Indonesians."[85] In any case, Amrozi stayed for only six months in Malaysia before returning to Tenggulun, where at twenty-three he married a local girl. This union did produce a daughter but floundered after only two years. Amrozi believed that his wife's parents, after—in his own words—"they learned the truth" and "realized that there was nothing to me," played a big role in the break-up.[86] Amrozi tried to pick up the pieces by re-enrolling in high school but again dropped out. Frustrated, he amused himself by vandalizing village graves, inspired apparently by his father's Salafi disdain for the Sufi-influenced Javanese *santri* tradition of grave worship. In 1987 and 1988, together with a local boy, Supriandi, Amrozi desecrated a "respected grave which was situated in a house in Tenggulun village"—an act that landed him in the Lamongan Police Station lockup for a week, much to his family's chagrin.[87] The next several years proved to be aimless ones, and Amrozi finally decided to marry a second time, but again, because of his restlessness, "going out all the time," as his second wife moaned later, this union too broke down, again after just two years.[88] Increasingly frustrated, Amrozi, after two failed marriages, reckoned that he could not continue in this way. He quit smoking, stopped watching movies, gave up "bad talk," and decided to cross the Melaka Strait yet again, this time to search out the revered Mukhlas. Unfortunately, when he turned up at the Pondok Pesantren Luqmanul Hakiem in Ulu Tiram, Johore State, Amrozi later recalled:

> I wanted to go this place, this brother of mine's place, to Muklas, but I wasn't accepted. He didn't believe in me. Perhaps he was afraid that I would create trouble.[89]

Amrozi took Mukhlas' rejection very badly. This proved to be a turning point along Amrozi's own Radical Pathway. He was, in Deikman's words, "dissatisfied, distressed," and at a "transition point" in his life. A later police psychiatric assessment would conclude that Amrozi was "simple" and "rather shallow," with an "intellectual ability lower than normal" and a "disordered attitude to work and planning." Significantly, the report would also observe that Amrozi had an "immature personality" and "tends to be "impulsive" and "easily influenced by others he respects or is in awe of."[90] This assessment is very revealing. It suggests that Amrozi was very likely what some experts would call an "ambient" personality. Psychologist Eric Zillmer and his colleagues, in a study of the Nazi war criminals on trial at Nuremberg, elaborated on this "problem-solving style" that they discovered among the Nuremberg defendants:

> [A]n unusually high number of the Nazis . . . tested as ambitent. Ambitents have *failed to develop a consistent preference or style in their coping behaviors* when confronted with difficult tasks. In other words, these are individuals who essentially *have no mind of their own. They rely heavily on others as well as on an external structure for guidance in problem solving.* Generally, this leads to less efficiency and more vacillation in decision-making operations [italics added].[91]

According to the above explanation, Amrozi was an ambient; he was assessed as having "a disordered attitude to work and planning," which suggests that he had no "consistent preference or style" in "problem solving." He had low intellectual ability and obviously was easily influenced by significant others, which suggests that he had "no mind of his own" and relied heavily on an "external structure for guidance in problem solving." In this sense, Amrozi, who genuinely idolized Mukhlas and likely saw him as a surrogate parent figure, needed Mukhlas to provide him with an "external structure of guidance in problem solving." The fact was that Amrozi was a classic example of someone who was temperamentally predisposed to "ride in the back seat of the car."[92] This personality trait, it should be noted, was probably buttressed by the large power-distance orientation of wider Javanese culture, expressed in "a pattern of dependence on seniors" and a "mental software" that "contains a strong need for such dependence."[93] Amrozi's ambient personality brought this cultural dependence on external guidance from his revered elder brother to a very pronounced level. To be fair, however, Amrozi was hardly the only individual in the regional JI firmament who seemed to "have no mind of their own." It is worth noting that several Singapore JI members turned to leaders like Singapore JI spiritual leader Ibrahim Maidin because they wished to "free themselves from endless searching as they found it stressful to be critical, evaluative and rational."[94] The fact that the Singapore "JI leaders had quoted from holy texts" appeared to have reassured them that "they could not go wrong."[95]

The sheer intellectual and moral "problem solving" challenges faced by both ambient personality types and the wider collectivist, large power-distance cultures in which they often find themselves embedded are getting more vexing by the day, a result of the worldwide phenomenon of globalization. Globalization has been usefully characterized as "worldwide integration through an ongoing, dynamic process that involves the interplay of free enterprise, democratic principles and human rights, the high-tech exchange of information, and movement of large numbers of people."[96] Although it is widely accepted that "the juggernaut of free enterprise, democracy, and technology offers the best chance of wealth creation," the key to "improving the human condition," globalization has had its downside as well.[97] By privileging "individualistic, impersonal, competitive, privatistic, and mobile" values and attitudes, globalization processes have inadvertently undermined traditional social units such as the family, clan, and voluntary associations.[98] More precisely, globalization—which in many non-Western societies is synonymous with Westernization—is destabilizing because it promotes the desacralization of society; encourages religious and moral relativism; places the onus on the individual to determine his "values, career, life style and moral system;" and most disconcertingly, undermines traditional ideas about sexuality and the status of women.[99] It should be recalled here that Amrozi found the sexual licentiousness of his Western colleagues in Malaysia—particularly toward Balinese women—upsetting. Michael Stevens puts Amrozi's visceral discomfort in broader perspective:

> For communitarian [i.e., collectivist] societies, keyed to historical continuity, group coherence and security, personal rootedness, and the affirmation of moral righteousness, empowering the individual is equated with rending society asunder.[100]

Globalization thus may inadvertently precipitate sociocultural dislocation at the aggregate level and psychosocial dysfunction at the unit level.[101] Hence, as Charles Selengut adds, to "follow the West is to become spiritually and psychologically homeless, without a transcendental anchor to provide security and safety during life's journey."[102] Ambient personalities, especially in collectivist cultures, simply may not be equipped to cope with what Jessica Stern calls "a surfeit of choice" because too much choice, "especially regarding identity, can be overwhelming and even frightening."[103] This is not at all an outlandish claim. The controversial ex-Muslim, Dutch Somali writer, and activist Ayaan Hirsi Ali recounted that her unmarried sister Haweya, who had seemed rather progressive in a Somali context after having an abortion, had found the "limitless freedoms" of the Netherlands, with its relatively lax and liberal attitudes toward sex and other aspects of social life, deeply unsettling. The extent of Haweya's psychological dislocation became clear one day when, to Ayaan's surprise, Haweya started wearing the headscarf while going out. When quizzed on why she was doing that, as she had "never been religious before," Haweya replied: "I have to be careful in this country. It's Godless. It will turn us into unbelievers." In an attempt to shore up her Muslim identity, Haweya began to pay more attention to her faith. As Ayaan recounts:

> Haweya began praying everyday. She had exactly the same questions as I did: Why was it that Holland could give its people so much better a life than any Muslim country we had seen? *But Haweya answered those questions by going back into religion.* She started reading Hasan al-Banna and Sayyid Qutb... she [also] sought answers in the Quran [italics added].[104]

Ayaan's diagnosis, apart from the possible trauma associated with Haweya's abortion (her second), was that perhaps Haweya "couldn't deal with individual freedom" and much preferred, like even Ayaan herself, to rely at times on "the comfortable, clear lines of doctrine and detailed rules."[105] Thus psychologists who study the appeal of religious dogma suggest that relinquishing "one's autonomy in return for absolute ideological security is a powerful motive."[106]

It is not that far-fetched to surmise that an ambient personality like Amrozi, like many other JI rank and file, not just in Java but throughout the collectivist societies of Southeast Asia that were subjected to the powerful forces of economic and especially cultural globalization (read Westernization), much preferred and *needed* an external structure for guidance in problem solving and "comfortable, clear lines of doctrine and detailed rules." Following Mukhlas' initial rejection, therefore, a dejected Amrozi returned to being a construction worker on sites all over Malaysia for a couple of years, but by his own admission, "somehow my heart was not in it."[107] After two years Amrozi tried to see Mukhlas again:

> Eventually I plucked up my courage and went back to Johor. I just stuck it out. I didn't have his permission, I just went to his place. When I finally got there I guess there was hope in this heart of mine. It was as if I was there to seek, what would you call it—to seek Allah's blessing.[108]

This time Mukhlas relented, took Amrozi in, and put him to work cleaning and helping out with the childrens' dormitory and other odd jobs around the place. Amrozi, finally feeling "very much at home," went on to buy into Darul Islamist ideology lock, stock, and barrel and underwent an observable personality change, swapping "his jeans for a Muslim tunic and his unkempt hairdo for a skullcap and a wispy beard."[109] By the late 1990s, following the fall of Soeharto, Amrozi and his third wife, a former cook from Pondok Pesantren Luqmanul Hakiem, returned to Tenggulun. Everyone was taken aback by the changes. One of his former wives marveled that Amrozi "was not the same man at all," and his new wife even "wore a full-face burkah."[110] Another of Amrozi's brothers, Khozin, described Amrozi's transformation:

> Before going to Malaysia he talked about driving fast, hanging out with friends, but after coming back he talked about *ulamas* who preach about Islam. Before he went to Malaysia when he heard the call to prayer he would keep working, but after Malaysia he would stop to pray.[111]

Becoming a Killer

Thus far we have discussed the various mechanisms that turned Amrozi from a free-spirited, not particularly observant Javanese Muslim into an apparently dedicated Darul Islamist. The next question is: what additional mechanisms enabled him to play his role in the October 12, 2002, attacks? Certainly his several-year stint in the relatively isolated environment of Al-Mukmin clone Pondok Pesantren Luqmanul Hakiem in Ulu Tiram, Malaysia, would have socialized him deeply into the virulent us-versus-them worldview of Darul Islamist ideology—an ideology that would have provided an ostensibly religious basis for his visceral racism toward Westerners.[112] Very much like Sungai Manggis in the north, Luqmanul Hakiem was another Darul Islamist "space" in Malaysia, and by the mid-1990s, the *pesantren* was a "key meeting place for the leaders and followers of JI."[113] Mukhlas, Amrozi, and another brother, Ali Imron, were living there together with the JI explosives expert Dulmatin. Furthermore, Ba'asyir, Hambali, and Imam Samudra "all commuted regularly" between Sungai Manggis and Ulu Tiram. Sungkar was also a frequent visitor to the *pesantren*, while other senior JI Afghan veterans like Zulkarnaen enrolled their children there.[114] Amrozi himself recalled first meeting Zulkarnaen at Luqmanul Hakiem in 1994 when the latter came down from Solo to see his children.[115] The Luqmanul Hakiem *pesantren*, until its abrupt closure in early 2002, enrolled 400 students ranging from five-year-olds in kindergarten to high school–level teenagers. Most of the teachers and students in the *pesantren* community were from Indonesia or Singapore. They lived commune-style, and as one Ulu Tiram resident observed very tellingly, they "lived and prayed apart" and "never mixed with other villagers."[116] Furthermore, the Luqmanul Hakiem staff, displaying all the controlling, near-pathological instincts of the "fundamentalist mentality" as described in the previous chapter, even sought to *synchronize* the Islam of the immediate Ulu Tiram environs with their preferred interpretation. Another resident complained:

They wouldn't mix with women who didn't wear the headscarf . . . if we wanted to mix with them, we couldn't go in there if our head was not covered. We were not allowed to talk loudly, weren't allowed to laugh, we had to look serious. . . . We're friendly, we like socializing and then they come here and tell us we're not allowed to do anything . . . weren't allowed to watch TV, weren't allowed to listen to the radio. . . . They said it's forbidden by Islamic law. Everything was forbidden by Islamic law.[117]

Decrying that this was the behavior of "fanatics" and certainly not "simple Islam," one man summed it up by branding the Luqmanul Hakiem community as "fanatics" and, more to the point, "Wahhabis."[118] It is not that hard to see how the thinking of marginal, ambient personalities like Amrozi would have been decisively captured and shaped by the dominant "group mind" prevailing within the otherworldly confines of Pondok Pesantren Luqmanul Hakiem.[119] Hence Amrozi's preexisting prejudice against white people was readily integrated and moreover intensified and given intellectual justification by Darul Islamism. R. S. Ezekiel's comments would have nicely captured the significant convergence between Amrozi's deep personal bigotry and the Darul Islamist virulent anti-Western agenda:

He believes the ideology literally, word for word—there is an Enemy, the Enemy is Evil. *He believes that ideology because he wants it: He wants the grounds for radical action.* He must have radical action. Violence is the language in which he can speak his message. . . . [italics added].[120]

The extent to which Amrozi had internalized Darul Islamism became apparent later, when he was arrested after the Bali attacks. Police raiding his house in Tenggulun village on November 5, 2002, discovered a cache of video compact discs with titles such as *Perang Salib Baru* (The New Crucifix Wars), *Abu Bakar Ba'asyir and the war in Bosnia,* and *Ambon— Jihad Proposal,* among others.[121] More to the point, Amrozi, when asked to explain the meaning of the video compact disc recordings, provided the familiar "the victims-must-victimize-the victimizer" stock response common to all convinced Darul Islamists, especially those influenced by Global Salafi *Jihad* perspectives:

USAMAH BIN LADEN explains that the Oppression and murder of Muslims carried out by the Jews and the Americans, especially of women and children, must be opposed because the [Hadith] forbids the killing of women and children. The flow of women and children's blood must be revenged [sic] because it is valuable as the blood of Jewish and American infidels.[122]

If Amrozi shared with Hambali the same ideological filters that consigned Americans, Jews, and Westerners to a permanent state of social death, did he also share the other social psychological mechanisms that nudged Hambali along his Radical Pathway toward the Bali attacks? On the surface, it would seem that the same factors of emotional distance, diffusion of responsibility, and the sense of anonymity conferred on Hambali by the wider JI Cell would also have worked in Amrozi's case, as the latter was, after all, a logistics support operative who was not directly involved in killing the Bali clubbers. However, this would not be an entirely accurate analysis, as it would omit the crucial contribution provided by a key defect of Amrozi's personality.

It is contended that the primary reason Amrozi was able to participate in the Bali terror attacks was that he very probably suffered from antisocial personality disorder (APD). A person who suffers from APD, a term devised by the American Psychiatric Association, is sometimes also called a "sociopath" (reflecting the impact of social and environmental factors) or "psychopath" (emphasizing the individual's personality structure).[123] James Waller elaborates:

> A pervasive pattern of disregard for, and violation of, the wishes, rights, or feelings of others characterizes this disorder. Persons with APD may blame the victims for being foolish, helpless, or deserving their fate; they may minimize the harmful consequences of their actions; or they may simply indicate complete indifference. Individuals with this disorder show little remorse for the consequences of their acts [italics added].[124]

Psychology professors Scott O. Lilienfeld and Hal Arkowitz add:

> Superficially charming, psychopaths tend to make a good first impression on others and often strike observers as remarkably normal. Yet they are self-centered, dishonest and undependable, and at times they engage in irresponsible behavior for no apparent reason than the sheer fun of it. Largely devoid of guilt, empathy and love, they have casual and callous interpersonal and romantic relationships. Psychopaths routinely offer excuses for their reckless and often outrageous actions. . . . They rarely learn from their mistakes or benefit from negative feedback, and they have difficulty inhibiting their impulses.[125]

It should be noted that the official psychiatric investigation of Amrozi on November 15, 2002, by Bali police reported that "the Subject is a normal individual with no indications of psychopathology."[126] This conclusion should be called into serious question and reviewed.[127] Such an assertion simply appears to fly in the face of several pieces of evidence pertaining to Amrozi's personality that conform to the descriptions of psychopathy offered above.

Despite his personal attractiveness to women and ostensible charm, two of his marriages failed largely because of his lack of serious commitment to his first two wives and the ensuing sentiment that he was undependable. Especially significant is the grave desecration affair. At one point Amrozi earned the not insignificant ire of his fellow Sufi-oriented villagers in Tenggulun for vandalizing graves considered sacred. Amrozi himself, after his arrest, recalled his old "pranks," laughing as he explained why he engaged in such antisocial activity. The excerpt is revealing:

> When there was a grave that was considered sacred, I dug it up, burnt it. People always got jittery about it. *Since way back I guess it's fair to say that I liked it when I could make other people upset.* . . . These were graves that were considered sacred, like the ones belonging to those clerics who spread religion to Indonesia, the ones people make monuments of. . . . Sometimes even after I had burnt it, they would rebuild it, then I would dismantle it, and they would still build it again. . . . There was often fabric laid out on graves considered to contain special powers, right? I would sometimes take away those pieces of fabric, and eventually when they keep on putting the fabric back, *sometimes I would shit on it* [italics added].[128]

This sounds like someone who engages in "irresponsible behavior for no apparent reason than the sheer fun of it." Moreover and more seriously, when told of the carnage he had helped inflict on the innocent victims at the Sari Club and Paddy's Bar, rather than express any hint of remorse, as would be the case with Ali Imron and even to an extent Mukhlas, Amrozi was fairly forthright—in a breathtakingly tasteless manner:

> I was very happy. . . . How can I describe it—it was like when I was still a bachelor, trying for a girl and you finally get to meet her, it was that sort of excitement. But this was even better.[129]

Finally, while Mukhlas expressed remorse for the deaths of Indonesian victims, Amrozi's callous, flippant quip was that "even if they didn't die there, they would die somewhere else, right?"[130] Amrozi *did not really need* the psychological defenses of emotional distance and diffusion of responsibility in helping him traverse his Radical Pathway to the Bali atrocities. He simply could not empathize with the suffering the bombs caused. Worse, as he himself admitted, he *enjoyed* it. In sum, Amrozi's intellectual marginality and ambient disposition rendered him susceptible to the intellectually and emotionally comforting, totalizing discourses of adored brother Mukhlas's Darul Islamism—a process of programming facilitated through Amrozi's deep immersion in the relatively cloistered ideological crucible of the Luqmanul Hakiem *pesantren*. In addition, his individual psychopathic tendencies meant that he faced little dissonance in playing a key role in the mass deaths of the Bali victims that fateful evening in October 2002. In Amrozi's case, therefore, the transition from Hater to Killer was a relatively natural progression. The case of Ali Imron, as we shall now see, could not be more different.

ALI IMRON

Becoming a Hater

Ali Imron bin Nurhasyim, born in 1970 in Tenggulun, the youngest in the Nurhasyim clan,[131] could be said to be a cross between brothers Mukhlas and Amrozi. Although as a teenager Imron shared the studious diligence of Mukhlas, in some ways he shared equally the early aimlessness of Amrozi. Again, the emotional anonymity of being part of a large family comprising eight biological siblings plus five additional step-siblings[132]—coupled with the fact that he was like neither Mukhlas, a star family performer, nor Amrozi, who was always at the center of attention (even if for all the wrong reasons) and their mother's pet—must have significantly intensified teenage Imron's esteem needs—particular the need for acceptance. To this end, the available biographical details suggest a picture of a young man intent on scouring his immediate family context for cues as to what he should be doing in order to gain such acceptance. Hence when we look closely at Ali Imron's personal Radical Pathway toward Bali, it seems that what truly marks him out as a distinct personality type from Amrozi and Mukhlas is his seemingly *overwhelming need to conform*: Ali Imron was in a sense, very susceptible to peer pressure. Social psychologists tell us that there are two main forms of conformity to peer pressure. The first is *normative* social influence. This occurs when individuals emulate their peers in order to avoid rejection, "especially in groups that are highly cohesive."[133] However, normative social influence often needs to be complemented by another form of conformity to peer pressure—*informational* social influence. This occurs when individuals emulate others simply to know what is "right" in various social contexts and "ascertain the norms" that should "guide" their "thoughts and behaviors."[134]

In Imron's case, it appears that the immediate social context strongly hinted that being a good student of Islam in general and studying at Pondok Pesantren Al-Mukmin in Solo, Central Java, in particular was the way to find favor in the sight of his parents. Hence by the time he was fifteen, and clearly a diligent, eager student, he dearly wished to emulate Mukhlas and another older brother, Amin Jabir, and leave Tenggulun to study at Al-Mukmin *pesantren* in Solo. Unfortunately, Imron was not permitted to do so by the patriarch Nurhasyim, as there was nobody left in the house. Amrozi—according to Imron, who tended to dislike his older brother—did not help matters because he was out most of the time, fooling around.[135]

Frustrated by this development and unsure of what to do next, Imron began to rebel. As he put it:

> Once I reached puberty it was a problem. My diligence greatly eroded. I started to ride on my brother Jafar's motorbike. . . . I was out of control—I was almost like Amrozi. . . . The only difference is I don't fool with girls. . . . This was back then, I was small, who would want to date a small boy? . . . I think my parents started to realize that their refusal to put me through the Islamic boarding school had created problems. My parents thought I was going to turn out like Amrozi.[136]

Imron, however, would finally get to go to Solo, but at the cost of losing a brother, Amin Jabir—the second-youngest in the Nurhasyim family. In 1987, a group of amateur climbers from Pondok Pesantren Al-Mukmin, including Amin Jabir, ran into bad weather while scaling Mount Lawu in Java. Beset by a storm and heavy fog, they ran out of water, and during the descent, sixteen people died.[137] The tragedy sparked an intriguing element of critical insight in Imron. Reflecting later on the incident, while in police custody, Imron tellingly admitted:

> It was pure miscalculation by those leading the climb. They had too much faith and not enough work and preparation was done. So they emphasized only faith—and ran out of everything while high in the mountain.[138]

Amin Jabir's demise caused his father Nurhasyim to relent on the question of allowing Imron to go off to Pondok Pesantren Al-Mukmin. At eighteen, Imron decamped to Solo and enrolled in the *pesantren* where Mukhlas had cut his religious and ideological teeth. An unexpected twist in Imron's Radical Pathway, however, soon developed. As this was the first time he had been away from home, Imron found himself overcome by a wave of overpowering homesickness. Hence he could muster enough emotional fortitude to last only *one month* in the spartan atmosphere of Al-Mukmin. But there was another factor. Imron frankly conceded:

> *I didn't feel at ease, I didn't feel at home with the teachings.* Even during that one month I felt I couldn't bear it any longer. I wanted to go home. *Those teachers at Ngruki [Al-Mukmin], they taught extreme lessons* [italics added].[139]

While the short-lived episode seemed to suggest that Imron was certainly not cut from the same hardy cloth as his big brother Mukhlas—at least not at that juncture—it suggested something more fundamental as well. In comparison to Mukhlas and certainly Amrozi, Imron was more of a critical thinker. This is precisely why he could admit his discomfort at the harsh, "extreme" content of Al-Mukmin teachings. Unlike Amrozi, Imron was no ambitent. He *did* have a mind of his own. The problem, as we shall see shortly, was that he never felt strong enough to voice his doubts openly and strongly.

Back in Tenggulun, it was obvious that Imron, tasting personal failure with his abrupt withdrawal from Al-Mukmin, had reached a transition point in his Radical Pathway. Depressed, he now lost interest in studying at the local Islamic boarding school where he was a day student, and his grades suffered. He skipped classes, stayed up late, and roamed around in motor cars. He was doing nothing of consequence, although he attempted to console himself that he was just passing through a teenage phase.[140] However, everything changed one day when Imron attended a meeting at his school where the preacher, who hailed from Jakarta, had been a veteran of the separatist struggle in Aceh. This man was an advocate of Middle Eastern Muslim Brotherhood teachings and spoke passionately about the sufferings being experienced by Muslims worldwide while showing videos of Palestine and Afghanistan. Imron credited that experience "as the beginning of my true conversion."[141] We can only speculate on exactly what transpired that day and the actual content of those videos to which Imron was exposed. Whatever did happen was profound enough to constitute for Imron a *chosen trauma*[142] powerful enough to compel him to act in putative defense of Islam itself. The sheer emotional trauma of atrocity propaganda and its potency as a mobilizing tool is not to be underestimated. The former British radical Ed Husain, who at one time was a skillful Islamist agitator, is unequivocal about the impact of such propaganda in this regard:

> Having incited the audience with my confrontational attitude [toward the enemies of Islam] I then played the video. In the dark lecture theatre there were sobs at what people were seeing; gasps of shock at what was going on two hours away from Heathrow airport: the serving of Muslim men's testicles on trays, Serbs slaughtering pregnant Muslim women, reports of group rape within the borders of Europe.[143]

Unsurprisingly, JI leaders themselves have relied heavily on atrocity propaganda in the form of homemade video compact discs. The Maluku conflict of 1999 to 2000 in particular provided much raw material for JI propagandists, who made video compact discs and distributed them across Southeast Asia, from Indonesia to the southern Philippines. These were shown during informal teaching sessions by JI clerics, and the "eager young men in attendance, duly incensed by what they had witnessed, were then briefed on how they could join the jihad."[144] Singapore JI leaders routinely employed fiery speeches to elicit an emotional response from members before requiring them to fill out surveys indicating what kinds of militant activities they wished to be involved in. "Having signed their names on the survey, members were not able to alter their decisions later on."[145]

It is a fact that this particular experience at the Tenggulun school very strongly nudged Imron further along his Radical Pathway to Bali 2002: driven by a visceral fear of group extinction, his concern with the welfare of his Group Tent began to overshadow his everyday parochial individual concerns; his sense of shared grievances with oppressed Muslims elsewhere was enhanced, and he began to identify with the stock Darul Islamist binary worldview with its crude us-them stereotypes more deeply.[146] To put it another way, that meeting impelled Imron to start treating as deeply personal "an attack or affront" not merely directed at his "physical self" but also at his Muslim "collective self."[147] To say that Imron was gripped by an overwhelming sense of urgency is not an overstatement. He literally wanted to turn over a new leaf then and there and decided to head off across the Melaka Strait to look for Mukhlas:

> After that meeting I didn't want to do anything but change my ways. . . . And there was no better way to change than to move to another place as far as possible. I had to go across the sea if necessary . . . to change from what I call that period of idle, wasted existence.[148]

Mukhlas, on hearing that Imron had arrived in Kuala Lumpur, promptly arranged to bring him south to Ulu Tiram. Mukhlas sensed that Imron was ready for greater things and sent him to Singapore to secure a visa for Pakistan. After that, Imron formally swore the *ba'iah* to Sungkar and Ba'asyir and was formally inducted into the JI network—although at the time it was still called Darul Islam. He was then sent off to Camp Saddah on the Afghan-Pakistani border for *jihadi* training. He was to spend three years there, where, like others before him, his immersion in a Global Salafi *Jihad*-leavened Darul Islamism was further deepened and intensified.[149]

On his return to Tenggulun, Imron promptly took up a teaching position in the local family-run Pondok Pesantren Al-Islam. Like Luqmanul Hakiem in Johore State in Malaysia, Al-Islam was an Al-Mukmin clone, with many Al-Mukmin alumni on its teaching staff.[150] Again like Luqmanul Hakiem in Malaysia, Al-Islam stuck out like a sore thumb in the surrounding East Javanese milieu. One village elder noted that the "people at that school weren't like people at other Islamic schools."[151] A Tenggulun village elder observed how Al-Islam pupils were obviously having a *jihadi* mindset drilled into them:

> Their education included military training, rifle drills and war games. . . . They usually came out to do their military training at night. It was like army training. They did it around eleven, twelve, one o'clock. It might have

gone on all night.... They practiced crawling along the ground, push-ups, marching and so on. And there was shooting practice.[152]

Very much a Darul Islamist "space" like Al-Mukmin and Luqmanul Hakiem, the "general climate" of Al-Islam was pregnant with crude, conspiratorial us-them imagery. A sign in English near the entrance to the *pesantren* boldly proclaimed: "Only for Muslim People," and a journalist who had managed to get into Al-Islam saw the words "mole," "spy," and "avenger" spelled out in English on the blackboard.[153] Immersion in such an environment only reinforced Imron's binary outlook. It was not surprising that he soon developed a fierce reputation for being an "inspiring orator," not above "seething outbursts about the alleged threat" from—to be expected from the Afghan-trained Darul Islamist—"the United States and the Jews."[154] Imron recalled that in the years he spent teaching at Al-Islam, he ensured that he always drummed into his charges that the Muslim world was under threat and *jihad* was incumbent upon them:

> When I returned I was an Afghan alumnus, so I thought it was, well, fitting for Afghan alumni to be dealing with jihad matters.... While I was teaching students at the boarding school I continued to plant the concept of jihad. I planted my radical thoughts on those students, both boys and girls.... Wherever I went, whatever was being discussed, I preached about jihad.[155]

When fighting between Christians and Muslims broke out in Ambon in the Maluku islands in January 1999, while Amrozi sent explosives to the Muslim militias, Imron descended upon Ambon personally to "preach to them about the real Islam."[156] The following August, Imron and Amrozi took part in the attack on the Philippine ambassador in Jakarta and then the Christmas Eve 2000 bombings of thirty churches throughout Indonesia. The Christmas Eve bombings planned by Hambali called for forty men working in eleven teams in eleven different cities throughout the Indonesian archipelago. Hambali and Ba'asyir had authorized the church bombings during the third meeting of the Rabitatul Mujahidin network in November 2000.[157] In a near–dress rehearsal for Bali two years later, Hambali worked out the Christmas Eve bombings in Kuala Lumpur along with Imam Samudra and Mukhlas, who was there to offer "spiritual guidance." Subsequently, Hambali arrived in the Egypt hotel in Surabaya to brief the foot soldiers on the plan as well. Amrozi and Imron were there. Imron later recounted:

> We had a meeting there and [Hambali] told us all about his jihad program.... I happily welcomed the program because I wanted to do a real jihad just like he explained. It immediately hooked me, I readily, promptly, accepted.[158]

It would be tempting to assert at this juncture that by the Christmas Eve bombings of 2000, Imron had arrived at the point in his individual Radical Pathway when he was a true believer in the Darul Islamist Cause of the JI network—ready to play an active, no-questions-asked part in the Bali attacks two years down the road. We have seen that Hambali was shielded from the actual carnage by emotional distance, while Amrozi lacked empathy with the victims. The question now is: what psychic forces impelled Ali Imron himself to take part? Although emotional distance—cultural, moral, and mechanical—could have played some role, that would not have been the full picture. The available evidence suggests that Imron had a mind of his own—for example, he initially decided to drop out of Al-Mukmin after just one month because the teachings were too extreme. Moreover, he admitted that one reason why his brother Amin Jabir had passed away during that ill-fated trek up the slopes of Mount Lawu was the overemphasis of the Al-Mukmin instructors on blind faith at the expense of adequate real-world preparation for a mountain climb. Imron was no ambitent personality. He could think and make critical judgments. So why did he go down the JI route? Of course, we could point to the intensifying, focusing impact of the experience at his local boarding school when he witnessed with his own eyes the oppression of Muslims in Afghanistan and Palestine, his three-year stint in Camp Saddah with other *jihadis* the world over, and the time spent immersed in the Darul Islamist "space" of Pondok Pesantren Al-Islam. The contention here, however, is that Ali Imron was not as committed a true believer as he may have appeared to be at first sight.

Becoming a Killer

According to social psychologist Herbert Kelman and sociologist V. Lee Hamilton, there are *degrees of social influence*, and they identify three such states: compliance, identification, and internalization.[159] In compliance, "one obeys authority, doing what one perceives that others want done, in order to receive a positive response from the authority." In other words, people "perform a behavior not because they agree with it but because its expression is necessary to producing a desired social effect."[160] Compliant behavior in this sense is not a result of one's internal beliefs and occurs only when close observation by authority figures is prevailing.[161] In Imron's case, the reason for studying at Al-Mukmin was his desire for the approval of his father, Nurhasyim. Imron had observed the high status that his older brother, Mukhlas, a well-known Al-Mukmin alumnus, enjoyed in the sight of their father and desired that as well. However, it was obvious after one month that he was only *complying* with this behavioral norm to seek his father's approval and that he actually could not personally stomach the extreme beliefs of Al-Mukmin teachers. The question then arises: did Imron "harden" later on? After all, he appeared to be an extremely gung-ho

anti-Western orator while teaching at Pondok Pesantren Al-Islam and planting thoughts of *jihad* in his young charges, and during the session with
Hambali in the Egypt hotel in Surabaya in late 2000, he seemed prepared
for *jihad*. Surface appearances, however, were deceptive in Imron's case. At
that point in late 2000, he had *identified* with the JI network program but
had not necessarily *internalized* it. What is the difference between "identification" and "internalization?" Waller is worth quoting here:

> In *identification*, one copies behavior that seems to go with a particular
> role. Though one may gradually come to believe in the copied behavior,
> the behavior is acted out only when one is playing the role.... *Behaviors
> adopted through identification remain tied to a continuing relationship with
> the authority and are stable only as long as the person operates in a social
> environment that is relatively unchanging* [italics added].[162]

In other words, until after the Bali attacks, Imron was only *acting out* the
role of committed JI militant. The belief system of Darul Islamist ideology
never actually sunk deep roots into his psyche, as in the cases of Imam
Samudra and Mukhlas. As long as Imron was in the company of, or in close
communication with, fellow Darul Islamists/JI militants, he could perhaps
even persuade himself that he was a true believer. But he was not, as he had
not *internalized* virulent Darul Islamist ideology and made it "congruent
with one's value system."[163] If Imron had truly *internalized* Darul Islamist
ideology and its incipient dehumanizing binary worldview, he would have
remained deeply committed to its key premises despite later being removed
physically from the company of fellow believers. This was clearly not the
case with Ali Imron. The ideological rot was apparent even before the Bali
attacks. Immediately after the Christmas Eve 2000 bombs detonated between 8:30 and 10:00 PM, killing 19 people and injuring 120 across the
Indonesian archipelago, Imam Samudra reassembled the Cell to go over the
evening's operations. Imron admitted:

> We realized that there were other human beings that we were attacking and
> we didn't want to think much about it at that point.... We had decided
> that it was jihad so we didn't want to think about it. To be involved in
> jihad we need to have enemies, right? I dared not think about anything. And
> anyway we were bound by the jemaah.... We were bound by the sacred
> *bai'at*, so that's it—not much questions asked.[164]

Despite quite apparent misgivings about the bombings, any further critical insight on Imron's part was obviously smothered by the *cult-like* atmosphere within the Cell. It would be apposite at this juncture to elaborate
on the dynamics of the cult. The difference between a cult and a wider

charismatic group may be elucidated by adapting more of Geert Hofstede's analytical terminology. Whereas in a cult, a smaller number of people are in close and regular contact with one another, in the charismatic group, which Galanter says can number in the hundreds or thousands, larger numbers of people may not necessarily be in direct contact with one another, but nevertheless strongly share common ideals and aspirations.[165] A religious cult in essence possesses four distinguishing characteristics that generate powerful social psychological pressures on its members: dependence on a leader, compliance with the group; suppression of dissent, and finally, devaluation of outsiders.[166] In Imron's case, cultlike pressures clearly existed within the JI Cell that enforced compliance with rationalizing group norms ("this is jihad" and being "bound by the sacred *bai'at*"), devalued outsiders as "enemies," and suppressed dissent. Nevertheless, Imron's inner dissonance continued to intensify. Following the Bali attacks two years later, the principals, on being arrested, displayed an interesting array of reactions. Amrozi showed utterly no remorse for the Bali victims, while Mukhlas declared: "This is jihad, not drugs," and that "we are not sorry at all."[167] For his part, Imam Samudra informed police that he "feared only Allah," and although he was sorry for the deaths of Muslims, he was "grateful" that "Americans" and "Christians" had been killed.[168] By stark contrast, however, Ali Imron, who became a lone fugitive after the attacks and was thus released from the social psychological pressures of the cultlike setting of the Bali Cell, confessed that he had been "relieved to be caught" and admitted:

> *After I became a fugitive that's when I snapped. My thoughts and beliefs changed. I knew I was wrong.* It wasn't supposed to be the way it turned out. I looked back at the history of the Prophet and our Muslim predecessors and I realized there was no such kind of jihad. . . . So when I was caught by the authorities I didn't resist, because I felt guilty, I knew that what I did was wrong [italics added].[169]

A very reasonable next set of questions would then be: why had Imron not awakened from his *jihadi* stupor earlier? Was this plea of remorse an attempt to secure a lighter sentence? While this factor cannot be ruled out entirely, it still cannot cloak the surprisingly tenuous hold that Darul Islamism ultimately appeared to have on him. He was clearly a waverer, which raises the issue of why he remained embedded in the Darul Islamist milieu for so long. The RP Framework may suggest some answers. On one hand, being very much a product of the collectivist Javanese *Culture*, Imron's desire to avoid the *shame* of being perceived to be letting the Cell down may have trumped the nascent *guilt* about his involvement in what was being planned. On the other hand, reinforcing the pull of Culture was surely Imron's *Individual Personality, Situated* within the psychological crucible of the Cell.

What we are talking about here is the well-documented *power of the small group* to induce obedience. Sigmund Freud used to warn that we should "never underestimate the need to obey."[170] Put another way, as long as he was immersed in a generalized Darul Islamist milieu, and more importantly, in close physical contact with the JI Bali Cell, Imron was for all intents and purposes the *psychological prisoner of a violent religious cult*. As early as 1895, the French sociologist Gustav le Bon warned about the mentally and volitionally homogenizing and even energizing power of the face-to-face group context, which promoted:

> the disappearance of the conscious personality, the predominance of the unconscious personality, the turning by means of suggestion and contagion of feelings and ideas in an identical direction, the tendency to immediately transform the suggested ideas into acts.[171]

More recently, the well-known Stanford social psychologist Philip Zimbardo argued:

> *Individual behavior is largely under the control of social forces and environmental contingencies* rather than personality traits, character, will power or other empirically unvalidated constructs [italics added].[172]

The upshot of the analyses of "situationists" such as Zimbardo is that relatively ordinary people—like Ali Imron—under the right mix of circumstances can actively engage in antisocial and harmful activities, including terrorism. One does not have to be a sociopath to kill. Under the sheer "power of the situational context," such as immersion in a cult-like environment in which dissent is suppressed and there is total dependence on a charismatic leader, individual human beings regress into an "agentic state." In short, as Kressel asserts, what "really matters is not who you are but where you are."[173] This calls to mind the renowned Yale professor Stanley Milgram and his well known "obedience-to-authority" experiments that gave rise to the concept of the *agentic state*. Milgram secured volunteers for what were actually "sham experiments, carried out in a seemingly legitimate psychology laboratory."[174] As Galanter summarizes aptly:

> Typically, the volunteer was instructed by the "researcher" to help condition a second subject played by an actor by administering electric shocks in a study on learning. As the experiment progressed, the volunteer was expected to give the learner increasingly strong electric shocks—the volunteer was not aware that the shock was simulated. Most volunteers inflicted the shock without questioning the propriety of the undertaking, even when it appeared to cause considerable pain to the learner subjects.[175]

Galanter stresses—importantly—that these "were ordinary people, yet they followed the rules set by the experimenter's authority without being constrained by the values they presumably held."[176] Milgram made several points: first, obedience and not personal aggression is the key to human destructiveness. Second, although personality, social class, and background may influence slightly the tendency to obey authority, the impulse to obey is very common, regardless of gender, era, culture, nationality, educational level, personality attributes, and religion. Third, people obey because they assume an "agentic state," in which they "relinquish personal responsibility to an authority figure" perceived as legitimate. Fourth—and this is the key—people "obey evil commands because they are overwhelmed by the situations in which they find themselves" rather than because "they lack character or appropriate morality."[177] It is telling in this regard that just before the Bali attacks, Imron began to display doubts about the impending operation. Intent on seeking an excuse to pull out, he told Cell leader Imam Samudra that he had to go back to Al-Islam *pesantren* to mark exam papers. Samudra, however, acting like, in Imron's words, a "tough man," compelled him to stay.[178] Imron seems to have lacked the inner strength to overcome the objections of his senior Samudra in particular and the overall "power of the situation" more generally.[179] Closely related to the agentic state idea is that of "deindividuation." James Waller explains that deindividuation refers to "a state of relative anonymity in which a person cannot be identified as a particular individual but only as a group member."[180] The concept also refers to the phenomenon of "the submergence of the individual in situation-specific group norms."[181] Such submergence confers a sense of anonymity and a consequent lack of accountability among group members. Individual volition is impaired, resulting in the inability to evaluate the ultimate consequences of one's own actions carefully and thoughtfully.[182] All this increases the chances of "extraordinary evil" occurring.[183]

When one examines Ali Imron's Radical Pathway closely, one thing that truly stands out is the sheer number of occasions he is found in a group context. From his youth in the highly collectivist, large power-distance Javanese village milieu, to his three-year stint in Afghanistan, to his years teaching at Pondok Pesantren Al-Islam, to his time moving around with the JI Cell and his participation in Ambon as well as the Philippine ambassador and Christmas Eve attacks of 2000 and of course Bali in October 2002, he was *never* physically and mentally separated from the Darul Islamist/JI social milieu for an appreciable amount of time—long enough for him to take stock of and critically evaluate his beliefs and values. The fact remains that Ali Imron was a relatively intelligent young man who—while he could think for himself—nonetheless could never overcome the subcultural, ideological, intellectual, and emotional hold of the Darul Islamic/Darul Islamist/JI milieu. Until Bali, he remained by and large a relatively deinviduated person. Unlike Hambali, Imron comes across as someone with an *external* locus of control, a person who on balance is shaped by environmental circumstances rather than someone who is an aggressive shaper of them. It was only after the Bali strikes, while in custody and detached from both the Darul Islamist ideological milieu and the cultlike pressures of the JI Bali Cell, that he was able to "re-individuate." He recanted his Darul Islamist beliefs publicly— not that big a leap, as he had never fully internalized them, unlike Mukhlas, Hambali, and others—expressing remorse for his role in the attacks and admitting that the "people in the Sari Club were not our enemy, they were not soldiers prepared for war."[184] Furthermore, Imron wrote a formal letter of repentance that he circulated to his former students in the Al-Islam *pesantren*, warning them that "jihad is a kind of disease."[185] He even wanted the police to publicize widely that he considered his "previous teachings" as completely wrong.[186] It was all, unfortunately, much too little, much too late.

ARNASAN

Becoming a Hater

Of the two Javanese Muslims who blew themselves up in Bali, adequate open-source information is available for only one of them, Arnasan, alias Iqbal. What is known is that Arnasan had become involved with the JI Cell more than a year before the Bali attacks in October 2002. Imam Samudra, like the good recruiter that he was, was always on the lookout for new talent to induct into the JI network. To this end, he set up a small study circle in Banten near his birthplace, Serang, in West Java. Samudra first attracted an Al-Mukmin graduate, Abdul Rauf, who in turn brought in four young men from the small town of Malimping, just south of Serang.[187] The four were Yudi, Amin, Agus, and Arnasan. These four and Abdul Rauf comprised a unit called Team Lima. Especially after the success of the Christmas Eve 2000 bombings, Samudra felt the need to raise JI operations to a whole new level of lethality and commitment to the Cause: suicide attacks. Team Lima was to be JI's suicide squad.[188] From the start Samudra pulled out all the stops in seeking to indoctrinate his charges, who, as was common to the area, were "brought up in the folklore of the old Darul Islam movement."[189] During the study circle meetings, Samudra unsurprisingly sought to intensify and focus the inchoate Darul Islamic subcultural sentiments and beliefs of these young men into the full-blown, consciously articulated Darul Islamist ideology. Samudra deliberately linked local conflicts such as the Christian-Muslim fighting in Ambon with the Global Salafi *Jihad*, including the 9/11 attacks. As he later told his Indonesian police interrogators, Samudra claimed that he merely presented Team Lima "with the facts, and then considered the facts in the light of the Koran and the Sunnah" together "with the views of the religious scholars, especially concerning the jihad."[190] Samudra also emphasized somewhat self-servingly that the "decision to take part was up to them and that nobody "forced them to do it."[191] At any rate, Samudra opened the eyes of these impressionable country boys with his knowledge of "computers and the internet" and his "war stories from Afghanistan" and drilled into them the notion that *jihad* was everything. After several months had passed, Arnasan seemed to Samudra "the most prominent in spirit and motivation."[192] Arnasan, whom Samudra addressed as "Iqbal" and recalled as "about 163 cm tall, of medium build, straight hair, reddish-brown skin," spoke with a "West Javanese accent," was a "bachelor,"[193] came from an extremely poor background and was in fact the "poorest of the boys" in Team Lima. He lived with his parents in a shack with no electricity just out-side town, where they shared a single rice paddy with a neighbor. Because his parents could not even afford school fees, Arnasan had had to drop out after only his second year of junior high school. Ali Imron, who met Arnasan just before the Bali bombing, described him later as a thoroughly unremarkable "plump boy" with a "dark, pimply, wrinkled and sad face."[194]

After more than a year of indoctrinating and training Team Lima, Samudra decided to send his charges out on a real mission to test their relative commitment levels: a bank robbery to raise funds for the coming Bali operation. Al Qaeda had already sent funding to JI for the impending Bali operation; hence, the point of this particular exercise was to see "how far" Samudra's "young novices would go."[195] Samudra instructed Team Lima to rob the Chinese-owned Elitah Indah goldsmith's shop in Serang. Samudra justified the heist on grounds of *fa'i*—that is, taking back what the "Chinese infidels" had wrongfully sequestered from the Muslims.[196] From a psychological standpoint, what Samudra was doing, consciously or uncon-sciously, was exploiting what social psychologists call the *foot-in-the-door* effect. This refers to the psychological reality that "it is easier to gain com-pliance with a large request if one first gets someone to go along with a much smaller request."[197] The Princeton social psychologist John Darley puts it very well:

> The essence of the process involves causing individuals, under pressure, to take small steps along a continuum that ends with evildoing. Each step is so small as to be essentially continuous with previous ones; after each step, the individual is positioned to take the next one. *The individual's morality follows rather than leads* [italics added].[198]

In the event, while two of Team Lima stood guard outside the Elitah Indah shop, Arnasan and the others, armed with handguns loaned to them by Samudra, assaulted the shop and escaped on motorbikes with "five million rupiah and 2.5 kilograms of gold."[199] The gold was later sold for cash, and the total heist of 400 million rupiah was set aside for the Bali bombing.[200] By late September 2002, Team Lima had entered the final phase of their training. The five boys took a bus to Solo, where Samudra had rented a house to plan for the operation. It was there that Samudra primed them to become *syahid* or martyrs. Samudra later revealed:

> We discussed jihad and the plans for *syahid* bombings in Bali.... I conveyed to them the condition of oppressed Muslims... especially the slaughter committed by American terrorists and their allies towards other Muslim countries.[201]

After an intense week of "preaching, prayer and indoctrination," on October 1 Samudra directly confronted each individual in Team Lima.[202] The moment had come, and Samudra, demonstrating a keen insight into the benefits of reverse psychology, asked:

> I asked them, Brothers, are you or are you not capable of going on jihad on behalf of Muslims with a martyr's bombing? I told them that they shouldn't do it if they felt pressured, or to be seen to be courageous, or to gain popularity, or for any other bad reasons. They should do it only for Allah.[203]

Among other "benefits," Samudra assured the five youth that "they could bring along their parents to Paradise"—something that would have struck a chord with the five "impoverished, simplistic recruits."[204] As it turned out, however, not one member of Team Lima was ready to sacrifice his life on behalf of Muslims—no one, that is, except for Arnasan.[205] Samudra, addressing Arnasan by his other moniker, Iqbal, simply asked: "Bal, is the martyr bomber ready?"[206] Arnasan replied in the affirmative.[207] Two days before the bombings, on October 10, Samudra sent the rest of Team Lima home to Serang to await another "jihad assignment" and instructed Arnasan to compose a will.[208] Arnasan did so, handing it to Ali Imron, and also composed good-bye notes to family and friends. One of these notes read:

> I want to say sorry to you. But all I want to do is commit myself to jihad.... I ask for all your prayers [because] there is so much work that must be completed for the sake of the struggle. I pray that my martyrdom will be the trigger for the growth of the mujahideen... if you all truly want to create a return to glory... you must spill your blood, in order that you are not all ashamed before Allah.[209]

Becoming a Killer

As we know, Arnasan subsequently immolated himself—and scores of other people in the process as well. What made "sad-faced" Arnasan carry out such a macabre act? A first attempt at an explanation must include the impact of the post-Afghanistan Darul Islamist ideology that Samudra had spent literally months drilling into him. Samudra himself spelled out the key elements of this binary worldview. It is illustrated in his emotionally charged justification for the Bali atrocity, which is so telling that it is worth citing at length:

> To oppose the barbarity of the US army of the Cross and its allies . . . to take revenge for the pain of . . . weak men, women and babies who died without sin when thousands of tonnes of bombs were dropped in Afghanistan in September 2001 [sic] . . . during Ramadan. . . . To carry out a [sic] my responsibility to wage a global jihad against Jews and Christians throughout the world. . . . As a manifestation of Islamic solidarity between Moslems, not limited by geographic boundaries. To carry out Allah's order in the Book of An-nisa, verses 74–76, which concerns the obligation to defend weak men, weak women, and innocent babies, who are always the targets of the barbarous actions of the American terrorists and their allies. . . . *So that the American terrorists and their allies understand that the blood of Moslems is expensive and valuable*; and cannot be—is forbidden to be— toyed with and made a target of American terrorists and their allies [italics added].[210]

Complementing this ideological justification and thus ostensible religious legitimacy of the proposed *jihadi* action in Bali would have been Samudra's employment of techniques designed to gradually increase the *moral distance* of the Bali bombers from the Bali clubbers. This is an important point, because of all the JI Bali Cell members considered in this study, Arnasan was the one who actually physically engaged in the killing of other human beings. Increasing moral distance meant, in essence, the disengaging of socially mandated "self-sanctions" that prevent human beings from taking the lives of other human beings. Social psychologist Albert Bandura reminds us that "to slaughter in cold blood innocent women and children in buses, department stores, and in airports" requires "intensive psychological training" in the "moral disengagement" of these self-sanctions. This is the only way to "create the capacity to kill innocent human beings."[211] Military psychologist Dave Grossman concurs, noting that killing other human beings, even in combat, is an extremely traumatic experience, and despite media depictions to the contrary, it is not that easy a task.[212] Bandura notes that one powerful way to relax self-sanctions is by "cognitively restructuring the moral value of killing, so that the killing can be done free from self-censuring restraints."[213] JI leaders like Samudra have always cognitively reconstrued their attacks on Western targets as part of a fully justified and legitimate defensive *jihad*. The September 2004 JI strike on the Australian embassy in Jakarta, furthermore, was presented as part of a noble *jihad* to compel the "Christian government in Australia" to withdraw its troops from the U.S.-led Coalition occupying Iraq.[214] A second mechanism for disengaging the inner restraints against killing human beings is what Bandura calls "euphemistic labeling," which "provides a convenient device for masking reprehensible activities or even conferring a respectable status on them."[215] To this end JI, like violent Islamist groups elsewhere, employed the term "*jihad*," which has a very respectable pedigree in Islamic history, to mask what for all intents and purposes was the mass murder of civilians. Euphemistic labeling was used by JI leaders in other contexts. As shown, both Samudra and even the late Abdullah Sungkar were not beyond justifying criminal activity on the part of their acolytes by recasting such behavior as *fa'i*, or the "robbing the infidels or enemies of Islam to secure funds for defending the faith."[216]

Third, Bandura argues that "people behave in injurious ways they normally repudiate if a legitimate authority accepts responsibility for the consequences of their conduct."[217] This is a variant of the "diffusion of responsibility" effect mentioned earlier. In this respect, several Malaysian and Singaporean JI militants have mentioned Al Qaeda leader Osama bin Laden's February 1998 *fatwa* declaring *jihad* on the Jewish-Crusader alliance as justification for their own terror activities, while it is clear from interrogation reports that JI militants took special care to seek spiritual sanction for key operations from JI *amir* Ba'asyir.[218] Finally, Bandura observes that self-sanctions against "cruel conduct can be disengaged or blunted by divesting people of human qualities." In a very important passage, he notes:

> Once dehumanized, the potential victims are no longer viewed as persons with feelings, hopes, and concerns but as subhuman objects. They are portrayed as mindless "savages," "gooks" ... and the like. Subhumans are regarded as insensitive to maltreatment and capable of being influenced only by harsh methods.[219]

In particular, systematic *linguistic dehumanization* of the enemy has always been a feature of mass killings or genocides throughout human history. James Waller recalls:

> In the Holocaust, for instance, the Nazis redefines Jews as "bacilli," "parasites," "vermins," "demons," "syphilis," "cancer," "excrement," "filth," "tuberculosis," and "plague."[220]

The eminent Harvard psychology professor Steven Pinker adds, somewhat starkly, that such use of "pejorative names" can "flip a mental switch" and cause an outsider to be seen as a "non-person," thereby "making it as easy for someone to torture or kill him as it is for us to boil a lobster alive."[221] In this respect, it is especially telling that Mukhlas himself declared that all Westerners were "dirty animals and insects that need to be wiped out,"[222] while Imam Samudra referred to Jews, Americans, and white people variously as "whiteys,"[223] "blood-sucking monsters,"[224] and "American terrorists and their allies."[225] Amrozi evinced his utter dehumanization of his Bali victims when he shrugged off the suggestion that the JI Cell had killed Australians instead of Americans by quipping: "Australians, Americans, whatever—they are all white people."[226] For his part, Hambali referred to Westerners as "white meat."[227] It is obvious that within the minds of key Bali Cell members, the flesh-and-blood people they were about to kill were a socially dead "them" and were utterly outside the bounds of the "moral circle" of the Darul Islamic "us."[228]

Because all Team Lima members were exposed to Samudra's hate-programming, one key question arises: why did Arnasan *alone* proceed down his Radical Pathway to self-immolation? Clearly, the dehumanizing impact of Darul Islamist ideology alone is not a sufficient explanation and other factors are needed to explain Arnasan's final progress down his Radical Pathway to his self-immolation in the name of God. One possible additional explanation is that Arnasan's inclement economic circumstances generated *frustration*, and this was the necessary added impetus for his subsequent actions. However, the ways in which objective societal conditions give rise to frustration are complex. Psychoanalyst Willard Gaylin informs us:

> Feeling deprived bears no relationship to the actual amount of comfort or goods that a person may possess. One can be surrounded with all the indulgences of the affluent society and still feel deprived. Contrary to this, we can observe people existing in great poverty, where each expenditure must be measured and considered, every nutrient stored and rationed, who still do not feel deprived.[229]

Gaylin states that "a sense of deprivation thrives on differentials: when others have what we do not." In other words, it is a "relative feeling, more closely associated with entitlement than want."[230] In like vein, but with a focus on "relative deprivation," Kressel notes that individuals are "especially likely to feel frustrated" if they have or receive less than what other people similar to them receive.[231] We do know that Arnasan's life prospects were not great—he came from the poorest family in Team Lima and had no real education. Whereas Hambali came from a dirt-poor background as well, the available evidence suggests that he had two advantages over Arnasan: inner drive—or, more technically, a strong internal locus of control—plus genuine intelligence. With these two assets, he was able to rise out of his circumstances—albeit by being upwardly mobile in a terrorist organization. Arnasan, on the other hand, based on available evidence, seemed to lack drive and self-belief and appeared to share Amrozi's ambient personality, seeking an external structure of guidance in problem solving. The upshot is that no matter how "frustrated" Arnasan may have felt about his unpromising life prospects, he was ill equipped—and importantly, most likely recognized that he was ill equipped—to do much about it. Hence Arnasan's "sad" demeanor may be more instructive than is apparent to most analysts. Although it is no longer possible, of course, for a definitive clinical diagnosis to be conducted by professional psychiatrists, it may not be too far-fetched to suggest that Arnasan may have been *clinically depressed*. If so, this would have been very important, and brings our attention back to the importance of Existential Identity and universal Human Nature in our RP Framework.

Research shows that all human beings, in order to be happy and enjoy high levels of self-esteem, need to feel in control of their destiny. Frustration about one's persistent inability to shape one's circumstances can precipitate helplessness, meaninglessness, and despair, all of which form the ingredients for clinical depression—a serious psychological disorder in the form of a prolonged state of sadness and hopelessness. Interestingly, some studies have shown that a "complex link" exists between clinical depression, hate, and aggression. Depression can provoke hostility toward others deemed to be responsible for one's severe circumstances. Anger, revenge, and violence are in fact "primitive antidotes" for depression, and hatred and revenge can give an individual a *sense of purpose* that may counter his or her "hopelessness and grief" at the overpowering sense of feeling trapped.[232] Ultimately, at the emotional core of depression is a very strong sense of low self-esteem. Recent advances in the brain and mind sciences viz. cognitive neuroscience, evolutionary biology, and evolutionary psychology inform us that the persistent low self-esteem associated with clinical depression has consequences for an important part of the brain called the *limbic system*. The human brain is made up of the hindbrain, midbrain, and forebrain. While the hindbrain coordinates breathing, heartbeat, and body movements, the midbrain regulates sleep and arousal. Hindbrain and midbrain together comprise the brain stem.[233] The limbic system, together with the cerebral cortex, form the forebrain. The large cerebral cortex is the "primary seat of consciousness," integrating information from the senses, directing voluntary motor activity, and integrating the higher functions of speech and motivation.[234] The limbic system, the other part of the forebrain, is the "master traffic-control complex that regulates emotional response as well as the integration and transfer of sensory information."[235] The emotional function of the limbic system is what makes it important in our analysis. The limbic system comprises the hypothalamus, hippocampus, thalamus, and amygdala.[236] The grape-sized amygdala is linked to the body's sensory systems and constantly scans the information flowing through them, looking for signs of "threat or pain, whether physical or mental"; in fact, the amygdala plays a role in many emotions, including hate, fear, joy, and love.[237] The limbic system can also be considered part of the so-called "reptomammalian brain": some neuroscientists argue that the human brain is divisible in terms of overall cognitive functioning. It comprises an ancient reptomammalian part at the back of the skull and the more recently evolved "new mammalian" part in front that is dominated by the huge, advanced neocortex, a part of the cerebral cortex.[238] According to the science journalist Rush W. Dozier Jr., the older reptomammalian component can also be termed the Primitive Neural System and the new, more recently evolved mammalian brain the Advanced Neural System. In the normal human brain, the more sophisticated, abstract information processing, including language, philosophy, and meaning systems, is done up front in the Advanced Neural System. What the Primitive Neural System does—importantly—is take the descriptive terms of complex language generated up front and imbue it with "limbic stereotypes" of enormous "emotional significance," because the "reptomammalian mind marks such stereotypes as either enhancing or threatening our survival and reproduction."[239]

Dozier observes that "violent hatred has its roots in the most ancient areas of the brain" and is "part of our reptomammalian nature that first evolved in the bleak kill-or-be-killed environment of millions of years ago."[240] For our purposes, the importance of the Primitive Neural System is that "hate is a product of the limbic system," which, as Dozier reiterates, "has been programmed to carry out the prime evolutionary imperatives of survival and reproduction."[241] Dozier explains the importance of the amygdala and the limbic system:

> The amygdala and related limbic structures are responsible for detecting both danger and opportunity—the snake in the grass and the quickest way to escape from it. Once the amygdala marks something like snakes as a serious threat, its reaction is difficult to change because the limbic system is the seat of our primitive survival responses. People with a severe snake phobia who know full well that garter snakes are harmless still can't help being afraid. The limbic system has seized control of their behavior and the rational mind can't make it let go.[242]

Dozier adds that in comparison to the Advanced Neural System, the more primitive limbic system tends to think in an extremely different way, and significantly, amygdala-driven areas of the limbic system cannot conceptualize uniqueness very well. In short, the limbic system, and the wider Primitive Neural System of which it is a component, tends on the whole to work with stereotypes. It is thus no accident that *hatred and stereotyping go together—* they are both products of the limbic system. The point is that "the racist hates all blacks, all whites, all Jews, all Arabs, all Christians, all Serbs, all Croats" because the "hater sees someone, first and foremost, as a stereotype, and unique individual qualities are of little or no importance."[243] This is, in a sense, the neurophysiologic explanation for the binary worldview of the JI militant.

In mentally and emotionally healthy human beings, the Advanced Neural System keeps the Primitive Neural System in check thanks to firm neocortical control that mutes "visceral rage" at some perceived injustice into "principled outrage," thereby making "enlightened behavior possible."[244] However, if for some reason control shifts from the Advanced to the Primitive Neural System, causing a person to cede overall cognitive control to his reptomammalian nature, then the limbic stereotypes he carries deep in his head could generate hatred and possibly even destructive antisocial acts. One such triggering factor is deep immersion in a hate-filled, paranoid meaning system. Dozier elaborates:

> An intricate, paranoid meaning system can be tied to primitive stereotypes embodied in general descriptive terms such as *Latino, Jew or black....* These elaborate meaning systems are not, however, governed by the complex mind but by the reptomammalian mind that contains the stereotypes they rationalize.[245]

Dozier adds that one can notice this "primitive control" if one tries to "reason with people infected by this kind of hate."[246] He continues:

> *They will continually spin out arguments, excuses, and paranoid ideas in a determined effort to protect their underlying prejudices and hostility.* Their advanced neural system has been enslaved by their primitive fear and hatred and is almost powerless to serve as an objective check on these rationalizations, which are constantly nourished by the reptomammalian view of the world. The primitive neural system has concluded that the objects of this stereotyped hate are a threat to survival and reproduction.... *Under the right circumstances, as with suicidal terrorists, such hate rationales can trigger savage aggression* [italics added].[247]

This is why Alderdice laments that "[r]ational argument is a weak lever in the face of profound violence and hate."[248] The above description sheds light on how the immersion of an intellectually and affectively susceptible individual in a hate-filled meaning system or ideology rife with us-them divisions can lead to extremely adverse consequences:

> Our limbic system has evolved a powerful tendency to *blindly interpret any meaning system that we deeply believe in as substantially enhancing our survival and reproduction.* Someone who wholeheartedly converts to a particular religion or political ideology, for example, is likely to experience strong primal feelings of joy and well-being coupled with an exciting new sense of purpose. This is true even if the belief system has elements that are bizarre or self-destructive [italics added].[249]

In a nutshell, a cognitive and affective cocktail of low self-esteem, "us-them divisions," and "hate-filled meaning systems" would surely prompt the limbic system to detect a threat to survival and reproduction and automatically shift control of thoughts, feelings, and behavior from the Advanced to the Primitive Neural System. It is the contention here that by the time of the Bali bombing, "sad-faced" Arnasan's personal frustration, helplessness, and low esteem, coupled with his intensive indoctrination by Imam Samudra into the hate-filled meaning system of Darul Islamist ideology, probably released forces within his mind that caused him to cede cognitive control to his Primitive Neural System. Quite possibly, Arnasan would have regarded at some subliminal level that "violence can be exciting as well as energizing" and "a compelling distraction from the anguish of depression."[250] He would have been in a *limbic state*, in which he would have *categorized*—quite possibly to a far more visceral extent than the other haters in the JI Cell—the clubbers in the Sari Club and Paddy's Bar not as human beings with parents and siblings and children but rather as dehumanized "American terrorists and their allies" or "bloodsucking monsters." This would have explained his ability to disengage all moral self-sanctions and kill them in cold blood. However, this does not fully explain Arnasan's willingness to *die in the process as well*.

If, as discussed, taking another human being's life is not easily done, certainly taking one's own life is an even more unthinkable prospect. The Primitive Neural System is hard-wired to preserve one's life through the well-known "fight-or-flight" set of physiologic responses, first researched by Walter B. Cannon.[251] In discussing the reasons for suicide attacks since the 1980s, Robert Pape makes the argument that rather than religious factors, the primary motivation is political. He states that historically, militarily weaker insurgent groups have used the tactic to force more powerful foreign forces out of their land.[252] One should, however, make an analytical distinction between militant leaders who wish to employ suicide attacks for politico-strategic reasons and the actual suicide attackers themselves, who may be driven by nonmaterialist factors, but more intangible, psychological ones. One such intangible factor may be what Don J. Feeney, Jr. calls *entrancement*. Feeney argues that entrancement is akin to an altered state of consciousness. In this state, the subject suspends his critical faculties, loses touch somewhat with reality, and cedes volitional control to some idealized authority figure.[253] This certainly seems to describe Arnasan's state of mind on one hand and his clearly dependent relationship with Samudra on the other. Additionally, Sweeney's comments about the suicide attacker's tenuous grasp of reality imply that it may not be an overstatement to suggest that not only was the clinically depressed Arnasan in a limbic state, but he was probably *delusional* as well. Psychoanalyst Willard Gaylin defines a delusion as "a false *belief* that entails an abandonment of all reality testing."[254] Importantly, Gaylin points out that a "psychotic delusion" can be generated by "affective (emotional) disorders like depression."[255] After all, in Arnasan's own words, cited earlier, he had prayed that "my martyrdom will be the trigger for the growth of the mujahideen" and informed his relatives in deadly earnestness that "if you all truly want to create a return to glory," it would simply be necessary to "spill your blood, in order that you are not all ashamed before Allah." In sum, perhaps to an even greater extent than other Bali Cell members, Arnasan was truly living out the alternate reality of what F. Bruno calls a "fantasy war."[256] Hence on October 12, 2002, Arnasan, alias Iqbal, of Malimping, West Java, driven inexorably forward through an immensely potent combination of clinical depression, ideological indoctrination, and a limbic, delusional state of mind, traversed the remaining length of his personal Radical Pathway to a murderous, fiery, hellish end.

CONCLUSION

This chapter has attempted the immensely difficult task of reconstructing the inner worlds and motivations of four key individuals in the JI Cell that bombed Bali: Hambali, Amrozi, Ali Imron, and Arnasan. It should be obvious by now that even when we examine a single JI terrorist cell—analogous to a cluster of Flowers within the wider Bouquet of Darul Islam—it is simply not possible to pin down the profile of an individual and the common process by which he is likely become radicalized. *There are, in short, not one, but many Radical Pathways.* To be sure, all four came from strong Darul Islamic subcultural backgrounds and shared a collective mental programming that could later be honed into a virulent anti-Christian, anti-Western ideology by the likes of Abdullah Sungkar, Abu Bakar Ba'syir, and Imam Samudra. In addition, all four had generally unfavorable socioeconomic backgrounds, with perhaps Hambali and Arnasan, relatively speaking, the worst off. But that is where the commonalities end. Hambali managed to claw his way out of his socioeconomic quagmire to become a very influential JI leader. Arnasan, possessed of far less nimbleness of mind, could not. Similarly, Amrozi and Ali Imron may have been brothers, but the similarities ended there. Amrozi was clearly an ambitent personality with virtually no mind of his own who relied heavily on Mukhlas for moral, religious, and ideological direction. By contrast, Ali Imron displayed evidence of an independent-mindedness very early on but, driven by his strong desire to win acceptance from his father and Mukhlas, gravitated toward Darul Islamism. Moreover, while Amrozi was also quite possibly a psychopath who had no compunction in playing a role in the mass murder of the Bali victims, Ali Imron displayed very evident remorse after the attacks and seemed to give the impression that while he was in the JI Bali Cell he was utterly deindividuated and could not overcome the cultlike psychological pressures that prevented critical reflection on what he was doing. Amrozi played a role in killing because he did not care; Ali Imron, despite Darul Islamist conditioning, nevertheless cared at some level but lacked the inner resources to *prevent* himself from playing a role in the atrocity. Similarly, Hambali was able to play his part because his lofty organizational position helped him maintain mechanical distance from his victims; this was reinforced by the moral distance programmed into him by the us-them dehumanization inherent in Darul Islamism. Arnasan killed "up close and personal" because he was likely in a limbic state buttressed by a delusion that he was on a fast track to Paradise. To reiterate: four different individuals; four different Radical Pathways.

The implication of this analysis—unfortunately for those who seek neat answers to complex problems—is that wider studies that eschew the notion of a single, overarching terrorist profile could not be more right. The common, larger factors that may compel people to nail their colors to a terrorist network like JI, viz. a subcultural milieu dominated by deeply collectivist, large power-distance, and strong uncertainty-avoidance outlooks; as well as a shared history of conflict, such as the Darul Islam struggle, may be highly suggestive markers of *possible* radicalization, but only up to a point. As many analysts have pointed out, not every young Javanese Muslim who went to Al-Mukmin—the ideological ground zero of Darul Islamism—became a radicalized JI militant. Hence, for instance, shutting down Al-Mukmin (and/or other similar JI-inspired *pesantren*), while tempting, would quite possibly unleash a severe political backlash against the secular government of current President Bambang Susilo Yudhoyono, as it would be transcendentalized by Islamists and possibly even traditionalist Muslims alike as evidence of a sinister campaign to undermine Islam in the archipelago. Likely the former would argue that Islam itself was being attacked, and the latter would complain about the lack of respect for an educational institution with deep roots in Javanese Muslim culture. This raises the question: are there any effective counterradicalization strategies that can be deployed instead? The answer to this is complex and needs careful unpacking in the final chapter.

5

Blocking Radical Pathways—Some Implications for Policy

On October 22, 2007, Abu Bakar Ba'asyir addressed a crowd of young people in a meeting in East Java, organized by the Persatuan Pemuda Islam Pantura or Java North Coast Islamic Youth Group. Displaying all the usual dehumanizing rhetoric of the virulent JI variety of Darul Islamism, Ba'asyir likened non-Muslim tourists in Bali as "worms, snakes, maggots—those are animals that crawl"; castigated the immorality of the "Australian infidels"; and even called upon young Javanese youth to "beat up" foreigners who dared to venture into the area and "not tolerate them."[1] He declared that Muslims in Indonesia should "reject the laws of the nation's parliament" and insisted that "following state laws that contradicted Islamic Shariah law was an act of blasphemy."[2] Tellingly, he encouraged his rapt listeners not to "be scared if you are called a hardliner Muslim," as "it must be like that."[3] It would seem that Ba'asyir the craftsman was out selling knives once more and—although he would no doubt deny it, as usual—was busily paving more "Radical Pathways" toward future acts of JI militancy and terrorism. Hence, blocking such Radical Pathways from developing remains a pressing policy issue. Throughout this book we have sought to isolate such Radical Pathways that lead more or less ordinary individuals toward degrees of involvement in violent, terrorist behavior. This was attempted to shed light on how certain Javanese Muslims associated with the Jemaah Islamiyah network, namely Abu Bakar Ba'asyir, Mukhlas, Imam Samudra, Hambali, Amrozi, Ali Imron, and Arnasan, developed the virulent binary worldview inherent to Darul Islamist ideology. This worldview—the product of the complex interaction between diverse historical, political, cultural, social psychological, and both innate and individualized psychological processes—caused them to play some indirect or direct role in the Bali bombing of October 12, 2002.

In a sense, this book confirms the conventional wisdom that trying to explain how and why an individual engages to some degree in violent terrorist acts is an extremely complex affair. Yet this study breaks new ground in that it has adapted the seminal work of the Dutch social psychologist Geert Hofstede and generated the so-called Radical Pathways or RP Framework. This Framework has guided the entire analysis, examining how Existential Identity Anxiety—in essence, the primal fear of group extinction—was amplified in a multitude of ways through constant interaction with Culture and the various factors captured under the Situated Individual Personality to produce highly individualized and idiosyncratic radicalization experiences in different JI militants and leaders. Furthermore, we adapted and applied certain botanical metaphors developed by Hofstede to the Javanese context: we saw how the "Bouquet" of Darul Islamic subculture, which arose out of the intermingling and intertwining of the "Branches" from the "Trees" of Javanese Islam, namely *santri* traditionalism, modernism, and Arabized modernism, as well as the enduring impact of S. M. Kartosoewirjo's Darul Islam revolt against the Republican government, provided critical if somewhat amorphous "learned ways of thinking, feeling and acting." These were later funneled and amplified, or "intensified and focused," by politically oriented Darul Islam movement activists, among whose number included Ba'asyir and Sungkar, into the more consciously systematized political ideology of Darul Islamism. These "Darul Islamists," as we termed them, today form what is popularly known as the "Darul Islam movement." More technically, though, the Darul Islamists comprise a charismatic group with a shared belief system, a relatively strong sense of social cohesiveness, and an adherence to group behavioral norms. They are held together affectively, despite subsequent factionalization, by a common, almost mystical allegiance and loyalty to the memory of the martyred charismatic DI Imam Kartosoewirjo. The core tenets of Darul Islamism have included the existential fear of group extinction; a rigid, binary worldview producing potent, categorical, us-them thinking; a powerful sense of moral entitlement and historic victimization; a focus on personalized socialization of new recruits into an exclusive order; and above all, the underlying but unmistakable political aspiration to ensure the dominance of Islam vis-à-vis all comers. The Darul Islamists of JI are not actually a spiritual movement but a political one; they are driven by a spiritualized politics of mimetic envy.

It was from the wider Darul Islamist charismatic group that the social networks of *jemaah islamiyah* associated with Sungkar and Ba'asyir emerged. Such *jemaah islamiyah* were further radicalized by the thoroughly virulent JI version of Darul Islamism propagated in more or less informal ideological spaces within institutions such as Al-Mukmin *pesantren* in Solo, Central Java; Al-Islam *pesantren* in Lamongan, East Java; Luqmanul Hakiem *pesantren* in Ulu Tiram, Johore State; and even the secluded kampong in Sungai Manggis in Selangor State at the time Hambali and Ba'asyir lived there. We saw how the emotional and ideological impact of participation in the Global Salafi Jihad in Afghanistan in the 1980s caused the key ideologues of Darul Islamism and, from January 1993, the offshoot JI network to expand their ambitions. They henceforth sought not just an Indonesian Islamic State but also a transnational caliphate in Southeast Asia. Following the Al Qaeda lead, they incorporated the "far enemy" of the "American terrorists and their allies" into the list of enemies of Indonesian Islam, a list previously dominated by the forces of the "near enemy"—the secular Indonesian Republic of first Soekarno and then later Soeharto. By the 1990s, JI had been globalized, and it was this global outlook of JI's virulent, dehumanizing Darul Islamist ideology—in conjunction with the individualized factors driving the militants we encountered in the previous chapter—that led to the formation of the Bali Cell, which for all intents and purposes functioned like a violent religious cult. The personalities of the dominant Imam Samudra, the ambitent Amrozi, the compliant Ali Imron, and the delusional Arnasan reinforced one another in a small, cult-like environment that induced group compliance and suppressed dissent while intensifying and focusing the dehumanizing devaluation of Westerners—a process that ultimately culminated in the Bali atrocity.

THE POST-BALI JI: THE CURRENT CHALLENGE

In this final chapter we need to address the issue of what, if anything, can be done to neutralize the JI threat. More than six years after the Bali attacks of October 2002, the problem of JI remains real, if somewhat evolved. The massive security force crackdown on JI militants after the 2002 Bali attacks did not prevent three more deadly strikes: in August 2003 on the Jakarta Marriott, in September 2004 outside the Australian embassy in the capital, and in Bali again on October 1, 2005.[4] Despite losses of key operational leaders such as Hambali, Mukhlas, and Imam Samudra and more recently JI *amir* and Poso operations chief Zarkasih[5] and military commander Abu Dujana[6] in June 2007—as well as the breakup of the old regional *mantiqi* regional administrative structure and cessation of direct leadership links with Al Qaeda on the Arabic-speaking Dujana's capture—the JI network has not quite crumbled.[7] Displaying a protean-like quality, JI just keeps finding replacements in leaders and manpower, while metastasizing and adapting. The major 2007 arrests of key JI militants led to the discovery of a new, simplified JI administrative structure. Instead of the four *mantiqis* covering Southeast Asia and Australia, there was only a single administrative structure centered on Indonesia with three divisions: one for East Indonesia, one for West Indonesia, and one for Poso in Central Sulawesi.[8] Moreover, at the time of this writing, it seems that the network has split: a mainstream faction, to all intents and purposes led by Ba'asyir, who was released from prison in June 2006, has opted to rebuild and consolidate, aiming to establish the old Darul Islam goal of an Islamic State in Indonesia itself and dropping the idea of the regional caliphate.[9] The mainstream leadership has sought to mobilize political support for the Islamic State through open activism as well as—taking a leaf from the PKS playbook—building a series of elementary schools for both fund-raising and long-term recruitment purposes. These schools apparently differ from the Pondok Pesantren Al-Mukmin model, as the former have a "broader curriculum."[10] Ba'asyir's mainstream faction also continues to exploit its deep roots in the Javanese strongholds of the historic Darul Islam movement—the Darul Islamic subcultural Bouquet, so to speak—sourcing funds and, importantly, recruits, through "family networks, business associates and a small number of Islamic colleges."[11]

This mainstream JI faction should not be hastily seen as newly "moderate" in its attitude toward violence, though. Its apparent decision to avoid large and spectacular Bali-like bomb attacks against Westerners is because of pragmatic concerns that Muslim casualties could erode support from sympathetic constituencies.[12] The mainstream JI has focused its energies instead on building support and boosting recruitment in conflict zones such as in Poso, Central Sulawesi. Christian-Muslim fighting in Poso claimed 2000 lives between 1999 and the signing of a peace accord in December 2001. Violence flared up again in 2003, and in October 2005 three Christian schoolgirls were brutally beheaded in a crime that shocked the nation.[13] Ansyaad Mbai, head of the counter-terrorism desk at the Indonesian Ministry for Political, Legal and Security Affairs, reported in the first quarter of 2007 that JI desires to turn strife-torn Poso into a base of operations through ideologically legitimated terror attacks that foment a wider religious conflict—which could in turn generate a flow of recruits to the cause. The aim has been to persuade Poso Muslims that it is "permitted to kill non-Muslims and infidels" in pursuit of an Islamic State.[14] It is worth keeping in mind that if Muslim casualties could be avoided, religious justifications were explicitly offered, and "benefits outweighed disadvantages," many mainstream JI would support further bomb attacks against Western and infidel targets.[15]

A smaller, extremely violent, anti-Western "pro-bombing" faction, led by the Malaysian Noordin Mohammed Top, remains at large at the time of this writing. Impatient with the comparatively "more subtle Islamic revolution" approach of the JI mainstream,[16] Noordin's so-called Tanzim Qaedat Al-Jihad faction,[17] composed of his personalized network of small, autonomous cells, prefers a "strike now" approach. In fact, militants in Noordin's faction, many of whom were recruited from Java,[18] hold that "if you want the slow track to heaven, join JI; if you want the fast track, join Noordin."[19] Noordin's network has been estimated to run into the hundreds, comprising militants who are relatively less well-trained and imbued more with a "jihadist mindset than religious knowledge or organizational commitment."[20] Noordin's Al Qaeda–influenced preference for "indiscriminate anti-Western attacks" has in fact alarmed the mainstream JI, which fears that the maverick militant leader's "confrontational approach would lead to a demonising of Islam and jeopardize its long-term goal."[21] The mainstream JI leaders have thus sought to rein in Noordin's faction and "choke off its support base"[22] by criticizing Osama bin Laden's important February 1998 *fatwa* calling for attacks on Western civilians in defense of the faith.[23] In any case, Noordin's operatives have been instructed to strike at least once a year to demonstrate their defiance and continuing potential in the face of "extreme pressure" from the Indonesian authorities.[24] The attacks need not necessarily be large ones either, and may be planned and carried out by "small cells without central control"—a concept called "uncontrolled decentralization" that has been spelled out in a terrorist manual circulating in Indonesia in the past couple of years.[25] It is worth noting that the May 2005 bombings of a market in Tentena, a Christian town in Central Sulawesi, which killed 22 people, were apparently carried out without central direction, as the bombers "simply adopted a local agenda."[26] Little wonder then that as late as October 2007, leading terrorism analyst Sidney Jones warned that the "biggest threat to Western targets and civilians is no longer from an attack sanctioned by the JI leaders but from the militant breakaway groups" such as Noordin's faction.[27] One should not forget either that other key JI leaders such as Zulkarnaen[28] and Umar Patek could form nodes around which additional violent, autonomous factions pursuing their own customized Darul Islamist agendas could coalesce as well.[29]

To reiterate a point made in the first chapter, counter-*terrorist* strategies privileging "hard" law enforcement measures such as killing or capturing terrorists, interdicting terror financing, imposing tighter border and immigration controls, harnessing technological solutions, and disrupting flows of weapons, explosives, and other material remain important. In this vein, counter-terrorist operational methodologies—such as the formation of the American- and Australian-trained antiterrorist police unit Detachment (or Densus 88)—have genuinely been successful in killing and capturing key JI militants.[30] Not for nothing did the Australian Federal Police Commissioner Mick Keelty laud the Indonesian National Police, of which Densus 88 is a part, for its successes against JI since October 2002.[31] There may well be a need for more resources and manpower to be funnelled to Densus 88, partly to reduce its reliance on the less well-trained Brimob paramilitary police unit in raids against militant hideouts, though.[32] In addition, other counter-terrorist policies, such as stricter sentencing for terrorism crimes and reducing corruption in Indonesian prisons, are also important. Ba'asyir, for instance, served only twenty-six of thirty months for his alleged involvement in the October 2002 bombings and later had his conviction overturned altogether.[33] Moreover, the problem of poorly educated, -trained, and -paid prison wardens, in addition to overcrowded jails, is another serious problem with wider implications for the fight against JI. Convicted Bali bombers Imam Samudra, Mukhlas, and Amrozi, although in Bali's Kerobokan prison facility, were actually able to run businesses like selling vouchers for mobile phone airtime, which helped them forge ties with regular criminals and through the latter gain access to "external funding from a range of sources."[34] Imam Samudra was able to influence a Bali warden to smuggle into the jail a laptop with which he issued calls for *jihad* over the Internet and that was supposedly "used in the lead-up to the second Bali bombing" as well.[35] Samudra even secured use of a mobile phone for communication with followers outside.[36] More seriously, ordinary criminals in Kerobokan were "converted to the violent jihadi cause" of the three Bali bombers, and when released, these "newly fanatical criminals" often disappeared from "the police anti-terrorism radar," as they had not been considered religious "hardliners."[37] Similarly, prior to his release from Jakarta's Cipanang prison in June 2006, Ba'asyir was able to build up a strong support base among the inmates as well.[38] Another problem that emerged was that convicted militants were allowed to spend their jail terms translating "Arabic jihadist manuals" that were subsequently distributed outside as books and pamphlets and also posted on the Internet.[39] While part of the problem with prisons can be addressed by legal and institutional means, such as imposing tighter controls on the activities of convicted militants and their contact with the outside world,[40] that is only part of the solution. The challenge is more profound.

Javanese culture, with its emphasis on collectivism and a large power-distance orientation, in tandem with the powerful appeal of the more focused and consciously articulated Darul Islamist ideology, ensures that JI leaders who deliberately portray themselves as victimized defenders of Islam would easily enjoy and therefore exploit a certain ascribed prestige and high status among both regular inmates and wardens. Although this can pose problems, it can also be exploited by the authorities as well. Abu Dujana, for instance, the JI operational commander captured in June 2007, is apparently greeted as "Teacher" by his prison guards, while his cell in the Brimob headquarters outside Jakarta has air-conditioning, a queen-size bed, and a sofa set.[41] This is part of the so-called "soft approach" by the Indonesian authorities to secure information from leaders like Dujana, a strategy that includes financial assistance to his family.[42] Both the "soft approach" to Abu Dujana as much as the ability of the convicted Bali bombers to continue the virtually unfettered pursuit of their Darul Islamist ideological agenda in prison suggest that in the end, counter-*terrorist* measures aimed at protecting against the *physical* threat posed by JI terrorism can bring one only so far. Countering the *metaphysical* threat of the wider Darul Islamist ideology that feeds upon the Javanese cultural norms that render prison wardens, inmates, and other Javanese and Indonesian young men vulnerable to the influence of the likes of Ba'asyir, Samudra, Mukhlas, and Dujana is a far more important and challenging task. This in turn requires broader-based, creative counter-*terrorism* approaches that seek to counter "not only the tactic of terrorism" but, *inter alia*, "the ideology that spawns it" as well.[43] In this respect, the cardinal aim of a counter-*terrorism* strategy must be to neuter the *radicalization* processes—or Radical Pathways—by which more or less ordinary people become transformed into fully indoctrinated terrorists committed to the employment of violence to further their aims. The rest of this chapter will attempt to critically examine various possible strategies with a view to identifying the most appropriate means of "blocking" Radical Pathways from developing in the Indonesian context.

The first important point to note is that a key part of blocking Radical Pathways from developing must be the provision of good governance. This must be aimed at creating sufficient political space for articulation of, and the capacity to address, interests and grievances, as well as reducing poverty and economic disparities throughout the archipelago but especially in regions with a history of conflict.[44] However, as the distinguished authors of a recent Commonwealth report have concluded, "material inequality does not mean people automatically protest, let alone choose violence."[45] Instead, it is precisely when such structural factors are combined with perceived profound disrespect for and threats to group identity that violence likely breaks out.[46] Thus an unavoidable and large aspect of blocking Radical Pathways must include coping with the problem of Existential Identity Anxiety—as we have seen, the primal force underlying radicalization within the JI network. The task therefore must be mitigating this Existential Identity Anxiety and the ways in which it is amplified to dangerous levels through the intervention of the various elements of the RP Framework: Existential Identity, Culture, and the Situated Individual Personality. In this regard, scanning the available literature suggests that treading on the familiar and well-worn policy path of "winning hearts and minds" is one potential tool for reducing Existential Identity Anxiety and hence blocking Radical Pathways from developing. A closer reexamination of the meaning of this concept is warranted, though. The phrase "hearts and minds" is widely considered to have been popularized by the controversial if effective British High Commissioner in colonial Malaya, General Sir Gerald Templer, at the height of the insurrection by the Communist Party of Malaya in the 1950s[47]—a "nauseating phrase," Templer later conceded in 1968, that "I think I invented."[48] In Malaya, winning hearts and minds was operationalized, *inter alia*, through the promulgation of policies aimed at improving the rule of law, reducing poverty, uplifting living conditions, and generating greater economic opportunities in tandem with calibrating the use of military force and the promotion of population-friendly attitudes and behavior on the part of government officials and security forces, which taken together were designed to wean the rural Chinese community—the constituency most vulnerable to Communist intimidation and blandishments—away from the latter's clutches.[49]

In a sense, what the colonial and later independent Malayan govern-ment eventually succeeded in doing was *cognitively immunizing*[50] a critical mass of the rural Chinese against Communist narratives. This effort began to bear fruit after 1954 and was so successful that support for the Commu-nists evaporated to such an extent as to compel its leadership to demobilize by the end of the decade.[51] In effect, rather than *win* the hearts and minds of the rural Chinese, what the government in Malaya did was *deny* them to the Communists. Rather than winning the deep-seated affections of the rural Chinese—which would have been an uphill task anyway, as the gov-ernment was dominated by urbanized ethnic Malays with the support of the politically conscious urban Chinese merchant class—what the Malayan authorities did, with great effect in the second half of the 1950s, was to prevent the Communist narrative from being *internalized* and *personalized* by the rural Chinese, thereby producing attitudes and behavior in support of the Communist cause.[52] In developing options for lessening Existential Identity Anxiety and hence blocking Radical Pathways in the Indonesian context, therefore, it would be useful to keep in mind that the common thread tying the options together is the goal of cognitive immunization of masses of young Javanese against Darul Islamist ideological narratives. That would be the key.

More precisely, we can think of two levels of cognitive immunization. *Primary* cognitive immunization can be considered to consist of short-term policies directed at the Darul Islamist charismatic group, including militants of the JI network who are at heart, as we have seen, Darul Islamists them-selves. We shall explore in this respect two measures: first, attacking the credibility of the key JI leaders so as to undercut their popular appeal and hence ability to recruit foot soldiers; and second, the so-called "creeping de-radicalization" policy currently being adopted by the Indonesian police in which what we may call the "Good Radicals"—rather than the conven-tional wisdom of deploying "moderate Muslim scholars"—are sought to dialogue with the "Bad Radicals" so as to persuade the latter to reform themselves. *Secondary* cognitive immunization against the Darul Islamist binary worldview and narrative would consist of policies targeted at not just the Darul Islamist charismatic group, but importantly the wider Darul Islamic subculture, the so-called Bouquet, the historic constituency of con-cern from which the Darul Islamist charismatic group emerged. In this regard we will explore and evaluate medium- to longer-term options for cognitive immunization, such as promoting an *integrated* U.S. public diplomacy ef-fort; creating greater opportunities for interfaith dialogue and cross-faith projects; expanding educational opportunities with a view to promoting critical thinking and a sense of shared humanity across faith boundaries; and the appreciation that one need not be pigeonholed into any identity category but can simultaneously possess multiple identities. We shall argue that the longer-term success of such measures in rendering Javanese and Indonesian Islam resistant to virulent ideological mutations such as "Al Qaedaized" Darul Islamism, as it were, requires generating a broad-based willingness among *santri* Muslims to critique both the form and substance of Arabized modernism in the Indonesian milieu. Finally, three possible philosophical end-states of a potentially generation-long educational process that promotes critical thought in both secular and Islamic education will be explored—states of mind that would render the young Javanese of the future relatively resilient to Darul Islamist–type ideological narratives that could generate pathways to future Balis.

PRIMARY COGNITIVE IMMUNIZATION

Undermining the JI "Story"[53]

It is instructive that during the Emergency in Malaya, the crack Psychological Warfare Section of the Government Information Services, led by the legendary Malayan Chinese propagandist C. C. Too, always tried to split the CPM rank and file guerrillas from their leaders.[54] The emphasis in psychological warfare or psywar efforts was on emphasizing, very deliberately, the precise ways in which the CPM leaders lived it up in the Malayan jungle at the expense of their often scared and hungry foot soldiers. Deliberate care was taken not to paint the rank and file as evil. The line taken instead was that the guerrillas were essentially honorable men who had been misled by the evil CPM leadership.[55] It should be noted that with regard to attacking the personal standing of the CPM leaders, C. C. Too ensured that everything said in government propaganda was true and verifiable. That did not mean, however, that he pulled his punches. In May 1952 Too released a psychological warfare (psywar) leaflet written by a surrendered CPM guerrilla, Ching Kien. Ching Kien first reminded the rank and file of the hardships of life in the jungle:

> Comrades! You can see that we never have full meals, warm clothing, or secure accommodation in the jungle. When we get sick there is no medicine.

He then very deliberately pointed an accusatory finger at the leaders:

> Comrades! You can see how the Political Commissar of our Independent Platoon keeps all the new watches, plastic cloth and fountain pens for himself and only lets us have what he does not want any more. At the same time, is there any of you who has ever tasted the nutritive food he keeps for his own consumption? Are Political Commissars and upper ranks the only human beings, are we not human beings too?

Building rhetorical momentum, Ching Kien then castigated the leaders' lack of concern for their own foot soldiers:

> When the lower ranks fall sick and ask for assistance, they will be regarded as being unable to bear hardships, as being too argumentative, in short, as exhibiting "bad manifestations."

Ching Kien's accusation culminated with an attack that touched on an extremely raw nerve:

> Comrades! The upper ranks can make love in their secret huts, but if you want to find a lady friend, then you will have to wait until there is any left over from the upper ranks.[56]

More than fifty years later, the late C. C. Too's psywar techniques may be illustrative of creative ways of employing psywar in undermining the JI "Story," thereby undercutting its attractiveness to potential recruits. One way, as the Malayan example suggests, would be to drive a wedge between JI leaders on the one hand and JI foot soldiers and potential recruits from the wider Darul Islamist charismatic group on the other by exploiting contradictions between the pious rhetoric of certain JI leaders and their actual behavior. This "wedge strategy" would have to be executed with great care, though. In the collectivist, large power-distance Javanese milieu within which JI is embedded, "seniors" seen to have both Islamic learning, like Abu Bakar Ba'asyir, and military training in Afghanistan, such as Imam Samudra, would enjoy high prestige and a sense of immunity from the criticisms of outsiders.[57] Nevertheless, so-called psywar opportunities do present themselves. It is known that Imam Samudra's laptop computer hard drive had pornographic material on it, specifically photographs of "naked western women."[58] This fact can be weaved by credible ex-JI leaders such as Nasir Abbas (see below) into a powerful "Counter-Story" of Samudra's rank hypocrisy in targeting Bali for being "a place of sin" while he entertained himself in his spare time by looking at nude women.[59] Moreover, Samudra's manipulation of the young, impressionable boys of Team Lima for martyrdom attacks can in turn be integrated into a wider narrative about how Samudra is not all that different from his counterparts in Pakistan, where, for instance, it is known that many *jihadi* leaders live luxuriously while foot soldiers are sent to be "cannon fodder" in Kashmir.[60] A potent message could be put across that Samudra and perhaps other JI leaders such as Noordin Top are concerned above all else with power and revenge, with the ethical essence of the Qu'ran relegated to a secondary, less crucial consideration. Testimony from abroad, such as that of the former British radical Ed Husain, is instructive here. Husain asserts that so intent are British Islamists in seeking power that they pay little attention to matters of the soul.

While portraying "signs of piety to maintain a standing" among followers, many Islamist leaders have in fact ceased to be "observant" Muslims. While ensuring that their foot soldiers have (as the CPM in 1950s Malaya used to say) the "correct cognition" of the situation and understand the importance of bringing about the establishment of the Islamic State, these Islamists are not interested in developing the "Islamicness of their Islamic recruits" but are content "to use these same recruits to promote a seemingly Islamic cause."[61] It could similarly be suggested in Indonesia that for the JI leaders like Samudra and Noordin Top, the ultimate end of striking back at the "American terrorists and their allies" through attacks like Bali so as to victimize their erstwhile Western victimizers evidently justifies *any* means—including sacrificing the hapless lives of impressionable young men like Arnasan.

There are other psywar opportunities as well, if one knows where to look. The video testimony of JI militants detained overseas in Singapore and Malaysia, shown during Ba'asyir's Jakarta trial from April to September 2003—for his alleged involvement with JI and a plot to overthrow the government—was criticized in some quarters because of controversy over whether the evidence was coerced.[62] However, a point that has been overlooked is that both the testimony and Ba'asyir's reactions to it constituted excellent psywar material. The spectacle of Ba'asyir's stony-faced refusal to acknowledge publicly his former acolytes in court, while one incarcerated senior Malaysian national but Singapore-based militant, Faiz Abu Bakar Bafana, broke down and wept while admitting that he had regarded Ba'asyir "like a father"[63] and declaring publicly "no matter what, I love you, Ustaz,"[64] was the stuff of such high theater that an Indonesian police equivalent of the cunning C. C. Too would have had a field day with it. Again, the Counter-Story of a JI leadership so single-mindedly driven by their quest for power that they exploited and made use of people and then discarded them when they were no longer of use could have been—and could still be, for that matter—solidly established with such yet-to-be-mined material. Finally, the fact that recent JI attacks in Jakarta generated significant Indonesian Muslim "collateral damage" also presents a potentially powerful psywar opportunity. The August 5, 2003, attack on the J. W. Marriott hotel killed mainly Muslims,[65] as did the September 9, 2004, car bomb outside the Australian embassy in Jakarta.[66] These two episodes represent "political oxygen" generated by JI that can be exploited to reinforce the Counter-Story of a morally decrepit and inept leadership causing unnecessary harm to the very community they claim to be championing in their quest for symbolic empowerment. In fact, these two bombing episodes have already been exploited by Indonesian police officials with the help of ex-JI militants (see below) to undermine the JI Story and drive a wedge between its leaders on one hand and the rank and file and potential recruits on the other.[67]

Finally, in addition to undercutting the moral legitimacy and credibility of JI leaders, another way in which the JI Story can be undermined is the most obvious: closing down the public spaces that enable the extreme, dehumanizing binary worldview that represents JI's version of Darul Islamism to be articulated. In fact, this is something that the Indonesian authorities are already doing. On one hand, "moderate" Muslim organizations like NU and Muhammadiyah are encouraged to "spread their moderate ideology to the public" through the "media, public gatherings and schools."[68] However, as the then-Head of Densus 88 pointed out in October 2007, the "groups" that "originated from Darul Islam, such as: Al Jemaah al Islamiyah, Kompak, Jundullah, Majelis Mujahidin Indonesia"—in other words, the key organized and interrelated social constellations within the Darul Islamist charismatic group that propagate the most virulent versions of Darul Islamism—"are monitored very closely," and ways are found to limit "their access to the public" in order "that we prevent them from spreading their faith."[69] Ultimately, while monitoring the public propagation of the JI Story has merits, more enduring results are likely to be achieved through a massive, well-orchestrated, and well-coordinated psywar campaign against the JI leadership—both its mainstream faction and the Noordin splinter network. The aim should not be to censor them but rather "censure them" for their power-driven opportunism and reprehensible, dehumanizing worldviews passed off as respectable Islamic belief.[70] Willard Gaylin reminds us of the criticality of this task:

> The greater danger will always lie with those who would cynically manipulate and exploit . . . misery, those who would organize and encourage hatred for their political ends. We must attend to them, the preachers and organizers of hatred.[71]

The question now is: what modalities should the psywar campaign take to undermine the JI leadership and its Story? While some otherwise knowledgeable analysts argue that modern publishing, the Internet, and satellite television "are far more effective and influential conveyors of ideas than a few *pesantren*,"[72] one should not take this too far. Indonesian observers who are close to the Darul Islamist charismatic group of which the JI network remains an integral part caution that the Internet, although a good means of communicating ideas, is not yet that influential in Indonesia.[73] A major problem is a lack of efficient countrywide connectivity—access to affordable personal computers, Internet connections and devices, telephone lines, and modems. It was estimated that only 2.4 percent of the population had Internet access in 2004, and "[m]ost of these users are in the city of Jakarta or elsewhere on Java."[74] As such, observers argue for the greater efficacy of the "open house meeting" within the ranks of the Darul Islamist charismatic group itself. This is an important argument that we must now address.[75]

DEPLOYING THE "GOOD RADICALS" RATHER THAN THE "MODERATES" TO SPEAK TO THE "BAD RADICALS"

It has been suggested that cognitively immunizing the militants and activists who are part of the Darul Islamist charismatic group against the rabid vision and wanton targeting philosophy of either the mainstream JI or Noordin's faction—or even attempting to persuade active JI militants to give up their beliefs—cannot involve exposing them to the rhetorical blandishments of moderate Muslim scholars in Indonesia or from abroad. This may seem counterintuitive at first sight, as many analysts have been calling, particularly after September 11, 2001, for the "moderate Muslim" scholars to be empowered to speak up loudly and clearly.[76] At face value, this makes absolute sense. Many moderate Muslim scholars are extremely well versed in the 1,400-year-old tradition of Islamic scholarship dating back to the time of the Prophet and can run theological circles around most Islamists and Salafis, who are relative theological "amateurs" in the first case[77] or highly selective in their selection and interpretation of texts in the latter.[78] In the Indonesian milieu, the well-known moderate Muslim historian and scholar Professor Azyumardi Azra of Indonesia's top state Islamic tertiary institution, the State Islamic University (UIN) Syarif Hidayatullah Jakarta, is forthright in insisting that "it is time for moderate Muslim leaders to speak more clearly and loudly that a literal interpretation of Islam will only lead to an extremism that is unacceptable to Islam" and that "Islam can not condone, let alone justify, any kind of violent and terrorist act."[79] Azra has consistently maintained that "the moderate Muslim leaders and organizations are more than willing to rally behind" the Indonesian government in "opposition against any kind of religious extremism and radicalism." He insists that both the traditionalist Nahdlatual Ulama and modernist Muhammadiyah, the two largest and most influential Muslim mass organizations in Indonesia, have always maintained that "since the September 11, 2001 tragedy in the United States . . . Indonesian Islam cannot accept any kind of religious extremism."[80] Moderate Muslim scholars, it could be argued, should take a more aggressive public stance in discussing topics such as various understandings of *jihad*; ways to reconcile the obligations of dual citizenship in a national state as well as a trans-national *ummah*; and the challenges—and rewards—of practicing one's faith within a modern, secular, multireligious society. More nuanced public discussion of and clarification by progressive moderate scholars of the various interpretations of the important Darul Islam or House of Islam concept might also be helpful. As the renowned, if somewhat controversial, Egyptian-born, UK-based scholar Tariq Ramadan suggests, it is simply outdated to "consider

Europe and other 'non-Muslim' countries as lands of darkness, the *dar al-harb*, and therefore unsafe for Muslims."[81] Ramadan suggests that *ulama* and professionals should form national, regional, or international committees to discuss openly these and other questions.[82] A Javanese modernist organization such as Muhammadiyah seems especially well placed to promote what the Tunisian scholar Rachid Ghannoushi calls a "realistic fundamentalism" that seeks to reject a binary "us-versus-them" worldview, revive Islamic values in all spheres of life while grounding them in current realities, and celebrate the value of religious pluralism.[83]

Although on *prima facie* evidence, deploying the moderate scholars of Javanese and Indonesian Islam as well as well-known foreign scholars in the effort to cognitively immunize the rank and file of the Darul Islamist charismatic group makes complete good sense, in reality, and perhaps counterintuitively, it only augments the Existential Identity Anxiety of the latter. It should not be forgotten that from the Darul Islamist vantage point, the traditionalists of NU, and to a large extent even the modernists of Muhamadiyah represent competing, deep-rooted, and even adversarial subcultural Trees in the Garden of Indonesian Islam. The Darul Islamists, of which JI remains an inescapable part, would *never* want to engage seriously with the ideas of a traditionalist like Gus Dur, who believes in an Indonesianized Islam and who is deeply influenced by Sufi mysticism. Neither would they be very open to the intellectual blandishments of *santri* modernists like the late Nurcholish Madjid (also known as Cak Nur) for accepting and embracing religious pluralism in Indonesia. To committed Darul Islamists like Abu Bakar Ba'asyir, Mukhlas, and Imam Samudra, both Gus Dur and Cak Nur, giant intellectual icons of Javanese Islam, would be regarded with great suspicion, even scorn. The Darul Islam movement spokesman Al Chaidar, when asked to assess the value of moderate Muslim scholars in speaking to the Darul Islamist rank and file, including the JI militants, was scathing:

> Whenever Muhammadiyah or NU try to convey message to the Jemaah Islamiyah, the Jemaah Islamiyah person just keep laughing, what they are doing [sic], they are all will be in hell. . . . [84]

Chaidar considered that moderate scholars who are world famous, such as Azra, as well as other liberal Muslim scholars from the well-regarded Liberal Islam Network led by Ulil Abshar Abdalla, are, from the vantage point of the Darul Islamist charismatic group, a "bothering," a "rock in the shoes," and "not effective at all."[85] Tito Karnavian, a respected senior Densus 88 officer, confirmed to this writer in November 2007 that moderate Muslim scholars were, to the JI militants, regarded as "infidel," "*kafir*," and "working for the government."[86] Furthermore, Chaidar claimed that Darul Islam movement activists and JI militants consider "Muhammadiyah and NU" as even "worse than the Christian" interlocutors because the former are seen as *munafiq*, or hypocrites, who do not practice or promote a true Islam.[87] As for bringing in well-renowned moderate scholars from overseas, Chaidar cautioned that Islamic scholars from the United States would not be trusted ("this is the teacher of Cak Nur") or respected.[88] He pointed out that scholars from the Middle East, particularly Egypt, Jordan, and especially Yemen, would have more standing with Darul Islamist activists and JI rank and file. Interestingly, Chaidar added that Osama bin Laden aside, Saudi scholars would not be welcome, as "many of the JI and DI" considered "that Salafi is created by the Jews [sic]."[89]

Chaidar, who had been in direct contact with JI leaders like Noordin Top, Zulkarnaen, and others and was familiar with their thinking, argued instead that a much better approach would be to get ex–JI militants to talk to detained JI members and current Darul Islamist activists who may be tempted to take a detour down the JI road. A very good example of this approach is the use Indonesian police have made of Mohammed Nasir bin Abbas (Nasir Abbas), formerly JI Mantiqi 3 leader and brother-in-law of Mukhlas. Nasir, born in Singapore but a Malaysian national,[90] had been in one of the earliest batches sent out by Sungkar and Ba'asyir to Afghanistan in the mid-1980s. He became a trainer at Camp Saddah and taught later recruits such as Ali Imron and Imam Samudra. In the early 1990s, Nasir returned to Southeast Asia and was made Mantiqi 3 leader, in charge of the Philippines, where JI's training areas in Mindanao were located. Between 1993 and 1996, moreover, brokering an agreement with Moro Islamic Liberation Front (MILF) leader Hashim Salamat, an "old friend" of Sungkar, Nasir set up and ran Camp Hudaibiyah within the MILF Abubakar training complex in Mindanao. JI's Indonesian recruits cycled through Hudaibiyah for training in weapons, explosives, and regular and guerrilla warfare.[91] From the independent-minded Nasir's perspective, the rot set in the day he received a *fatwa* from Hambali and Ba'asyir that endorsed Osama bin Laden's February 1998 ruling authorizing the killing of American and Western non-combatants.[92] As Nasir later explained:

> I heard there was a decree brought down by Hambali that was passed to him by Abu Bakar Bashir. The decree was allegedly from Osama, urging Muslims to defend themselves from the Americans. The Americans had persecuted Muslims all over and had even killed the Muslims. The decree said it was alright to kill Americans even though they were not armed. We were also told that we could kill women and children and other civilians. The decree was given to all the Mantiqis.[93]

This decree forced the Mantiqi 3 leader into some serious soul-searching. He later admitted that he had "personally read a photocopy of the decree" and felt strongly that "something was not right." He consequently did not relay the decree to his Mantiqi 3 charges, thinking to himself that if it was "the American leadership that we are after," then why should JI "attack the innocent," which could well include Muslim civilians?[94] Nasir's qualms grew stronger after Hambali masterminded the Christmas Eve 2000 bombings. Nasir observed that "to me it was murder and I never understood the meaning of jihad in such acts, especially when civilians were the victims."[95] Subsequently, when the October 2002 Bali attacks were staged, Nasir was livid and made it clear within JI circles that "this was not the way. Jihad is not like that. It is about protecting Islam if it is under attack."[96] Against such a backdrop, when Nasir was arrested by the Indonesian police in April 2003, he had few qualms in turning against his former colleagues.[97] What helped from a legal perspective was that in comparison with other senior JI militants, Nasir had not been involved in the major attacks and was arrested for the relatively minor infraction of using a fake identity. In fact, in prison Nasir responded positively to the efforts of the Indonesian police to address his personal and family problems and decided to turn against his former comrades in the JI network. If he had chosen to go back to Malaysia, he would have been immediately detained without trial under the Malaysian Internal Security Act. It made more sense for him to remain in Indonesia and cooperate with the police.[98] Nasir's unique insights into and knowledge of the inner workings of the JI network were responsible, according to some reports, for almost half of the arrests that took place after the Bali bombings of 2002. He has also participated in talks aimed at debunking JI's Darul Islamist storyline on university campuses, at "selected pesantrens,"[99] and in prisons.[100] Nasir even wrote a book exposing JI for the terrorist organization that it is,[101] in which he debunked Imam Samudra's views that the Bali bombing of 2002 was a legitimate *jihad*.[102]

Certainly co-opting "Good" Radicals like the ex-JI militant Nasir Abbas has had merit. Within Darul Islamist and JI circles, a "hierarchy" of sorts exists, in which those seniors seen to have a good grasp of Arabic and "Islamic teachings" and "knowledge in military" affairs tend to be listened to and respected—something very much reinforced by the large power-distance orientation of Javanese culture more generally.[103] People like Nasir, precisely because they have been active in the network and know what they are talking about—and more importantly, will be *seen* to know what they are talking about—are very useful in warning youth from the traditional Darul Islamic heartlands, potential future Arnasans and Ali Imrons, perhaps, of the dangers of blindly treading down the JI path. This is not that new a departure either. Fifty years ago the British were employing surrendered senior CPM guerrillas, like the well-known State Committee Member Lam Swee, in precisely the role Nasir Abbas is playing now, with solid results among vulnerable rural Chinese.[104] When Nasir talks to JI militants already in prison, moreover, he reports that the "story of his detention and overnight conversion," which he presents as "a parable of pragmatism," seems to grab their attention[105] after initial suspicions are overcome.[106] The Indonesian police refer to this strategy of employing people like Nasir "to deradicalise junior members" as "creeping deradicalization."[107] Nasir has apparently successfully recruited to his cause other "respected" detained senior JI militants such as Ali Imron and Mubarok—both of whom were involved in the 2002 Bali bombing and had military experience in Afghanistan and thus possess the requisite "street cred" among Darul Islamists more generally and the younger JI militants in particular.[108] The three of them have sought to wean away from the JI ideological sway "prisoners," "ex-prisoners," and "potential" JI recruits, particularly "those trained in Afghanistan and Mindanao."[109] For instance, a meeting was held just outside Jakarta not long ago in which Nasir, Imron, and Mubarok invited forty JI members for a police-facilitated debate on their struggle. A very encouraging thirty-eight of the forty invitees turned up, and in addition to providing the police with the valuable opportunity to gain insights into the Darul Islamism of these JI men, it also, importantly, provided the latter with the chance to see that the police officers were not quite the disembodied, abstract "evil troops" of the secular, un-Islamic Indonesian government, as their ideology had taught them to believe. Furthermore, the invitees engaged with Nasir, Imron, and Mubarok on how JI's worldview contradicted basic tenets of the Qu'ran and the Hadith literature and how the 2003 J. W. Marriott and 2004 Australian Jakarta embassy attacks had killed Muslims—apparently a potent line of attack. The upshot of the meeting was that at the very least, the JI invitees, while still committed to pursuing a *shariah*-based Indonesian State, appeared persuaded that nonviolent means were superior to violent approaches.[110]

There are limitations, however. Nasir is unlikely to make much headway with the JI hard-core, both within and outside prison. His attempts to persuade the incarcerated Mukhlas, incidentally his brother-in-law, that "killing unarmed civilians" is a "shameful thing" and "not jihad in Islam," was rebutted by the latter, who countered that "America killed our civilians in Chechnya and Afghanistan" and "we are taking revenge on them."[111] Both men "ended up shouting at each other."[112] In addition, hard-core JI militants still at large tend to view Nasir as a "traitor" and "infidel"[113]— not least because Nasir is seen as "too close to the government" and a "co-opted person"[114]—and rather than being effective in winning them over, he is likely to be harmed by them, given half the chance. In fact, he has to move around under police protection for fear of precisely such reprisals. Whereas the police do not wish for Nasir to speak at Pondok Pesantren Al-Mukmin, which is seen as a "JI base,"[115] more dangerously, Noordin Top is apparently out to eliminate Nasir.[116] This fact of being seen as a "traitor" has been shrewdly used by the Indonesian police to encourage Nasir to work harder in attracting more militants away from JI, thereby dividing and further weakening the network.[117] It would help, Chaidar noted, if the Indonesian broadcast media knew how to make better use of Nasir's talents by eschewing overly long questions and and not cutting him off before he even made his points.[118] Moreover, Nasir's efforts at creeping deradicalization are effective to the extent that they are also accompanied, as Sidney Jones points out, by "police economic assistance" to detainee families.[119]

In addition to engaging senior ex-JI militants like Nasir Abbas in "creeping deradicalization" efforts, a variant of the co-opting the "Good Radicals" approach that has been suggested by insiders such as Chaidar is the promotion of internal dialogue within the Darul Islamist charismatic group, particularly between its DI and JI elements. Chaidar observed in January 2006 that the old Darul Islam political movement is heavily splintered into about eighteen factions, of which fifteen are nonviolent and three are violent. JI, he asserted, recruits its foot soldiers, including its suicide bombers, from the violent DI factions.[120] He informed this writer that "many of the DI people have been recruited by Noordin Top."[121] Chaidar pointed out that the international community should not overlook the potential of the nonviolent factions of DI in deradicalization efforts because "they are the only group who stand against or resist against the Jemaah Islamiyah and only them [sic] could communicate in the same language"; hence "whenever the Darul Islam people talk," JI militants "will hear, they will listen."[122] Chaidar told the present writer that the main problem with the JI militants is that they "have not many places for intellectual exercise" and "contemplation time."[123] To rectify this, Chaidar suggested that the DI could be asked to organize what he called a "critical workshop" in the form of an "open house meeting" to enable JI and DI members to discuss "sensitive issues" and hear "alternative" perspectives on these matters. As Chaidar put it:

> We just open the discourse, we just open a kind of discussion of everything and let them talk. And let all the people give feedback, just like that and then it will become a kind of dialogue. It's as simple as that.[124]

Chaidar suggested that topics to be discussed at such internal dialogues could range from, *inter alia*, issues such as the ability of Muslims to practice their faith in a secular political system and not an Islamic State; the status of non-Muslims in an Islamic State; the meaning of *jihad*; "the next jihad"; "what is the future war of Muslims"; Islamic solutions to Indonesia's current crisis; and even "how to overcome the terrorism" threat.[125] Chaidar's point is that the JI militants simply need more opportunities to open up their intellectual horizons somewhat and break out of the extremely violent, dehumanizing, binary worldview fostered by the JI variety of Darul Islamism. The overriding aim of such internal "critical workshops" within the Darul Islamist charismatic group would be to draw back the JI individual from a "terrorist" who uses violence all the time to a DI "radical" who uses violence in a more restrained fashion, under "certain conditions" that are "specific."[126] The idea would be to "domesticate the radical, the terrorist or new recruit person of the JI."[127] Chaidar pointed out that the fifteen nonviolent factions of DI do not buy into the Global Salafi Jihad–influenced JI storyline that the Muslim world is now at war with America and the West or, as Osama bin Laden argues in the February 1998 *fatwa* that influenced Hambali, that Western civilians are legitimate targets of *jihad*. Instead, the nonviolent DI factions have indicated that DI members can only take up arms when their Imams declare war, and even when that happens, strict limits on targeting are to be observed: only combatants should be killed, not non-combatants like women and children.[128] Nasir Abbas's views on *jihad* are to some extent in the mold of the nonviolent DI factions: it is not that armed *jihad* is not permissible under any circumstances, but that it is, although under certain strict conditions, such as "on the battlefield in defence of Islam," and that civilians should not be targeted. When asked in a May 2007 interview if, had the Al Qaeda *fatwa* not emerged, he still would have been part of the JI network, "training soldiers to go to kill the infidels somewhere in the world," Nasir freely—and tellingly—admitted: "I think so, yeah."[129]

Nasir's comment is pungent with significance about the limitations of the "Co-opting the Good Radicals" approach. He—and for that matter the nonviolent DI factions—has not eschewed armed *jihad* but merely recognizes restraints on its implementation. The right to employ armed violence in pursuit of the Islamic State in Indonesia—the historic goal of the old Darul Islam movement, a.k.a. the Darul Islamist charismatic group—remains a potential instrument to be employed at the "right time," "the proper time," against "America or against the government of the Republic of Indonesia."[130] It is thus very important to recognize that meetings where the "Good Radicals" engage the "Bad Radicals" in debate, even if successful in compelling JI militants to rethink their position on *jihad*, are purely *palliative* in nature. Although Nasir Abbas may be sincere in his "mission," whenever he meets potential JI recruits, "to open their minds," there are limits as to how far the mental opening can go.[131] There is every possibility, after all, that given some future concatenation of events and circumstances, JI militants would quite simply resume their violent ways—perhaps even joined by their DI cousins, should their leaders decide to declare hostilities. The real problem is that the Darul Islamist charismatic group—which includes Nasir Abbas and the nonviolent DI factions mentioned by Chaidar—remain "radical in their heads"; that is, to varying degrees they think, feel, and act in accordance with the stock us-versus-them, good-versus-evil, Darul Islamist worldview that makes them all—to differing extents, to be sure—walking time-bombs. The Co-opting the "Good" Radical option not only does not even remotely begin to address this latent problem, but it is powerless to prevent future cohorts of young Muslims from not merely the Darul Islamist charismatic group, but also the wider Darul Islamic strongholds in Java, from being socialized within various ideological spaces into the binary, black-and-white world of Darul Islamism of either the DI or the rabid, even more violent JI variety. Employing co-opted Good Radicals in a creeping deradicalization exercise represents simply *ideological containment*; the strategy encourages the acceptance of restraints on armed *jihad* or better, nonviolent paths toward the goal of an Islamic State in Indonesia. This begs the larger question, however, of whether even nonviolent approaches to an Islamic State can be seen as optimal from the perspective of non-Muslims. As the earlier analysis of the ostensibly nonviolent Ba'asyir's binary worldview shows, the answer is no, because of the deeply rooted, xenophobic us-versus-them dynamic that would almost certainly animate an Islamic regime based on Darul Islamist principles. This would be unsurprising, given the *strong uncertainty-avoidance cultural outlook* that Arabized modernism especially has bequeathed to Darul Islamism itself. The upshot of all this is simple: dealing with the root problem of the strong uncertainty-avoidance orientation at the core of Darul Islamism is beyond the purview of short-term, primary cognitive immunization efforts. It instead requires complementary, longer-range, secondary cognitive immunization measures, directed not only at the Darul Islamist charismatic group, but especially at the wider Darul Islamic subculture in Java. The aim must be to reduce the longer-term cognitive vulnerability of young Javanese men—future Ali Imrons, if you like—to the virulent Darul Islamist view of the world. The stock solution is to encourage critical thought aimed at opening up their worldviews through various modalities that we shall now address.

SECONDARY COGNITIVE IMMUNIZATION

Promoting a Face-to-Face Dialogue of "Humankinds"

As noted previously, one should make a distinction between the *pesantren*, religious boarding schools linked with the traditionalists of NU, and the *madrasah* or Islamic religious schools usually associated with the modernist Muhammadiyah. While in the past, the *pesantren* used to be located in rural areas, today they are increasingly established in the urban centers. Furthermore, the *pesantren* have moved out of the Java heartlands and spread to Sumatra, Kalimantan, Sulawesi, and other islands. Today's *pesantren* are no longer merely centers of Islamic education, but also provide instruction in some secular subjects, similar to *madrasah*. *Pesantren* even provide vocational training up to university level, while, as Azyumardi Azra points out, conducting "programs and activities related to economic development, social welfare, appropriate technologies for rural area, etc."[132] Since the 1980s, moreover, large numbers of new Islamic schools and *madrasah*, such as the Sekolah Islam al-Azhar, SMU[133] Madania, and SMU al-Izhar, have been set up and have won public acclaim as "*sekolah Islam unggulan*" (quality Islamic schools). These tend to be attended mostly by children of the Muslim elite. In addition, Azra notes that, nowadays, nongovernmental organizations (NGOs) and the so-called *Majlis Ta'lim,* or religious group discussions in offices and society at large, are additional ways progressive Islamic teaching gets disseminated.[134] Thanks to the 1989 Indonesian Educational Law, moreover, the standards of instruction in both the *madrasah* and *pesantren* networks have been required to be equivalent to those of the "secular schools" and must employ the national curricula issued by the Ministries of National Education and of Religious Affairs. Azra is adamant that it "is inaccurate to assume that the *madrasah*s and *pesantren*s have their own curriculum" that would "allow them to teach subjects according to the whims of their teachers or the foundations that own them."[135] Nevertheless, the fact remains that there *are* outliers that do not fit neatly into this rather rosy picture. Room was left in the 1989 legislation, as Farish Noor tells us, for "private Islamic education to be provided by non-state agencies."[136] As part of this development, what Greg Fealy and Anthony Bubalo refer to as "radical jihadist *pesantren,*" very small in number, have emerged, constituting "less than one percent of the more than 30,000 *pesantren*" that dot the Indonesian archipelago.[137]

Included in this small number, as we have seen, are the deliberately cloistered ideological spaces of Darul Islamism located within the compounds of Pondok Pesantren Al-Mukmin and Pondok Pesantren Al-Islam in Indonesia. As we saw in Chapter Three, an ideological space need not actually be the entire institution; certainly in the complex case of Al Mukmin, it seems that "a pattern of close-knit cells or circles of students and teachers" within the wider institution constituted the Darul Islamist space.[138] For that matter, ideological spaces existed across the Melaka Strait in neighboring Malaysia as well, in the remote Luqmanul Hakiem *pesantren* in Ulu Tiram in Johore State, and to an extent in the secluded kampong in Sungai Manggis in Selangor State, where Hambali and Ba'asyir were neighbors. Within such spaces, some people from the Darul Islamic heartlands of Java had their amorphous Darul Islamic beliefs and sentiments "intensified and focused" into the consciously held political ideology of Darul Islamism. Because of cult-like psychological processes working within such ideological spaces within relatively remote environments, critical, independent thought was not encouraged in the process of manufacturing the common Darul Islamist group mind. As the specific case of Ali Imron shows, suspension of one's critical faculties can lead to disastrous consequences. A major consequence of a lack of critical, independent thought within such hermetically sealed-off ideological spaces within *pesantren* such as Al-Mukmin and Al-Islam is that the normal ethnocentrism of its students—as we have seen, a legacy of Existential Identity—tends to develop over time into extreme categorical thinking toward outsiders. Whether they are Christians, Americans, Australians, or Jews, they tend to be abstracted, denuded of any notion of humanity, and stereotyped. This sort of black-and-white, us-versus-them, binary worldview structures and underlies Darul Islamist ideology, which dehumanizes non-Muslims and using subtle operant conditioning processes[139] consigns them to a state of social death—a situation that in some cases lubricates the slide toward atrocities such as genocide and mass-casualty terrorism. If the amorphous cultural prejudices extant in a society are strong—that is, if there is a strong uncertainty-avoidance outlook in that culture—the resulting xenophobia and prejudices toward outsiders could well be exploited down the road by hate-entrepreneurs for nefarious purposes. The Dutch-Somali activist Ayaan Hirsi Ali, reflecting on her youth in Saudi Arabia, provides a telling illustration of how the strong uncertainty avoidance of the Saudi culture results in a rabid anti-Semitism:

> In Saudi Arabia, everything bad was the fault of the Jews. When the air conditioner broke or suddenly the tap stopped running, the Saudi women next door used to say the Jews did it. The children next door were taught to pray for the health of their parents and the destruction of the Jews. Later, when we went to school, our teachers lamented at length all the evil things Jews had done and planned to do against Muslims.[140]

The curious thing was that at the time, the young Ayaan had *never met a Jew* and neither had her young Saudi classmates.[141] It is not prohibitively hard to imagine how such abstract, categorical thinking, when developed at an early age and sharpened and deepened at school and in a wider community of prejudice, can later render an individual susceptible to destructive worldviews and ideologies such as Global Salafi Jihad and Darul Islamism.

This is precisely why *structured, face-to-face interfaith activities* are important. The aim of these events should not be to create a meaningless talking shop for moderate Muslim leaders to meet and engage with non-Muslim counterparts. Fealy and Bubalo are correct in asserting that beyond a symbolic value, little would be attained, as those from both sides who attend would tend to believe in the idea of interfaith meetings anyway.[142] Instead, the aim of structured, face-to-face interfaith activity in the Indonesian context must be to provide opportunities for the Darul Islamist charismatic group, as well as young people—especially *pesantren* and university students—from the Darul Islamic heartlands of Java, to enjoy meaningful face-to-face interaction with different "humankinds,"[143] and to expose them to a wider world of *difference*. The idea would simply be to *open up the worldview*[144] of these young people, break the cognitive filters imposed by inchoate Darul Islamic prejudices or more consciously held Darul Islamist ideology, and expose them to the shared flesh-and-blood humanity of non-Muslims. In Dave Grossman's terms, such meetings would help reduce "cultural distance," and over time, as the sense of a common humanity steadily increases, help reduce the "moral distance" that infuses the devaluation of non-Muslims as well.[145] The Darul Islam movement spokesman, Al Chaidar, himself noted that simply providing structured opportunities for face-to-face interaction with Christians and discussing the topics of "love" and "peace" would be more educational for JI militants than getting them to meet high-profile Indonesian traditionalist and modernist scholars.[146] Opening up the worldviews of not only the organized DI and JI factions, but also of young people from the historic Javanese constituencies of the Darul Islam movement to the rich diversity of humankind outside Java and Indonesia may be helpful. In particular, focused, face-to-face interfaith activities could lead over time to greater mutual "respect and understanding."[147] A recent Commonwealth Commission Report shed some useful light on what is meant by "respect":

> [R]espect is about acknowledging a common humanity, and a preparedness to treat everyone, no matter how different their world views, with the dignity they deserve because of their humanity.... There is an important distinction to make between respecting persons (and their right to hold their own views) and indiscriminately respecting what they believe in or how they behave. *We can show respect for others without agreeing with their particular doctrines or their actions* [italics added].[148]

Furthermore, "understanding does not necessarily involve agreement with the views or beliefs others hold."[149] Rather:

> Understanding implies an ability to grasp what someone else is saying in order to get to the heart of what they are trying to communicate. To do this requires a willingness to put aside one's own preconceived notions in order to appreciate their world view. *Understanding, therefore, involves the acknowledgement that one's own culture and experience are not the only models for thinking and acting* [italics added].[150]

Intergroup respect and understanding—by acknowledging identity-group differences while simultaneously accepting the reality of a wider common, basic and irreducible humanity—has two strategic benefits. First, it could play a role in dampening Existential Identity Anxiety—the primal animating force at the heart of religious radicalization. After all, if essential identities and boundaries are seen by identity group members to be respected, then a collective visceral fear of imminent group extinction is unlikely to gestate. Second, this in turn creates conditions for reaching out meaningfully across identity-group boundaries. Although the structural forces of history and geopolitics have stabilized the boundaries between the great monotheistic faiths, it does not at all follow that cross-boundary cooperation is impossible. In other words, people need not be forever pigeonholed into "Christians," "Muslims," or "Jews" with no possibility of commingling, sometimes profoundly, across faith and other humankind lines. Nobel Laureate Amartya Sen, the chairperson of the Commonwealth Commission whose Report is already cited, has in this regard rejected reductionist, "solitarist" views of "human identity," arguing instead that the latter has an "inescapable plurality."[151] Ordinary people, cross-culturally worldwide, can and do quite spontaneously cycle through different "humankinds," sometimes even on a daily basis, depending on environmental stimuli and demands.[152] As Sen explains:

> The same person can, for example, be a British citizen, of Malaysian origin, with Chinese racial characteristics, a stockbroker, a nonvegetarian, an asthmatic, a linguist, a bodybuilder, a poet, an opponent of abortion, a bird-watcher, an astrologer, and one who believes that God created Darwin to test the gullible.[153]

Sen's point is that "we do belong to many different groups, in one way or another, and each of these collectivities can give a person a potentially important identity."[154] What we must do is exercise reason and choice to "decide whether a particular group to which we belong is—or is not—important for us."[155] Michael Ignatieff, who followed the Balkan Wars of the 1990s closely, agrees that it is vitally important for individuals in zones wracked by identity-based conflict to "fly free of the nets of nationality, religion and language" and to "force a separation between what the tribe told you to be and what you truly are."[156] The question has to be asked: do the arguments of Sen and Ignatieff for individual human beings to take ownership of their identity make sense in the context of the current discussion? As discussed in the first chapter, Existential Identity concerns prompt each individual to seek psychic refuge within a stable, high-prestige Group Tent to shore up his own self-esteem. Moreover, in the Indonesian context, Javanese Culture reflects both collectivist and large power-distance dimensions. The impact of these two sets of factors would suggest that within the Darul Islamic heartlands of Java, the scope for individual agency in determining personal identity is severely curtailed. What the elders, *kyai*, and Imams lay down as the "correct" path for group and by inference personal success would be followed. On the one hand, however, as we saw in the case of Hambali in the previous chapter, "internals," that is, individuals who possess an internal locus of control, even if they are born into a collectivist culture where hierarchy and harmony are valued and the opinion of seniors and elders prevails, can and do buck the trend and carve out customized personal identities and life trajectories for themselves.[157] Moreover, while both Hofstede[158] and Sen[159] suggest that cultural factors are important but never deterministic, identity group boundaries, while basic and important, are not necessarily ossified either.

Social psychological research confirms this fact. In 1954, twenty-two normal eleven-year-old boys with similar cultural, physical, and status backgrounds took part in a three-week study conducted by the renowned Turkish-American social psychologist Muzafer Sherif in Robbers Cave, Oklahoma. The boys, on arrival, were randomly assigned to two different groups who were then sent to separate cabins. The cabins were far apart from each other so as to reduce intergroup contact and promote bonding within each separate group. Over the course of a week, each of these two groups developed a distinct subcultural identity and appointed a leader. One group called itself the Rattlers and the other, the Eagles. Sherif and his team then pitted the two groups against each other in deliberately contrived, zero-sum activities, such that "one group's gain was always the other group's loss."[160] Very quickly, strong feelings of hostility developed between the Rattlers and the Eagles. It got so bad that the members of both groups could not even enjoy a "benign noncompetitive activity" like watching a movie without name-calling and fighting breaking out.[161] The famous Robbers Cave experiment, as Berreby informs us, show that "what shaped each boy's tribal sense" was not "what he *was*, but what he was *doing*."[162] In other words, social group boundaries need not be based on supposedly immutable *ascribed* identities such as religion but could also coalesce as a response to the *prevailing situation*. In 1963, the social psychologist Lutfy N. Diab conducted an experiment based on Sherif's Robbers Cave experiment, this time with eleven-year-old boys in Beirut. Eight were Christians and ten were Muslims. Berreby recounts:

> Not surprisingly, given the historic tensions in Lebanon, fighting broke out between the two teams of campers, the Blue Ghosts and the Red Genies. After three Genies threatened a Blue Ghost with knives stolen from the camp kitchen, Diab decided he had to break up the camp.[163]

As Berreby observes, though, the fighting was *not* along religious lines:

> The Blue Ghosts consisted of five Muslims and four Christians; so did the Red Genies. The three Genies with the knives were all Christians, but so was their Blue Ghost victim.

Berreby adds that fourteen of the eighteen campers "had come from fiercely religious schools," and in the camp, "separated from the outside world," they could quite "easily have chosen to see themselves as Christian versus Muslim." Instead, they chose the socially constructed humankind categories "Ghost versus Genie."[164]

What this suggests is that structured activities, in which young Javanese Muslims from historic Darul Islamic communities and non-Muslims work together in *mixed-faith groups* on common tasks, could produce revealing results. The Commonwealth Commission Report cited earlier backs this claim:

> Social psychologists confirm what common sense suggests: *people who work together when young in circumstances of equality and mutual dependence across races, religions and ethnicities, tend to be less prejudiced than those who do not.* Similarly, in the area of employment, integrating government workplaces and enforcing anti-discrimination laws in the private sector can lead to developing cross-group linkages outside the workplace [italics added].[165]

The Report adds that "encouraging young people not only to study together but to play sports, engage in community activities, make music, and otherwise work together across groups" can all open up worldviews and foster intergroup respect and understanding.[166] Berreby nails the point elegantly in asserting that "there are circumstances in which face-to-face experience with people overcomes doctrines about our bonds to people we never met."[167] Social psychologist James Waller agrees and explains at length why structured, face-to-face, cross-faith activity clearly evinces the "power of personalization":

> *Humanizing, decategorizing, or personalizing others all create a powerful self-restraining effect.* It is difficult to mistreat a person who has an actual identity, with flesh and blood and family, without suffering a significant level of personal distress and self-condemnation. . . . [The] power of personalization [can] counteract cruel conduct and . . . promote a strong sense of social obligation [italics added].[168]

Berreby gives a further good example of the importance of *face-to-face contact* between people of different faiths. In 1481, a Jewish rabbi recorded in his diary that he met a group of Christians on a ship from Palestine to Italy. The only shared "humankind" they had was the fact that were all literally in the same boat as passengers en route to Italy. The rabbi got to know the Christians, who assumed he was a Christian merchant. "But after they heard that I was a Jew, they were much astounded, but still, because of their former love for me they could not change their attitude."[169] In short, face-to-face interaction between the Christians and this Jewish rabbi enabled the former to transcend whatever existing biased stereotypes they had toward Jews and instead feel respect and act upon a shared humanity. In sum, if we accept that young people from the Javanese districts and villages that were base areas for Kartosoewirjo's Darul Islam movement or from families whose relatives had fought with the DI and who may have contemporary kinship and personal but not necessarily institutional links with the JI network are susceptible to the "radical jihadist" sentiments encoded in Darul Islamist ideology, then creating opportunities for them to participate in regular, structured, face-to-face interfaith meetings, dialogues, and cooperative activities may not be a bad idea. Certainly, the Indonesian government is not new to the idea of interfaith dialogue, as it hosted the Bali Interfaith Dialogue within the multilateral framework of the Asia-Europe Meeting (ASEM) in July 2005. The resultant Bali Declaration on Building Interfaith Harmony within the International Community called for, *inter alia*, promoting "cross-cultural awareness and understanding at all levels of society, particularly among the young."[170] Moreover, the Second Asia-Europe Youth Interfaith Dialogue, part of the ASEM Youth Dialogue series, was scheduled to be held in Lembang, West Java, in June 2008. This was co-organized with the Indonesian Ministry of Foreign Affairs, the Ministry of Religious Affairs and Youth, and the NU Central Board.[171] Nevertheless, recent online activity among Indonesian youth suggests that much more needs to be done to decrease "radical violence" through promoting respect and understanding between Indonesian Muslims and Christians, especially through education.[172]

In sum, promoting face-to-face dialogue of "humankinds"—to employ Berreby's apt phrase—could well be one of the best ways over time to gradually erode the *strong uncertainty-avoidance orientation* that so well characterizes the collective mental programming of the wider subculture, the Hofstedean Bouquet, so to speak, of Darul Islam. In other words, gradually, young people from this particular subculture may come to see that what is different, as Hofstede well may put it, is not necessarily dangerous.[173] The end result would be well worth it: cognitive immunization against the internalization and personalization of Darul Islamist narratives of Jews, Crusaders, and their *kuffar* allies in both the government and society of Indonesia out to destroy Islam. The religious scholar William Sloane Coffin:

> *What is intolerable is for difference to become idolatrous....* No human being's identity is exhausted by his or her gender, race, ethnic origin, or national loyalty. Human beings are fully human only when they find the universal in the particular, when the [sic] recognize that *all people have more in common than they have in conflict....* Human rights are more important than the politics of identity, and *religious people should be notorious boundary crossers* [italics added].[174]

Through frequent interfaith boundary crossings and structured face-to-face interactions over time, vulnerable young people in the Darul Islamic heartlands of Java can somewhat soften if not "alter who is a 'we' and who is a 'they'"—and in doing so, "undermine a contributing force to the social death" of outsiders[175]—a slippery slope that often leads to atrocities like Bali.

Toward an Integrated U.S. Public Diplomacy Effort

Because the "US terrorists and their allies" seem to be the stock enemy identified in JI's post-Afghan *jihad* Darul Islamist ideology, exemplified by the fact that JI had struck Bali attempting to kill American civilians, it could be suggested that a major secondary cognitive immunization initiative would have to be enhanced U.S. public diplomacy efforts. These could be stepped up to counter misleading stereotypes about America and the West—stereotypes that boost JI recruitment and reinforce the kind of "limbically" driven primitive thinking that fuels disastrous terrorist attacks against Western targets in Indonesia and Southeast Asia. That the United States has a serious image problem in a big Muslim country like Indonesia is pretty much incontestable. A June 2003 Pew survey found that an overwhelming 83 percent of Indonesian Muslims—mainly relatively laid-back *abangan* Muslims—had an unfavorable impression of the United States.[176] More recent Pew Global Attitudes surveys find that Indonesian Muslim attitudes toward "the US and American foreign policy also tend to be quite negative."[177] This image of the United States as duplicitous explains why some Indonesian Muslims believed that the Central Intelligence Agency (CIA) was behind both the September 11, 2001, World Trade Center attack as well as the Bali blasts of October 12, 2002.[178] Similarly, following the Jakarta Marriott bombing of August 2003, a number of Indonesians believed that the CIA again perpetrated the attack, inventing the supposedly fictitious JI organization to mask the real U.S. aim of discrediting Islam, destabilizing Indonesia, and taking control of the country.[179] Among many average Indonesian university students, ever since the U.S. invasion of Iraq in March 2003, there has been "growing acceptance" of the notion that the Islamic world is under attack by Western forces such as the United States and, crucially, "must be defended—with violence if necessary."[180] A recent 2007 Pew survey found that Indonesian Muslims, along with Muslims in other countries, actually felt that the "United States could become a military threat to their country someday."[181] Certainly, the Bush administration identified the need for boosting its global public image among Muslims early on. Hence following the invasion of Iraq in March 2003, Washington tried to ensure that its public diplomacy highlighted in great detail how America has genuinely helped alleviate the plight of Muslims in Bosnia, Afghanistan, and now Iraq.[182] There have been missteps, though. A U.S.$15-million public relations campaign, sponsored by the State Department and produced by the advertising firm McCann-Erickson, showcased the lives of Muslims in America—but featured no Southeast Asian Muslims. This had the unintended effect of making Indonesian Muslims watching the advertisements upset that the State Department appeared to believe that "Muslims only lived in Arab countries and only those Muslims migrated to the United States."[183] In the years following her appointment in 2005, Karen Hughes, a longtime Bush confidante and Undersecretary of State for Public Diplomacy and Public Affairs, doubled the U.S. public diplomacy budget to about U.S.$900 million annually, sent Arabic speakers to do a large number of interviews with Arab media, and inaugurated a number of programs to boost the U.S. image with the world's Muslims. However, when she left office at the end of 2007, she acknowledged that polls had not shown any improvement in the world's view of the United States, and in Indonesia itself, the continuing Iraq imbroglio had contributed to 70 percent of Indonesians having an unfavorable view of Washington. Hughes pointed to the widespread negative reactions to the intervention in Iraq and the Israel-Palestinian conflict as key problems, but another point she made, which tends to be overlooked but has very important implications for cognitive immunization efforts worldwide and certainly in Indonesia, is that Iraqi civilian casualties at the hands of U.S. forces or private security contractors constituted "negative events" that "never help," either.[184] In other words, public diplomacy must involve a positive *integration* of rhetoric and actual deeds on the ground. This requires elaboration.

Hughes was referring to the incident in September 2007 in which the prominent private security contractor Blackwater, which deployed at the time an estimated 1,000 personnel in Iraq and enjoyed U.S.$800 million in government contracts, killed eight Iraqi civilians in a Baghdad firefight after a convoy of its personnel came under fire. The problem was that this was not an isolated case and that Blackwater personnel had been involved in previous incidents resulting in the deaths of Iraqis, and this, together with its general aggressive posture toward the population, had generated a strong sense of resentment on the part of ordinary Iraqis that as private contractors and not regular U.S. troops, they were somehow above the law.[185] In making reference to the Blackwater episode, Hughes was likely arguing that dealing with the technical and political challenges of getting the U.S. public diplomacy machinery in order was only one aspect of the problem. She had a point. Washington officials need to recognize that they could very well undercut their own finely honed and technically brilliant public diplomacy message by inadvertently generating "political oxygen" that could be exploited by radical Islamists worldwide for propaganda purposes. Such political oxygen is generated every single time an air strike or military operation accidentally kills, injures, or brutalizes Afghan or Iraqi civilians. Thanks to near-instantaneous transmission of such errors worldwide through the likes of especially Al-Jazeera and the Internet, such political oxygen only helps radical Islamist networks—such as JI in Indonesia—sustain the rabid anti-Americanism at the core of radical Islamist ideology. We have seen how Imam Samudra, for example, had justified the Bali attacks as revenge for the crimes of the "American terrorists and their allies" against innocent Muslim civilians in Afghanistan and have heard his refrain, common to all radical Islamist militants, that the blood of Muslims is not cheap.[186] The Darul Islam movement spokesperson, Al Chaidar, moreover informed this writer that both JI and their DI cousins think "very much" about the U.S. interventions in Iraq and Afghanistan. The extent to which the Iraq war is *personalized* in DI and possibly even more so in JI circles was exposed when Chaidar recounted the following about a friend of his, "a Darul Islam person":

> [He] was praying at that time and mentioning something to the god. And he is crying very much for that moment, mentioning many time about the . . . situation in Iraq; please save the mujahideen in Iraq and please give more power to the mujahideen and please send your own mujahideen from Heaven to be on the earth of Iraq [sic].[187]

Unfortunately, that the political importance of calibrating military force in the highly globalized, ventilated Iraqi theater of operations does not appear widely appreciated is attested to by the fact that private security contractors aside, regular U.S. commanders do not seem to have trained their troops to cope well with threats in an urban environment where civilians are relatively plentiful.[188] In general, the use of firepower in military operations does not seem to have been adequately calibrated so that "collateral damage" is greatly minimized. Rather, the penchant of U.S. commanders for operational war-fighting employing high technology and massive firepower in operations appears to have been carried over from Vietnam.[189] This operational war-fighting focus has led to considerable civilian casualties—a case in point being the U.S. military's notorious Fallujah campaign of 2004 that resulted in 600 Iraqi civilian deaths and the virtual "Talibanization" of the city thereafter.[190]

Compounding matters and playing right into the hands of radical Islamist propagandists everywhere have been the insensitive attitudes and behavior of U.S. forces toward Iraqi civilians. While some formations like the Marine and Airborne units have made the effort to treat the locals with respect, others, such as the 4th Infantry Division, have tended to abuse, break into the homes of, and intimidate Muslim civilians in ways that only fuelled the insurgency. Much seems to have depended on the personality of individual commanders.[191] Joshua Key, a U.S. army deserter from the 3rd Armored Cavalry Regiment, complained that the physical and psychological stresses of operating in a counterinsurgency environment where the enemy was not easily detected was made even worse because his commanders encouraged the troops to deal with their frustrations by "constantly" reminding them "that all Iraqis were our enemies, civilians included."[192] This created a general climate of permissiveness in which "it was tempting to steal, no big deal to punch, and easy to kill."[193] The general attitude was that: "We were Americans in Iraq and we could do anything we wanted to do."[194] Such attitudes probably help explain the infamous 2004 Abu Ghraib prison scandal in which Iraqi prisoners were subjected to "sadistic, blatant and wanton criminal abuses" at the hands of their U.S. military captors.[195] It should be evident that in the age of the camera phone, satellite television, and the Internet, such attitudes and behavior can no longer be hidden but are transmitted across Iraq and for that matter worldwide near-instantaneously. They can hence serve as a godsend not just to Iraqi insurgents but also to JI recruiters in Java in their quest to point out to future Amrozis, Ali Imrons, and Arnasans some new American perfidy against innocent Muslim women and children. United States commanders should note the example of 1950s Malaya, where the police and military were told to employ "minimum force" as well as be more "propaganda-minded" in their everyday dealings with the strategic rural Chinese community so as to gradually wean them away from the Communist Party of Malaya (CPM) guerrillas.[196] Put differently, precisely because radical Islamist networks like JI emphasize the notion that "the blood of Muslims is not cheap" as a means of generating the kind of primitive thinking among angry young Muslims that can fuel terrorist atrocities against Western civilians, counterinsurgency and counter-terrorist operations must always be guided by the minimum force principle.[197] It is heartening, at least in this respect, that the Indonesian police—in particular the crack Densus 88 unit—have understood that in counter-terrorist operations, "any use of force must be controllable, measurable and accounted for," and that "any mistake of the government, such as excessive force, can be capitalized by terrorists to gain support."[198] It cannot be overstated: because the JI version of Darul Islamism sees the United States and the West as enemies, and not only the secular Indonesian government, it is imperative that the U.S. military take a leaf from their current Indonesian police counterparts or study the Malayan example on the political importance of minimum force in the utterly ventilated counterinsurgency campaigns in Iraq and Afghanistan. If the United States fails to do so, this will further reinforce the Darul Islamist "Story" of, as Samudra put it, the "US army of the Cross and its allies" hell-bent on subjugating and brutalizing the Muslim world—it was such a narrative that helped pave the way to the massive Western civilian casualties in Bali.[199] Recently, some attempt to reform U.S. counterinsurgency tactics has been evident, fortunately.[200]

This is not to imply that effective and nuanced public diplomacy campaigns are not needed. They do play a significant role in promoting the genuinely positive impact the United States is making on the world in general and in Indonesia in particular—such as the well-received humanitarian relief efforts following the devastating Indian Ocean tsunami of December 26, 2004.[201] Unfortunately, it must be conceded that even if public diplomacy efforts are buttressed by more "propaganda-minded" and calibrated military operations in Iraq and Afghanistan, it would be unwise to place too much reliance on the enhanced public diplomacy card. The true political value of strong and effective U.S. public diplomacy is really to render the pro–United States tilt of President Susilo Bambang Yudhoyono more palatable to his nationalistic secular republican constituencies while hardening his flanks against attacks from the Indonesian parliamentary Islamists. It should be reiterated that U.S. public diplomacy efforts, no matter how enhanced, can never "win" the hearts and minds of the religiously observant Javanese Muslim masses, especially those from the Darul Islamic heartlands of Java. What is relatively more achievable, rather, is the less ambitious goal of cognitive immunization—preventing the personalization and internalization of virulent Darul Islamist narratives of the type spun by Ba'asyir and Imam Samudra. What concerns elders and *kyais* and their social networks in the historic constituencies where the Darul Islam movement flourished in Java and what animates to a far more pronounced extent their ideologically driven Darul Islamist cousins in DI, and even more virulently so in JI, is a primordial fear that their identities are being utterly submerged under the relentless cultural assault of U.S.- and Western-dominated globalization. To recall, the theological cousins of the Darul Islamic subcultural community, the Salafis and the Islamists, share a broadly similar anxiety. The former *Far Eastern Economic Review* Jakarta correspondent Sadanand Dhume captures this impeccably by contrasting the relatively *weak uncertainty-avoidance* outlook of the majority Javanese *abangan* with the closed, insular mindsets of the Islamists—one strain of Arabized modernism:

> The masses, with their love of Manchester United, Korean pop and Bollywood blockbusters, show a cheerful openness to the rest of the world at odds with Islamism's monochrome fealty to the Middle East and its aversion to music and art.[202]

The Darul Islamists, Salafis, and Islamists—as discussed, all linked in various ways to a common Arabized modernist Tree in the Garden of Indonesian Islam—do not want to be poor copies of Americans and other Westerners and will take considerable steps to maintain their perceived cultural authenticity and uniqueness. Their affective, theological, and ideological affinity with "high Arabian Islam"—expressed in dress, diet, rituals, and political activism—is one manifestation of this attitude. Terrorism of the JI kind is another, extreme example. It is precisely the deep-seated fear of the limitless freedoms and superiority of American and Western cultural, moral, philosophical, and political systems that prompts the overcompensating psychic mechanisms inherent in the theology of Salafism—and in the derivative ideology of Islamism and its customized, localized variant of Darul Islamism—to kick into overdrive. The fundamentalist—that is, the controlling and supremacist—impulse that is inherent to all three epistemic systems is a *reaction* to the secular, homogenizing, liberal democratic, and capitalist modernity at the core of what America and the West stand for. This reaction is a negative reflex, a constitutive aspect of what the Arabized modernists and their affiliates are and represent. Khaled Abou El-Fadl concurs, observing that the "puritans' anti-Westernism is a core part of their reaction to modernity as well as a central part of their identity."[203] This is why a smart, *integrated* U.S. public diplomacy campaign worldwide that synchronizes Washington's rhetoric with actual policy and actions on the ground, especially in media-saturated Muslim war zones like Iraq and Afghanistan, still cannot win neutral Muslim hearts and minds. It can only *try to deny* the latter to the radical Islamists as well. United States public diplomacy remains a defensive instrument, a vitally necessary but still insufficient weapon in the cognitive immunization arsenal.

THE REAL ROLE OF MODERATE MUSLIM SCHOLARS AND EDUCATIONISTS: ENCOURAGING THE DEVELOPMENT OF CRITICAL, INDEPENDENT THOUGHT

The discussion thus far suggests that the Darul Islamist charismatic group and its associated JI mainstream and Noordin Top networks, and wider still, the communities in Java that were ideological ground zero of Kartosoewirjo's Darul Islam movement, are key constituencies of concern toward which cognitive immunization efforts should be directed. Primary cognitive immunization efforts should be directed at the DI and JI networks that comprise the Darul Islamist charismatic group in order to persuade militants to eschew violence in pursuit of the Islamic State as well as the extreme Global Salafi Jihad ideology that encourages a form of autonomous *jihad* that legitimizes mass civilian casualty attacks against Westerners and their *kuffar* allies. Primary cognitive immunization approaches would also include undermining the rabidly virulent JI Story and undercutting the moral standing and hence appeal of JI leaders. Secondary cognitive immunization measures, on the other hand, involving structured, face-to-face, interfaith activity as well as an integrated U.S. public diplomacy that promotes politically sensitive counterinsurgency tactics in media-saturated and thus utterly ventilated Muslim conflict zones, while also targeting the Darul Islamist charismatic group, should widen the focus to include measures directed at the Darul Islamic heartlands of Java. It would be apposite at this juncture to suggest—at the real risk of political incorrectness—that secondary cognitive immunization measures, to be truly effective down the road, also cannot ignore the potent influence on these two constituencies of concern of the strong uncertainty outlook orientation that is common to their related Salafi and Islamist cousins. Arabized modernists, whether Salafi or Islamist, will never accept a dilution of their sense of religio-cultural purity and superiority built on their hermetically sealed off, all-encompassing notions of Islam. Attempts by non-Muslims, whether Indonesians or Westerners, to transform

Arabized modernists so that they practice a redefined faith that accords with what non-Muslims feel comfortable with would only backfire, generating fears of impending cultural assimilation and group extinction—the stuff of the very Existential Identity Anxiety we have been exploring in this study.[204] The same logic applies to the Darul Islamist charismatic group and the wider communities that comprise Darul Islamic subculture. This is why Amartya Sen's suggestion of promoting instead a mindset that appreciates and understands "the many other identities that Muslims also have"[205] makes more sense.

In general, it would seem that encouraging the opening up of world-views of the coming generations of young people within the Darul Islamist charismatic group and the wider Darul Islamic heartlands, so that they may be equipped to embrace the reality of identity plurality, requires the promotion of *critical, independent thought*. The ultimate aim of secondary cognitive immunization efforts in this regard would be to encourage the development of young Muslim minds—despite immersion within a collectivist, large power-distance cultural context—that are nimble enough to "fly free of the nets of nationality, religion and language" and to "force a separation between what the tribe told you to be and what you truly are," as Ignatieff eloquently states.[206] The noted scholar of comparative religion Charles Kimball agrees with this sentiment. He has warned:

> *Intellectual freedom, personal integrity, and common sense are indispensable in authentic religion*. . . . Any religious group that largely withdraws from society needs *to ensure that people can think and make important decisions for themselves*. A segregated group in which the thinking and critical decisions reside with one or a few people, particularly when apocalyptic teaching is involved, is a disaster waiting to happen [italics added].[207]

Kimball's warning captures nicely the essence of the phenomenon we have analyzed in this study: religio-cultural communities within collectivist, large power-distance societies, possessed with a strong uncertainty-avoidance outlook shaped by both tradition and a history of conflict, developing Existential Identity Anxiety in the face of the perceived onslaught of secularization and Westernization. This primordial anxiety over Group Tent welfare in turn gives rise to organized charismatic groups driven by an ideology structured by a binary worldview, in turn spinning off smaller, more extreme networks of cells that develop cult-like thinking among its members. When these cult-like networks of cells within the charismatic group transmute themselves due to inclement socio-political circumstances into highly radicalized entities driven by ever more virulent versions of the parent ideology, all manner of mayhem will break out. The need for individuals within small groups or cells to develop the capacity to question received wisdom and combat cult-like thinking is thus an important countervailing factor against dangerous "group-think"[208] processes. This, however, is not something that can be expected to develop spontaneously in collectivist, large power-distance societies that emphasize compliance with the group and its seniors.[209]

In fact, as the case of Ali Imron shows, an individual in a collectivist milieu who does display elements of critical thought and has doubts about the small group's proposed course of action may still quite likely buckle under the combined psychic pressures of the *innate* human need to obey the authority of the small-group leadership he is part of—viz. Milgram—plus the *learned* cultural expectation that he do so. Despite this, however, we need to remind ourselves that ultimately, small groups can either be good or bad. In other words, "group interaction is a social amplifier that strengthens the pre-existing signals of the individuals in the group—whether good or evil."[210] Hence while a single individual with a dissenting view may well be drowned out in a small group context, *several* individuals with the same dissenting view may well be able to change the group's thinking. As we have seen, culture, while very important, is not deterministic. Culture interacts with an individual's human personality attributes—Hambali and his internal locus of control comes to mind—and the sum total of his personal experiences in various idiosyncratic ways. Hence even in a collectivist society, not everyone will think, feel, and act the same way all the time. Nobody in a collectivist milieu need be an unthinking automaton. Cult-like thinking in a collectivist milieu, therefore, especially cult-like thinking oriented toward the perpetration of evil behavior, *can* be defeated if there is a sufficient critical mass of independent-minded members willing to articulate dissenting views. In other words, if the bigots in a small group dominate, that group will likely behave in a bigoted fashion, but if the "givers" in that same group dominate discussion, that group will become more "philantropic"— there exists "a psychological continuity between people acting as individuals and people acting as group members."[211] Education aimed at encouraging critical, independent thought in a collectivist milieu is hence fully feasible and entirely justified. In this regard, Ayaan Hirsi Ali's contention that that should "be no schools indoctrinating poor kids with a hostile view of life" based upon the "superstitions their parents subscribe to" is especially apposite.[212]

This is where the true value of the "moderate" Muslim scholars— Indonesian or otherwise—could well play a strategic role in opening up the worldviews of young people, in particularly the wider Darul Islamic constituencies of Java. The Indonesian government has long recognized the potential value of such scholars in education. In the 1970s, President Soeharto, conscious of the rise of campus-based Islamist movements in Indonesia inspired by similar occurrences in the Middle East, sought to bring Islamic education, hitherto largely unregulated and left to the likes of private Islamic groups such as NU and Muhammadiyah, under greater central oversight.

To this end, continuing earlier initiatives by his predecessor Soekarno to upgrade Islamic education, the Soeharto government created the first National Academies for Islamic Studies (*Institut Agama Islam Negeri* or IAIN), research institutes funded by the Ministry of Religious Affairs charged with some teaching roles, somewhat on par with colleges and universities. These IAINs readily absorbed *pesantren* and *madrasah* graduates who wished to further their Islamic studies.[213] The 1989 Education Law further formalized the status of the IAINs.[214] Eminent moderate scholar Azyumardi Azra, writing in 2003, noted there were thirteen IAIN and thirty-three State Islamic Colleges (Sekolah Tinggi Agama Islam or STAIN) scattered in various cities throughout the Indonesian archipelago.[215] A big step toward promoting critical approaches to the study of religion was taken in 1994 when the IAINs introduced the foundation course *"Pendekatan Terhadap Pengajian Islam* (Approach to Islamic Studies)."[216] Farish Noor explains the significance of this development:

> The aim of the IAIN reforms was to demonstrate that the scholar had to *research* religion, not just study it. The core courses introduced from the 1990s were all based on the humanities: Sociology, Anthropology, History, Discourse Analysis, Linguistics and Semiotics, Philosophy and the basic modes of empirical research and fieldwork research methods. These were the tools used to study religion in general and Islam in particular.[217]

In fact, in 1994 it was announced by the Ministry of Religious Affairs that the IAINs would be converted to full National Islamic Universities (UIN).[218] In May 2002, subsequently, IAIN Sharif Hidayatullah in Jakarta was converted into a full-fledged university (UIN). UIN Jakarta has faculty not just in Islamic studies, but also in economics, science and technology, and psychology.[219] IAIN Sunan Kalijaga in Jogjakarta and STAIN Malang were upgraded to UIN status two years later.[220] In 2007, UIN Sunan Kalijaga students in the Islamic Studies department were "studying the Qu'ran and Hadith using the tools of discourse analysis and critical theory," and they and students at other UIN were studying works, translated into *Bahasa* Indonesia, of progressive, even liberal Muslim scholars such as Abdullahi an-Naim, Ebrahim Moosa, and Nasr Abu Zayd.[221] Little wonder that Azra opines that these UIN and other state-funded Islamic higher educational institutions have begun to play a crucial role in the "modernization of Muslim society."[222] Very importantly, as a result of their "rational" and "non-denominational" approaches to Islam, the critically minded graduates of the STAIN, IAIN, and now the UIN have been increasingly recognized by Indonesian society as having a "progressive, inclusive, and tolerant view of Islam."[223] They are well placed to "think for themselves, think objectively, critically and scientifically so that they can cope with the demands of the age they live in."[224]

Perhaps somewhat counterintuitively, Azra observes by way of contrast that many students and graduates of "secular" universities such as the University of Indonesia (UI) or the Bandung Institute of Technology (Institut Teknologi Bandung or ITB) tend to be "more literal in their view and understanding of Islam."[225] Amin Abdullah, the rector of UIN Sunan Kalijaga, agrees that UIN graduates "have turned out to be more moderate (politically) than the graduates of the secular universities, some of whom have turned into literal-minded conservative Islamists in their own personal struggles to 'rediscover Islam' for themselves."[226] Sri Yunanto, executive director of the nongovernmental Ridep Institute in Jakarta, offers more insight into this phenomenon, and his views are worth quoting at length:

> The activists who join militant movements are those having simple understanding, not to say "poor understanding [sic], of Islamic teaching with "one track mind" style of thinking character. *With such character, they [emphasize] more on obedience and loyalty than criticism and logical argument. They view that Islam is a religion to obey and to implement, not to argue.* Based on such simple understanding, they claim that their understanding [represents] "true Islam" ... [and the Islam of Muslims who are active in] Muhammadiyah and NU are seen as "polluted Islam or not true Islam." It is not surprising to see that radical Islamist groups like MMI, LJ [Lasker Jihad], Hizbuttahrir and Dakwah Kampus [Campus Islam] movements appeal [to] university students from Science department[s] as they have been accustomed [to] the style of "one track mind" thinking [italics added].[227]

Sri Yunanto's latter comment requires elaboration. One of the curious phenomena that one encounters in the study of Muslim radicalization worldwide, not just in Indonesia, is the unusual, counterintuitive correlation between an advanced education in the technical sciences and radicalism. Analysts have noted that many Islamists have "advanced education," while a "disproportionate number of terrorists and suicide bombers" possess a "higher education, often in engineering and the sciences."[228] Ramzi Yousef, the Al Qaeda operative who planned the 1993 New York World Trade Center attack, for instance, studied computer-aided electrical engineering in Swansea, Wales.[229] Hambali's close friend, the former Al Qaeda operations chief Khalid Sheikh Mohammad, graduated with a mechanical engineering degree from North Carolina Agricultural and State University in the United States.[230] Within the JI network in Southeast Asia, the Indonesian Agus Dwikarna, who also had leadership roles in MMI and DDII, is a civil engineer by training.[231] Malaysian JI operative Shamsul Bahri Hussein read applied mechanics at Dundee.[232] Another Malaysian, Yazid Sufaat, who apparently tried to acquire anthrax and develop biological weapons for Al Qaeda, was a 1987 biochemistry graduate from California State University in Sacramento.[233] One should not forget yet another Malaysian, the late

Dr. Azahari Husin, the top JI bomb-maker who wrote the network's bomb manual and was involved in the Bali, Jakarta Marriott, and Jakarta Australian embassy bombings. Husin studied in Adelaide for four years in the 1970s, secured an engineering degree in Malaysia, and later received a PhD in statistical modeling from Reading University in the 1980s. He taught at Universiti Teknologi Malaysia (UTM) before going underground in 2001.[234] Azahari was tracked down and killed by Densus 88 in a firefight in November 2005.[235]

Why do some well-educated individuals like Azahari Husin, who have lived and studied to the highest levels in the West and been presumably exposed to Enlightenment rationalism and the disciplines of scientific enquiry, embark on Radical Pathways toward extremism and ultimately terrorism? One explanation offered by Moojan Momen is the psychological need for "certainty." While certainty is *professionally* important to technical people because they have to be very precise in mechanical tasks such as building a bridge or designing ships and aircraft, it is possible that certainty is *psychologically* important as well. Scientists and engineers—let us call them technical people—tend to be *concrete/objective* individuals by nature. Concrete/objective people, personality theorists tell us, tend to "prefer a concrete way of perceiving the world, are down-to-earth; perhaps simple and possibly simplistic," and strongly "solution-oriented." Conversely, the *abstract/intuitive* individual tends to be creative in his problem solving, is willing to explore hunches and new ideas, is imaginative, likes change, and is problem-oriented. Ronald Johnson pithily suggests that while abstract people see "what could be," concrete people see "what is."[236] This strong need for certainty and solutions means that "when scientists (especially from the physical sciences) and engineers become religious they often tend towards fundamentalist religion."[237] Such *techno-fundamentalists* can tolerate "no ambiguities, no equivocations, no reservations, and no criticism"[238] because ambiguity is "deeply unsatisfactory" to the techno-fundamentalist psyche.[239] That largely certainty- and solution-oriented natural or physical scientists tend to be more religious than generally abstract/intuitive social scientists such as sociologists and psychologists has been borne out by the research findings of the psychologists of religion Benjamin Beit-Hallahmi and Michael Argyle. They have postulated the so-called "scholarly distance" thesis to explain the relative differences in religiosity levels between natural scientists on the one hand and social scientists on the other:

> The reason, in psychological terms, is that the natural sciences apply critical thinking to nature; the human sciences ask critical questions about culture, tradition and beliefs. The mere fact of choosing human society or behavior as the object of study reflects a curiosity about basic social beliefs and conventions and a readiness to reject them. Physical scientists, who are at a greater scholarly distance, *may be able to compartmentalize their science and religion more easily* [italics added].[240]

This may explain why a 1997 survey of biologists, physicists, and mathematicians reported that when asked if they believed in a personal God who communicates with humankind, *40 percent* answered affirmatively. Francis S. Collins, the eminent scientist who directed the Human Genome Project, points out that "spiritual belief among scientists" is "more prevalent than many realize."[241]

While some technical people may be psychologically hard-wired to tend toward dogma and certainty in matters of religion, it seems equally true that religious fundamentalists, for their part, tend toward technical subjects by choice as well. The renowned scholar of Islamic Law Khaled Abou El Fadl points out that the Islamist/Salafi "puritans" of the Middle East seek "modernism" but not "modernity," which is seen as Western and corrupt.[242] Puritans hold that the pathway to modernization leads *backwards* to the time of the Prophet. Science and technology are regarded as the means to achieve this quest to recreate the "golden age of Islam," *sans* the Western culture that created that very same science and technology:

> Muslims should learn the technology and science invented by the West, but in order to resist Western culture, Muslims should not seek to study the social sciences or humanities. This is the reason that a large number of puritans come to the West to study, but invariably focus their studies on the physical sciences, including computer science, and *entirely ignore the social sciences and humanities* [italics added].[243]

El Fadl shows that with "the majority" of the Salafi and Islamist "puritan leadership comprised [sic] of people who studied the physical sciences, such as medicine, engineering, and computer science"—they then, being by nature concrete/objective individuals—"anchor themselves in the objectivity and certitude that comes from empiricism."[244] This empiricist mindset in turn conditions them to hold certain assumptions about matters of faith:

> [A] group of very specific commandments and rules delineate and define the straight path of God, and there is no room in this outlook for reason-based moral or ethical speculative thought.... God is manifested through a set of clear and precise legal commands that cover nearly all aspects of life, and the sole purpose of human beings is to realize the Divine manifestation by dutifully and faithfully implementing the Divine law.... This fairly technical and legalistic way of life is considered inherently superior to all others, and the followers of any other way are [categorized as] either infidels (*kuffar*), hypocrites (*munafiqun*), or the iniquitous (*fasiqun*).[245]

The Salafi or Islamist techno-fundamentalists' strongly held intellectual and emotional fixation with what Malise Ruthven calls "monodimensional or literalist readings of scripture" contrasts sharply with their "counterparts in the arts and humanities whose training requires them to approach texts multidimensionally, exploring contradictions and ambiguities."[246] El Fadl adds that "empirically unquantifiable" elements such as "human dignity, love, mercy and compassion" are also all but ignored.[247] The real-world impact of this techno-fundamentalism cannot be overstated. Khalid Duran has wryly commented on the "odd" fact that in Egypt, "Islamic fundamentalism" has always had "strongest appeal among engineers," and "they always say the Muslim Brotherhood is really the Engineering Brotherhood."[248] Noting the rigid empiricism implicit in the fundamentalist mentality of the Brotherhood Islamists, Duran elaborates:

> Engineers don't exercise their fantasy and imagination. Everything is precise and mathematical. They don't study what we call "the humanities." Consequently when it comes to issues that involve religion and personal emotion, they tend to see things in very stark terms.[249]

El Fadl also complains that "self-proclaimed experts" in the shape of "engineers, medical doctors, and physical scientists," including the "leaders" of the "Muslim Brotherhood and al-Qa'ida," have sought to make authoritative interpretations on Islamic Law—despite the fact that they are generally "unfamiliar with the precedents and accomplishments of past generations" of Islamic scholars in developing Islamic jurisprudence.[250] At any rate, there is a high proportion of Salafi and Islamist activists in the Middle East with backgrounds in the hard sciences and engineering. On university campuses in Iran and Egypt, for instance, such activists constitute "25 percent of humanities students, but 60 to 80 percent of students in medicine, engineering and science."[251] These individuals, who enjoy a high social status as modern professionals within their deeply collectivist, large power-distance cultures, can well be expected to take the lead in shaping the future of Islam in that part of the world—with attendant huge implications for the ability of the Islamic faith to keep pace with modernity. Justifying this assertion requires a quick digression into the basic differences between the *shariah* and *fiqh*, the two key aspects of Islamic Law. *Shariah* is the "eternal, immutable, and unchanging law as it exists in the mind of God."[252] The task of human beings, El Fadl avers, is to "strive and struggle to realize God's law to the best of their abilities." By contrast, *fiqh* is the human law, the attempt by humans to "reach and fulfill the eternal law as it exists in God's mind." El Fadl argues that "*fiqh* is not itself Divine, because it is the product of human efforts"—hence *fiqh*, unlike *shariah*, is "not eternal, immutable, or unchanging" but is human and thus "subject to error, alterable and contingent."[253] The issue is that while most moderate Muslim scholars hold that because of the complexity of life in an ever-changing world, the scope for human *fiqh* must be broad enough to cope with changing realities, dogmatic and rigid

Salafi/Islamist puritans demur. They argue instead that for most matters, "God has revealed a precise and exact law," and all that is required is for Muslims to obey and comply.[254] As El Fadl explains:

> According to the puritans, 90 percent of what they consider the revealed law is not open to debate or discussion, alteration or change. Only 10 percent of the law is open to debate and differences of opinion... *fiqh* is applicable to no more than 10 percent of all legally pertinent issues.[255]

This position is of course not acceptable to extremely learned, moderate scholars like El Fadl, who justifiably asks why then would God confer *free will* on his human subjects? He insists instead that the whole point of "legal analysis is not to unthinkingly and blindly implement a set of technical rules, but to seek after the ultimate objectives of the Qur'an." He adds that the "particular and specific rules" as set forth in the Qur'an "are not objectives in themselves," but rather dependent on "particular historical circumstances that might or might not exist in the modern age."[256] In fact, all four Islamic *madhabs* or jurisprudential schools agreed that the overriding, timeless aim of the *shariah* has been to "serve the best interests of human beings." El Fadl:

> Because puritans do not think of the specific rules as demonstrative examples but as objectives in themselves, they seek to implement the rules *regardless of whether their application will enhance or undermine Qur'anic principles* such as justice, equity, and mercy [italics added].[257]

Hence, to puritan Salafis and Islamists, using "reason" to seek to adapt Islamic law to modern conditions is "absolute anathema" because to them, all that "Muslims need to do is find the law and apply it strictly and faithfully, and that is the end of the process."[258]

This analysis of the moderate-puritan theological debate is not irrelevant to our overall discussion. For one thing, the Darul Islamist puritan Abu Bakar Ba'asyir would never agree with El Fadl's assertion that the *shariah* exists to serve the best interests of human beings. In a May 2007 interview at Pondok Pesantren Al-Mukmin, he insisted that "Muslims need to bend our ways to suit Islam, and not the other way round."[259] It can be asserted here that if Salafi and Islamist techno-fundamentalists and leaders with their narrow, puritan focus gain the upper hand in shaping the future trajectory of Islam in Indonesia, let alone the Middle East, then the implications for long-term cognitive immunization efforts—and by implication, counter-radicalization strategy would be dire indeed. We are not of course directly equating Arabized modernist Islam in Indonesia with terrorism. Nevertheless, we cannot entirely dismiss the notion that a theological Radical Pathway runs from Arabized modernism through Darul Islamism and finally to JI terrorism. El Fadl is unequivocal in this regard:

Militant groups such as al-Qa'ida or the Taliban, despite their ability to commit highly visible acts of violence, are a sociological and intellectual marginality in Islam. However, these groups are in fact extreme manifestations of more prevalent intellectual and theological currents in modern Islam. *In my view, they are extreme manifestations of the rather widespread theological orientation of Puritanism* [italics added].[260]

This is precisely why Ayaan Hirsi Ali, who had been deeply active in the Muslim Brotherhood earlier in her life, on hearing about the September 11, 2001, terrorist attacks in New York and Washington D.C., recalled that the extremist ideology driving the hijackers was not all that alien to Muslims:

[September 11 lead hijacker, the Egyptian] Mohamed Atta was exactly my age. I felt as though I knew him, and in fact I did know many people like him.... There were tens of thousands of people, in Africa, the Middle East—even in Holland—who thought this way. Every devout Muslim who aspired to practice genuine Islam—the Muslim Brotherhood Islam, the Islam of the Medina Quran schools—*even if they didn't actively support the attacks, they must have approved of them.* This wasn't just a band of frustrated Egyptian architects in Hamburg. It was much bigger than that, and it had nothing to do with frustration. *It was about belief* [italics added].[261]

Leading traditionalist leader and former president Gus Dur himself seems fully aware that while Indonesia needs to fully exploit modern science and technology to power the country's economic development, heavy investment in technical education needs to be balanced by the provision of adequate opportunities for students in the technical university campuses especially to be educated in modern techniques of Islamic scholarship. Gus Dur complains that because many young technical students "have not been trained in the rich disciplines of Islamic scholarship," they tend to bring to "their reflection on their faith the same sort of simple modelling and formulistic thinking that they have learnt as students of engineering or other applied sciences."[262] As a result, these students take a "more or less literalistic approach to the textual sources of Islam" and use these texts "in a reductionistic fashion without being able to undertake, or even appreciate, the subtly-nuanced task of interpretation required of them."[263] Gus Dur opines that these confident, smart, but relatively intellectually blinkered young men need proper training to understand how documents from "the 7th to 8th centuries, from the tribal Arab society among the desert sands," are to be "applied correctly to the very different world that we live in today."[264] If they are not taught, Gus Dur worries, "how to approach their faith with the intellectual sophistication that the demands of the modern world require of them," then when "alienation, loneliness and the search for identity encroach upon them," they will be vulnerable to the "formalistic understanding of Islamic law" that breeds "violent radicalism."[265] He therefore asserts that a real problem is that "precious few young Muslims from developing nations have the privilege of undertaking liberal arts courses in Western universities."[266] Gus Dur's call for expanded liberal arts education in Indonesian universities, particularly the secular, technically oriented ones, is not unique. Khalid Duran believes that "having an education in literature or politics or sociology seems to inoculate you against the appeals of fundamentalism."[267] Roy Mottahedeh similarly argues for a strong liberal arts emphasis that encourages critical thinking and writing "about both the human and scientific spheres."[268]

In sum, as seen within Indonesia today, leading Islamic tertiary institutions like UIN Sunan Kalijaga (UINSUKA) as well as the Universitas Muhammadiyah Surakarta (UMS) have engaged with modern Western liberal arts disciplines in an attempt to provide graduates with enhanced critical thinking skills. The religious studies curricula of these institutions include courses on hermeneutics, sociology, discourse analysis, critical theory, and deconstruction.[269] The challenge now is to expand such modern techniques to the secular university campuses to provide technical students from the heartlands of Darul Islam in Java with the critical analytical tools to cognitively immunize themselves against "ideological and/or religious dogmatism."[270] In particular, the standard of Islamic education on secular university campuses must be raised so as to turn such students away from a "one track" fixation with a "text-based religiosity that is often literalist, fundamentalist and conservative," not to mention manipulated for "sectarian or political ends."[271] To this end, expansion of humanities education in fields such as hermeneutics and textual analysis can assist technical and other students on secular university campuses such as ITB and UI to avoid falling prey to the cynical efforts of "dogmatic conservative-literalists" to effect a "closure of meaning" and foster a selective interpretation of texts in pursuit of "their political-ideological agendas."[272] The impact of humanities education in gradually opening up the worldview of Islamists and encouraging "critical thinking and fresh interpretations" is important and has been documented.[273] This is not at all lost on a "dogmatic conservative-literalist" like Ba'asyir, who told his interlocutor, the well-known Malaysian scholar Farish A. Noor, that he regards all these new fields as Jewish-led schemes to "confuse" the faith of true Muslims and enervate them so that they can be easily dominated.[274]

CRITICAL THOUGHT AND THE THEOLOGICAL CONTAINMENT OF ARABIZED MODERNIST ISLAM

At any rate, the systematic promotion of critical independent thought among young people hailing from the Darul Islamic subcultural zones of

Java (incorporating the smaller number of ideological Darul Islamists) is a secondary cognitive immunization strategy whose effects will not be apparent for years—possibly a generation. It cannot be overemphasized either that developing the capacity to think and act independently—to open up one's worldview and "force a separation between what the tribe told you to be and what you truly are"—cannot be expected to come very readily within a highly collectivist, large power-distance culture like that of the Javanese. What a long-term educational strategy to promote critical thinking should aim to achieve, however, is not so much cultural transformation—theoretically possible over generations[275] but utterly problematic on moral, political, and quite simply pragmatic grounds—but rather *theological containment*. That is, over time, the strategy should help tip the balance in the historic internal contest between Javanized and Arabized Islam in favor of the former. As we have seen, the key distinction between the *abangan*, the *santri* traditionalists, and modernists on the one hand, and the Arabized modernist Salafis, Islamists, and for that matter the theologically and ideologically affiliated Darul Islamists on the other, is the cultural dimension of uncertainty avoidance. The former group can cope with and embrace ambiguity and difference. They hence represent the tolerant, "smiling face" of Indonesian Islam.[276] The latter group, with its deeply ingrained strong uncertainty-avoidance outlook, are, as discussed, radical theological synchronizers in the case of the Salafis, power-seeking activists in the case of the Islamists, and violent militants in the case of particularly the JI network, driven by a particularly virulent, Qaedaist-shaped version of Darul Islamism. If tolerant Indonesian Islam is to be salvaged and allowed to prosper well into the future, its Arabized modernist strain would have to be *theologically contained*.

At first sight, this assertion may make strike some observers as both politically incorrect and utterly antithetical to the ideals of a multicultural, newly liberal democratic state like Indonesia. The rules of the liberal democratic game work, however, only if all sides agree to abide by the rules of the constitutionally instituted authority. With the exception of those putatively Islamist political parties that have, according to current evidence, apparently been willing to nuance their Islamization agendas to accommodate competing secular and other political interests,[277] the track record of *unreconstructed, binary-minded radical Islamists everywhere*, in Indonesia or Europe, suggests that they are thoroughly committed to subverting and overthrowing the very system that gives them abundant political space and freedom of worship. They are not even coy about this. In democratic Indonesia, Abu Bakar Ba'asyir himself openly defined religious and political pluralism as a state of affairs in which Muslims "can be tolerant of the non-Muslims," but only after "you have them under your control and governance."[278] The upshot of all this is that liberal multiculturalism must have its limits,[279] and governments, in cooperation with more enlightened sections of Muslim civil society, must cooperate to find ways and means of *undermining destructive, religiously inspired political ideologies—while simultaneously containing the wider theologies that birth them in the first place.* This is morally justified, as frankly some species of religion can be socially, politically, and ethically harmful, especially to non-believers.[280] In the Indonesian context, this does not at all imply seeking to transform Arabized modernist Islam itself—as noted, a self-defeating strategy bound to reinforce the very Existential Identity Anxiety that fuels the slide into extremism. It does, however, imply encouraging and equipping young Javanese to critically evaluate the central tenets of Arabized Islamic modernism. To reiterate: it is not at all being suggested here that such a task will come easily to young people born into a culture that is strongly collectivist and in which respect for senior religious figures, especially those of Hadrami Arab descent, is very deeply ingrained. Breaking free of transgenerationally transmitted, deeply imbibed cultural attitudes and entrenched cognitive filters can be very difficult. Even after the former British radical Ed Husain had quit the Islamist Hizbut Tahrir movement, he admitted that the "indoctrination of the Hizb was powerful and it was many years before I was completely free of it."[281] Much to his chagrin, although he had left the Hizb movement, immediately after the September 11, 2001, attacks in the United States he realized that the born-again "spiritual Muslim" in him had utterly failed to sense the "remnants of the arrogant sleeper Islamist still residing within." He admitted that although he had "consciously tried to decontaminate" his thinking, there were "aspects of Islamist political strategies" that he still regarded as "normal":

> [A]n acceptance of terrorism, an unconscious belief that those who "opposed Islam" were somehow less than human and thus expendable in the Islamist pursuit of political dominion over palm and pine.[282]

Ayaan Hirsi Ali, recounting her own painful experience of theological escape, confesses that cultural conditioning is "very powerful, and it takes great energy and force of mind and will to break out of it."[283] She explained later that leaving a faith and culture is like leaving a "mental cage":

> At first, when you open the door, the caged bird stays inside: it is frightened. It has internalized its imprisonment. It takes time for the bird to escape, even after someone has opened the doors to its cage.[284]

Nevertheless, although leaving a culture and adopting new mental software is extremely difficult, *it is not impossible.* Containing the influence of Arabized modernism in the Darul Islamic heartlands of Java can proceed apace. It could involve programs aimed at fostering a critical engagement with the theology and contemporary lived realities of modern Arabized modernist Islam, a.k.a. Wahhabism. The specific modalities of such critical engagement could include current staples such as books, newspaper articles, and magazines, as well as *intrafaith* seminars and forums on television or in the form of public events. Sri Yunanto of the Ridep Institute, a Jakarta-based NGO, brought together liberal and moderate Muslims from the Liberal Islam Network and Muhammadiyah and more radical but nonviolent Islamists from MMI and Hizbut Tahrir and the Pondok Pesantren Al-Mukmin alumni association IKAPIM in an intrafaith workshop to thrash out issues such as corruption, poverty, the low quality of education in the archipelago, and communal conflict and terrorism.[285] It is suggested here that a concerted effort now be made to subject Arabized modernist Islam to critical scrutiny in similar forums. A systematic series of public debates between moderate scholars and activists from the likes of LIPIA, DDII, Persis, and Al-Irsyad (not DI or JI activists and militants, though) can be held on secular university campuses such as UI and ITB. The aim of these would be to provide multiple opportunities for open debate on assertions by moderate scholars such as Khaled Abou El Fadl that the Wahhabis practice a very selective approach to the rulings of the strict, literalist Hanbali school of jurisprudence, choosing those rulings that "confirm their worldview and ideology."[286] Moderate scholars, such as Mochamad Nur Ichwan of UIN Sunan Kalijaga, articulate similar complaints within the Indonesian context.[287] El Fadl, incidentally, makes no secret of his intellectual disdain for Wahhabism:

> In [the puritan] paradigm, one often encounters a simplistic attitude that assumes that the Qur'an and Sunna are full of formulas, and that the only thing missing in the equation is the will and determination to apply the correct formula to the appropriate problem. This attitude induces puritans to treat the tradition as a vending machine of sorts.[288]

The Wahhabi puritans, he adds, feel that there is a "ready-made solution in the sources for every problem that confronts people." The essence of the puritan approach, he concludes, is that if the "lived reality" clashes with the "puritan pretense," the puritans "conclude that the solution is most certainly correct, and it is the people who must be all wrong."[289] This is precisely why Ba'asyir told Malaysian analyst Farish Noor that "Muslims need to bend our ways to suit Islam, and not the other way 'round."[290] As for the Arabized modernists in their Salafi, Islamist, and related Darul Islamist incarnations, there is only one correct interpretation of Islam, they have it, and the rest should come on board. In any case, even if the rest fail to do so, Arabized modernists will find ways and means to impose their epistemic reality on one and all, other Muslims and non-Muslims alike. It is "in the nature," says Ed Husain of the Arabized modernist version of "Islam," that "it must dominate."[291]

Buttressing these critical theological and intellectual examinations of Arabized modernist Islam should be factual strategic information campaigns aimed at opening up the worldview of those Javanese young people who admire the Arabized modernists and informing them about the blatant ethnic and class prejudice—the product of both strong uncertainty-avoidance and large power-distance orientations—against fellow Muslims who are not Arab. Ayaan Hirsi Ali, of Somalian extraction, lived as a child in Saudi Arabia, and her recollections reveal a strong degree of obsessive-compulsiveness within the collective Saudi Arab mental software—a mental disposition that strongly underlies religious fundamentalism:

> Everything in Saudi Arabia was about sin. You weren't naughty; you were sinful. You weren't clean; you were pure. The word *haram*, forbidden, was something we heard everyday. Taking a bus with men was *haram*. Boys and girls playing together was *haram*. When we played with the other girls in the courtyard of the Quran school, if our white headscarves shook loose, that was *haram*, too, even if there were no boys around.[292]

Such ingrained categorical thinking expressed itself in social relations at the *madrasah* where Ayaan and her sister were studying. In such an environment, "for the first time," she thought of the other students as white and herself as "black." Additionally, Ayaan and her sister Haweya were called *abid*, meaning slave. "Being called a slave," she recounted, "the racial prejudice this term conveyed," was "a big part" of what she "hated in Saudi Arabia."[293] Of course, Ayaan met Saudis who were gracious, but in the main, "to be a foreigner, and moreover a black foreigner, meant you were barely human."[294] She recalled that while at the *madrasah*, she was always picked on because she was the only black child. When she was struck with a ruler, the Egyptian teacher called her "*Aswad Abda*: black slave-girl." Ayaan was blunt: "I hated Saudi Arabia."[295] This is not just one person's biased view. Briton Ed Husain also spent a few years in Saudi Arabia, working with the British Council in Jeddah. He reported that the Saudi Arabs to whom he taught English "often used the word 'nigger' to describe black people."[296] Before long he felt the full impact of the strong Arab large power-distance, highly collectivist, and strong uncertainty-avoidance outlooks, expressed in the "social structure that Saudis imposed on their foreign workforce," which had the "following pecking order":

> Americans were at the top, followed by Brits, then other Europeans, then Lebanese, Syrians, Egyptians, Yemenis, and other Arabs, followed by the Sudanese. Asians (Filipinos, Indians, Pakistanis, Bangladeshis) were at the bottom of the pile, above only poor black Africans from Chad, mainly staying beyond their pilgrimage visas.[297]

In particular, Husain soon learned to grow a goatee and speak his good Arabic in public so as to hide his Asian ethnicity and pass off as a rather brown-hued Arab. As he put it:

> I refused to be pigeon-holed by Arab racism, to be seen as an inferior *hindi*, or Indian. In the racist Arab psyche, *hindi* is as pejorative as *kuffar*. In countless gatherings I silently sat and listened to racist caricatures of a billion people by Saudi bigots.[298]

Ayaan Hirsi Ali observed that her well-educated Somali father Abeh, who always told his children that one must always seek to understand "the spirit" behind the overt "rules" of the Qur'an—complained that what was practiced in Saudi Arabia was "not Islam," but rather the "Saudis, perverting Islam."[299] Although Abeh was a Muslim, he "hated Saudi judges and Saudi law" and regarded the routine public floggings, executions, amputations, and stoning of miscreants as "all barbaric, all Arab desert culture."[300]

These perspectives are some far from exhaustive examples of what the Campus Islam groups on secular university campuses and *pesantren* students alike need to think deeply about, and to which their leaders are urged to publicly respond. Intellectuals from LIPIA, DDII, Persis, and Al-Irsyad should be given every opportunity to debate these ideas as well. Ba'asyir himself, now a teacher at Pondok Pesantren Al-Mukmin, should be asked to respond to, justify, and rebut these ideas in public forums, perhaps in seminars held within the *pesantren* and open to all comers. The mass-market popular media also have a big role to play in a bid to "promote transparency and public criticism" of Arabized modernism and the ways in which such a theological system could contribute and has in fact contributed to the excesses of violent Islamists in Indonesia and globally.[301] What would be potentially interesting is how the Arabized modernists in Indonesia would respond to the blatant Arab racism against Asians who are fellow Muslims. After all, are not all Muslims part of the same global *ummah*, and nationality and culture unimportant? The blatant reality of Arab prejudice against outsiders was one powerful reason that convinced ex-Islamist Ed Husain that the stock Islamist propaganda line of creating one united global *ummah* "seemed so juvenile now":

> It was only in the comfort of Britain that Islamists could come out with such radical, utopian slogans as one government, one ever-expanding country, for the Muslim nation. The racist reality of the Arab psyche would never accept black and white people as equal.[302]

Of course, the Salafis and Islamists may well holler loudly in protest and the Darul Islamists—particularly of the JI variety—may make threats if such ideas are publicly discussed in Indonesia, but this would only drive home the point, and further underscore the need for young people in Java and across the archipelago for that matter, to open up their worldviews and "force a separation between what the [Arabized modernist] tribe told [them] to be and what [they] truly are." To further aid this process, creative ways of subjecting Arabized modernism to critical scrutiny in a form palatable for a mass market need to be devised. After all, as today's Salafi, Islamist, and Darul Islamist ideologues spread their message through Web sites, video compact discs, DVDs, and cassette tapes of vivid sermons, there is no reason why a secondary cognitive immunization strategy should ignore the potential of the adroit exploitation of such media. Ayaan Hirsi Ali again:

> Political speeches are fine, but it's time now for satire, art, for movies and books. Creative people with a dissident message need to get beyond the mental block that prevents them from treating religion like any other subject—and from treating Islam like any other religion. They need to get their own message across with pictures, not just with words, to people who don't literally or metaphorically, speak their language.[303]

POSSIBLE PHILOSOPHICAL END-STATES: ATHEISM AND *ABANGAN* NOMINALISM, SUFISM, AND "REALISTIC MODERNISM"

Gazing into a metaphorical crystal ball, suppose that a longer-term, secondary cognitive immunization campaign targeted at Javanese communities historically susceptible to Darul Islamist ideological mobilization and aimed at promoting critical thinking as an emergent cultural habit within a traditionally collectivist, large power-distance milieu was successful. What would the metrics of success be precisely? While the reduction of religiously inspired terrorism and conflict to insignificant levels is an obvious indicator, another could possibly be the configuration of philosophical end-states extant in the Indonesian body politic a generation hence. Four probable if not necessarily exhaustive possibilities that spring to mind could be atheism, *abangan* nominalism, a Sufist resurgence, and what we may call realistic modernism. It is possible that the better-educated graduates of secular university campuses— those with a strong internal locus of control—may develop an interest in atheism as opposed to theism. Atheism as a philosophy appears to have gathered momentum in the post–September 11, 2001, era. Popular writers such as Richard Dawkins and Sam Harris have come out to argue that monotheistic religion is in fact evil and must be held ultimately responsible for the attacks in New York and Washington and other instances of terrorism across all faith lines. The British zoologist Dawkins, for instance, in his much-discussed book *The God Delusion*, argues that religious faith itself—not merely religious extremism—is irrational, infantile, and can lead to violence. He promotes atheism instead as an alternative worldview that is superior to religious faith in promoting moral, rational, civilized, and importantly, tolerant living in the globalized, multicultural societies of today.[304] For his part, the American philosopher Sam Harris agrees with Dawkins that it is religion itself and not merely its extreme forms that is the root cause of religious violence and terrorism; like Dawkins, he insists that it is possible to live ethical, meaningful lives that express tolerance of those unlike ourselves purely through the application of reason, love, and honesty.[305] Ayaan Hirsi Ali's own personal journey from her Muslim Brotherhood–influenced Islamic faith is both poignant and telling. Following the September 11 attacks, Ayaan's longtime misgivings about her faith resurfaced, and she felt that she could no longer "avoid seeing the totalitarianism, the pure moral framework, that is Islam."[306] She felt that the faith "regulates every detail of life and subjugates free will."[307] She found herself thinking that "true Islam, as a rigid belief system and moral framework, leads to cruelty."[308] This is how she thought the September 11 hijackers saw the world, which was "divided between 'Us' and "Them',," and "if you don't accept Islam you should perish."[309] She later read the book *The Atheist Manifesto* and realized that she had become an atheist. Her thoughts are worth quoting at length:

> It felt right. There was no pain, but a real clarity. The long process of seeing the flaws in my belief structure and carefully tiptoeing around the frayed edges as parts of it were torn out, piece by piece—that was all over. The angels, watching from my shoulders; the mental tension about having sex without marriage, and drinking alcohol, and not observing any religious obligations—they were gone. The ever-present prospect of hellfire lifted, and my horizon seemed broader. God, Satan, angels: these were figments of human imagination. From now on I could step firmly on the ground that was under my feet and navigate based on my own reason and self-respect. My moral compass was within myself, not in the pages of a sacred book.[310]

Ayaan, who had studied political science in the Netherlands, began to find her belief system increasingly shaped by the great Enlightenment thinkers such as "Spinoza, Locke, Kant, Mill, Voltaire—and the modern ones, Russell and Popper, with my full attention, not just as a class assignment."[311] Popper, it seems, greatly influenced her with his observation that "all life is problem solving," and as "there are no absolutes," the only way we can progress is through "critical thought."[312] Both Dawkins[313] and Harris[314] echo Ayaan's call for the promotion of critical thinking and the utter rejection of absolutist religious dogma. For that matter, the respected *Guardian* journalist Francis Wheen holds that all forms of dogma, not just religious ones, should be subject to unapologetic critical scrutiny—in the true spirit of the Enlightenment.[315]

To be sure, Ayaan's unconventional and at times controversial views on Islam have caused her to be regarded as an "Enlightenment fundamentalist."[316] In any case, apart from a few adventurous young people, driven as noted by a very strong internal locus of control, it is not very likely that atheism—with its heavily self-referencing, individualist connotations—will be a widely popular intellectual choice within the deeply mystical and collectivist Javanese milieu. As explained in the first chapter, most individuals born into collectivist societies tend to behave in ways that seek to preserve established group norms rather than acting on "an individually developed conscience that functions as an inner pilot."[317] Such individuals in collectivist societies are mainly *interdependent* rather than independent entities.[318] Rather than outright atheism, therefore, perhaps what is more likely—if secondary cognitive immunization efforts are successful in the Darul Islamic heartlands in the coming generation—is a gradual decline in deeply self-conscious religiosity in favor of the *abangan* nominalism that has always characterized the wider Garden of Indonesian Islam. In this scenario, rather than embrace a single dominant and all-encompassing identity—Islam—young people would be comfortable with multiple identities in which Islam is but one of several coexisting modes of self-identification.[319] This development would facilitate an intensification of structured, multidimensional, cross-group interactions in all spheres, strengthening Indonesian civil society as a whole. As the Commonwealth Commission Report puts it:

> [C]ivil society groups and organisations can bring together people on the basis of identities they share, not those that have previously divided them. When people meet, for example, as journalists, business people, educationalists or trade union members, and when they are drawn from both sides of previous divisions, they not only bring with them a ready-made network of contacts but also a means of communicating with those contacts [italics added].[320]

It is worth reiterating, nonetheless, that because of the specific dispositional makeup and life circumstances of a few individuals in the Indonesian milieu—the Situated Individual Personality factor in our RP Framework—they may well go the way of Ayaan, adopting atheism as a personal creed. Ayaan herself, after all, emerged originally from a deeply collectivist Somali cultural milieu.[321]

Quite apart from atheism and *abangan* nominalism as philosophical end-states, it is possible as well that a successful secondary cognitive immunization campaign within the Darul Islamic subcultural Bouquet could beget a softer interpretation of Islam that replaces the concept of an "angry God"[322] who is "full of vengeance, a legislator, a controller, a punisher"[323] with the idea that God is love.[324] In this respect, a renaissance of Sufist *santri* traditionalism could be in the cards. It should not be forgotten that

Sufism has very deep roots in the Indonesian archipelago, including Java. It has been suggested that the Indian Muslim merchants who first brought Islam to the archipelago were themselves Sufis or were deeply influenced by Sufis.[325] This notion of inveterate Darul Islamic heartlanders giving up the collective binary worldview that is the product of a strong uncertainty-avoidance cultural orientation and embracing tolerant Sufism is not entirely far-fetched. As noted, Kartosoewirjo—Ba'asyir's hero, no less—was a dedicated Sufi mystic, and Sufi-influenced Javanese traditionalism was one of the remote sources of Darul Islamic subculture in Java—one thinks especially of the emphasis on personalized transfer of knowledge from *kyai* to student within closed social networks.[326] Today, moreover, hard-nosed Islamists elsewhere have been known to become Sufis as well. Ed Husain, for instance, through his own searching and critical inquiry, found that, in contrast to the soulless Islamism of the Hizb movement in the United Kingdom, which essentially presented a heavily politicized Islam that was "an alternative to Marxism," Sufism offered an Islam "deeply rooted in Muslim scholarship, introspection, and spiritual enrichment."[327] Husain noted that "in a world full of material competition, fashion, individualism, immediacy, display, youth, wealth, glamour, and concentration on all that is external," Sufism taught something else entirely:

> We were to turn *inside* and attempt to cleanse our hearts of feelings of anger, enmity, arrogance, envy, rancour, jealousy and other vices that distance us from the truth and put us into conflict with creation. Once God is in the heart, then the limbs respond smoothly to his worship. Without a pure heart, worship is burdensome and tiring.[328]

Moreover, Husain found that while the Islamists talked about the Prophet a great deal, they focused on his *political* role and did not really flesh out his character and personality. By contrast, "no other Muslim group" brought the Prophet "to life as the Sufis did." In the company of Sufis, Husain met people who "internalized every single one of the Prophet's traits: happiness, compassion, love, fairness, gentility, and an aura of inner contentment."[329] Down the road, therefore, the attractive, spiritually healing potentialities of a resurgent, tolerant Sufism within the Darul Islamic heartlands of Java, the fruit of successful cognitive immunization strategies aimed at the theological containment of Arabized modernism, cannot be ruled out.

A final, important philosophical end-state of a long-term campaign to open up the worldviews of young Javanese could be what we may call "realistic modernism." While Indonesia remains largely *abangan*-dominated, with some recent estimates putting the percentage of this community as comprising between 50 and 70 percent of the Indonesian population as a whole,[330] there is little doubt that there has been a steady increase in Muslim religiosity since the 1970s, especially in urban areas, due to "rapid social and economic change."[331] Azyumardi Azra notes the emergence of new "tendencies in religious observance, new institutions, new Muslim groups, and new Islamic life-styles" along with more "new mosques with new architecture" enjoying "full congregations, mostly youth."[332] Moreover, more Muslims have gone on the *haj* to Mecca and have dipped deeper into their pockets to provide "religious alms and donations" to their "poorer and deprived co-religionists."[333] Fealy, White, and Hooker note that many more Indonesian Muslims are "well educated, urban dwelling," and "professionally employed" compared with their predecessors in the 1950s and 1960s.[334] This is why Azra considers the 1980s as the decade when the "new Muslim middle class" emerged in Indonesia.[335] This evident "santrinization" of Indonesian Islam, however, has been more cultural than political: while many Islamic political parties were established in Indonesia after Soeharto's fall from power in May 1998, they were unable to secure decisive shares of the nationwide vote, either in the 1999 or 2004 elections, suggesting that Muslims in Indonesia appear to "differentiate Islam as a religion from its political manifestations."[336] Hence Azra is forthright in asserting that "it is a myth to exaggerate the strength and influence of the Islamists" in Indonesia.[337] The rise of the new Muslim middle class, nevertheless, has prompted some scholars to suggest that the old distinction between the *santri* traditionalists and modernists is blurring, and "the ritual and doctrinal differences" between them are "now widely regarded as inconsequential."[338] Some of these scholars suggest that this "convergence" has given rise to "neo-modernism," which "combines the respect for classical learning with a receptivity to modern, including Western, influences."[339]

What neo-modernism represents in a metaphorical sense is an *intertwining* of the Trees of Javanese traditionalism and Javanese modernism within the wider Garden of Indonesian Islam. This study suggests that what is needed is an additional convergence, or blurring of boundaries, between Javanese Islam, with its relatively weak uncertainty-avoidance outlook, and Arabized modernist Islam, with its deeply ingrained abhorrence of difference. It is precisely because of the latter cultural trait that one Branch of the Tree of Arabized modernist Islam, Salafism, seeks to radically synchronize all other expressions of Islam with its self-declared "correct" version, while the other Branch, the Islamists, seeks power so as to impose its preferred vision of the perfect Islamic society from above. What is common to both is a strong uncertainty-avoidance outlook expressed in an ingrained basic discomfort with that which is dissimilar. While the Darul Islamists, as we have seen, possess remote traces of *santri* traditionalist influences in their theological "DNA," they nevertheless remain the close cousins of the Salafis and Islamists and share the same basic inability and unwillingness to either cope with or accept difference. One result of this has been the emergence of the violent JI network from within its ranks. In a generation's time, secondary cognitive immunization efforts involving opening up the worldview of the members of the Darul Islamist charismatic group as well as the wider

Javanese Darul Islamic communities from which they emerged, in addition to fostering the growth of atheism, *abangan* nominalism, and Sufism, may also encourage what we may call a *realistic modernism*—adapting a phrase from the Tunisian Islamic scholar Rachid Ghannoushi. There would be three key characteristics of realistic modernism in the Indonesian context. First, the emphasis would be on loving a merciful God and not on fearing a vengeful, hard-to-please God—something that is psychologically functional and needed as a means of avoiding a harmful drift towards overbearing legalism and a neurotic preoccupation with avoiding sin in all circumstances and at all costs, particularly in relation to matters of sexual morality.[340] El Fadl argues that the "impact of Islam upon the world today should be humanistic" in that it should promote a "religious orientation that focuses on ending human suffering" and that "believes that human well-being and progress is a Godly task."[341]

Second, realistic modernism would be, as the term implies, "realistic." It would actively seek to revive Islamic values in all spheres of life—*while making sure to ground them in current realities*. This goes back to the earlier discussion on *shariah* and *fiqh*. While *shariah* is God's law and immutable, *fiqh* is humanly devised and is not. Realistic modernists would thus reject the puritan notion that for 90 percent of all legally pertinent matters, God has decreed an immutable position. Rather, the realistic modernists would seek to go beyond the letter of the law and "seek after the ultimate objectives of the Qur'an." As Abeh, Ayaan Hirsi's father, once told her, it's "the spirit" behind the "rules" of the Qur'an that truly matters. After all, as El Fadl observes, the "rules" as set forth in the Qur'an for unique "historical circumstances" may not be relevant today.[342] Ultimately, through the disciplined exercise of scholarly, informed legal analysis that seeks out the timeless "spirit" behind the historically contingent "rules," realistic modernist intellectuals would want to keep the great faith of Islam vital and alive, constantly evolving and growing to keep pace with "new challenges and changed conditions."[343] This realistic modernist emphasis on the practical requirements of "lived Islam" rather than the "imagined Islam" of puritans essentially translates into the willingness to apply reason in all matters of faith.[344] At one level, it would mean accepting the notion that Muslims do not need an Islamic State to practice their faith effectively; a secular, liberal democratic system would do just as well—a position that has long been articulated by Gus Dur in the Indonesian context.[345] At a more basic level, it would mean openly recognizing, as Pondok Pesantren Al-Mukmin graduate Noor Huda Ismail did, the *sheer impracticality* of the Darul Islamist binary worldview in the working world:

> Ngruki's teachings proved *unrealistic in the real world*, especially the emphasis on the strict interpretation of Islam that was at complete odds with the environment where we ended up working. After graduation, I had to obtain a personal identification card from the government, the same

government I was taught to disregard. I chose to further my studies at two
government-run universities, where I had to sing the national anthem and
respect the national flag. All of this was necessary to start a successful career
[italics added].[346]

Realistic modernists would also be well equipped to mount a doctrinal challenge to Indonesian Islamists and Salafis who would want to suffocate and
stultify social life in Java, Sumatra, and the rest of the country, and radically
synchronize it with the "simple, desert form of Islam" found in the Middle East.[347] The attempts in 2006 by the Muslim Brotherhood–influenced
Islamists of PKS to push through legislation in the national parliament to
prosecute "women in miniskirts or couples caught kissing in public" is in this
respect a worrying trend that should be watched.[348] Gus Dur, who would
be a strong natural ally of the realistic modernists, put the issue in sensible
perspective: "Young people like to kiss each other," and just "because old
people don't do it doesn't mean it's wrong."[349] Finally, and importantly, realistic modernism—in line with the relatively weaker uncertainty-avoidance
orientation and capacity for accepting difference of Javanese culture—would
champion religious pluralism. The following remarks of the late Nurcholish
Madjid or Cak Nur, the leading Javanese modernist intellectual, could provide a basis for the tolerant realistic modernist stance on religious pluralism:

> A command of God to all followers of scripture everywhere declares that
> if they are truly people of faith and piety, God will forgive them all their
> sins and send them the eternal joys of heaven. Later, another command to
> Jews and Christians—*which directly or indirectly shows a recognition of
> the existence of their religion and teachings*—promises abundant prosperity
> from above (the sky) and from beneath their feet (the earth) if they truly
> uphold the teachings of the Torah and the Gospels along with the teachings
> that God has revealed to them. . . . *Regardless of differing religious means,
> methods or paths to God, the God we want to approach is nonetheless the
> same God, the one Almighty God.* . . . That is the God of *all humankind,
> without exception* [italics added].[350]

It should be noted that the Javanese modernist Cak Nur was once considered
Natsir Muda or the Young Natsir, after Mohammad Natsir, the former Arabized modernist leader who played a key role in Persis, Masjumi, DDII, and
later LIPIA.[351] The historical fact that a key Javanese modernist could at one
time be seen to be the heir to a key Arabized modernist suggests that realistic
modernism—the product of the blurring of the boundaries between Javanese
traditionalism and modernism on one hand and Arabized modernism on the
other—would not necessarily represent that far-fetched a vision. Hence theologically containing and diluting the hard theological core of Arabized
modernism is a reachable long-term goal that moderate Muslim scholars

should be encouraged to undertake. Blocking future Radical Pathways from developing might well depend on it.

TAKING STOCK—AND A FINAL NOTE

Using the key personalities involved in Bali bombings of October 2002 as a case study, this book has sought to prompt fresh ways of thinking about how, in the main, more or less ordinary people could embark on so-called Radical Pathways toward extremism and terrorist behavior. By developing the Radical Pathways or RP Framework, comprising Existential Identity, Culture, and the Situated Individual Personality—a framework incorporating historical, geopolitical, and ideational forces through our conceptualization of Darul Islamic subculture and the political ideology of Darul Islamism—we have tried to discern the diverse ways in which the likes of key JI militants such as Imam Samudra, Amrozi, Ali Imron, and Arnasan, with the direct or indirect encouragement of the likes of Abu Bakar Ba'asyir, Mukhlas, and Hambali, came together to form the JI Cell that attacked Bali. We have found that effectively countering such Radical Pathways requires that we move beyond rather simplistic and hackneyed suggestions to win over Muslim hearts and minds. To summarize, we have argued rather that the Darul Islamist charismatic group and its associated JI mainstream and Noordin Top networks—and casting the analytical net wider, the communities in Java from which the Darul Islam movement emerged—should be the targets of a systematic cognitive immunization campaign. To be precise, such a campaign should be designed to cognitively immunize young people from these "collectivities at risk" against the blandishments of Darul Islamist ideology with its underlying binary worldview that dangerously dehumanizes unbelievers. Primary cognitive immunization efforts should be directed at the DI and JI networks that make up the Darul Islamist charismatic group in order to persuade militants to abjure violence in pursuit of the Islamic State, as well as to reject the violent Global Salafi Jihad ideology that legitimized the Bali attacks of October 2002 and subsequent JI strikes as well. Primary cognitive immunization approaches must also embrace efforts to undermine the moral standing of JI leaders and hence their message. Secondary cognitive immunization measures, on the other hand, would be directed not just at the Darul Islamist charismatic group but also at the wider Darul Islamic heartlands of Java. These would involve structured, face-to-face interfaith activity as well as integrated U.S. public diplomacy that promotes politically sensitive counterinsurgency tactics in media-saturated Muslim war zones like Iraq and Afghanistan. We also argued that in the long run, effective secondary cognitive immunization requires encouraging the opening up of worldviews of the coming generations of young people within the Darul Islamist charismatic group, and even more so in the wider Darul Islamic heartlands, through the promotion of critical, independent thought so as to "force a separation between what the tribe told you to be and what you truly are." We noted that the ultimate aim in encouraging the widespread development of the capacity for critical thought within the Javanese collectivist, large power-distance cultural milieu must be the long-term theological containment of Arabized modernist Islam, expressed in the forms of Salafism (or Wahhabism) and Islamism—both of which have deeply shaped the strong uncertainty-avoidance outlook that resides at the core of the Darul Islamic subculture and its stepchild, the political ideology of Darul Islamism.

Of the postulated philosophical end-states of secondary cognitive immunization strategies among future generations of young people in the Darul Islamic heartlands, we argued that atheism would likely not be widely appealing, but a revival of *abangan* nominalism and Sufism would probably be more so, along with, importantly, a dilution of Arabized modernism through its deliberate synthesis with Javanese traditionalism and modernism to generate what we called realistic modernism. The thrust of realistic modernism would be an emphasis on the return to the fundamentals of the Qu'ran and the Sunnah that the classic modernists call for, but all the while married to the recognition of the need to continually update the *fiqh* to ensure that the humanistic intent of Islamic law is never sacrificed at the altar of legalistic determinism and selective interpretations driven by power considerations. We may say that at the core of realistic modernism would be not be the weak uncertainty-avoidance outlook of the Sufis and traditionalists or the strong one of the Arabized modernists but rather a *moderate uncertainty-avoidance* orientation that is closer to the more conservative elements of the Muhammadiyah movement today. In the final analysis, as Charles Kimball rightly reminds us, non-Muslims need not and really should not attempt to tell Muslims in Java what or what not to do, as "all the resources needed for reform can be found at the heart of the major religious traditions."[352] Hence, let the Javanese Muslims deal with Darul Islamism by digging deep into their rich indigenous traditions. Finally, it is worth remembering one encouraging fact: a big part of the solution to the threat of religious radicalization, as we have seen in this study, seems to be the simplest one: teaching people from the time they are young to think for themselves.[353]

The great nineteenth-century Prussian philosopher of war Carl von Clausewitz famously stated: "Everything in war is very simple, but the simplest thing is very difficult." It would seem that the same idea applies to the complex challenge of blocking Radical Pathways from developing in Indonesia. While encouraging the development of critical independent thought among young people in the Darul Islamic heartlands sounds straightforward enough, operationalizing this approach will not be easy. The devil, as they say, is in the details. This study has shown that undertaking research into the task of neutralizing the threat of violent, religiously inspired militancy and terrorism requires recognition of the multiple causes of the phenomenon and by implication the necessity of the adoption of a multidisciplinary approach. No single discipline can by itself throw up the necessary insights to guide analysts and policy makers and law enforcement officials who have to deal with the threat on a daily basis. Like the story of the blind men and the elephant, each discipline in isolation can shed only partial light on the overall problem. In this study, the insights of area studies, particularly the history of Islam in the Middle East and in Java, the domestic politics of Indonesia and the geopolitics of the Cold War in Southeast Asia, Islamic philosophy, cultural psychology, cross-cultural psychology, evolutionary psychology, social psychology, and even cognitive neuroscience were employed in order to produce analytically pertinent and hopefully *consilient* knowledge—to employ sociobiologist E. O. Wilson's term. In the future, consilient knowledge, the product of systematic interdisciplinary research, will be more important, not least in dealing with the threats of violent religious radicalization and particularly the emergent threats of "self-radicalization" and the so-called "home-grown terrorism" phenomenon. It is readily admitted here that the single analyst trawling the various disciplines for insights into the increasingly complex and multi-faceted radicalization problem can go only so far by his own efforts. There would come a point when he or she would simply lack the specialized training to extract any more meaningful insights from the disciplinary mix and would have to rely on other specialists for assistance. It is thus hoped that terrorism scholars working on Southeast Asia—the target of sometimes justified, but at other times smug and short-sighted attacks from area specialists, journalists, and other political scientists—would be given a fair shake and cooperated with on an interdisciplinary basis.[354] No one should think that they have a monopoly on knowledge. There is much to be said, to borrow a phrase from a popular book, for tapping the "wisdom of crowds."[355] If this *Radical Pathways* volume, blemishes and all, is able to encourage further movement in the direction of multidisciplinary research into the threat of violent religious radicalization in Southeast Asia—perhaps pivoting on the question of the wider applicability of the Radical Pathways Framework to other parts of the region and even beyond—then the effort will have been worth it.

Notes

PROLOGUE

1. Made Mangku Pastika, "The Uncovering of the Bali Blast Case" (presentation, Jakarta, January 20, 2003). The author gratefully acknowledges the International Center for Political Violence and Terrorism Research of the S. Rajaratnam School of International Studies, Nanyang Technological University, Singapore, for making a copy available.

2. Pastika, "The Uncovering of the Bali Blast Case." See also Ken Conboy, *The Second Front: Inside Asia's Most Dangerous Terrorist Network* (Jakarta: Equinox Publishing, 2006), 181–4.

3. Sally Neighbour, *In the Shadow of Swords: On the Trail of Terrorism from Afghanistan to Australia* (Sydney: HarperCollins, 2004), 288–9.

4. For details of the so-called Singapore plot, see *The Jemaah Islamiyah Arrests and the Threat of Terrorism*, cmnd. 2 of 2003 (January 2003), 26–8. Hereafter Singapore WP.

5. Conboy, *The Second Front*, 163–4.

6. Neighbour, *In the Shadow of Swords*, 288–9.

7. Conboy, *The Second Front*, 185. Neighbour, *In the Shadow of Swords*, 294–6.

8. David Greecy interview in *Bombali*. Directed by Phil Craig and Steve Westh. Perth, Western Australia: Electric Pictures Productions and Brook Lapping Productions, 2006.

9. Neighbour, *In the Shadow of Swords*, 297.

10. Ibid.

11. Ibid., 298.

12. *Bombali.*

13. Pastika, "The Uncovering of the Bali Blast Case."

14. *Bombali.*

15. Pastika, "Uncovering of the Bali Blast Case."

16. Conboy, *The Second Front*, 186.

17. Kelly McEvers, "Visiting the Space Where the Sari Club Used to Be," *Slate.com*, posted November 2, 2005, http://www.slate.com/id/2128835/entry/2128838/ (accessed August 9, 2008).

18. Conboy, *The Second Front*, 186.

19. Pastika, "Uncovering of the Bali Blast Case;" Conboy, *The Second Front*, 186.

20. *Bombali.*

CHAPTER 1

1. "Police Seek Bombers' Names," *BBC News*, October 3, 2005, http://news.bbc.co.uk/2/hi/asia-pacific/4302982.stm (accessed September 3, 2007).

2. Peter Chalk and William Rosenau, "Southeast Asia the Second Front of Global Terror?" *The Nation Multimedia.com* (Thailand), September 21, 2006, http://www.nationmultimedia.com/specials/south2years/sep2106.php (accessed September 3, 2007).

3. Peter Chalk, "Al Qaeda and its Links to Terrorist Groups in Asia," in *The New Terrorism: Anatomy, Trends and Counter-Strategies*, ed. Andrew Tan and Kumar Ramakrishna (Singapore: Eastern Universities Press, 2002), 117.

4. Twelve people were killed and nearly 150 injured. See "Marriott Blast Suspects Named," *CNN.com*, August 19, 2003, http://www.cnn.com/2003/WORLD/asiapcf/southeast/08/19/indonesia.arrests.names/index.html (accessed September 3, 2007).

5. Nine people were killed. "JI Responsible for Jakarta Bombing: Statement," *ABC News Online* (Australia), September 10, 2004, http://www.abc.net.au/news/newsitems/200409/s1196027.htm (accessed September 3. 2007).

6. For instance, see Chalk, "Al Qaeda and its Links to Terrorist Groups in Asia," 112–8; Anthony L. Smith, "Terrorism and the Political Landscape in Indonesia: The Fragile Post-Bali Consensus," in *Terrorism and Violence in Southeast Asia: Transnational Challenges to States and Regional Stability*, ed. Paul J. Smith (New York: M. E. Sharpe, 2005), 104–9; Greg Fealy, "Islamic Radicalism in Indonesia: The Faltering Revival?" *Southeast Asian Affairs 2004* (Singapore: Institute of Southeast Asian Studies, 2004), 104–21; Joseph Chinyong Liow, "Muslim Resistance in Southern Thailand and Southern Philippines: Religion, Ideology, and Politics," *East-West Center Policy Studies* 24 (Washington, D.C: East-West Center, 2006).

7. "Philippines: Extremist Groups Target Civilians," *Human Rights Watch*, July 30, 2007, http://hrw.org/english/docs/2007/07/27/philip16515.htm (accessed September 3, 2007).

8. For an informative and recent American assessment of the strategic importance of Southeast Asia, see Walter Lohman, "Guidelines for US Policy in Southeast Asia," *Backgrounder* 2017 (Washington D.C: The Heritage Foundation, March 20, 2007).

9. See United Nations Office of Drug and Crime (UNODC), "Definitions of Terrorism," http://www.unodc.org/unodc/terrorism_definitions.html (accessed August 16, 2007).

10. UNODC, "Definitions of Terrorism."

11. Walter Laqueur, *No End to War: Terrorism in the Twenty-First Century* (New York: Continuum, 2003), 233.

12. David C. Rapoport, "The Fourth Wave: September 11 in the History of Terrorism," *Current History* 100 (2001): 419–24.

13. Steven Simon and Daniel Benjamin, "The Terror," *Survival* 43 (2001–2): 5. See also their *The Age of Sacred Terror* (New York: Random House, 2002), ix.

14. Laqueur, *No End to War*, 232–3.

15. UNODC, "Definitions of Terrorism."

16. Laqueur, *No End to War*, 233.

17. Jessica Stern, *Terror in the Name of God: Why Religious Militants Kill* (New York: HarperCollins, 2003), xx–xxi.

18. Cited in Carlyle A. Thayer, "Al-Qaeda and Political Terrorism in Southeast Asia," in Smith, *Terrorism and Violence in Southeast Asia*, 81.

19. See "National Exclusive: Hezbollah Leader Hassan Nasrallah Talks With Former US Diplomats on Israel, Prisoners and Hezbollah's Founding," *Democracy Now* Web site, July 28, 2006, http://www.democracynow.org/article.pl?sid=06/07/28/1440244 (accessed August 16, 2007).

20. See John M. Whiteley's 1988 interview with Brian M. Jenkins, "Terrorists Want a Lot of People Watching, Not a Lot of People Dead," *Quest for Peace* Web site, University of California at Irvine, http://www.lib.uci.edu/quest/index.php?page=jenkins (accessed August 20, 2007).

21. See Thomas Perry Thornton, "Terror as a Weapon of Political Agitation," in *Internal War*, ed. Harry Eckstein (New York: The Free Press, 1964), 83. A detailed discussion is found in Kumar Ramakrishna, *Emergency Propaganda: The Winning of Malayan Hearts and Minds 1948–1958* (Richmond: Curzon, 2002), 12–17.

22. Thornton, "Terror as a Weapon of Political Agitation," 83.

23. See Alex P. Schmid and Janny de Graaf, *Violence as Communication: Insurgent Terrorism and the Western News Media* (London: Sage, 1982), 12; and Grant Wardlaw, *Political Terrorism: Theory, Tactics and Counter-Measures*, 2nd ed. (Cambridge: Cambridge University Press, 1989), 20–21.

24. Benjamin and Simon, *Age of Sacred Terror*, 40.

25. Bruce Hoffman, "The Emergence of the New Terrorism," in Tan and Ramakrishna, *The New Terrorism*, 45.

26. Ibid., 30.

27. Alain Bauer, criminologist at Sorbonne University in France, has even recently asserted that "terrorism has become war." See Mitchell D. Silber and Arvin Bhatt, *Radicalization in the West: The Homegrown Threat* (New York: New York Police Department Intelligence Division, 2007), 13.

28. Gavin Cameron, "Terrorism and Weapons of Mass Destruction: Prospects and Problems," in Tan and Ramakrishna, *The New Terrorism*, 50–72.

29. Laqueur, *No End to War*, 238.

30. Jonathan T. Drummond, "From the Northwest Imperative to Global Jihad: Social Psychological Aspects of the Construction of the Enemy, Political Violence,

and Terror," in *The Psychology of Terrorism*, ed. Chris E. Stout (Westport: Praeger, 2002), vol. 1, *A Public Understanding*, 54.

31. Michael J. Stevens, "The Unanticipated Consequences of Globalization: Contextualizing Terrorism," in Stout, *Psychology of Terrorism*, vol. 3, *Theoretical Understandings and Perspectives*, 37.

32. James Waller, *Becoming Evil: How Ordinary People Commit Genocide and Mass Killing* (New York: Oxford University Press, 2005), 16.

33. Ibid.

34. Drummond, "From the Northwest Imperative to Global Jihad," in Stout, *Psychology of Terrorism*, vol. 1, 51.

35. John E. Mack, "Looking Beyond Terrorism: Transcending the Mind of Enmity," in Stout, *Psychology of Terrorism*, vol. 1, 174.

36. This incident on March 11, 2004, was perpetrated by a Moroccan cell with Al Qaeda links. A total of 191 people were killed. See "Madrid Remembers Train Bombings," *BBC News*, March 11, 2005, http://news.bbc.co.uk/2/hi/europe/4338727.stm (accessed September 4, 2007).

37. Waller, *Becoming Evil*, 16–17.

38. Steven Pinker, *The Blank Slate: The Modern Denial of Human Nature* (London: Penguin, 2003), 179–80.

39. Andrew Silke, "Becoming a Terrorist," in *Terrorists, Victims and Society: Psychological Perspectives on Terrorism and its Consequences*, ed. Andrew Silke (Chichester, UK: Wiley, 2003), 31.

40. Ibid., 32.

41. John M. Davis, "Countering International Terrorism: Perspectives from International Psychology," in Stout, *Psychology of Terrorism*, vol. 4, *Programs and Practices in Response and Prevention*, 33.

42. Ba'asyir has been interviewed by, for instance, Scott Atran, a research scientist at the National Center for Scientific Research in Paris and the University of Michigan. See Scott Atran, "In Indonesia, Democracy is Not Enough," *NYTimes.com*, October 5, 2005, http://www.nytimes.com/2005/10/05/opinion/05atran.html?pagewanted=1&ei=5088&en=6e98aa49e50af97a&ex=1286164800&partner=rssnyt&emc=rss (accessed September 4, 2007). Ba'asyir has also granted interviews to the Malaysian political scientist Farish Noor. See Farish A. Noor, "Interview with Abu Bakar Bashir: Jihad, Not Elections," *Politik Pop*, August 18, 2006, http://politikpop.blogspot.com/2006/08/interview-with-abu-bakar-bashir.html (accessed September 4, 2007).

43. "Indonesian Defence Minister Says Hambali No Longer 'Useful'," *Kabar-Indonesia*, October 9, 2006, http://72.14.253.104/search?q=cache:TR00V6_TOpYJ:www.kabar-irian.info/pipermail/kabar-indonesia/2006-October/012152.html+hambali,+no+access&hl=en&ct=clnk&cd=1&gl=sg (accessed August 24, 2007).

44. John Sidel, *Riots, Pogroms, Jihad: Religious Violence in Indonesia* (Singapore: NUS Press, 2007), x.

45. Natasha Hamilton-Hart, "Terrorism in Southeast Asia: Expert Analysis, Myopia and Fantas," *The Pacific Review* 18 (2005): 308.

46. David Martin Jones and Michael L. R. Smith, "Is There a Sovietology of Southeast Asian Studies?" *International Affairs* 77 (2001): 843–65.

47. Verity Edwards and Cameron Stewart, "Professor Warned Off Terrorist Trip," *Australian*, September 13, 2006, http://www.theaustralian.news.com.au/story/0,20867,20402378–12332,00.html (accessed August 9, 2008).

48. Hamilton-Hart, "Terrorism in Southeast Asia," 310.

49. See notes 2 and 3 above for bibliographic information on the accounts by Neighbour and Conboy.

50. Harper Lee, *To Kill a Mockingbird* (New York: Harper Perennial Modern Classics, 2006).

51. Martha Crenshaw, "Questions to be Answered, Research to be Done, Knowledge to be Applied," in *Origins of Terrorism: Psychologies, Ideologies, Theologies, States of Mind*, ed. Walter Reich (Washington D.C: Woodrow Wilson Center Press, 1998), 247.

52. Hamilton-Hart, "Terrorism in Southeast Asia," 319.

53. Christopher R. Browning, *Ordinary Men: Reserve Police Battalion 101 and the Final Solution in Poland* (New York: HarperCollins, 1992).

54. Neil J. Kressel, *Mass Hate: The Global Rise of Genocide and Terror*, rev. and updated ed. (Cambridge, Mass.: Westview Press, 2002); Alan C. Elms, *Uncovering Lives: The Uneasy Alliance of Biography and Psychology* (New York and Oxford: Oxford University Press, 1994); Willard Gaylin, *Hatred: The Psychological Descent into Violence* (New York: Public Affairs, 2003).

55. Elms, *Uncovering Lives*, 5.

56. Cited in Waller, *Becoming Evil*, viii.

57. E. O. Wilson, *Consilience: The Unity of Knowledge* (New York: Vintage Books, 1999), 13.

58. Ibid., 13–14.

59. Ibid., 8.

60. Peter Chalk, "Separatism and Southeast Asia: The Islamic Factor in Southern Thailand, Mindanao and Aceh," *Studies in Conflict and Terrorism* 24 (2001): 241–69.

61. Syed Serajul Islam, *The Politics of Islamic Identity in Southeast Asia* (Singapore: Thomson Learning, 2005), 295.

62. Smith, ed., *Terrorism and Violence in Southeast Asia*; Kumar Ramakrishna and See Seng Tan, eds., *After Bali: The Threat of Terrorism in Southeast Asia* (Singapore: World Scientific, 2003).

63. Rohan Gunaratna, *Inside Al Qaeda: Global Network of Terror* (London: Christopher Hurst, 2002), 174–203; Zachary Abuza, *Militant Islam in Southeast Asia; Crucible of Terror* (Boulder, Colo.: Lynne Rienner, 2003); Maria Ressa, *Seeds of Terror: An Eye-Witness Account of Al Qaeda's Newest Center of Operations in Southeast Asia* (New York: Free Press, 2003); Bilveer Singh, *The Talibanization of Southeast Asia: Losing the War on Terror to Islamist Extremists* (Westport, Conn.: Praeger Security International, 2007); and the numerous reports by Sidney Jones's International Crisis Group. A good example of Jones's ICG output is *How the Jemaah Islamiyah Terrorist Network Operates*, Asia Report 43 (Jakarta, Brussels: International Crisis Group, December 11, 2002).

64. Conboy, *The Second Front*; Neighbour, *In the Shadow of Swords*; Mike Millard, *Jihad in Paradise: Islam and Politics in Southeast Asia* (New York: M. E. Sharpe, 2004); Tracy Dahlby, *Allah's Torch: A Report from Behind the Scenes in Asia's War on Terror* (New York: William Morrow, 2005).

65. Greg Barton, *Jemaah Islamiyah: Radical Islamism in Indonesia* (Singapore: Singapore University Press, 2005); Anthony Bubalo and Greg Fealy, *Joining the Caravan? The Middle East, Islamism and Indonesia* (Alexandria, NSW: The Lowy Institute for International Policy, 2005).

66. Sidel, *Riots, Pogroms, Jihad*.

67. Ibid., xi.

68. Thayer, "Al-Qaeda and Political Terrorism in Southeast Asia," in Smith, *Terrorism and Violence in Southeast Asia*, 83–4.

69. Hamilton-Hart, "Terrorism in Southeast Asia," 320.

70. Walter Reich, "Understanding Terrorist Behavior: The Limits and Opportunities of Psychological Enquiry," in Reich, *Origins of Terrorism*, 267.

71. Ibid., 276.

72. Tom Allard, "Head of JI 'Captured'," *smh.com.au* (Australia), June 15, 2007, http://www.smh.com.au/news/world/head-of-ji-captured/2007/06/15/1181414530007.html?s_cid=rss_smh (accessed September 3, 2007).

73. Mark Forbes, "Radicals in Retreat," *theage.com.au* (Australia), August 26, 2007, http://www.theage.com.au/news/in-depth/radicals-in-retreat/2007/08/25/1187462586317.html (accessed September 3, 2007).

74. The distinction between counter-terrorist and counter-terrorism approaches is elaborated in Kumar Ramakrishna, "US Strategy in Southeast Asia: Counter-Terrorist or Counter-Terrorism?" in Ramakrishna and Tan, *After Bali*, 306.

75. Peter B. Smith, Michael Harris Bond, and Cigdem Kagitcibasi, *Understanding Social Psychology Across Cultures: Living and Working in a Changing World* (London: Sage, 2006), 33.

76. Smith et al., *Understanding Social Psychology Across Cultures*, 33–4. See also Hofstede, *Culture's Consequences: International Differences in Work-Related Values* (Beverly Hills: Sage, 1980).

77. Geert Hofstede and Gert Jan Hofstede, *Cultures and Organizations: Software of the Mind* (New York: McGraw-Hill, 2005), 23.

78. Ibid., 22–3.

79. Ibid., 32. For the methodology employed by Schwartz, see Smith et al., *Understanding Social Psychology Across Cultures*, 38–44.

80. Smith et al., *Understanding Social Psychology Across Cultures*, 45.

81. Ibid.

82. Hofstede and Hofstede, *Cultures and Organizations*, p. 33.

83. Ibid.

84. Smith et al., *Understanding Social Psychology Across Cultures*, 45.

85. Ibid., 45–6. It should be noted that this particular study by Trompenaars, Smith, and Dugan did not clearly distinguish between the individual and nation level of analysis, and strictly speaking cannot be classed as entirely identical to the distinctly nation-level values studies as those done by Hofstede, Schwartz, and Inglehart. See also Hofstede and Hofstede, *Cultures and Organizations*, 32–3.

86. Hofstede and Hofstede, *Cultures and Organizations*, 2–3.

87. Ibid., 4.

88. Ibid., 3.

89. Smith et al., *Understanding Social Psychology Across Cultures*, 47–55.

90. Cited in ibid., 74.

91. Cited in ibid.

92. Ibid.

93. J. Hayes and C. W. Allinson, "Cognitive Style and the Theory and Practice of Individual and Collective Learning in Organisations," *Human Relations* 51 (1998): 850.

94. Smith et al., *Understanding Social Psychology Across Cultures*, 75.

95. Ibid.

96. Hofstede and Hofstede, *Cultures and Organizations*, 16.

97. Ibid., 9–10.

98. Ibid., 3.

99. Ayaan Hirsi Ali, *The Caged Virgin: A Muslim Woman's Cry for Reason* (London: The Free Press, 2006), 31.

100. Ibid., 98.

101. Brigitte Gabriel, *Because They Hate: A Survivor of Islamic Terror Warns America* (New York: St. Martin's Press, 2006), 15.

102. Ibid.

103. Ibid.

104. Hofstede and Hofstede, *Cultures and Organizations*, 2.

105. For a brief, early attempt to suggest the applicability of the Hofstede framework to the study of terrorism, see Olufemi A. Lawal, "Social-Psychological Considerations in the Emergence and Growth of Terrorism," in Stout, *Psychology of Terrorism*, vol. 4, 26–7.

106. Hofstede and Hofstede, *Cultures and Organizations*, 23.

107. Ibid., 46.

108. Ibid., 76.

109. Ibid., 167.

110. Ibid., 51–7.

111. Ibid., 43–4.

112. Ibid., 75.

113. Ibid., 86–7.

114. Ibid., 89–90.

115. Ibid., 78–9.

116. Ibid., 83.

117. Ibid., 189.

118. Ibid., 203.

119. Abd Samad Moussaoui, with Florence Bouquillat, *Zacarias Moussaoui: The Making of a Terrorist*, trans. Simon Pleasance and Fronza Woods (London: Serpent's Tail, 2003), 59.

120. Silber and Bhatt, *Radicalization in the West*.

121. Hofstede and Hofstede, *Cultures and Organizations*, 174.

122. Ibid.

123. Ibid., 195–9.

124. Ibid., 203.

125. Ibid.

126. Ibid., 196–7.

127. Ibid., 197.

128. Ibid., 4–5.

129. Ibid., 4.

130. Ibid., 5.

131. Ibid.

132. I am grateful to Professor Khong Yuen Foong for suggesting the use of the term "Existential Identity."

133. Waller, *Becoming Evil*, 149.

134. Pinker, *Blank Slate*, 142.

135. Waller, *Becoming Evil*, 145.

136. Ibid., 145–6.

137. Ibid., 147.

138. Ibid., 146–7.

139. Cited in ibid., 147.

140. Ibid., 146.

141. Wilson, *Consilience*, 138.

142. Ibid., 163.

143. Ibid.

144. See Robert Winston, *Human Instinct: How Our Primeval Impulses Shape Our Modern Lives* (London: Bantam Books, 2003), 40.

145. Waller, *Becoming Evil*, 147.

146. Ibid., 148.

147. Cited in ibid. See also Winston, *Human Instinct*, 39–42.

148. Waller, *Becoming Evil*, 149.

149. Ibid., 150–51.

150. Ibid., 151.

151. David Berreby, *Us and Them: Understanding Your Tribal Mind* (New York and Boston: Little, Brown and Company, 2005), 311.

152. Elliot Sober and David Sloan Wilson cited in Waller, *Becoming Evil*, 152.

153. Waller, *Becoming Evil*, 152.

154. Ibid., 153.

155. See Rush W. Dozier, Jr., *Why We Hate: Understanding, Curbing and Eliminating Hate in Ourselves and Our World* (New York: Contemporary Books, 2002), 40–41.

156. Ibid., 40.

157. Kressel, *Mass Hate*, 211.

158. Henri Tajfel and Joseph P. Forgas, "Social Categorization: Cognitions, Values and Groups," in *Stereotypes and Prejudice: Essential Readings*, ed. Charles Stangor (Philadelphia: Psychology Press, 2000), 49–63.

159. Waller, *Becoming Evil*, 239.

160. Berreby, *Us and Them*, 211.

161. Waller, *Becoming Evil*, 239–40.

162. Ibid., 240.

163. Berreby, *Us and Them*, 52–3.

164. Waller, *Becoming Evil*, 240.

165. For a very good discussion of the concept and its application to the Balkans conflicts of the 1990s, see Michael Ignatieff, *The Warrior's Honor: Ethnic War and the Modern Conscience* (New York: Owl Books, 1997), 34–71.

166. Waller, *Becoming Evil*, 240.

167. Ibid., 240.

168. Kressel, *Mass Hate*, 211.

169. Sumner cited in Berreby, *Us and Them*, 211.

170. Kressel, *Mass Hate*, 199.

171. Waller, *Becoming Evil*, 154.

172. Ibid., 154–5.

173. Ibid., 155.

174. Kressel, *Mass Hate*, 200.

175. Waller, *Becoming Evil*, 155.

176. Ibid.

177. Alister McGrath, with Joanna Collicutt McGrath, *The Dawkins Delusion? Atheist Fundamentalism and the Denial of the Divine* (London: Society for Promoting Christian Knowledge, 2007), 51.

178. Timothy Gallimore, "Unresolved Trauma: Fuel for the Cycle of Violence and Terrorism," in Strout, *Psychology of Terrorism,* vol. 2, *Clinical Aspects and Responses*, 147.

179. Waller, *Becoming Evil*, 242.

180. Psychoanalyst Vamik Volkan credits Erik H. Erikson for making the concept of "identity" a key domain for research. See Vamik Volkan, *Killing in the Name of Identity: A Study of Bloody Conflicts* (Charlottesville, Va.: Pitchstone, 2006), 14.

181. Fathali M. Moghaddam, *From the Terrorists' Point of View: What They Experience and Why They Come to Destroy* (London and Westport: Praeger Security International, 2006), 23.

182. Ibid., 26.

183. Stevens, "The Unanticipated Consequences of Globalization," in Stout, *Psychology of Terrorism,* vol. 3, 44.

184. Moghaddam, *From the Terrorists' Point of View*, 27.

185. Joseph S. Nye, Jr., *Bound to Lead: The Changing Nature of American Power* (New York: Basic Books, 1991). For a more recent critical comment on the way the administration of George W. Bush has not fully appreciated the importance of soft power, especially in its approach to the Iraq issue, see also Joseph S. Nye Jr., "Propaganda isn't the Way: Soft Power," *International Herald Tribune*, January 10, 2003, available online at http://www.ksg.harvard.edu/news/opeds/2003/nye_soft_power_iht_011003.htm (accessed October 11, 2007).

186. Moghaddam, *From the Terrorists' Point of View,* 27.

187. Ibid., 28.

188. Ibid.

189. Volkan, *Killing in the Name of Identity,* 69–70.

190. Ibid.

191. Stevens, "the Unanticipated Consequences of Globalization," in Stout, *Psychology of Terrorism*, vol. 3, 45.

192. Lord Alderdice, "The Individual, the Group and the Psychology of Terrorism," *International Review of Psychiatry* 19 (2007): 203.

193. Ibid., 204.

194. Volkan, *Killing in the Name of Identity,* 70–85.

195. See Kumar Ramakrishna, "The (Psychic) Roots of Religious Violence in South and Southeast Asia," in *Religion and Conflict in South and Southeast Asia: Disrupting Violence*, ed. Linell E. Cady and Sheldon W. Simon (New York: Routledge, 2007), 126.

196. Cited in Kressel, *Mass Hate*, 28.

197. Alderdice, "The Individual, the Group and the Psychology of Terrorism," 204.

198. Volkan, *Killing in the Name of Identity*, 200.

199. Cited in Sidel, *Riots, Pogroms, Jihad*, 13.

200. Mack C. Stirling, "Violent Religion: Rene Girard's Theory of Culture," in *The Destructive Power of Religion: Violence in Judaism, Christianity and Islam*, ed. J. Harold Ellens (Westport, Conn.: Praeger, 2004), vol. 2, *Religion, Psychology, and Violence*, 12.

201. Ramakrishna, "The (Psychic) Roots of Religious Violence," 125–6.

202. Stirling, "Violent Religion," 15.

203. Ibid., 17–18.

204. Hofstede and Hofstede, *Cultures and Organizations*, 306.

205. Ibid.

CHAPTER 2

1. This is not to deny that Al Qaeda's global *jihad* ideology did have an impact on senior JI militants who fought with the *mujahidin* in Afghanistan in the late 1980s and that there were both personal and operational links forged between Al Qaeda and JI operatives subsequently. See Abuza, *Militant Islam in Southeast Asia*, 121–87; Rohan Gunaratna, "Understanding Al Qaeda and its Network in Southeast Asia," in Ramakrishna and Tan, *After Bali*, 117–32; Barton, *Jemaah Islamiyah*, 7–24.

2. Javanese society represents the majority of Indonesian Muslims. Hence in this work "Javanese Islam" and "Indonesian Islam" will be used interchangeably. See Noorhaidi Hasan, "Islamic Militancy, Sharia, and Democratic Consolidation in Post-Suharto Indonesia," Working Paper 143 (Singapore: S. Rajaratnam School of International Studies, October 23, 2007), p. 8, n. 7.

3. Barbara Watson Andaya, "Religious Developments in Southeast Asia, c. 1500–1800," in *The Cambridge History of Southeast Asia*, vol. 1, pt. 2, *From c. 1500 to c. 1800*, ed. Nicholas Tarling (Cambridge: Cambridge University Press, 1999), 171. Hereafter abbreviated as *CHSEA*.

4. Ibid., 170–71.

5. Robert Day McAmis, *Malay Muslims: The History and Challenge of Resurgent Islam in Southeast Asia* (Grand Rapids, Michigan: William B. Eerdmans, 2002), 13.

6. Andaya, "Religious Developments in Southeast Asia," Tarling, *CHSEA*, vol. 1, pt. 2, 170.

7. Ibid., 171.

8. Greg Fealy, Virginia Hooker, and Sally White, "Indonesia," in *Voices of Islam in Southeast Asia: A Contemporary Sourcebook*, ed. Greg Fealy and Virginia Hooker (Singapore: Institute of Southeast Asian Studies, 2006), 41.

9. Andaya, "Religious Developments in Southeast Asia," in Tarling, *CHSEA*, vol. 1, pt. 2, 172.

10. Ibid.

11. Ibid., 173.

12. Ibid.

13. See also Joel S. Kahn, *Other Malays: Nationalism and Cosmopolitanism in the Malay World* (Singapore: Singapore University Press, 2006), 21; McAmis, *Malay Muslims,* 47.

14. For a detailed account of the impact of the Sumatra-based Srivijaya and Java-centred Majapahit kingdoms on the development of the eclectic Javanese Hindu-Buddhist worldview between the seventh and fourteenth centuries C.E., see Keith W. Taylor, "The Early Kingdoms," in Tarling, *CHSEA,* vol. 1, pt. 1, *From Early Times to circa 1500,* 173–81.

15. Mark R. Woodward, "The 'Slametan': Textual Knowledge and Ritual Performance in Central Javanese Islam," *History of Religions* 28 (1988): 54–89.

16. Andaya, "Religious Developments in Southeast Asia," in Tarling, *CHSEA,* vol. 1, pt. 2, 174.

17. Ibid.

18. Ibid., 175.

19. Ibid.

20. Ibid., 176.

21. Ibid.

22. Peter N. Stearns and William L. Langer, eds., *The Encyclopedia of World History,* rev. ed. (New York: Houghton Mifflin, 2001), 373.

23. Andaya, "Religious Developments in Southeast Asia," in Tarling, *CHSEA,* vol. 1, pt. 2, 176–7.

24. Ibid., 181.

25. McAmis, *Malay Muslims,* 17.

26. Anthony Nutting, *The Arabs: A Narrative History from Mohammed to the Present* (New York: Mentor, 1964), 18.

27. Raphael Patai, *The Arab Mind,* rev. ed., with an updated foreword by Norwell B. De Atkine (New York: Heatherleigh Press, 2007), 79.

28. Nutting, *The Arabs,* 18.

29. Ibid., 19.

30. Patai, *The Arab Mind,* 78–9.

31. Ibid., 82.

32. Nutting, *The Arabs,* 19.

33. Ibid.

34. Ibid., 22.

35. Ibid., 22–3.

36. Ibid., 39.

37. Reuven Firestone, *Jihad: The Origins of Holy War in Islam* (New York: Oxford University Press, 1999), 26–7.

38. Nutting, *The Arabs,* 17.

39. Ibid.

40. Ibid., 18.

41. Ibid., 25.

42. Ibid.

43. Firestone, *Jihad,* 27.

44. Nutting, *The Arabs,* 26.

45. Firestone, *Jihad,* 20.

46. Nutting, *The Arabs,* 27.

47. Ibid., 27–8.

48. Ibid., 37.

49. Firestone, *Jihad*, 117–21.

50. Ibid., 124–5.

51. Nutting, *The Arabs*, 37.

52. Richard Fletcher, *The Cross and the Crescent: The Dramatic Story of the Earliest Encounters Between Christians and Muslims* (London: Penguin, 2004), 13.

53. Ibid., 14–15.

54. Mark A. Gabriel, *Journey Into the Mind of an Islamic Terrorist: Why They Hate Us and How We Can Change Their Minds* (Lake Mary, Florida: Frontline, 2006), 144. Gabriel, a convert to Christianity, was a devout Muslim who grew up in Egypt, earned a doctorate in Islamic history and culture, and taught at the prestigious Al-Azhar University in Cairo.

55. Ibid.

56. Graham E. Fuller, *The Future of Political Islam* (New York: Palgrave Macmillan, 2003), 51.

57. Angel M. Rabasa et al., *The Muslim World After 9/11* (Santa Monica: Rand, 2004), 22.

58. Gabriel, *Journey into the Mind of an Islamic Terrorist,* 145.

59. Ibid., 148.

60. Rabasa et al., *The Muslim World After 9/11*, 22; Andaya, "Religious Developments in Southeast Asia," in Tarling, *CHSEA*, vol. 1, pt. 2, 179.

61. Andaya, "Religious Developments in Southeast Asia," in Tarling, *CHSEA*, vol. 1, pt. 2, 178.

62. Ibid.

63. Ibid., 177, 181.

64. Ibid., 179.

65. Reynaldo Ileto, "Religion and Anti-Colonial Movements," in Tarling, *CHSEA*, vol. 2, pt. 1, *From c. 1800 to the 1930s*, 203.

66. Ibid.

67. Ibid., 204.

68. Ibid.

69. Ibid.

70. Peter Bellwood, "Southeast Asia Before History," in Tarling, *CHSEA*, vol. 1, pt. 1, 57.

71. Ibid., 94.

72. See Jeffrey Sachs, "Notes on a New Sociology of Economic Development," in *Culture Matters: How Values Shape Human Progress*, ed. Lawrence E. Harrison and Samuel P. Huntington (New York: Basic Books, 2000), 32.

73. Kenneth R. Hall, "Economic History of Early Southeast Asia," in Tarling, *CHSEA*, vol. 1, pt. 1, 187.

74. Ibid.

75. Hofstede and Hofstede, *Cultures and Organizations*, 69.

76. Hall, "Economic History of Early Southeast Asia," in Tarling, *CHSEA*, vol. 1, pt. 1, 219.

77. Azyumardi Azra, "The Megawati Presidency: The Challenge of Political Islam" (paper presented at the "Joint Forum on the First 100 Days of the Megawati Presidency," organized by the Institute of Southeast Asian Studies [Singapore] and

the Center for Strategic and International Studies [Jakarta], Singapore, November 1, 2001).

78. Harold Crouch, "Radical Islam in Indonesia: Some Misperceptions," in *Islamic Terrorism in Indonesia: Myths and Realities*, ed. Marika Vicziany and David Wright-Neville (Melbourne: Monash University Press, 2005), 34–36. See also Azyumardi Azra, "Bali and Southeast Asian Islam: Debunking the Myths," in Ramakrishna and Tan, *After Bali*, 39–40.

79. Fealy, Hooker, and White, "Indonesia," 39–41. See also Hasan, "Islamic Militancy, Sharia, and Democratic Consolidation in Post-Suharto Indonesia," p. 8, n. 7.

80. Fealy, Hooker, and White, "Indonesia," 39–40.

81. Ibid., 40.

82. Howard M. Federspiel, *Indonesian Muslim Intellectuals of the 20th Century* (Singapore: Institute of Southeast Asian Studies, 2006), 5.

83. Ibid.

84. Fealy, Hooker, and White, "Indonesia," 40.

85. I am grateful to my colleague, the Muslim scholar Ustaz Muhammad Haniff Hassan, of the Rajaratnam School's International Centre for Political Violence and Terrorism Research, for this explanation.

86. Fealy, Hooker, and White, "Indonesia," 40.

87. Rabasa et al., *The Muslim World After 9/11*, 21.

88. Ibid.

89. See Mark R. Woodward's Introduction to Speech by Abdurrahman Wahid, "Islam Pluralism and Democracy," Consortium for Strategic Communication, Arizona State University, April 19, 2007, 2. See also "The 1993 Ramon Magsaysay Award for Community Leadership: Biography of Abdurrahman Wahid," September 1993, http://www.rmaf.org.ph/Awardees/Biography/BiographyWahidAbd.htm (accessed August 10, 2008).

90. Mark R. Woodward, "President Gus Dur: Indonesia, Islam and *Reformasi*," n.d., http://web.archive.org/web/20030219093713/http://www.asu.edu/clas/asian/pubs/woodward.htm (accessed October 18, 2007).

91. Abdurrahman Wahid, "Indigenizing Islam," Extract 15-2, in Fealy and Hooker, *Voices of Islam in Southeast Asia*, 417.

92. John L. Esposito and John O. Voll, eds., *Makers of Contemporary Islam* (New York: Oxford University Press, 2001), 204–7.

93. Federspiel, *Indonesian Muslim Intellectuals*, 16.

94. Khaled Abou El Fadl, *The Great Theft: Wrestling Islam From the Extremists* (New York: HarperSanFrancisco, 2005), 75–6.

95. Ibid., 76.

96. See Waller's comment that the "in-group" can encompass "small, face-to-face groupings of family and friends to "large social categories such as race, ethnicity, gender, or religion." Waller, *Becoming Evil*, 239.

97. John L. Esposito, *Unholy War: Terror in the Name of Islam* (New York: Oxford University Press, 2002), 78–9.

98. Kahn, *Other Malays*, 96.

99. Fealy, Hooker, and White, "Indonesia," 42.

100. Kahn, *Other Malays*, 94.

101. Ibid., 95.

102. Andaya, "Religious Developments in Southeast Asia," in Tarling, *CHSEA,* vol. 1, pt. 2, 214.

103. Ibid., 214–15.

104. Ibid., 215.

105. Ibid.

106. Federspiel, *Indonesian Muslim Intellectuals,* 15.

107. Nutting, *The Arabs,* 224.

108. Esposito, *Unholy War,* 47.

109. Hamid Algar, *Wahhabism: A Critical Essay* (New York: Islamic Publications International, 2002), 20–21.

110. Ibid.

111. El Fadl, *The Great Theft,* 45.

112. Ibid., 46.

113. Ibid., 46–7.

114. Hofstede and Hofstede, *Cultures and Organizations,* 163.

115. J. Kathirithamby-Wells, "The Age of Transition: The Mid-Eighteenth to the Early Nineteenth Centuries," in Tarling, *CHSEA,* vol. 1, pt. 2, 262.

116. Azra, "Bali and Southeast Asian Islam," in Ramakrishna and Tans, *After Bali,* 46–7.

117. Fealy, Hooker, and White, "Indonesia," 42.

118. Federspiel, *Indonesian Muslim Intellectuals,* 16–17.

119. Ibid., 17–19.

120. Fealy, Hooker, and White, "Indonesia," 40–41.

121. Kahn, *Other Malays,* 95.

122. Federspiel, *Indonesian Muslim Intellectuals,* 29.

123. Fealy, Hooker, and White, "Indonesia," 44.

124. Sidel, *Riots, Pogroms, Jihad,* 37.

125. Ibid.

126. Fealy, Hooker, and White, "Indonesia," 44.

127. Federspiel, *Indonesian Muslim Intellectuals,* 29.

128. Fealy, Hooker, and White, "Indonesia," 44.

129. Federspiel, *Indonesian Muslim Intellectuals,* 33.

130. Ibid.

131. Woodward Introduction to Wahid's "Islam Pluralism and Democracy," 4.

132. Sidel, *Riots, Pogroms, Jihad,* 37–8.

133. Ibid., 38.

134. Cited in ibid.

135. Federspiel, *Indonesian Muslim Intellectuals,* 33.

136. Sidel, *Riots, Pogroms, Jihad,* 38.

137. See Extract 15-20 in Fealy and Hooker, *Voices of Islam in Southeast Asia,* 453–4.

138. See Extract 11-4 in Fealy and Hooker, *Voices of Islam in Southeast Asia,* 149–50.

139. See Azyumardi Azra, "The Transmission of Islamic Reformism to Indonesia: Networks of Middle Eastern and Malay-Indonesian Ulama in the 17th and 18th Centuries" (PhD diss., Columbia University, 1992).

140. Azra, "Bali and Southeast Asian Islam," in Ramakrishna and Tan, *After Bali*, 43.

141. Sidel, *Riots, Pogroms, Jihad*, 203.

142. Martin van Bruinessen, "'Traditionalist' and 'Islamist' Pesantren in Contemporary Indonesia" (paper presented at the workshop The Madrasa in Asia: Transnational Linkages and Alleged or Real Political Activities, organized by the International Institute for the Study of Islam in the Modern World [ISIM], Leiden, Netherlands, May 24–25, 2004).

143. Sidel, *Riots, Pogroms, Jihad*, 203.

144. Ibid.

145. Ibid., 204.

146. Federspiel, *Indonesian Muslim Intellectuals*, 39.

147. Ibid., 39–40.

148. Ibid., 51.

149. Ibid.

150. Fealy, Hooker, and White, "Indonesia," 47.

151. Federspiel, *Indonesian Muslim Intellectuals*, 46.

152. Ibid., 52.

153. Ibid., 33, 53.

154. "Rais Wins More Support," *Laksamana.Net* (Indonesia), June 8, 2004, http://www.laksamana.net/vnews.cfm?ncat=2&news_id=7123 (accessed August 12, 2004).

155. Yong Mun Cheong, "The Political Structures of the Independent States," in Tarling, ed., *CHSEA*, vol. 2, pt. 2, *From World War Two to the Present*, 94–6.

156. *Why Salafism and Terrorism Mostly Don't Mix*, Asia Report 83 (Jakarta/Brussels: International Crisis Group, September 13, 2004), 6.

157. Ibid., 7.

158. Martin van Bruinessen, "Indonesia's Ulama and Politics: Caught Between Legitimizing the Status Quo and Searching for Alternatives," *Prisma: The Indonesian Indicator* 49 (1990): 52–69.

159. "Rais Wins More Support;" Hasan, "Islamic Militancy, *Sharia*, and Democratic Consolidation," 8.

160. van Bruinessen, "Indonesia's Ulama and Politics."

161. Sidel, *Riots, Pogroms, Jihad*, 206; Hasan, "Islamic Militancy, *Sharia*, and Democratic Consolidation," 6.

162. *Why Salafism and Terrorism Mostly Don't Mix*, 6–7.

163. Hasan, "Islamic Militancy, *Sharia*, and Democratic Consolidation," 8.

164. Bubalo and Fealy, *Joining the Caravan?* 57.

165. Ibid., 58.

166. Ibid.

167. *Why Salafism and Terrorism Mostly Don't Mix*, 6–8. Also Bubalo and Fealy, *Joining the Caravan?* 58.

168. Ibid.

169. El Fadl, *The Great Theft*, 76.

170. Ibid.

171. Ibid.

172. Ibid.

173. Ibid., 78.

174. Ibid.

175. Ibid., 75, 79.

176. Ibid., 75.

177. Ibid., 86.

178. Ibid., 52.

179. Bubalo and Fealy, *Joining the Caravan?* 57.

180. Alan Sipress, "Indonesia's Radical Arabs Raise Suspicions of Moderate Countrymen," *Washington Post*, January 9, 2003.

181. Ibid.

182. Ibid.

183. Ibid.; Sidel, *Riots, Pogroms, Jihad*, 205. It should of course be recognized that being of Hadrami Arab descent does not *ipso facto* make one a radical. After all, many Indonesians of Arab descent have made positive contributions to Indonesian society and politics, such as former Indonesian Foreign Minister Ali Alatas, for instance. As we have discussed, Culture is not the only element shaping individual behavior or orientations.

184. Sipress, "Indonesia's Radical Arabs Raise Suspicions of Moderate Countrymen."

185. Patricia Martinez, "Deconstructing *Jihad*: Southeast Asian Contexts," in Ramakrishna and Tan, *After Bali*, 73–4.

186. Dahlby, *Allah's Torch*, 191–2.

187. Ed Husain, *The Islamist: Why I Joined Radical Islam in Britain, What I Saw Inside and Why I Left* (London: Penguin, 2007), 71.

188. Cited in Kahn, *Other Malays*, 96.

189. Bubalo and Fealy, *Joining the Caravan?* 40–41.

190. Ibid., 60.

191. David Thaler, "The Middle East: The Cradle of the Muslim World," in Rabasa et al., *The Muslim World After 9/11*, 91.

192. Bubalo and Fealy, *Joining the Caravan?* 13.

193. Ibid., 14.

194. Ibid., 13.

195. Ibid., 14.

196. Ibid., 57–8.

197. Ibid., 58.

198. Ibid.

199. Sidney Jones, "Terrorism and 'Radical Islam' in Indonesia," in Vicziany and Wright-Neville, *Islamic Terrorism in Indonesia*, 4.

200. Bubalo and Fealy, *Joining the Caravan?* 59.

201. Fealy, Hooker, and White, "Indonesia," 48; Hasan, "Islamic Militancy, *Sharia,* and Democratic Consolidation," 6.

202. Bubalo and Fealy, *Joining the Caravan?* 67.

203. Author interview with Al Chaidar, January 8, 2006.

204. Ibid.

205. Bubalo and Fealy, *Joining the Caravan?* 67–8.

206. Fealy, Hooker, and White, "Indonesia," 49; Bubalo and Fealy, *Joining the Caravan?* 69.

207. Bubalo and Fealy, *Joining the Caravan?* 70–71.

208. Fealy, Hooker, and White, "Indonesia," 48. For more on the origins of the HTI in Indonesia, see Hasan, "Islamic Militancy, *Sharia,* and Democratic Consolidation," 2–3.

209. Hasan, "Islamic Militancy, *Sharia,* and Democratic Consolidation," 7.

210. Barbara D. Metcalf, "'Traditionalist Islamic Activism: Deoband, Tablighis, and Talibs" (Institute for the Study of Islam in the Modern World [ISIM] Annual Lecture, Leiden University, Netherlands, November 23, 2001).

211. Daniel Pipes, *Militant Islam Reaches America* (New York: W. W. Norton, 2003), 8.

212. Ibid.

213. Metcalf, "Traditionalist Islamic Activism."

214. Pipes, *Militant Islam,* 8–9.

CHAPTER 3

1. Greg Fealy, "Half a Century of Violent Jihad in Indonesia: A Historical and Ideological Comparison of Darul Islam and Jema'ah Islamiyah," in Vicziany and Wright-Neville, *Islamic Terrorism in Indonesia*, 18.

2. Ibid., 17.

3. Fealy, "Islamic Radicalism in Indonesia," 111.

4. Fealy, "Half a Century of Violent Jihad in Indonesia," in Vicziany and Wright-Neville, *Islamic Terrorism in Indonesia*, 15.

5. C. Van Dijk, *Rebellion Under the Banner of Islam: The Darul Islam in Indonesia* (The Hague: Martinus Nijhoff, 1981), 20.

6. See Ibid., 21–2. See also Hiroko Horikoshi, "The Dar Ul-Islam Movement in West Java: An Experience in the Historical Process," *Indonesia* 20 (1975): 73.

7. Van Dijk, *Rebellion Under the Banner of Islam*, 22–3.

8. Federspiel, *Indonesian Muslim Intellectuals*, 14.

9. Ibid.

10. "Glossary," in Fealy and Hooker, *Voices of Islam in Southeast Asia,* xlvii.

11. Federspiel, *Indonesian Muslim Intellectuals*, 15.

12. Ibid., 21.

13. Fealy and Hooker, *Voices of Islam in Southeast Asia*, 215, 228, n. 22.

14. Van Dijk, *Rebellion Under the Banner of Islam*, 24; Horikoshi, "The Dar Ul-Islam Movement in West Java," 62.

15. Federspiel, *Indonesian Muslim Intellectuals,* 21.

16. Ibid., 23.

17. Ibid.

18. Sidel, *Riots, Pogroms, Jihad*, 215.

19. Van Dijk, *Rebellion Under the Banner of Islam*, 23.

20. Ibid., 24.

21. Horikoshi, "The Dar Ul-Islam Movement in West Java," 73, n. 63; Ileto, "Religion and Anti-Colonial Movements," in Tarling, *CHSEA,* vol. 2, pt. 1, 236.

22. Paul Kratoska and Ben Batson, "Nationalism and Modernist Reform," in Tarling, *CHSEA,* vol. 2, pt. 1, 264.

23. Van Dijk, *Rebellion Under the Banner of Islam*, 24.

24. Federspiel, *Indonesian Muslim Intellectuals, 25.*

25. Van Dijk, *Rebellion Under the Banner of Islam*, 26.

26. Horikoshi, "The Dar Ul-Islam Movement in West Java," 62.

27. Van Dijk, *Rebellion Under the Banner of Islam*, 25–6.

28. Ibid., 26.

29. Federspiel, *Indonesian Muslim Intellectual*, 41.

30. Van Dijk, *Rebellion Under the Banner of Islam*, 30.

31. Ibid., 31.

32. Ibid., 33.

33. Ibid., 33–4; Federspiel, *Indonesian Muslim Intellectuals*, 42.

34. Federspiel, *Indonesian Muslim Intellectuals*, 42.

35. Van Dijk, *Rebellion Under the Banner of Islam*, 34.

36. Federspiel, *Indonesian Muslim Intellectuals*, 42.

37. Horikoshi, "The Dar Ul-Islam Movement in West Java," 63; Van Dijk, *Rebellion Under the Banner of Islam*, 35.

38. Van Dijk, *Rebellion Under the Banner of Islam*, 36.

39. Ibid., 28–9, 36.

40. Horikoshi, "The Dar Ul-Islam Movement in West Java," 63; Van Dijk, *Rebellion Under the Banner of Islam*, 36–8.

41. Van Dijk, *Rebellion Under the Banner of Islam*, 38; Federspiel, *Indonesian Muslim Intellectuals*, 42.

42. Horikoshi, "The Dar Ul-Islam Movement in West Java," 63.

43. Ibid.

44. Ibid., 64.

45. Ibid.

46. Van Dijk, *Rebellion Under the Banner of Islam*, 39.

47. Federspiel, *Indonesian Muslim Intellectuals*, 42.

48. Van Dijk, *Rebellion Under the Banner of Islam*, 39.

49. Horikoshi, "The Dar Ul-Islam Movement in West Java," 64.

50. Van Dijk, *Rebellion Under the Banner of Islam*, 43.

51. Ibid.

52. Neighbour, *In the Shadow of Swords*, 9.

53. Fealy, "Half a Century of Violent Jihad in Indonesia," in Vicziany and Wright-Neville, *Islamic Terrorism in Indonesia*, 17.

54. Horikoshi, "The Dar Ul-Islam Movement in West Java," 71–2.

55. Fealy, "Half a Century of Violent Jihad in Indonesia," in Vicziany and Wright-Neville, *Islamic Terrorism in Indonesia*, 17; Neighbour, *In the Shadow of Swords*, 9.

56. Neighbour, *In the Shadow of Swords*, 9.

57. See Chapter One.

58. Van Dijk, *Rebellion Under the Banner of Islam*, 21.

59. Ibid., 27–8.

60. Smith et al., *Understanding Social Psychology Across Cultures*, 98.

61. See Kressel, *Mass Hate*, 203–4.

62. Horikoshi, "The Dar Ul-Islam Movement in West Java," 73.

63. Stewart Bell, *The Martyr's Oath: The Apprenticeship of a Homegrown Terrorist* (Mississauga, Ontario: John Wiley and Sons Canada Ltd., 2005), 57.

64. In fact, Bell was talking about Mohammed Mansour Jabarah, the Canadian-Kuwaiti Al Qaeda terrorist who played a strategic role in the JI Singapore plot to

attack Western targets in the city-state in late 2001. For details of Jabarah's role in the Singapore plot, see the Singapore WP, 27–8.

65. Horikoshi, "The Dar Ul-Islam Movement in West Java," 74.

66. See Charles Selengut, *Sacred Fury: Understanding Religious Violence* (Walnut Creek, Calif.: Altamira Press, 2003), 65–7.

67. Ibid., 67–8.

68. Ibid., 68.

69. Moojan Momen, "Fundamentalism and Liberalism: Towards an Understanding of the Dichotomy," *Bahai Studies Review* 2 (1992), http://www.breacais. demon.co.uk/abs/bsr02/22_momen_fundamentalism.htm (accessed April 1, 2008).

70. Ibid.

71. J. Harold Ellens, "Fundamentalism, Orthodoxy and Violence," in Ellens, *Destructive Power of Religion*, vol. 4, *Contemporary Views on Spirituality and Violence*, 120.

72. Stuart Sim, *Fundamentalist World: The New Dark Age of Dogma* (Cambridge: Icon Books, 2004), 29.

73. Ibid., 100.

74. Van Dijk, *Rebellion Under the Banner of Islam*, 27–8.

75. Ibid., 28; Horikoshi, "The Dar Ul-Islam Movement in West Java," 74.

76. Horikoshi, "The Dar Ul-Islam Movement in West Java," 74.

77. Ibid.

78. Fealy, "Half a Century of Violent Jihad in Indonesia," in Vicziany and Wright-Neville, *Islamic Terrorism in Indonesia*, 23.

79. Horikoshi, "The Dar Ul-Islam Movement in West Java," 73–4.

80. Van Dijk, *Rebellion Under the Banner of Islam*, 29.

81. Horikoshi, "The Dar Ul-Islam Movement in West Java," 75.

82. Van Dijk, *Rebellion Under the Banner of Islam*, 45.

83. Originally Soekarno had wanted Belief in God to be the last pillar, but due to pressure from the Muslim leaders, this pillar became the first instead. See Van Dijk, *Rebellion Under the Banner of Islam*, 45–7.

84. Ibid., 46.

85. Ibid., 48.

86. Ibid., 58.

87. Ibid., 59–62.

88. David Kilcullen, "Globalization and the Development of Indonesian Counterinsurgency Tactics," *Small Wars and Insurgencies* 17 (2006): 47.

89. Horikoshi, "The Dar Ul-Islam Movement in West Java," 71–2.

90. Fealy, "Half a Century of Violent Jihad in Indonesia," in Vicziany and Wright-Neville, *Islamic Terrorism in Indonesia*, 21.

91. Ibid.

92. Ibid.

93. Ibid., 22.

94. The full quote is: "The tree of liberty must be refreshed from time to time with the blood of patriots and tyrants. It is it's natural manure." See "Thomas Jefferson," *Bartleby.com*, http://www.bartleby.com/73/1065.html (accessed April 1, 2008).

95. Fealy, "Half a Century of Violent Jihad in Indonesia," in Vicziany and Wright-Neville, *Islamic Terrorism in Indonesia*, 22.

96. Kilcullen, "Globalization and the Development of Indonesian Counterinsurgency Tactics," 49–53.

97. Horikoshi, "The Dar Ul-Islam Movement in West Java," 77.

98. M. C. Ricklefs, *A History of Modern Indonesia Since c. 1300*, 2nd ed. (Stanford: Stanford University Press, 1993), 286.

99. Fealy, "Half a Century of Violent Jihad in Indonesia," in Vicziany and Wright-Neville, *Islamic Terrorism in Indonesia*, 24.

100. Ibid.

101. Chaidar interview.

102. Chaidar interview.

103. Chaidar interview.

104. M. Tito Karnavian, "Rehabilitative Program of Terrorists in Indonesia" (workshop presentation, London, November 8, 2007).

105. Sidel, *Riots, Pogroms, Jihad*, 38.

106. Tim Behrend, "Meeting Abubakar Ba'asyir," December 23, 2002, http://www.arts.auckland.ac.nz/asia/tbehrend/meet-abb.htm (accessed 2003).

107. Karnavian, "Rehabilitative Program of Terrorists in Indonesia."

108. Waller, *Becoming Evil*, 183.

109. Chaidar interview.

110. Chaidar interview.

111. My use of the term "Darul Islamic subculture" is similar to the way terrorism expert Louise Richardson uses the term "enabling community." See Louise Richardson, *What Terrorists Want: Understanding the Terrorist Threat* (London: John Murray, 2006), 14, 31.

112. A phrase borrowed from the psychoanalyst Willard Gaylin. See Gaylin, *Hatred*, 244.

113. Neighbour, *In the Shadow of Swords*, 7.

114. Ibid., 8.

115. Ibid.

116. Ibid., 11.

117. Ibid., 12; Sidel, *Riots, Pogroms, Jihad*, 203.

118. Neighbour, *In the Shadow of Swords*, 12.

119. Ibid., 9.

120. Ba'asyir in ibid.

121. Ibid., 11.

122. Volkan, *Killing in the Name Of Identity*, 154.

123. Sidel, *Riots, Pogroms, Jihad*, 48–9.

124. Neighbour, *In the Shadow of Swords*, 13.

125. Bilveer Singh, "The Emergence of the Jemaah Islamiyah Threat in Southeast Asia: External Linkages and Influences" (paper presented at a workshop on International Terrorism in Southeast Asia and Likely Implications for South Asia, organized by the Observer Research Foundation, New Delhi, India, April 28–29, 2004).

126. Blontank Poer, "Tracking the Roots of Jamaah Islamiyah," *Jakarta Post*, March 8, 2003.

127. Farish A. Noor, "Ngruki Revisited: Modernity and Its Discontents at the Pondok Pesantren al-Mukmin of Ngruki, Surakarta," Working Paper 139 (Singapore: S. Rajaratnam School of International Studies, October 1, 2007), 5–6.

128. Poer, "Tracking the Roots."

129. Bilveer Singh, "Emergence."

130. Martin van Bruinessen, "The Violent Fringes of Indonesia's Radical Islam," http://www.let.uu.nl/~martin.vanbruinessen/personal/publications/violent_fringe.htm (accessed July 29, 2004).

131. Neighbour, *In the Shadow of Swords*, 26.

132. Azra, "Bali and Southeast Asian Islam," in Ramakrishna and Tan, *After Bali*, 44.

133. Esposito, *Unholy War*, 53.

134. van Bruinessen, "The Violent Fringes of Indonesia's Radical Islam."

135. Tim Behrend, "Reading Past the Myth: Public Teachings of Abu Bakar Ba'asyir," February 19, 2003, http://www.arts.auckland.ac.nz/asia/tbehrend/abb-myth.htm (accessed April 30, 2004).

136. Sidel, *Riots, Pogroms, Jihad*, 55.

137. Ibid., 55–6; Neighbour, *In the Shadow of Swords*, 27.

138. Sidel, *Riots, Pogroms, Jihad*, 56.

139. Neighbour, *In the Shadow of Swords*, 27.

140. Bilveer Singh, "Emergence"; Neighbour, *In the Shadow of Swords*, 28.

141. Neighbour, *In the Shadow of Swords*, 28.

142. "Abu Bakar Bashir: The Malaysian Connection," *Tempo* (Indonesia), November 9, 2002.

143. Ibid.

144. Behrend, "Reading Past the Myth."

145. Poer, "Tracking the Roots."

146. El Fadl, *The Great Theft*, 82.

147. Ibid.

148. Esposito, *Unholy War*, 56.

149. Qutb cited in ibid., 60.

150. Selengut, *Sacred Fury*, 80.

151. Marc Sageman, *Understanding Terror Networks* (Philadelphia: University of Pennsylvania Press, 2004), 16.

152. Esposito, *Unholy War*, 62.

153. Mark Juergensmeyer, *Terror in the Mind of God: The Global Rise of Religious Violence*, updated ed. with a new preface (Berkeley and Los Angeles: University of California Press, 2000), 81.

154. Ibid.

155. Ibid.

156. Sageman, *Understanding Terror Networks*, 16.

157. Van Bruinessen, "Violent Fringes of Indonesia's Radical Islam."

158. Poer, "Tracking the Roots."

159. Sageman, *Understanding Terror Networks*, 17.

160. Azzam cited in Malise Ruthven, *A Fury for God: The Islamist Attack on America* (New York: Granta, 2002), 203.

161. Sageman, *Understanding Terror Networks*, 18.

162. Ibid.

163. Ibid.

164. Poer, "Tracking the Roots."

165. Behrend, "Reading Past the Myth."

166. Poer, "Tracking the Roots."

167. Ibid.

168. Fealy, Hooker, and White, "Indonesia," 362.

169. Fealy, "Islamic Radicalism," 112.

170. Bilveer Singh, "Emergence."

171. Fealy, "Islamic Radicalism," 112.

172. Chaidar interview.

173. Farish A. Noor, "Ngruki Revisited," 8.

174. Ibid.

175. Ibid., 8–9.

176. Usmar Anza, "Islamic Education: A Brief History of Madrassas with Comments on Curricula and Current Pedagogical Practices," unpublished paper, March 2003.

177. Behrend, "Meeting Abubakar Ba'asyir." See also Clifford Geertz, "The Near East in the Far East: On Islam in Indonesia," Occasional Paper 12 (Princeton: Institute for Advanced Study, December 2001), 6.

178. Van Bruinessen, "'Traditionalist' and "Islamist' Pesantren in Contemporary Indonesia."

179. Farish A. Noor, "Ngruki Revisited," 9.

180. Pondok Pesantren Al-Mukmin presentation by Noor Huda (NH) Ismail at the Institute of Defence and Strategic Studies (IDSS), Nanyang Technological University, Singapore, April 8, 2005. Hereafter NH Ismail IDSS Talk.

181. Farish A. Noor, "Ngruki Revisited," 11.

182. Farish A. Noor, "Ngruki Revisited," 12–13; NH Ismail IDSS Talk.

183. Farish A. Noor, "Ngruki Revisited," 11.

184. Ibid.

185. Ibid., 11–12.

186. Ibid., 15.

187. Ibid.

188. The phrase is Martin van Bruinessen's. See Van Bruinessen, "'Traditionalist' and 'Islamist' Pesantren in Contemporary Indonesia."

189. NH Ismail IDSS Talk. See also Farish A. Noor, "Ngruki Revisited," 29.

190. Noor Huda Ismail, "Ngruki: It is a Terrorism School?" *Jakarta Post*, March 14–15, 2005, also available on former Indonesian President Abdurrahman Wahid's official Web site, http://www.gusdur.net/english/index.php?option=com_content&task=view&id=699&Itemid=1 (accessed August 11, 2008).

191. NH Ismail IDSS Talk.

192. NH Ismail, "Ngruki: It is a Terrorism School?"

193. NH Ismail IDSS Talk.

194. Ibid.

195. NH Ismail, "Ngruki: It is a Terrorism School?"

196. Zalman Mohamed Yusof and Mohammad Ishak, "Inside a JI School," *New Paper on Sunday* (Singapore), January 4, 2004.

197. Neighbour, *In the Shadow of Swords*, 6.

198. Dahlby, *Allah's Torch*, 229.

199. Ibid.

200. Farish A. Noor, "Ngruki Revisited," 15, n. 8.

201. Ibid., 16, 29.

202. Ibid., 18.

203. In July 2008, Ba'asyir split from the MMI after an internal leadership dispute and two months later inaugurated a new organization, Jemaah Anshorut Tauhid, with himself as the *amir*. "Ba'asyir Declares New Political Islamist Group," *Jakarta Post*, September 17, 2008.

204. John E. Mack, "Looking Beyond Terrorism: Transcending the Mind of Enmity," in Stout, *Psychology of Terrorism*, vol. 1, 176. I would also like to acknowledge my appreciation of the insights into Indonesian radical Islamist worldviews of my former colleague Ms. Faizah Samat.

205. Ba'asyir in Neighbour, *In the Shadow of Swords*, 1.

206. Ba'asyir in ibid., 2.

207. For a discussion of *"dhimmitude,"* see Robert Spencer, *Onward Muslim Soldiers: How Jihad Still Threatens America and the West* (Washington, D.C.: Regnery, 2003), 7.

208. Behrend, "Reading Past the Myth."

209. Farish A. Noor, "Ngruki Revisited," 20.

210. Behrend, "Meeting Abubakar Ba'asyir."

211. Farish A. Noor, "Ngruki Revisited," 21, 23.

212. Farish A. Noor, "Ngruki Revisited," 21.

213. Farish A. Noor, "Ngruki Revisited," 25, n. 24; Neighbour, *In the Shadow of Swords*, 11.

214. Farish A. Noor, "Ngruki Revisited," 6.

215. Farish Noor, "Fire and Brimstone: Face to Face with the Mujahedeens of Indonesia," *Asia Inc*, January/February 2007, 32.

216. Ibid.

217. Farish A. Noor, "Ngruki Revisited," 15.

218. *Jemaah Islamiyah in Southeast Asia: Damaged But Still Dangerous*, Asia Report 63 (Jakarta/Brussels: International Crisis Group, August 26, 2003), 26.

219. Fealy, "Islamic Radicalism," 113.

220. J. Harold Ellens, "The Dynamics of Prejudice," in Ellens, *Destructive Power of Religion*, vol. 2, 96.

221. Gaylin, *Hatred*, 24.

222. Ibid., 26.

223. Ibid.

224. Ibid., 28.

225. Ibid.

226. Cited in Clark McCauley, "Psychological Issues in Understanding Terrorism and the Response to Terrorism," in Stout, *Psychology of Terrorism*, vol. 3, 7.

227. Gaylin, *Hatred*, 26–27.

228. Ibid., 27.

229. Ibid., 245–6.

230. Ibid., 244.

231. Waller, *Becoming Evil*, 237.

232. Farish Noor, "Ngruki Revisited," 5.

233. NH Ismail IDSS Talk.

234. Yusof and Ishak, "Inside a JI School."

235. Farish Noor, "Ngruki Revisited," 14.

236. Charles Kimball, *When Religion Becomes Evil* (New York: HarperCollins, 2003), 74.

237. Drummond, "From the Northwest Imperative to Global Jihad," in Stout, *Psychology of Terrorism,* vol. 1, 76.

238. Timothy Mapes, "Indonesian School Gives High Marks to Students Embracing Intolerance," *Asian Wall Street Journal,* September 2, 2003.

239. Dahlby, *Allah's Torch,* 232.

240. Anthony Paul, "Enduring the Other's Other," *Straits Times* (Singapore), December 4, 2003.

241. Lt. Col. Dave Grossman, *On Killing: The Psychological Cost of Learning to Kill in War and Society* (New York: Back Bay Books, 1996), 313.

242. Ibid., xviii.

243. Ibid., 88.

244. Albert Bandura, "Mechanisms of Moral Disengagement," in Reich, *Origins of Terrorism,* 163.

245. Grossman, *On Killing,* xix.

246. David Sloan Wilson, *Evolution for Everyone: How Darwin's Theory Can Change the Way We Think About Ourselves* (New York; Delta Trade, 2008), 285–6.

247. Husain, *Islamist,* 178.

248. Cited in Neighbour, *In the Shadow of Swords,* 14–15.

249. Behrend, "Meeting Abubakar Ba'asyir;" Richard C. Paddock, "Terror Network's Academic Outposts," *Los Angeles Times,* April 1, 2003.

250. *Jemaah Islamiyah in Southeast Asia: Damaged But Still Dangerous,* 26.

251. Wong Chun Wai and Lourdes Charles, "More than 100 Marriages Involve Key JI Member," *The Star Online* (Malaysia), September 7, 2004, http://thestar.com.my/news/archives/story.asp?ppath=%5C2004%5C9% (accessed September 11, 2004).

252. *Jemaah Islamiyah in Southeast Asia: Damaged But Still Dangerous,* 26–7.

253. Marc Galanter, *Cults: Faith, Healing, and Coercion,* 2nd ed. (New York: Oxford University Press, 1999), 4.

254. Ibid.

255. Cited in Benjamin Beit-Hallahmi and Michael Argyle, *The Psychology of Religious Behavior, Belief and Experience* (New York: Routledge, 1997), 243.

256. Fealy, Hooker, and White, "Indonesia," 377.

257. John Dawson, "The Bali Bombers: What Motivates Death Worship?" *Capitalism Magazine,* October 19, 2003, http://www.capmag.com/article.asp?ID=3000 (accessed September 1, 2004).

258. Mukhlas Statement, Bali Region Police Detective Directorate, December 14, 2002.

259. Neighbour, *In the Shadow of Swords,* 17.

260. Ibid., 21.

261. Ibid.

262. Mukhlas Statement, Bali Region Police Detective Directorate, December 13, 2002.

263. Neighbour, *In the Shadow of Swords,* 22.

264. Ibid., 21.

265. Ibid., 22.

266. Alderdice, "The Individual, the Group and the Psychology of Terrorism," 202.

267. Mukhlas, December 13, 2002, Statement; Neighbour, *In the Shadow of Swords*, 26.

268. Fealy, Hooker, and White, "Indonesia," 377.

269. Mukhlas, December 13, 2002, Statement.

270. Ibid.; Neighbour, *In the Shadow of Swords*, 42.

271. Mukhlas, December 13, 2002, Statement.

272. Volkan, *Killing in the Name of Identity*, 215.

273. Mukhlas in Neighbour, *In the Shadow of Swords*, 50–51.

274. Mukhlas, December 13, 2002, Statement.

275. Ibid.; Neighbour, *In the Shadow of Swords*, 58.

276. Mukhlas, December 13, 2002, Statement.

277. Ibid.

278. "Mukhlas," Extract 14-6, in Fealy and Hooker, *Voices of Islam in Southeast Asia*, 380–1.

279. Ibid., 381.

280. Juergensmeyer, *Terror in the Mind of God*, 184.

281. "Mukhlas," Extract 14-6, in Fealy and Hooker, *Voices of Islam in Southeast Asia*, 378.

282. Elms cited in Kressel, *Mass Hate*, 225.

283. Imam Samudra Police Interview, November 29, 2002; Dawson, "Bali Bombers."

284. Neighbour, *In the Shadow of Swords*, 80.

285. Imam Samudra, November 29, 2002, Interview.

286. Neighbour, *In the Shadow of Swords*, 81–2.

287. Ibid., 82.

288. Muhammad Haniff Hassan, "Imam Samudra's Justification for Bali Bombing," *Studies in Conflict and Terrorism* 30 (2007): 1034.

289. Dan Murphy, "How Al Qaeda Lit the Bali Fuse," pt. 3, *Christian Science Monitor*, June 19, 2003.

290. Neighbour, *In the Shadow of Swords*, 82.

291. Ibid.

292. Hassan, "Imam Samudra's Justification for Bali Bombing," 1034.

293. Neighbour, *In the Shadow of Swords*, 82.

294. Cited in Kressel, *Mass Hate*, 199.

295. Murphy, "How Al Qaeda Lit the Bali Fuse," pt. 3.

296. Ibid.

297. Neighbour, *In the Shadow of Swords*, 83.

298. Ibid., 86–7.

299. Ibid., 85.

300. Ibid., 88.

301. Imam Samudra, November 29, 2002, Interview.

302. Mukhlas December 13, 2002, Statement.

303. Fealy, Hooker, and White, "Indonesia," 373.

304. Imam Samudra, *Aku Melawan Teroris* [I Fight the Terrorists] (Solo: Jazeera, 2004).

305. Fealy, Hooker, and White, "Indonesia," 373.

306. Greg Fealy and Virginia Hooker have usefully compiled extracts from Samudra's 2004 book. See "Imam Samudra," Extract 14-5, in Fealy and Hooker, *Voices of Islam in Southeast Asia*, 374–5.

307. Samudra, *Aku Melawan Teroris*, 108.

308. "Imam Samudra," Extract 14-5, in Fealy and Hooker, *Voices of Islam in Southeast Asia*, 375.

309. " . . . and fight the Pagans all together as they fight you all together. But know that Allah is with those who restrain themselves (*Sura* 9:36)." Unless otherwise stated, all Qu'ranic citations are from *The Holy Qu'ran*, translated by Abdullah Yusuf Ali (Ware, Hertfordshire: Wordsworth Editions, 2000). Ali's rendition of the Qu'ran is considered among the best in the English language.

310. "Imam Samudra," Extract 14-5, in Fealy and Hooker, *Voices of Islam in Southeast Asia*, 376.

311. Ibid.

312. Ibid., 377.

313. "Fight in the cause of Allah those who fight against you, but do not transgress limits; for Allah loveth not transgressors (*Sura* 2:190)," Samudra, *Aku Melawan Teroris*, 115–6.

314. Imam Samudra, November 29, 2002, Interview.

315. "Imam Samudra," Extract 14-5, in Fealy and Hooker, *Voices of Islam in Southeast Asia*, 376.

316. Imam Samudra, November 29, 2002, Interview.

317. "International Martyrs' Battalion," Extract 14-4, in Fealy and Hooker, *Voices of Islam in Southeast Asia*, 370–72. Samudra is believed to be the author of this document.

318. Hassan, "Imam Samudra's Justification for Bali Bombing," 1035.

319. Samudra, *Aku Melawan Teroris*, 123–4.

320. See also Hassan, "Imam Samudra's Justification for Bali Bombing," 1035.

321. Ibid., 1036.

322. Ibid., 1037.

323. See also ibid., 1036.

324. See ibid., 1037.

325. Juergensmeyer, *Terror in the Mind of God*, 214.

326. Sidel, *Riots, Pogroms, Jihad*, 207.

327. Fealy, "Islamic Radicalism," 111–2.

328. Chaidar interview.

329. See the comments by 1989 Al-Mukmin graduate Muhammad Wildan in Farish A. Noor, "Ngruki Revisited," 28.

CHAPTER 4

1. John Horgan interviewed by Steve Ayan in Annette Schaefer, "Inside the Terrorist Mind," *Scientific American Mind* (December 2007/January 2008), 79.

2. Crenshaw, "Questions to be Answered," in Reich, *Origins of Terrorism*, 247.

3. Rex A. Hudson et al., *Who Becomes a Terrorist and Why: The 1999 Government Report on Profiling Terrorists* (Guilford, Conn.: The Lyons Press, 2002).

4. Horgan in Schaefer, "Inside the Terrorist Mind," 78.

5. Walter Reich, "Understanding Terrorist Behavior," in Reich, *Origins of Terrorism,* 276.

6. Silke, "Becoming a Terrorist," 31-2.

7. Schaefer, "Inside the Terrorist Mind," 77.

8. "Reporter Daniel Pearl is Dead, Killed by His Captors in Pakistan," *Wall Street Journal Online*, http://online.wsj.com/public/resources/documents/pearl-022102.htm (accessed April 1, 2008).

9. Schaefer, "Inside the Terrorist Mind," 77.

10. Cited in ibid., 79.

11. Cited in ibid.

12. Edwards and Stewart, "Professor Warned Off Terrorist Trip."

13. Conboy, *The Second Front*, 46; Neighbour, *In the Shadow of Swords*, 38.

14. See chapter 2.

15. Neighbour, *In the Shadow of Swords*, 38–9.

16. Ibid., 39.

17. Ibid.; Conboy, *The Second Front*, 46–7.

18. Husain, *Islamist,* 35.

19. Ibid.

20. Neighbour, *In the Shadow of Swords*, 228.

21. Ibid., 39.

22. Conboy, *The Second Front*, 47.

23. Ibid., 46

24. Neighbour, *In the Shadow of Swords*, 38.

25. Ibid., 39.

26. Conboy, *The Second Front*, 47.

27. Ibid.; Neighbour, *In the Shadow of Swords*, 39.

28. Conboy, *The Second Front*, 47.

29. Ibid.; Neighbour, *In the Shadow of Swords*, 39.

30. Conboy, *The Second Front*, 47.

31. Matthew Alper, *The "God" Part of the Brain: A Scientific Interpretation of Human Spirituality and God* (Naperville, Ill.: Sourcebooks Inc., 2006), 171.

32. Ibid., 175.

33. Conboy, *The Second Front*, 46.

34. Arthur J. Deikman, *Them and Us: Cult Thinking and the Terrorist Threat* (Berkeley: Bay Tree Publishing, 2003), 9.

35. Ibid., 8–9.

36. Ibid., 9.

37. Ibid., 6.

38. Ibid., 2.

39. Alper, *The "God" Part of the Brain*, 174.

40. Ibid.

41. Conboy, *The Second Front*, 47.

42. Ibid., 53.

43. Neighbour, *In the Shadow of Swords*, 47, 51.

44. Ibid., 46–7.

45. Ibid., 47; Conboy, *The Second Front*, 48.

46. According to political psychologist Jerrold M. Post, all terrorists commonly seem to be willing to "subordinate their individual identity to a collective identity." See Shaefer, "Inside the Terrorist Mind," 76.

47. Conboy, *The Second Front*, 49.

48. Neighbour, *In the Shadow of Swords*, 39.

49. Ibid., 40.

50. Ibid.

51. Ibid.

52. Ibid., 40–41.

53. Ibid., 51.

54. Smith et al., *Understanding Social Psychology Across Cultures*, 98. See also the discussion on Kartosoewirjo in the previous chapter.

55. Neighbour, *In the Shadow of Swords*, 167.

56. Waller, *Becoming Evil*, 193.

57. Neighbour, *In the Shadow of Swords*, 168.

58. Also called Kumpulan Mujahidin Malaysia.

59. Chaidar interview.

60. Neighbour, *In the Shadow of Swords*, 219.

61. Singapore WP, 4–7.

62. Waller, *Becoming Evil*, 237.

63. Ibid., 240.

64. Ibid.

65. Ibid., 243.

66. See Chapter Three.

67. Waller, *Becoming Evil*, 243.

68. See Bandura, "Mechanisms of Moral Disengagement," in Reich, *Origins of Terrorism*, 161.

69. Grossman, *On Killing*, 160.

70. Cited in ibid., 151.

71. Ibid., 152.

72. Discussed in Waller, *Becoming Evil*, 32.

73. Bandura, "Mechanisms of Moral Disengagement," in Reich, *Origins of Terrorism*, 176.

74. Ibid.

75. Grossman, *On Killing*, 151.

76. "Official Report of Confrontation," Balinese Police Force, Detective Directorate, November 15, 2002 (witnessed by Silvester Tendean of Gubeng, Surabaya). Other Indonesian documents produced on the same day record Amrozi's date of birth as July 5, 1962: "Results of Psychological Investigation," November 15, 2002. Local administrative errors and inefficiencies are, however, not unknown in the Indonesian bureaucratic context.

77. Neighbour, *In the Shadow of Swords*, 18.

78. Ibid., 18, 23.

79. Ibid., 32.

80. Ibid., 23.

81. Ibid., 18.

82. Ibid., 18, 23; "Results of Psychological Investigation," November 15, 2002.

83. Neighbour, *In the Shadow of Swords*, 23.

84. Ibid., 33.

85. Millard, *Jihad in Paradise*, 140.

86. Neighbour, *In the Shadow of Swords*, 33.

87. "Official Report of Further Interrogation," Balinese Police Force, Directorate of Detectives, December 14, 2002; Neighbour, *In the Shadow of Swords*, 33.

88. Neighbour, *In the Shadow of Swords*, 61.

89. Amrozi in ibid.

90. Ibid., 23; "Results of Psychological Investigation," November 15, 2002.

91. Waller, *Becoming Evil*, 73–4.

92. Deikman, *Them and Us*, 9.

93. Hofstede and Hofstede, *Cultures and Organizations*, 51–7.

94. Singapore WP, 17.

95. Ibid.

96. Stevens, "The Unanticipated Consequences of Globalization," in Stout, *Psychology of Terrorism*, vol. 3, 37–8.

97. Ibid., 38.

98. Ibid., 39.

99. Selengut, *Sacred Fury*, 157–8.

100. Stevens, "The Unanticipated Consequences of Globalization," in Stout, *Psychology of Terrorism*, vol. 3, 40.

101. Ibid.

102. Selengut, *Sacred Fury*, 158.

103. Stern, *Terror in the Name of God*, 69.

104. Ayaan Hirsi Ali, *Infidel: My Life* (London: The Free Press, 2007), 247–8.

105. Ibid., 248.

106. Beit-Hallahmi and Argyle, *Psychology of Religious Behavior*, 115.

107. Neighbour, *In the Shadow of Swords*, 61.

108. Amrozi in ibid., 61–2.

109. Ibid., 62.

110. Ibid., 156–7.

111. Khozin in ibid., 157.

112. Millard, *Jihad in Paradise*, 75.

113. Neighbour, *In the Shadow of Swords*, 126.

114. Ibid.

115. "Official Report of Further Interrogation," Balinese Police Force, Directorate of Detectives, December 13, 2002.

116. Neighbour, *In the Shadow of Swords*, 60.

117. Cited in ibid., 59.

118. Ibid., 60.

119. Jerrold M. Post, "Terrorist Psycho-Logic: Terrorist Behavior as a Product of Psychological Forces," in Reich, *Origins of Terrorism*, 33.

120. Ezekiel cited in Timothy Gallimore, "Unresolved Trauma: Fuel for the Cycle of Violence and Terrorism," in Stout, *Psychology of Terrorism*, vol. 2, 153.

121. "Official Report of Further Interrogation," Balinese Police Force, Directorate of Detectives, November 26, 2002. Ambon is the capital of the Maluku islands where Christian-Muslim fighting broke out between 1999 and 2002. JI elements were involved in the conflict.

122. "Official Report of Further Interrogation," November 26, 2002.

123. Waller, *Becoming Evil*, 69–70.

124. Ibid., 70.

125. Scott O. Lilienfeld and Hal Arkowitz, "What 'Psychopath' Means: It Is Not Quite What You May Think," *Scientific American Mind*, 80.

126. "Results of Psychological Investigation," November 15, 2002.

127. Ibid. The problem is that this document does not provide details of any psychological testing protocols that Amrozi may have undergone. It is not clear therefore whether a rigorous assessment was made of Amrozi's psychological disposition or if a highly subjective, hurried assessment was done so as not to impede the criminal investigation.

128. Amrozi in Neighbour, *In the Shadow of Swords*, 33–4.

129. Amrozi in ibid., 299.

130. Ibid., 298–9.

131. Ibid., 18. That is, the youngest of the children from the union between Nurhasyim and first wife Tariyem.

132. Imron's biological siblings were Alimah, Afiyah, Mohamad Khozin, Djafar [Jafar] Sodiq, Mukhlas, Amrozi, and Amin Jabir (who died in 1987). His stepsiblings, from his father Nurhasyim's union with a second wife, were Tafsir, Asyarifah, Sumyah, Na Imah, and Fauzi. Mukhlas, December 13, 2002, Statement.

133. Waller, *Becoming Evil*, 218.

134. Ibid., 219–20.

135. Neighbour, *In the Shadow of Swords*, 33.

136. Imron in ibid., 34.

137. Mukhlas, December 13, 2002, Statement; Neighbour, *In the Shadow of Swords*, 34.

138. Imron in Neighbour, *In the Shadow of Swords,* 34.

139. Imron in ibid., 61.

140. Ibid., 62.

141. Imron in ibid.

142. See Chapter Three.

143. Husain, *Islamist*, 74.

144. Dan Murphy, "How Al Qaeda Lit the Bali Fuse," pt. 2, *Christian Science Monitor*, June 18, 2003.

145. Singapore WP, 16.

146. The theoretical dynamics of such a process is captured in Stevens, "Unanticipated Consequences," in Stout, *Psychology of Terrorism*, vol. 3, 45.

147. Drummond, "From the Northwest Imperative to Global Jihad," in Stout, *Psychology of Terrorism*, vol. 1, 60, 75.

148. Imron in Neighbour, *In the Shadow of Swords*, 62.

149. Ibid., 63.

150. Conboy, *The Second Front*, 116.

151. Neighbour, *In the Shadow of Swords*, 19.

152. Cited in ibid., 20.

153. Ibid.

154. Conboy, *The Second Front*, 116.

155. Imron in Neighbour, *In the Shadow of Swords*, 157.

156. Ibid., 218.

157. Ibid., 220.
158. Imron in ibid., 222.
159. Discussed in Waller, *Becoming Evil*, 225–6.
160. Ibid., 225–6.
161. Ibid., 226.
162. Ibid.
163. Ibid.
164. Imron in Neighbour, *In the Shadow of Swords*, 225–6.
165. Hofstede and Hofstede, *Cultures and Organizations*, 377, n. 2.
166. Deikman, *Them and Us*, 52.
167. Neighbour, *In the Shadow of Swords*, 309.
168. Ibid., 298.
169. Imron in ibid., 308.
170. Freud cited in Grossman, *On Killing*, 142.
171. Discussed in Deikman, *Them and Us*, 56.
172. Zimbardo in Waller, *Becoming Evil*, 203.
173. Kressel, *Mass Hate*, 149.
174. Galanter, *Cults*, 143.
175. Ibid., 143–4.
176. Ibid., 144.
177. Kressel, *Mass Hate*, 146–7.
178. Imron in Neighbour, *In the Shadow of Swords*, 290.
179. Kressel, *Mass Hate*, 145.
180. Waller, *Becoming Evil*, 216.
181. Ibid.
182. Bandura, "Mechanisms of Moral Disengagement," in Reich, *Origins of Terrorism*, 176.
183. Waller, *Becoming Evil*, 216.
184. *Bombali.*
185. Ibid.
186. Ibid.
187. Neighbour, *In the Shadow of Swords*, 276.
188. Conboy, *The Second Front*, 180.
189. Neighbour, *In the Shadow of Swords*, 276.
190. Imam Samudra, November 29, 2002, Interview.
191. Ibid.
192. Neighbour, *In the Shadow of Swords*, 276.
193. Imam Samudra, November 29, 2002, Interview.
194. Neighbour, *In the Shadow of Swords*, 276.
195. Ibid., 277.
196. Imam Samudra, November 29, 2002, Interview.
197. Kressel, *Mass Hate*, 133.
198. Waller, *Becoming Evil*, 206.
199. Neighbour, *In the Shadow of Swords*, 277.
200. Ibid. See also Conboy, *The Second Front*, 180–81.
201. Samudra in Neighbour, *In the Shadow of Swords*, 282.
202. Conboy, *The Second Front*, 180.
203. Samudra in Neighbour, *In the Shadow of Swords*, 282.

204. Conboy, *The Second Front*, 180.

205. Ibid., 180–81.

206. Samudra in Neighbour, *In the Shadow of Swords*, 283.

207. Ibid.

208. Imam Samudra, December 16, 2002, Police Interview.

209. Arnasan in Neighbour, *In the Shadow of Swords*, 292.

210. Imam Samudra, November 29, 2002, Interview.

211. Bandura, "Mechanisms of Moral Disengagement," in Reich, *Origins of Terrorism*, 163.

212. Grossman, *On Killing*, 88.

213. Bandura, "Mechanisms of Moral Disengagement," in Reich, *Origins of Terrorism*, 164.

214. See the full text of the "Statement of the Jama'ah al-Islamia in East Asia on the Jakarta Blast," September 9, 2004, found in Kumar Ramakrishna, "'Constructing' the Jemaah Islamiyah Terrorist: A Preliminary Inquiry," Working Paper 71 (Singapore: Institute of Defence and Strategic Studies, October 2004), 19.

215. Bandura, "Mechanisms of Moral Disengagement," in Reich, *Origins of Terrorism*, 169–70.

216. *Jemaah Islamiyah in Southeast Asia: Damaged But Still Dangerous*, 24.

217. Bandura, "Mechanisms of Moral Disengagement," in Reich, *Origins of Terrorism*, 173.

218. Ramakrishna, "'Constructing' the Jemaah Islamiyah Terrorist," 44.

219. Bandura, "Mechanisms of Moral Disengagement," in Reich, *Origins of Terrorism*, 180–81.

220. Waller, *Becoming Evil*, 246.

221. Pinker, *Blank Slate*, 321

222. Ramakrishna, "'Constructing' the Jemaah Islamiyah Terrorist," 45.

223. Imam Samudra, December 16, 2002, Police Interview.

224. "Imam Samudra," Extract 14-5, in Fealy and Hooker, *Voices of Islam in Southeast Asia*, 377.

225. Imam Samudra, November 29, 2002, Interview.

226. Ramakrishna, "'Constructing' the Jemaah Islamiyah Terrorist," 45.

227. Kathy Marks, "First Suspect Stands Trial for Attack on 'White Meat' in Bali Blast," *The Independent* (UK), May 10, 2003, http://findarticles.com/p/articles/mi_qn4158/is_20030510/ai_n12684197/pg_1 (accessed February 8, 2008).

228. See Pinker, *Blank Slate*, 320.

229. Gaylin, *Hatred*, 46.

230. Ibid., 48.

231. Kressel, *Mass Hate*, 209.

232. Dozier, *Why We Hate*, 109–11.

233. Wilson, *Consilience*, 116–17.

234. Ibid., 117.

235. Ibid.

236. Ibid.

237. Dozier, *Why We Hate*, 6.

238. Ibid., 9, 58.

239. Ibid., 63–4 .

240. Ibid., 66.

241. Ibid., 17.
242. Ibid., 17.
243. Ibid., 20.
244. Ibid., 61.
245. Ibid., 63–4.
246. Ibid., 64.
247. Ibid.
248. Alderdice, "The Individual, the Group and the Psychology of Terrorism," 205.
249. Dozier, *Why We Hate*, 11.
250. Ibid., 111–12.
251. Gaylin, *Hatred*, 39.
252. Robert A. Pape, *Dying to Win: The Strategic Logic of Suicide Terrorism* (New York: Random House, 2005).
253. Don J. Feeney Jr., "Entrancement in Islamic Fundamentalism," in Stout, *Psychology of Terrorism*, vol. 3, 192–201.
254. Gaylin, *Hatred,* 122.
255. Ibid., 123.
256. Bruno cited in Franco Ferracuti, "Ideology and Repentance: Terrorism in Italy," in Reich, *Origins of Terrorism*, 60–61.

CHAPTER 5

1. Natasha Robinson, "Bashir Urges Attacks On 'Infidel' Australians," *Australian*, March 24, 2008.
2. Ibid.
3. Ibid.
4. Shefali Rekhi, "JI's Ability to Launch Attacks Curbed; Terrorist Group Has Lost Top Leaders But Threat Remains," *Straits Times* (Singapore), October 13, 2007.
5. Amy Chew, "Indonesian Police Capture JI Leader," *New Straits Times* (Malaysia), June 16, 2007.
6. Amy Chew, "Anti-Terror Police Now Set Sights on Asia's Most Wanted Militant," *South China Morning Post* (Hong Kong), August 7, 2007.
7. Natalie O'Brien, "JI Splinter Group Now Threatens Australians," *Australian*, October 8, 2007.
8. Leslie Lopez, "Key JI Men Poised to Fill Leadership Vacuum," *Straits Times*, August 8, 2007.
9. Azhar Ghani, "Forget Bombings . . . JI Changes Goals; Militant Group Gives Up Regional Aim to Focus on Creating an Islamic Nation, Sources Say," *Straits Times*, November 17, 2006.
10. Rekhi, "JI's Ability to Launch Attacks Curbed."
11. "Charting the Evolution of Jemaah Islamiyah," *South China Morning Post*, September 7, 2006.
12. Azhar Ghani, "JI terrorists Switch Focus to Local Sectarian Conflicts: They Feel Attacks on Western Targets Are Costly and Cause Outrage When Muslims Are Killed," *Straits Times*, May 4, 2007.

13. Amy Chew, "A Jemaah Islamiyah Surge Bodes Ill for Poso," *New Straits Times*, March 1, 2007.

14. Ibid.

15. Ghani, "JI Terrorists Switch Focus to Local Sectarian Conflicts."

16. Ghani, "Forget Bombings . . . JI Changes Goals."

17. "Charting the Evolution of Jemaah Islamiyah."

18. John McBeth, "Terrorist Tactics Changing in Indonesia," *Straits Times*, August 30, 2006.

19. Shefali Rekhi, "New Threat to Region: Do-It-Yourself Terrorists; Former JI Leader Noordin Is at Heart of New Cells," *Straits Times*, January 5, 2007.

20. Ibid.

21. Ghani, "Forget Bombings . . . JI Changes Goals."

22. Ibid.

23. Ibid.

24. McBeth, "Terrorist Tactics Changing in Indonesia."

25. "A JI Attack Every Year—Mastermind Commands," *Sydney Times* (Australia), September 12, 2006.

26. McBeth, "Terrorist Tactics Changing in Indonesia."

27. O'Brien, "JI Splinter Group Now Threatens Australians."

28. Rekhi, "JI's Ability to Launch Attacks Curbed."

29. "Philippine Military: Two Jemaah Islamiyah Bombers Now With Abu Sayyaf," *BBC Monitoring Asia Pacific–Political*, February 13, 2008.

30. Sadanand Dhume, "Step Up the Fight Against Islamism," *Far Eastern Economic Review* (July/August 2007), 10.

31. O'Brien, "JI Splinter Group Now Threatens Australians."

32. "Wounded But Still Dangerous: Terrorism in Southeast Asia," *Economist* (US Edition), June 16, 2007.

33. Ibid.

34. Stephen Fitzpatrick, "Corruption Threatens Anti-Terror Bid in Jails," *Australian*, November 20, 2007.

35. Ibid.; Mark Forbes, "Terrorism Network Commanded from Jail," *Sydney Morning Herald* (Australia), October 11, 2006.

36. Forbes, "Terrorism Network Commanded from Jail."

37. Fitzpatrick, "Corruption Threatens Anti-Terror Bid in Jails."

38. Ibid.

39. Forbes, "Terrorism Network Commanded from Jail."

40. Ibid.

41. Amy Chew, "Soft-Spoken Militant Has Steely View of the Future—Muslims Will Rule the World, Says Alleged JI Commander," *South China Morning Post*, August 7, 2007.

42. Lindsay Murdoch, "Terrorist Leader Warns of More Bali Bombings," *Sydney Morning Herald*, December 22, 2007.

43. Dhume, "Step Up the Fight," 7.

44. *Civil Paths to Peace: Report of the Commonwealth Commission on Respect and Understanding* (London: Commonwealth Secretariat, 2007), 39–53.

45. Ibid., 36.

46. Ibid., 36-8.

47. See Phillip Deery, "Malaya, 1948: Britain's 'Asian Cold War'?" The Cold War as Global Conflict Project, Working Paper 3 (New York: International Center for Advanced Studies, New York University, April 2002), 28. For an analysis on Templer, see Kumar Ramakrishna, "'Transmogrifying' Malaya: The Impact of Sir Gerald Templer (1952-54)," *Journal of Southeast Asian Studies* 32 (2001): 79–92.

48. Templer cited in Richard Stubbs, "Malayan Lessons in 'Hearts and Minds' Worth Revisiting," *Financial Times* (UK), July 28, 2006.

49. Ramakrishna, *Emergency Propaganda*, passim.

50. We are adapting the World Health Organization (WHO) definition of "immunization" as the "process whereby a person is made immune or resistant to an infectious disease." See WHO Web site, http://72.14.235.104/search?q=cache:pE5fxIkPPoQJ:www.who.int/topics/immunization/en/+immunization&hl=en&ct=clnk&cd=8&gl=sg (accessed February 27, 2008).

51. Ramakrishna, *Emergency Propaganda*, passim.

52. Kumar Ramakrishna, "Making Malaya Safe For Decolonization: The Rural Chinese Factor in the Counterinsurgency Campaign," in *The Transformation of Southeast Asia: International Perspectives on Decolonization*, ed. Marc Frey, Ronald W. Pruessen, and Tan Tai Yong (New York: M. E. Sharpe, 2003).

53. This section draws on and adapts ideas first elaborated in Kumar Ramakrishna, "It's the *Story*, Stupid: Developing a Counter-Strategy for Neutralizing Radical Islamism in Southeast Asia," *Countering Terrorist Ideologies Discussion Papers* (Wiltshire, UK: Advanced Research and Assessment Group, September 2005).

54. Kumar Ramakrishna, "The Making of a Malayan Propagandist: The Communists, the British and C. C. Too," *Journal of the Malaysian Branch of the Royal Asiatic Society* 73, pt. 1 (2000): 67–90.

55. Ramakrishna, *Emergency Propaganda*, 113–18; 198–9.

56. Ibid., 38–9.

57. On the high standing of seniors within JI and the trust placed on insiders, see Brig-General Bekto Suprapto, "De-Radicalisation Strategy and Practices in Indonesia" (seminar paper, London, October 2007). Suprapto was the head of Densus 88.

58. "Statement Claming Bali Bombings, Porn, Found on Suspect's Computer: Experts," *Jakarta Post*, July 7, 2003.

59. Ibid.

60. Stern, *Terror in the Name of God*, 136.

61. Husain, *Islamist*, 146–7.

62. Zachary Abuza, "The Trial of Abu Bakar Ba'asyir: A Test Case for Indonesia," *Jamestown Terrorism Monitor* 2 (2004), http://www.jamestown.org/terrorism/news/article.php?articleid=2368802 (accessed March 4, 2008); John Roberts, "Singapore Witnesses Bolster Flagging Jakarta Terrorist Trial," *World Socialist Web Site*, July 8, 2003, http://www.wsws.org/articles/2003/jul2003/indo-j08.shtml (accessed March 4, 2008).

63. Shawn Donnan, "Trial Witness Links Indonesian Cleric to Bombings," *FT.com* (UK), June 26, 2003, http://search.ft.com/search/article.html?id=030626004586 (accessed March 4, 2008).

64. Zuraidah Ibrahim, "Singapore JI Trio Accuse Bashir," *Straits Times*, June 27, 2003.

65. Steven Gutkin, "Asia Radicals Divided on Killing Muslims," Associated Press, December 9, 2003.

66. "2004 Australian Embassy Bombing," *Wikipedia*, page last modified February 28, 2008, http://en.wikipedia.org/wiki/2004_Australian_embassy_bombing (accessed March 4, 2008).

67. Interview with Col. M. Tito Karnavian, Head Intelligence, Densus 88, November 9, 2007, London, UK.

68. Suprapto, "De-Radicalisation Strategy."

69. Ibid.

70. Grossman, *On Killing*, 327.

71. Gaylin, *Hatred*, 247.

72. Bubalo and Fealy, *Joining the Caravan?* 104.

73. Chaidar interview.

74. Ismail Fahmi, "The Indonesian Digital Library Network Is Born to Struggle with the Digital Divide," *Bulletin of the American Society for Information Science and Technology* 28 (2002), http://www.asis.org/Bulletin/May-02/fahmi.html (accessed March 4, 2008).

75. Chaidar interview.

76. Angel M. Rabasa et al., *Building Moderate Muslim Networks* (Santa Monica, Calif.: Rand, 2007).

77. Husain, *Islamist*, 208.

78. El Fadl, *The Great Theft*, 152–3.

79. Azra, "Bali and Southeast Asian Islam," in Ramakrishna and Tan, *After Bali*. 53.

80. Ibid., 54.

81. Mafoot Simon, "A New Voice in Muslim Europe," *Straits Times*, August 6, 2003.

82. Ibid.

83. Kumar Ramakrishna, "US Strategy in Southeast Asia: Counter-Terrorist or Counter-Terrorism?" in Ramakrishna and Tan, *After Bali*, 327.

84. Chaidar interview.

85. Ibid.

86. Karnavian interview.

87. Chaidar interview.

88. Ibid.

89. Ibid.

90. Neighbour, *In the Shadow of Swords*, 107.

91. Ibid., 108.

92. "Switching Sides: Inside the Enemy Camp," CBS News *60 Minutes* program, May 6, 2007.

93. Nasir in Neighbour, *In the Shadow of Swords*, 176.

94. Ibid., 177.

95. Ibid., 227.

96. Nasir in ibid., 309.

97. Peter Taylor, "The Jihadi Who Turned 'Supergrass'," *BBC News*, September 13, 2006, http://news.bbc.co.uk/2/hi/programmes/5334594.stm (accessed February 27, 2008).

98. Karnavian interview.

99. Ibid.

100. "Switching Sides."

101. Nasir Abas, *Membongkar Jamaah Islamiyah: Pengakuan Mantan Anggota JI* [Uncovering Jemaah Islamiyah: Confessions of a Former JI Member] (Jakarta: Grafindo Khanazah Ilmu, 2005).

102. Mafoot Simon, "A Manual to Counter JI Ideology," *Straits Times*, September 26, 2006.

103. Karnavian interview; Suprapto, "De-Radicalisation Strategy."

104. Ramakrishna, *Emergency Propaganda*, 107–110.

105. Seth Mydans, "Nasir Abas, Terrorist Defector, Aids Indonesian Police," *New York Times*, February 29, 2008.

106. Andrew Harding, "The Bali Jihadist on a Peace Mission," *BBC News*, March 14, 2008.

107. Suprapto, "De-Radicalisation Strategy."

108. Karnavian interview.

109. Ibid.

110. Ibid.

111. Mydans, "Nasir Abas."

112. Ibid.

113. Harding, "The Bali Jihadist on a Peace Mission."

114. Chaidar interview.

115. Karnavian interview.

116. Taylor, "The Jihadi Who Turned 'Supergrass'."

117. Karnavian interview; Suprapto, "De-Radicalisation Strategy."

118. Chaidar interview.

119. Harding, "The Bali Jihadist on a Peace Mission."

120. Chaidar interview.

121. Ibid.

122. Ibid.

123. Ibid.

124. Ibid.

125. Ibid.

126. Ibid.

127. Ibid.

128. Ibid.

129. "Switching Sides."

130. Chaidar interview.

131. Harding, "The Bali Jihadist on a Peace Mission."

132. Azra, "Bali and Southeast Asian Islam," in Ramakrishna and Tan, *After Bali*, 42.

133. *Sekolah Menengah Umum* or middle-level school for later teens.

134. Azra, "Bali and Southeast Asian Islam," in Ramakrishna and Tan, *After Bali*, 41–2.

135. Ibid., 42.

136. Farish A. Noor, "Thinking the Unthinkable: The Modernization and Reform of Islamic Higher Education in Indonesia," Working Paper 152 (Singapore: S. Rajaratnam School of International Studies Working, February 15, 2008), 21.

137. Bubalo and Fealy, *Joining the Caravan?* 104.

138. Farish A. Noor, "Ngruki Revisited," 16, 29.

139. See the extended discussion in Chapter Three.

140. Ali, *Infidel,* 47.

141. Ibid.

142. Bubalo and Fealy, *Joining the Caravan?* 101.

143. This is David Berreby's phrase.

144. This is adapted from a telling phrase of Ed Husain's.

145. Grossman, *On Killing,* 160.

146. Chaidar interview.

147. *Civil Paths to Peace,* 16–17.

148. Ibid.

149. *Civil Paths to Peace,* 17.

150. Ibid.

151. Amartya Sen, *Identity and Violence: The Illusion of Destiny* (London: Allen Lane, 2006), 182.

152. Berreby, *Us and Them,* 323.

153. Sen, Identity and Violence, 24.

154. Ibid.

155. Ibid.

156. Ignatieff, *Warrior's Honor,* 166–7.

157. See Chapter Four.

158. Hofstede and Hofstede, *Cultures and Organizations,* 3.

159. Sen, *Identity and Violence,* 34.

160. Waller, *Becoming Evil,* 238.

161. Ibid.

162. Berreby, *Us and Them,* 178.

163. Ibid.

164. Ibid.

165. *Civil Paths to Peace,* 26.

166. Ibid.

167. Berreby, *Us and Them,* 179.

168. Waller, *Becoming Evil,* 274.

169. Berreby, *Us and Them,* 179.

170. ASEM "Bali Interfaith Dialogue," July 21–22, 2005, http://www.aseminfoboard.org/content/documents/050722_BaliDeclaration.pdf (accessed March 5, 2008).

171. "Second Asia-Europe Youth Interfaith Dialogue 2008," Asia-Europe Foundation Web site, http://www.asef.org/index.php?option=com_project&task=view&id=1079 (accessed March 5, 2008).

172. Saidiman, "Interfaith Dialogue Through Education System," posted November 21, 2007, available online at http://72.14.235.104/search?q=cache:ss5wf7Ab4k0J:saidiman.wordpress.com/2007/11/21/interfaith-dialog-through-education-system/+indonesia,+interfaith+dialogue,+young+people&hl=en&ct=clnk&cd=1&gl=sg (accessed March 5, 2008).

173. Hofstede and Hofstede, *Cultures and Organizations,* 163–205.

174. Cited in Kimball, *When Religion Becomes Evil,* 199.

175. Waller, *Becoming Evil,* 274.

176. Jane Perlez, "Saudis Quietly Promote Strict Islam in Indonesia," *New York Times*, July 5, 2003.

177. Richard Wike, Pew Global Attitudes Project, and Brian J. Grim, Pew Forum on Religion and Public Life, "Widespread Negativity: Muslims Distrust Westerners More Than Vice Versa," October 30, 2007, http://pewresearch.org/pubs/625/widespread-negativity (accessed February 26, 2008).

178. For instance, see the report on the views of Indonesian university students on the Bali blast investigations in Phil Zabriskie, "Did You Hear . . . ?" *Time (Asia)*, March 10, 2003.

179. Derwin Pereira, "Indonesian Terrorist Bombings: Fact and Fiction," *Straits Times*, August 15, 2003.

180. Elizabeth Fuller Collins, "Dakwah and Democracy: The Significance of Partai Keadilan and Hizbut Tahrir" (paper presented at the International Seminar on Islamic Militant Movements in Southeast Asia, Jakarta, July 22–23, 2003).

181. Wike and Grim, "Widespread Negativity."

182. Edmund F. Scherr, "US Aid Effort for Iraq Largest Since Marshall Plan," *Washington File*, March 26, 2003, available online at http://www.globalsecurity.org/wmd/library/news/iraq/2003/iraq-030326-usia05.htm (accessed February 26, 2008).

183. Jane Perlez, "Muslim-as-Apple-Pie Videos Greeted with Skepticism," *New York Times*, October 30, 2002.

184. Mark Silva, "Karen Hughes Leaves, Mission Not Accomplished," *The Swamp: Tribune's Washington Bureau*, October 30, 2007, http://www.swamppolitics.com/news/politics/blog/2007/10/karen_hughes_leaves_mission_no.html (accessed February 26, 2008).

185. Daniel Luban, "Blackwater Pays Price For Iraqi Firefight," *Asia Times Online*, September 19, 2007, http://www.atimes.com/atimes/Middle_East/II19Ak04.html (accessed February 26, 2008).

186. See Chapter Three.

187. Chaidar interview.

188. For a seminal discussion of the need for conventional armed forces to deal with state collapse and the rise of non-state armed groups, see Gen. Charles C. Krulak, "The Strategic Corporal: Leadership in the Three-Block War," *Marines Magazine* (January 1999), http://www.au.af.mil/au/awc/awcgate/usmc/strategic_corporal.htm (accessed February 26, 2008); see also Ignatieff, *Warrior's Honor,* 109–63; and Thomas X. Hammes, *The Sling and the Stone: On War in the 21st Century* (Osceola, Wis.: Zenith, 2004).

189. See Thomas E. Ricks, *Fiasco: The American Military Adventure in Iraq* (London: Penguin, 2007), 222, 260, passim.

190. Pepe Escobar, "The Islamic Emirate of Fallujah," *Asia Times Online*, July 15, 2004, http://atimes.com/atimes/Middle_East/FG15Ak01.html (accessed February 26, 2008).

191. Ricks, *Fiasco*, 232-3.

192. Joshua Key, as told to Lawrence Hill, *The Deserter's Tale: The Story of an Ordinary Soldier Who Walked Away from the War in Iraq* (New York: Atlantic Monthly Press, 2007), 99.

193. Ibid.

194. Ibid.

195. "Abu Ghraib Timeline," *CBC News Online* (Canada), February 18, 2005, http://www.cbc.ca/news/background/iraq/abughraib_timeline.html (accessed April 8, 2008).

196. See Ramakrishna, *Emergency Propaganda*, passim.

197. Thomas Mockaitis, *British Counterinsurgency, 1919-60* (London: Macmillan, 1990).

198. Suprapto, "De-Radicalisation Strategy."

199. Ramakrishna, "It's the *Story*, Stupid."

200. See *The US Army/Marine Corps Counterinsurgency Field Manual* (University of Chicago Press, 2007). Among other insights, the new manual suggests that "sometimes, the more force is used, the less effective it is." Two military officers and leading counterinsurgency theorists, the Australian David Kilcullen and the American John A. Nagl (who has studied the Malayan Emergency)—along with U.S. commander in Iraq, General David Petraeus—have been influential in helping the U.S. military revise its thinking on counterinsurgency. See Jim Michaels, "Petraeus Strategy Takes Aim at Post-Vietnam Mindset," *USA Today.Com,* March 7, 2007, http://www.usatoday.com/news/world/iraq/2007-03-07-petraeus_N.htm (accessed March 5, 2008).

201. "US Announces $350 million in Tsunami Aid," *MSNBC*, December 31, 2004, http://www.msnbc.msn.com/id/6767190/ (accessed February 26, 2008).

202. Dhume, "Step Up the Fight," 11.

203. El Fadl, *The Great Theft*, 173.

204. Sen, *Identity and Violence*, 180.

205. Ibid.

206. Ignatieff, *Warrior's Honor*, 166–7.

207. Kimball, *When Religion Becomes Evil*, 95.

208. A term coined by the psychologist Irving L. Janis to refer to the powerful pressures a small group can exert on its members to conform to the group's line of thinking. See Deikman, *Them and Us*, 101–2, 160–1.

209. Kressel, *Mass Hate*, 233.

210. Waller, *Becoming Evil*, 35.

211. Ibid., 35–6.

212. Ayaan Hirsi Ali and Samuel Huntington, "Culture Clash Continued," *New Perspectives Quarterly* (Winter 2007), 51.

213. Farish A. Noor, "Thinking the Unthinkable," 10, 17.

214. Ibid., 14.

215. Azra, "Bali and Southeast Asian Islam," in Ramakrishna and Tan, *After Bali*, 41.

216. Farish A. Noor, "Thinking the Unthinkable," 14.

217. Ibid., 23.

218. Ibid.

219. Azra, "Bali and Southeast Asian Islam," in Ramakrishna and Tan, *After Bali*, 41.

220. Farish A. Noor, "Thinking the Unthinkable," 28.

221. Ibid., 29.

222. Azra, "Bali and Southeast Asian Islam," in Ramakrishna and Tan, *After Bali*, 41.

223. Ibid.

224. Farish A. Noor discussion with Professor Akhmad Minhaji, Faculty of Shariah, UIN Sunan Kalijaga, in Farish A. Noor, "Thinking the Unthinkable," 53.

225. Azra, "Bali and Southeast Asian Islam," in Ramakrishna and Tan, *After Bali*, 41.

226. Farish A. Noor discussion with Professor Amin Abdullah, Rector, UIN Sunan Kalijaga, in Farish A. Noor, "Thinking the Unthinkable," 37.

227. Sri Yunanto, "The Rise of Radical Islamist Groups in Indonesia and the Political and Security Consequences of the Political Activities" (paper presented at the Interntional Conference on Democratization and the Issue of Terrorism in Indonesia, organized by the Department of International Relations, Parahyangan Catholic University and Konrad Adenauer Stiftung, Bandung, April 13, 2005).

228. Pipes, *Militant Islam*, 56.

229. Ruthven, *Fury for God*, 217.

230. "Khalid Sheikh Mohammed," *Biography.Com*, 2007, http://www.biography.com/search/article.do?id=241188 (accessed March 6, 2008).

231. "Indonesian Linked to Manila, Jakarta Bombings," *Laksamana.net*, July 6, 2002, http://www.laksamana.net/vnews.cfm?ncat=22&news_id=3127 (accessed September 11, 2004).

232. Michael Day and David Bamber, "Universities Spy for MI5 on Foreign Students," *news.telegraph.co.uk*, August 28, 2004, http://www.telegraph.com.uk/news/main.jhtml?xml=/news/2004/03/21/nspy21.xml&sSheet=/news/2004/03/21/ixnewstop.html (accessed September 11, 2004).

233. Maria Ressa, "Al Qaeda Operative Sought Anthrax," *CNN.com*, October 10, 2003, http://www.cnn.com/2003/WORLD/asiapcf/southeast/10/10alqaeda.anthrax (accessed September 21, 2004).

234. "Azahari: Professor, Bomb-Maker and Fanatic," *Channelnewsasia.com* (Singapore), September 10, 2004, http://www.channelnewsasia.com/stories/afp_asiapacific/view/105933/1/.html (accessed September 10, 2004); Dan Murphy, "Leaderless, Terror Group Still Potent," *Christian Science Monitor*, August 18, 2003.

235. "Top Terrorist Azahari Reported Killed In Raid," *Paras Indonesia*, November 9. 2005, http://www.parasindonesia.com/read.php?gid=119 (accessed March 11, 2008).

236. Ronald Johnson, "Psychoreligious Roots of Violence: The Search for the Concrete in a World of Abstractions," in Ellens, *Destructive Power of Religion*, vol. 4, 200–202.

237. Momen, "Fundamentalism and Liberalism."

238. Ibid.

239. Ibid.

240. Beit-Hallahmi and Argyle, *Psychology of Religious Behavior*, 181.

241. Francis S. Collins, *The Language of God: A Scientist Presents Evidence for Belief* (London: Pocket Books, 2007), 4. Collins considers himself a committed Christian as well.

242. El Fadl, *The Great Theft*, 171.

243. Ibid.

244. Ibid., 99.

245. Ibid., 98.

246. Ruthven, *Fury for God*, 103.

247. El Fadl, *The Great Theft*, 99.

248. See Steven Emerson, *American Jihad: The Terrorists Living Among Us* (New York: The Free Press, 2002), 172.

249. Ibid., 173.

250. El Fadl, *The Great Theft*, 38–9.

251. Beit-Hallahmi and Argyle, *Psychology of Religious Behavior*, 182.

252. El Fadl, *The Great Theft*, 150.

253. Ibid.

254. Ibid., 151.

255. Ibid.

256. Ibid., 156.

257. Ibid., 157.

258. Ibid.

259. Farish A. Noor interview with Ustaz Abu Bakar Ba'asyir at Pondok Pesantren Al-Mukmin, Ngruki, Surakarta, Indonesia, May 20-22, 2007.

260. El Fadl, *The Great Theft*, 101.

261. Ali, *Infidel*, 269–70.

262. Abdurrahman Wahid, "Best Way to Fight Islamic Extremism," *Sunday Times (*Singapore), April 14, 2002.

263. Ibid.

264. Ibid.

265. Ibid.

266. Ibid.

267. Emerson, *American Jihad*, 173.

268. Roy Mottahedeh, "Help Get Education Running Again," *The IHT Online*, February 13, 2002, www.iht.com/articles/47879.html (accessed February 20, 2002).

269. Farish A. Noor's Ba'asyir interview.

270. Farish A. Noor interview with Amin Abdullah, in "Thinking the Unthinkable," 38.

271. Farish A. Noor interview with Amin Abdullah, in ibid., 39.

272. Farish A. Noor interview with Mochamad Nur Ichwan, UIN Sunan Kalijaga, in ibid., 48.

273. Husain, *Islamist*, 154–64.

274. Farish A. Noor's Ba'asyir interview.

275. Hofstede and Hofstede, *Cultures and Organizations*, 13.

276. Azra, "Bali and Southeast Asian Islam," in Ramakrishna and Tan, *After Bali*, 45.

277. Examples of more nuanced Islamist political groupings are the Hizb al-Wasat in Egypt, which broke away from the Muslim Brotherhood, and the Justice and Development Party in Turkey, both of which have sought to carve out political space within, rather than seek the outright Islamization of, their respective national political systems. See Bubalo and Fealy, *Joining the Caravan?* 33–6.

278. Farish A. Noor's Ba'asyir interview.

279. Ian Buruma, *Murder in Amsterdam: The Death of Theo van Gogh and the Limits of Tolerance* (London: Atlantic, 2007), 34–5.

280. Neil J. Kressel, *Bad Faith: The Dangers of Religious Extremism* (New York: Prometheus Books, 2007), 243.

281. Husain, *Islamist*, 156.

282. Ibid., 202.

283. Ali, *Caged Virgin*, 31.

284. Ali, *Infidel*, 285–6.

285. S. Yunanto, "Darul Islam (DI) and Jemaah Islamiyah (JI): The Dynamics of Militant Islamic Movements in Indonesia" (paper presented at the International Seminar on Religion and Conflict, organized by Parahyangan Catholic University, Indonesia Conflict Study Network and Asia Links, Bandung, January 10–11, 2005).

286. El Fadl, *The Great Theft*, 152.

287. Farish A. Noor interview with Mochamad Nur Ichwan, in "Thinking the Unthinkable," 44.

288. El Fadl, *The Great Theft*, 154.

289. Ibid.

290. Farish A. Noor's Ba'asyir interview.

291. Husain, *Islamist*, 51.

292. Ali, *Infidel*, 42.

293. Ibid.

294. Ibid., 48.

295. Ibid., 48–49.

296. Husain, *Islamist*, 241.

297. Ibid., 238.

298. Ibid.

299. Ali, *Infidel*, 44.

300. Ibid., 43, 51.

301. Elena Pavlova, "An Ideological Response to Islamist Terrorism: Theoretical and Operational Overview," in *Terrorism in the Asia-Pacific: Threat and Response*, ed. Rohan Gunaratna (Singapore: Eastern Universities Press, 2003), 43.

302. Hussain, *Islamist*, 241.

303. Ali, *Infidel*, 307.

304. Richard Dawkins, *The God Delusion* (London: Bantam Press, 2006).

305. Sam Harris, *The End of Faith: Religion, Terror and the Future of Reason* (London: The Free Press, 2005).

306. Ali, *Infidel*, 272.

307. Ibid.

308. Ibid.

309. Ibid.

310. Ibid., 281.

311. Ibid., 282.

312. Ibid.

313. Dawkins, *God Delusion*, 281–308.

314. Harris, *End of Faith*, 225.

315. Francis Wheen, *How Mumbo-Jumbo Conquered the World* (London: Harper Perennial, 2004).

316. Buruma, *Murder in Amsterdam*, 27.

317. Hofstede and Hofstede, *Cultures and Organizations*, 89.

318. Smith et al., *Understanding Social Psychology Across Cultures*, 106–7.

319. Sen, *Identity and Violence*, 24–5.

320. Civil Paths to Peace, 42.

321. Ali, *Infidel*, 4–8.

322. Husain, *Islamist*, 143.

323. Ibid., 149.

324. El Fadl, *The Great Theft*, 277.

325. McAmis, *Malay Muslims*,17.

326. See Chapter Three.

327. Husain, *Islamist*, 189.

328. Ibid.

329. Ibid., 196–7.

330. Federspiel, *Indonesian Muslim Intellectuals*, 15.

331. Fealy, Hooker, and White, "Indonesia," 41.

332. Azra, "Bali and Southeast Asian Islam," in Ramakrishna and Tan, *After Bali*, 40.

333. Ibid.

334. Fealy, Hooker, and White, "Indonesia," 41.

335. Azra, "Bali and Southeast Asian Islam," in Ramakrishna and Tan, *After Bali*, 42.

336. Fealy, Hooker, and White, "Indonesia," 46.

337. Azra, "Bali and Southeast Asian Islam," in Ramakrishna and Tan, *After Bali*, 43.

338. Fealy, Hooker, and White, "Indonesia," 41.

339. Ibid.

340. Ali, *Caged Virgin*, 17–22.

341. El Fadl, *The Great Theft*, 281.

342. Ibid., 156.

343. Ibid., 283–4.

344. Ibid., 279.

345. Woodward, "President Gus Dur: Indonesia, Islam and *Reformasi*."

346. Ismail, "Ngruki: It is a Terrorism School?"

347. Husain, *Islamist*, 237.

348. Dhume, "Step Up the Fight," 6–7.

349. Bret Stephens, "An Interview with Abdurrahman Wahid," *Wall Street Journal*, April 7, 2007.

350. Extract 15-20, 'Nurcholish Madjid," in Fealy and Hooker, *Voices of Islam in Southeast Asia*, 455–6.

351. Extract 12.1.4, "Nurcholish Madjid," in ibid., 220.

352. Kimball, *When Religion Becomes Evil*, 188.

353. Ibid., 98.

354. For example, Michael Connors, "War on Error and the Southern Fire: How Terrorism Analysts Get it Wrong," *Critical Asian Studies* 38 (2006): 151–75; Hamilton-Hart, "Terrorism in Southeast Asia"; Michael Vatikiotis, "Terrorism and the Problem of Binary Vision," *Asia Times Online*, August 29, 2006, http://www.atimes.com/atimes/Southeast_Asia/HH29Ae01.html (accessed March 15, 2008). Strangely, while one of the key criticisms of terrorism analysts working on Southeast Asia is that they tend not to differentiate between species of Islam and Islamism, rather lumping "the good guys" and the "bad guys" together, it can equally be suggested that the critics do not always tease out adequately the very real differences

in approaches among the Southeast Asian terrorism analysts themselves! The latter are invariably lumped together into the often-lampooned monolithic category of "terrorism experts."

355. James Surowiecki, *The Wisdom of Crowds: Why the Many Are Smarter Than the Few* (London: Abacus, 2006).

Glossary of Key Terms and Phrases

abangan Muslim	nominal Muslim in Indonesia
abid	slave
al-Wala wal-Bara	the doctrine of solidarity between Muslims of the same persuasion and the avoidance of non-Muslims as well as Muslims of different sects
alim	a learned Islamic scholar
amir	commander or leader
aqidah	faith
bida	doctrinal innovation, deviation from Islamic tradition
dakwah	religious proselytization
dhimmi	non-Muslim living under the protection of an Islamic State
fasiqun	rebellious
fatwa	a legal opinion based on Islamic Law
fiqh	Islamic jurisprudence
Hadith	report of the words and deeds of the Prophet
haj	pilgrimage to Mecca
halal	permissible under Islamic Law
halaqah	small religious discussion group
haram	forbidden under Islamic Law
hijrah	flight or migration
Imam	spiritual leader of a Muslim community

jahiliyya	extreme disbelief in and ignorance of God, usually descriptive of the era before advent of Islam in Arabia
jihad	in essence, to strive to for moral excellence. The meaning ranges from a struggle for personal self-mastery over baser instincts to engaging in holy war
kaum muda	"Young group" of early twentieth-century Islamic reformists in Malay world
kaum tua	"Old group" of early twentieth-century Islamic conservative scholars in Malay world
kuffar	infidels
madrasah	modern religious school
Mahdi	the "guided one"
mujahidin	holy warrior engaged in *jihad*
munafiq	hypocrite
pesantren	religious boarding school
ratu adil	just king
santri Muslim	devout, observant Muslim in Indonesia
shariah	Islamic Law
shirk	apostasy
Sufism	Islamic mysticism
Sunnah	customs and precedents in Islam based on the Prophet's example
tariqa	Sufi order
ulama	plural of *alim*; learned Islamic scholars
usroh	small group or cell based on Egyptian Muslim Brotherhood model and adopted by the Tarbiyah movement in Indonesia
ustaz	religious teacher
wali	someone close to God; a saint
zikr	mystical, rhythmic chants in remembrance of God, characteristic of the Sufi tradition

Bibliography

BOOKS

Abbas, Nasir. *Membongkar Jamaah Islamiyah: Pengakuan Mantan Anggota JI* [Uncovering Jemaah Islamiyah: Confessions of a Former JI Member]. Jakarta: Grafindo Khanazah Ilmu, 2005.

Abuza, Zachary. *Militant Islam in Southeast Asia: Crucible of Terror*. Boulder, Colo.: Lynne Rienner, 2003.

Algar, Hamid. *Wahhabism: A Critical Essay*. New York: Islamic Publications International, 2002.

Ali, Ayaan Hirsi. *The Caged Virgin: A Muslim Woman's Cry for Reason*. London: The Free Press, 2006.

———. *Infidel: My Life*. London: The Free Press, 2007.

Alper, Matthew. *The "God" Part of the Brain: A Scientific Interpretation of Human Spirituality and God*. Naperville, Ill.: Sourcebooks Inc., 2006.

Barton, Greg. *Jemaah Islamiyah: Radical Islamism in Indonesia*. Singapore: Singapore University Press, 2005.

Beit-Hallahmi, Benjamin, and Michael Argyle. *The Psychology of Religious Behavior, Belief and Experience*. New York: Routledge, 1997.

Bell, Stewart. *The Martyr's Oath: The Apprenticeship of a Homegrown Terrorist*. Mississauga, Ontario: John Wiley and Sons Canada Ltd., 2005.

Berreby, David. *Us and Them: Understanding Your Tribal Mind*. New York and Boston: Little, Brown and Company, 2005.

Browning, Christopher R. *Ordinary Men: Reserve Police Battalion 101 and the Final Solution in Poland*. New York: HarperCollins, 1992.

Bubalo, Anthony and Greg Fealy. *Joining the Caravan? The Middle East, Islamism and Indonesia*, Alexandria, NSW: The Lowy Institute for International Policy, 2005.

Buruma, Ian. *Murder in Amsterdam: The Death of Theo van Gogh and the Limits of Tolerance*. London: Atlantic, 2007.

Collins, Francis S. *The Language of God: A Scientist Presents Evidence for Belief*. London: Pocket Books, 2007.

Conboy, Ken. *The Second Front: Inside Asia's Most Dangerous Terrorist Network*. Jakarta: Equinox Publishing, 2006.

Dahlby, Tracy. *Allah's Torch: A Report from Behind the Scenes in Asia's War on Terror*. New York: William Morrow, 2005.

Dawkins, Richard. *The God Delusion*. London: Bantam Press, 2006.

Deikman, Arthur J. *Them and Us: Cult Thinking and the Terrorist Threat*. Berkeley: Bay Tree Publishing, 2003.

Dozier, Jr., Rush W. *Why We Hate: Understanding, Curbing and Eliminating Hate in Ourselves and Our World*. New York: Contemporary Books, 2002.

El Fadl, Khaled Abou. *The Great Theft: Wrestling Islam From the Extremists*. New York: HarperSanFrancisco, 2005.

Elms, Alan C. *Uncovering Lives: The Uneasy Alliance of Biography and Psychology*. New York: Oxford University Press, 1994.

Emerson, Steven. *American Jihad: The Terrorists Living Among Us*. New York: The Free Press, 2002.

Esposito, John L., *Unholy War: Terror in the Name of Islam*. New York: Oxford University Press, 2002.

Esposito, John L., and John O. Voll, eds. *Makers of Contemporary Islam*. New York: Oxford University Press, 2001.

Federspiel, Howard M. *Indonesian Muslim Intellectuals of the 20th Century*. Singapore: Institute of Southeast Asian Studies, 2006.

Firestone, Reuven. *Jihad: The Origins of Holy War in Islam*. New York: Oxford University Press, 1999.

Fletcher, Richard. *The Cross and the Crescent: The Dramatic Story of the Earliest Encounters Between Christians and Muslims*. London: Penguin, 2004.

Fuller, Graham E. *The Future of Political Islam*. New York: Palgrave Macmillan, 2003.

Gabriel, Brigitte. *Because They Hate: A Survivor of Islamic Terror Warns America*. New York: St. Martin's Press, 2006.

Gabriel, Mark A. *Journey Into the Mind of an Islamic Terrorist: Why They Hate Us and How We Can Change Their Minds*. Lake Mary, Fla.: Frontline, 2006.

Galanter, Marc. *Cults: Faith, Healing, and Coercion*. 2nd ed. New York: Oxford University Press, 1999.

Gaylin, Willard. *Hatred: The Psychological Descent into Violence*. New York: Public Affairs, 2003.

Grossman, Lt. Col. Dave. *On Killing: The Psychological Cost of Learning to Kill in War and Society*. New York: Back Bay Books, 1996.

Gunaratna, Rohan. *Inside Al Qaeda: Global Network of Terror*. London: Christopher Hurst, 2002.

Hammes, Thomas X. *The Sling and the Stone: On War in the 21st Century*. Osceola, Wis.: Zenith, 2004.

Harris, Sam. *The End of Faith: Religion, Terror and the Future of Reason*. London: The Free Press, 2005.

Hofstede, Geert. *Culture's Consequences: International Differences in Work-Related Values*. Beverly Hills: Sage, 1980.

Hofstede, Geert, and Gert Jan Hofstede. *Cultures and Organizations: Software of the Mind*. New York: McGraw-Hill, 2005.

The Holy Qu'ran. Translated by Abdullah Yusuf Ali. Ware, Hertfordshire: Wordsworth Editions, 2000.

Hudson, Rex A., and Staff of the Federal Research Division of the Library of Congress. *Who Becomes a Terrorist and Why: The 1999 Government Report on Profiling Terrorists*. Guilford, Conn.: The Lyons Press, 2002.

Husain, Ed. *The Islamist: Why I Joined Radical Islam in Britain, What I Saw Inside and Why I Left*. London: Penguin, 2007.

Ignatieff, Michael. *The Warrior's Honor: Ethnic War and the Modern Conscience*. New York: Owl Books, 1997.

Islam, Syed Serajul. *The Politics of Islamic Identity in Southeast Asia*. Singapore: Thomson Learning, 2005.

Juergensmeyer, Mark. *Terror in the Mind of God: The Global Rise of Religious Violence*. Updated ed. with a new preface. Berkeley and Los Angeles: University of California Press, 2000.

Kahn, Joel S. *Other Malays: Nationalism and Cosmopolitanism in the Malay World*. Singapore: Singapore University Press, 2006.

Key, Joshua, as told to Lawrence Hill. *The Deserter's Tale: The Story of an Ordinary Soldier Who Walked Away from the War in Iraq*. New York: Atlantic Monthly Press, 2007.

Kimball, Charles. *When Religion Becomes Evil*. New York: HarperCollins, 2003.

Kressel, Neil J. *Mass Hate: The Global Rise of Genocide and Terror*. rev. and updated ed. Cambridge, Mass. Westview Press, 2002.

———. *Bad Faith: The Dangers of Religious Extremism*. New York: Prometheus Books, 2007.

Laqueur, Walter. *No End to War: Terrorism in the Twenty-First Century*. New York: Continuum, 2003.

Lee, Harper. *To Kill a Mockingbird*. New York: Harper Perennial Modern Classics, 2006.

McAmis, Robert Day. *Malay Muslims: The History and Challenge of Resurgent Islam in Southeast Asia*. Grand Rapids, Mich.: William B. Eerdmans, 2002.

McGrath, Alister, with Joanna Collicutt McGrath. *The Dawkins Delusion? Atheist Fundamentalism and the Denial of the Divine*. London: Society for Promoting Christian Knowledge, 2007.

Millard, Mike. *Jihad in Paradise: Islam and Politics in Southeast Asia*. New York: M. E. Sharpe, 2004.

Mockaitis, Thomas. *British Counterinsurgency, 1919–60*. London: Macmillan, 1990.

Moghaddam, Fathali M. *From the Terrorists' Point of View: What They Experience and Why They Come to Destroy*. Westport, Conn.: Praeger Security International, 2006.

Moussaoui, Abd Samad, with Florence Bouquillat. *Zacarias Moussaoui: The Making of a Terrorist.* Translated by Simon Pleasance and Fronza Woods. London: Serpent's Tail, 2003.

Neighbour, Sally. *In the Shadow of Swords: On the Trail of Terrorism from Afghanistan to Australia.* Sydney: HarperCollins, 2004.

Nutting, Anthony. *The Arabs: A Narrative History from Mohammed to the Present.* New York: Mentor, 1964.

Nye, Jr., Joseph S. *Bound to Lead: The Changing Nature of American Power.* New York: Basic Books, 1991.

Pape, Robert A. *Dying to Win: The Strategic Logic of Suicide Terrorism.* New York: Random House, 2005.

Patai, Raphael. *The Arab Mind.* Revised edition with an updated foreword by Norwell B. De Atkine. New York: Heatherleigh Press, 2007.

Pinker, Steven. *The Blank Slate: The Modern Denial of Human Nature.* London: Penguin, 2003.

Pipes, Daniel. *Militant Islam Reaches America.* New York: W. W. Norton, 2003.

Rabasa, Angel M., Cheryl Benard, Peter Chalk, C. Christine Fair, Theodore Karasik, Rollie Lal, Ian Lesser, and David Thaler. *The Muslim World After 9/11.* Santa Monica, Calif.: Rand, 2004.

Rabasa, Angel M., Cheryl Barnard, Lowell H. Schwartz, and Peter Sickle. *Building Moderate Muslim Networks.* Santa Monica, Calif.: Rand, 2007.

Ramakrishna, Kumar. *Emergency Propaganda: The Winning of Malayan Hearts and Minds 1948–1958.* Richmond, Surrey: Routledge Curzon, 2002.

Ressa, Maria. *Seeds of Terror: An Eye-Witness Account of Al Qaeda's Newest Center of Operations in Southeast Asia.* New York: Free Press, 2003.

Richardson, Louise. *What Terrorists Want: Understanding the Terrorist Threat.* London: John Murray, 2006.

Ricklefs, M. C. *A History of Modern Indonesia Since c. 1300.* 2nd ed. Stanford: Stanford University Press, 1993.

Ricks, Thomas E. *Fiasco: The American Military Adventure in Iraq.* London: Penguin, 2007.

Ruthven, Malise. *A Fury for God: The Islamist Attack on America.* New York: Granta, 2002.

Sageman, Marc. *Understanding Terror Networks.* Philadelphia: University of Pennsylvania Press, 2004.

Samudra, Imam. *Aku Melawan Teroris* [I Fight the Terrorists]. Solo: Jazeera, 2004.

Schmid, Alex P., and Janny de Graaf. *Violence as Communication: Insurgent Terrorism and the Western News Media.* London: Sage, 1982.

Selengut, Charles. *Sacred Fury: Understanding Religious Violence.* Walnut Creek, Calif.: Altamira Press, 2003.

Sen, Amartya. *Identity and Violence: The Illusion of Destiny.* London: Allen Lane, 2006.

Sidel, John. *Riots, Pogroms, Jihad: Religious Violence in Indonesia.* Singapore: NUS Press, 2007.

Sim, Stuart. *Fundamentalist World: The New Dark Age of Dogma.* Cambridge: Icon Books, 2004.

Simon, Steven, and Daniel Benjamin. *The Age of Sacred Terror.* New York: Random House, 2002.

Singh, Bilveer. *The Talibanization of Southeast Asia: Losing the War on Terror to Islamist Extremists*. Westport, Conn.: Praeger Security International, 2007.

Smith, Peter B., Michael Harris Bond and Cigdem Kagitcibasi. *Understanding Social Psychology Across Cultures: Living and Working in a Changing World*. London: Sage, 2006.

Spencer, Robert. *Onward Muslim Soldiers: How Jihad Still Threatens America and the West*. Washington, D.C.: Regnery, 2003.

Stearns, Peter N., and William L. Langer, eds. *The Encyclopedia of World History*. Rev. ed. New York: Houghton Mifflin, 2001.

Stern, Jessica. *Terror in the Name of God: Why Religious Militants Kill*. New York: HarperCollins, 2003.

Surowiecki, James. *The Wisdom of Crowds: Why the Many Are Smarter Than the Few*. London: Abacus, 2006.

The US Army/Marine Corps Counterinsurgency Field Manual. University of Chicago Press, 2007.

Van Dijk, C. *Rebellion Under the Banner of Islam: The Darul Islam in Indonesia*. The Hague: Martinus Nijhoff, 1981.

Volkan, Vamik. *Killing in the Name of Identity: A Study of Bloody Conflicts*. Charlottesville, Va.: Pitchstone, 2006.

Waller, James. *Becoming Evil: How Ordinary People Commit Genocide and Mass Killing*. New York: Oxford University Press, 2005.

Wardlaw, Grant. *Political Terrorism: Theory, Tactics and Counter-Measures*. 2nd ed. Cambridge: Cambridge University Press, 1989.

Wheen, Francis. *How Mumbo-Jumbo Conquered the World*. London: Harper Perennial, 2004.

Wilson, David Sloan. *Evolution for Everyone: How Darwin's Theory Can Change the Way We Think About Ourselves*. New York; Delta Trade, 2008.

Wilson, E. O. *Consilience: The Unity of Knowledge*. New York: Vintage Books, 1999.

Winston, Robert. *Human Instinct: How Our Primeval Impulses Shape Our Modern Lives*. London: Bantam Books, 2003.

BOOK CHAPTERS AND JOURNAL ARTICLES

Alderdice, Lord. "The Individual, the Group and the Psychology of Terrorism." *International Review of Psychiatry* 19 (2007): 201–209.

Ali, Ayaan Hirsi, and Samuel Huntington. "Culture Clash Continued." *New Perspectives Quarterly* (2007): 47–59.

Andaya, Barbara Watson. "Religious Developments in Southeast Asia, c. 1500–1800." In Tarling, *Cambridge History of Southeast Asia*, Vol. 1, Part 2, 164–227.

Azra, Azyumardi. "Bali and Southeast Asian Islam: Debunking the Myths." In Ramakrishna and Tan, *After Bali*, 39–57.

Bandura, Albert. "Mechanisms of Moral Disengagement." In Reich, *Origins of Terrorism*, 161–91.

Bellwood, Peter. "Southeast Asia Before History." In Tarling, *Cambridge History of Southeast Asia*, vol. pt. 1, 55–136.

Cameron, Gavin. "Terrorism and Weapons of Mass Destruction: Prospects and Problems." In Tan and Ramakrishna, *The New Terrorism*, 50–72.

Chalk, Peter. "Al Qaeda and its Links to Terrorist Groups in Asia." In Tan and Ramakrishna, *The New Terrorism*, 107–28.

———. "Separatism and Southeast Asia: The Islamic Factor in Southern Thailand, Mindanao and Aceh." *Studies in Conflict and Terrorism* 24 (2001): 241–69.

Connors, Michael. "War on Error and the Southern Fire: How Terrorism Analysts Get it Wrong." *Critical Asian Studies* 38 (2006): 151–75.

Crenshaw, Martha. "Questions to be Answered, Research to be Done, Knowledge to be Applied." In Reich, *Origins of Terrorism*, 247–60.

Crouch, Harold. "Radical Islam in Indonesia: Some Misperceptions." In Vicziany and Wright-Neville, *Islamic Terrorism in Indonesia*, 33–51.

Davis, John M. "Countering International Terrorism: Perspectives from International Psychology." In Stout, *Psychology of Terrorism*, vol. 4, 33–56.

Drummond, Jonathan T. "From the Northwest Imperative to Global Jihad: Social Psychological Aspects of the Construction of the Enemy, Political Violence, and Terror." In Stout, *Psychology of Terrorism*, vol. 1, 49–95.

Ellens, J. Harold, ed. *The Destructive Power of Religion: Violence in Judaism, Christianity and Islam*, vol. 2, *Religion, Psychology and Violence*. Westport, Conn.: Praeger, 2004.

———, ed. *The Destructive Power of Religion: Violence in Judaism, Christianity and Islam*, vol. 4, *Contemporary Views on Spirituality and Violence*. Westport, Conn.: Praeger, 2004.

———. "Fundamentalism, Orthodoxy and Violence." In Ellens, *Destructive Power of Religion*, vol. 4, 119–42.

———. "The Dynamics of Prejudice." In Ellens, *Destructive Power of Religion*, vol. 2, 85–98.

Fahmi, Ismail. "The Indonesian Digital Library Network is Born to Struggle with the Digital Divide." *Bulletin of the American Society for Information Science and Technology* 28 (2002), http://www.asis.org/Bulletin/May-02/fahmi.html (accessed March 4, 2008).

Fealy, Greg. "Islamic Radicalism in Indonesia: The Faltering Revival?" *Southeast Asian Affairs 2004*. Singapore: Institute of Southeast Asian Studies, 2004, 104–121.

———. "Half a Century of Violent Jihad in Indonesia: A Historical and Ideological Comparison of Darul Islam and Jema'ah Islamiyah." In Vicziany and Wright-Neville, *Islamic Terrorism in Indonesia*, 15–32.

———, Virginia Hooker, and Sally White, "Indonesia." In *Voices of Islam in Southeast Asia: A Contemporary Sourcebook*, edited by Greg Fealy and Virginia Hooker, 39–50. Singapore: Institute of Southeast Asian Studies, 2006.

Feeney, Don J. Jr. "Entrancement in Islamic Fundamentalism." In Stout, *Psychology of Terrorism*, vol. 3, 191–209.

Ferracuti, Franco. "Ideology and Repentance: Terrorism in Italy." In Reich, *Origins of Terrorism*, 59–64.

Gallimore, Timothy. "Unresolved Trauma: Fuel for the Cycle of Violence and Terrorism." In Stout, *Psychology of Terrorism*, vol. 2, 143–64.

Gunaratna, Rohan. "Understanding Al Qaeda and its Network in Southeast Asia." In Ramakrishna and Tan, *After Bali*, 117–32.

Hall, Kenneth R. "Economic History of Early Southeast Asia." In Tarling, *Cambridge History of Southeast Asia*, vol. 1, pt. 1, 183–275.

Hamilton-Hart, Natasha. "Terrorism in Southeast Asia: Expert Analysis, Myopia and Fantasy." *The Pacific Review* 18 (2005): 303–25.

Hassan, Muhammad Haniff. "Imam Samudra's Justification for Bali Bombing." *Studies in Conflict and Terrorism* 30 (2007): 1033–56.

Hayes, J., and C. W. Allinson. "Cognitive Style and the Theory and Practice of Individual and Collective Learning in Organisations." *Human Relations* 51 (1998): 847–71.

Hoffman, Bruce. "The Emergence of the New Terrorism." In Tan and Ramakrishna, *The New Terrorism*, 30–49.

Horikoshi, Hiroko. "The Dar Ul-Islam Movement in West Java: An Experience in the Historical Process." *Indonesia* 20 (1975): 58–86.

Ileto, Reynaldo. "Religion and Anti-Colonial Movements." In Tarling, *Cambridge History of Southeast Asia*, vol. 2, pt. 1, 193–244.

Johnson, Ronald. "Psychoreligious Roots of Violence: The Search for the Concrete in a World of Abstractions." In Ellens, *Destructive Power of Religion*, vol. 4, 195–210.

Jones, David Martin, and Michael L. R. Smith. "Is There a Sovietology of Southeast Asian Studies?" *International Affairs* 77 (October 2001): 843–65.

Jones, Sidney. "Terrorism and 'Radical Islam' in Indonesia." In Vicziany and Wright-Neville, *Islamic Terrorism in Indonesia*, 1–13.

Kathirithamby-Wells, J. "The Age of Transition: The Mid-Eighteenth to the Early Nineteenth Centuries." In Tarling, *Cambridge History of Southeast Asia*, vol. 1, pt. 2, 228–75.

Kilcullen, David. "Globalization and the Development of Indonesian Counterinsurgency Tactics." *Small Wars and Insurgencies* 17 (March 2006): 44–64.

Kratoska, Paul, and Ben Batson. "Nationalism and Modernist Reform." In Tarling, *Cambridge History of Southeast Asia*, vol. 2, pt. 1, 245–320.

Krulak, Gen. Charles C. "The Strategic Corporal: Leadership in the Three-Block War." *Marines Magazine* (Jan. 1999), http://www.au.af.mil/au/awc/awcgate/usmc/strategic_corporal.htm (accessed February 26, 2008).

Lawal, Olufemi A. "Social-Psychological Considerations in the Emergence and Growth of Terrorism." In Stout, *Psychology of Terrorism*, vol. 4, 23–32.

Mack, John E. "Looking Beyond Terrorism: Transcending the Mind of Enmity." In Stout, *Psychology of Terrorism*, vol. 1, 173–84.

Martinez, Patricia. "Deconstructing *Jihad*: Southeast Asian Contexts." In Ramakrishna and Tan, *After Bali*, 59–79.

McCauley, Clark. "Psychological Issues in Understanding Terrorism and the Response to Terrorism." In Stout, *Psychology of Terrorism*, vol. 3, 3–29.

Momen, Moojan. "Fundamentalism and Liberalism: Towards an Understanding of the Dichotomy." *Bahai Studies Review* 2 (1992), http://www.breacais.demon.co.uk/abs/bsr02/22_momen_fundamentalism.htm (accessed April 1, 2008).

Pavlova, Elena. "An Ideological Response to Islamist Terrorism: Theoretical and Operational Overview." In *Terrorism in the Asia-Pacific: Threat and Response*, edited by Rohan Gunaratna, 30–45. Singapore: Eastern Universities Press, 2003.

Post, Jerrold M. "Terrorist Psycho-Logic: Terrorist Behavior as a Product of Psychological Forces." In Reich, *Origins of Terrorism*, 25–40.

Ramakrishna, Kumar. "The Making of a Malayan Propagandist: The Communists, the British and C. C. Too." *Journal of the Malaysian Branch of the Royal Asiatic Society* 73, pt. 1 (2000): 67–90.

———. "'Transmogrifying' Malaya: The Impact of Sir Gerald Templer (1952–54)." *Journal of Southeast Asian Studies* 32 (2001): 79–92.

———. "US Strategy in Southeast Asia: Counter-Terrorist or Counter-Terrorism?" In Ramakrishna and Tan, *After Bali*, 305–37.

———. "Making Malaya Safe For Decolonization: The Rural Chinese Factor in the Counterinsurgency Campaign." In *The Transformation of Southeast Asia: International Perspectives on Decolonization*, edited by Marc Frey, Ronald W. Pruessen, and Tan Tai Yong, 161–79. New York: M. E. Sharpe, 2003.

———. "The (Psychic) Roots of Religious Violence in South and Southeast Asia." In *Religion and Conflict in South and Southeast Asia: Disrupting Violence*, edited by Linell E. Cady and Sheldon W. Simon, 122–34. New York: Routledge, 2007.

———, and See Seng Tan, eds. *After Bali: The Threat of Terrorism in Southeast Asia*. Singapore: World Scientific, 2003.

Rapoport, David C. "The Fourth Wave: September 11 in the History of Terrorism." *Current History* 100 (2001): 419–24.

Reich, Walter, ed. *Origins of Terrorism: Psychologies, Ideologies, Theologies, States of Mind*. Washington D.C.: Woodrow Wilson Center Press, 1998.

———. "Understanding Terrorist Behavior: The Limits and Opportunities of Psychological Enquiry." In Reich, *Origins of Terrorism*, 261–79.

Sachs, Jeffrey. "Notes on a New Sociology of Economic Development." In *Culture Matters: How Values Shape Human Progress*, edited by Lawrence E. Harrison and Samuel P. Huntington, 29–43. New York: Basic Books, 2000.

Silke, Andrew. "Becoming a Terrorist." In *Terrorists, Victims and Society: Psychological Perspectives on Terrorism and its Consequences*, edited by Andrew Silke, 29–53. Chichester, UK: Wiley, 2003.

Simon, Steven, and Daniel Benjamin. "The Terror." *Survival* 43 (2001–2): 5–18.

Smith, Anthony L. "Terrorism and the Political Landscape in Indonesia: The Fragile Post-Bali Consensus." In Smith, *Terrorism and Violence in Southeast Asia*, 98–121.

Smith, Paul J., ed. *Terrorism and Violence in Southeast Asia: Transnational Challenges to States and Regional Stability*. New York: M. E. Sharpe, 2005.

Stevens, Michael J. "The Unanticipated Consequences of Globalization: Contextualizing Terrorism." In Stout, *Psychology of Terrorism*, vol. 3, 31–56.

Stirling, Mack C. "Violent Religion: Rene Girard's Theory of Culture." In Ellens, *Destructive Power of Religion*, vol. 2, 11–50.

Stout, Chris E., ed. *A Public Understanding*, vol. 1, *The Psychology of Terrorism*. Westport, Conn.: Praeger, 2002.

———, ed. *Clinical Aspects and Responses*, vol. 2, *The Psychology of Terrorism*. Westport, Conn.: Praeger, 2002.

———, ed. *Theoretical Understandings and Perspectives*, vol. 3, *The Psychology of Terrorism*. Westport, Conn.: Praeger, 2002.

———, ed., *Programs and Practices in Response and Prevention*, vol. 4, *The Psychology of Terrorism*. Westport, Conn.: Praeger, 2002.

Tajfel, Henri, and Joseph P. Forgas. "Social Categorization: Cognitions, Values and Groups." In *Stereotypes and Prejudice: Essential Readings*, edited by Charles Stangor, 49–63. Philadelphia: Psychology Press, 2000.

Tan, Andrew, and Kumar Ramakrishna, eds. *The New Terrorism: Anatomy, Trends and Counter-Strategies*. Singapore: Eastern Universities Press, 2002.

Tarling, Nicholas, ed. *From Early Times to circa 1500*. vol. 1, pt. 1, *The Cambridge History of Southeast Asia*. Cambridge: Cambridge University Press, 1999.

———, ed. *From c. 1500 to c. 1800*. vol. 1, pt. 2, *The Cambridge History of Southeast Asia*. Cambridge: Cambridge University Press, 1999.

———, ed. *From c. 1800 to the 1930s*, vol. 2, pt. 1, *The Cambridge History of Southeast Asia*. Cambridge University Press, 1999.

———, ed. *From World War Two to the Present*, vol. 2, pt. 2, *The Cambridge History of Southeast Asia*. Cambridge: Cambridge University Press, 1999.

Taylor, Keith W. "The Early Kingdoms." In Tarling, *Cambridge History of Southeast Asia*, vol. 1, pt. 1, 137–82.

Thayer, Carlyle A. "Al-Qaeda and Political Terrorism in Southeast Asia." In Smith, *Terrorism and Violence in Southeast Asia*, 79–97.

Thornton, Thomas Perry. "Terror as a Weapon of Political Agitation." In *Internal War*, edited by Harry Eckstein, 71–99. New York: The Free Press, 1964.

Van Bruinessen, Martin. "Indonesia's Ulama and Politics: Caught Between Legitimizing the Status Quo and Searching for Alternatives." *Prisma: The Indonesian Indicator* 49 (1990): 52–69.

Vicziany, Marika, and David Wright-Neville, eds. *Islamic Terrorism in Indonesia: Myths and Realities*. Melbourne: Monash University Press, 2005.

Woodward, Mark R. "The 'Slametan': Textual Knowledge and Ritual Performance in Central Javanese Islam." *History of Religions* 28 (1988): 54–89.

Yong, Mun Cheong, "The Political Structures of the Independent States." In Tarling, *Cambridge History of Southeast Asia*, vol. 2, pt. 2, 59–137.

WORKING PAPERS AND POLICY ANALYSES

Abuza, Zachary. "The Trial of Abu Bakar Ba'asyir: A Test Case for Indonesia." *Jamestown Terrorism Monitor* 2 (2004), http://www.jamestown.org/terrorism/news/article.php?articleid=2368802 (accessed March 4, 2008).

Deery, Phillip. "Malaya, 1948: Britain's 'Asian Cold War'?" The Cold War as Global Conflict Project, Working Paper 3. New York: International Center for Advanced Studies, New York University, April 2002.

Geertz, Clifford. "The Near East in the Far East: On Islam in Indonesia." Occasional Paper 12. Princeton: Institute for Advanced Study, December 2001.

Hasan, Noorhaidi. "Islamic Militancy, Sharia, and Democratic Consolidation in Post-Suharto Indonesia." Working Paper 143. Singapore: S. Rajaratnam School of International Studies, October 23, 2007.

How the Jemaah Islamiyah Terrorist Network Operates. Asia Report 43. Jakarta/Brussels: International Crisis Group, December 11, 2002.

Jemaah Islamiyah in Southeast Asia: Damaged But Still Dangerous. Asia Report 63. Jakarta/Brussels: International Crisis Group, August 26, 2003.

Liow, Chinyong Joseph. "Muslim Resistance in Southern Thailand and Southern Philippines: Religion, Ideology, and Politics." *East-West Center Policy Studies* 24. Washington, D.C.: East-West Center, 2006.

Lohman, Walter. "Guidelines for US Policy in Southeast Asia." *Backgrounder* 2017. Washington D.C.: The Heritage Foundation, March 20, 2007.

Noor, Farish A. "Ngruki Revisited: Modernity and Its Discontents at the Pondok Pesantren al-Mukmin of Ngruki, Surakarta." Working Paper 139. Singapore: S. Rajaratnam School of International Studies, October 1, 2007.

———. "Thinking the Unthinkable: The Modernization and Reform of Islamic Higher Education in Indonesia." Working Paper 152. Singapore: S. Rajaratnam School of International Studies, February 15, 2008.

Ramakrishna, Kumar. "'Constructing' the Jemaah Islamiyah Terrorist: A Preliminary Inquiry." Working Paper 71. Singapore: Institute of Defence and Strategic Studies, October 2004.

———. "It's the *Story*, Stupid: Developing a Counter-Strategy for Neutralizing Radical Islamism in Southeast Asia." *Countering Terrorist Ideologies Discussion Papers*. Wiltshire, UK: Advanced Research and Assessment Group, September 2005.

Why Salafism and Terrorism Mostly Don't Mix. Asia Report 83. Jakarta/Brussels: International Crisis Group, September 13, 2004.

NEWSPAPER AND PERIODICAL ARTICLES/ONLINE NEWS SOURCES

"A JI Attack Every Year—Mastermind Commands." *Sydney Times*, September 12, 2006.

"Abu Bakar Bashir: The Malaysian Connection." *Tempo* (Indonesia), November 9, 2002.

"Abu Ghraib Timeline." *CBC News Online* (Canada), February 18, 2005, http://www.cbc.ca/news/background/iraq/abughraib_timeline.html (accessed April 8, 2008).

Allard, Tom. "Head of JI 'Captured.'" *smh.com.au* (Australia). June 15, 2007, http://www.smh.com.au/news/world/head-of-ji-captured/2007/06/15/1181414530007.html?s_cid=rss_smh (accessed September 3, 2007).

Atran, Scott. "In Indonesia, Democracy is Not Enough." *New York Times.com*, October 2, 2005, http://www.nytimes.com/2005/10/05/opinion/05atran.html?pagewanted=1&ei=5088&en=6e98aa49e50af97a&ex=1286164800&partner=rssnyt&emc=rss (accessed September 4, 2007).

"Azahari: Professor, Bomb-Maker and Fanatic." *Channelnewsasia.com* (Singapore), September 10, 2004, http://www.channelnewsasia.com/stories/afp_asiapacific/view/105933/1/.html (accessed September 10, 2004).

"Ba'asyir Declares New Political Islamist Group," *Jakarta Post*, September 17, 2008.

Behrend, Tim. "Meeting Abubakar Ba'asyir." December 23, 2002, http://www.arts.auckland.ac.nz/asia/tbehrend/meet-abb.htm (accessed 2003).

Behrend, Tim. "Reading Past the Myth: Public Teachings of Abu Bakar Ba'asyir." February 19, 2003, http://www.arts.auckland.ac.nz/asia/tbehrend/abb-myth.htm (accessed April 30, 2004).

Chalk Peter, and William Rosenau. "Southeast Asia the Second Front of Global Terror?" *The Nation Multimedia.com* (Thailand), September 21, 2006, http://www.nationmultimedia.com/specials/south2years/sep2106.php (accessed September 3, 2007).

"Charting the Evolution of Jemaah Islamiyah." *South China Morning Post* (Hong Kong), September 7, 2006.

Chew, Amy. "A Jemaah Islamiyah Surge Bodes Ill for Poso." *New Straits Times* (Malaysia), March 1, 2007.

————. "Indonesian Police Capture JI Leader." *New Straits Times* (Malaysia), June 16, 2007.

————. "Anti-Terror Police Now Set Sights on Asia's Most Wanted Militant." *South China Morning Post* (Hong Kong), August 7, 2007.

————. "Soft-Spoken Militant Has Steely View of the Future—Muslims Will Rule the World, Says Alleged JI Commander." *South China Morning Post* (Hong Kong), August 7, 2007.

Dawson, John. "The Bali Bombers: What Motivates Death Worship?" *Capitalism Magazine*, October 19, 2003, http://www.capmag.com/article.asp?ID=3000 (accessed September 1, 2004).

Day, Michael, and David Bamber. "Universities Spy for MI5 on Foreign Students." *news.telegraph.co.uk,* August 28, 2004, http://www.telegraph.co.uk/news/main.jhtml?xml=/news/2004/03/21/nspy21.xml&sSheet=/news/2004/03/21/ixnewstop.html (accessed September 11, 2004).

Dhume, Sadanand. "Step Up the Fight Against Islamism." *Far Eastern Economic Review,* July/August 2007.

Donnan, Shawn. "Trial Witness Links Indonesian Cleric to Bombings." *FT.com* (UK), June 26, 2003, http://search.ft.com/search/article.html?id=030626004586 (accessed March 4, 2008).

Edwards, Verity, and Cameron Stewart. "Professor Warned Off Terrorist Trip." *Australian*, September 13, 2006, http://www.theaustralian.news.com.au/story/0,20867,20402378-12332,00.html (accessed August 9, 2008).

Escobar, Pepe. "The Islamic Emirate of Fallujah." *Asia Times Online*, July 15, 2004, http://atimes.com/atimes/Middle_East/FG15Ak01.html (accessed February 26, 2008).

Fitzpatrick, Stephen. "Corruption Threatens Anti-Terror Bid in Jails." *Australian*, November 20, 2007.

Forbes, Mark. "Terrorism Network Commanded from Jail." *Sydney Morning Herald* (Australia), October 11, 2006.

————. "Radicals in Retreat." *theage.com.au* (Australia), August 26, 2007, http://www.theage.com.au/news/in-depth/radicals-in-retreat/2007/08/25/1187462586317.html (accessed September 3, 2007).

Ghani, Azhar. "Forget Bombings . . . JI Changes Goals; Militant Group Gives Up Regional Aim To Focus on Creating an Islamic Nation, Sources Say." *Straits Times* (Singapore), November 17, 2006.

————. "JI Terrorists Switch Focus to Local Sectarian Conflicts: They Feel Attacks on Western Targets Are Costly and Cause Outrage When Muslims Are Killed." *Straits Times* (Singapore), May 4, 2007.

Gutkin, Steven. "Asia Radicals Divided On Killing Muslims." Associated Press, December 9, 2003.

Harding, Andrew. "The Bali Jihadist on a Peace Mission." *BBC News*, March 14, 2008.

Ibrahim, Zuraidah. "Singapore JI Trio Accuse Bashir." *Straits Times* (Singapore), June 27, 2003.

"Indonesian Defence Minister Says Hambali No Longer 'Useful'." *Kabar-Indonesia*, October 9, 2006, http://72.14.253.104/search?q=cache:TR00V6_TOpYJ:www.kabar-irian.info/pipermail/kabar-indonesia/2006-October/012152.html+hambali,+no+access&hl=en&ct=clnk&cd=1&gl=sg (accessed August 24, 2007).

"Indonesian Linked to Manila, Jakarta Bombings." *Laksamana.Net,* July 6, 2002, http://www.laksamana.net/vnews.cfm?ncat=22&news_id=3127 (accessed September 11, 2004).

Ismail, Noor Huda. "Ngruki: It is a Terrorism School?" *Jakarta Post*, March 14–15, 2005, http://www.gusdur.net/english/index.php?option=com_content&task=view&id=699&Itemid=1 (accessed August 11, 2008).

Jenkins, Brian M. "Terrorists Want a Lot of People Watching, Not a Lot of People Dead." *Quest for Peace* Web site, University of California at Irvine, http://www.lib.uci.edu/quest/index.php?page=jenkins (accessed August 20, 2007).

"JI Responsible for Jakarta Bombing: Statement." *ABC News Online* (Australia), September 10, 2004, http://www.abc.net.au/news/newsitems/200409/s1196027.htm (accessed September 3, 2007).

"Khalid Sheikh Mohammed." *Biography.Com*, 2007, http://www.biography.com/search/article.do?id=241188 (accessed March 6, 2008).

Lilienfeld, Scott O., and Hal Arkowitz. "What 'Psychopath' Means: It Is Not Quite What You May Think." *Scientific American Mind*, December 2007/January 2008.

Lopez, Leslie. "Key JI Men Poised to Fill Leadership Vacuum." *Straits Times* (Singapore), August 8, 2007.

Luban, Daniel. "Blackwater Pays Price For Iraqi Firefight." *Asia Times Online*, September 19, 2007, http://www.atimes.com/atimes/Middle_East/II19Ak04.html (accessed February 26, 2008).

"Madrid Remembers Train Bombings." *BBC News*, March 11, 2005, http://news.bbc.co.uk/2/hi/europe/4338727.stm (accessed September 4, 2007).

Mapes, Timothy. "Indonesian School Gives High Marks to Students Embracing Intolerance." *Asian Wall Street Journal*, September 2, 2003.

Marks, Kathy. "First Suspect Stands Trial for Attack on 'White Meat' in Bali Blast." *Independent* (UK), May 10, 2003, http://findarticles.com/p/articles/mi_qn4158/is_20030510/ai_n12684197/pg_1 (accessed February 8, 2008).

"Marriott Blast Suspects Named." *CNN.com*, August 19, 2003, http://www.cnn.com/2003/WORLD/asiapcf/southeast/08/19/indonesia.arrests.names/index.html (accessed September 3, 2007).

McBeth, John. "Terrorist Tactics Changing in Indonesia." *Straits Times* (Singapore), August 30, 2006.

McEvers, Kelly. "Visiting the Space Where the Sari Club Used to Be." *Slate.com*, posted November 2, 2005.

Michaels, Jim. "Petraeus Strategy Takes aim at Post-Vietnam Mindset." *USA Today.Com,* March 7, 2007, http://www.usatoday.com/news/world/iraq/2007-03-07-petraeus_N.htm (accessed March 5, 2008).

"Top Terrorist Azahari Reported Killed In Raid." *Paras Indonesia*, November 9, 2005, http://www.parasindonesia.com/read.php?gid=119 (accessed March 11, 2008).

"US Announces $350 million in Tsunami Aid." *MSNBC*, December 31, 2004, http://www.msnbc.msn.com/id/6767190/ (accessed February 26, 2008).

Van Bruinessen, Martin. "The Violent Fringes of Indonesia's Radical Islam." December 2002, http://www.let.uu.nl/~martin.vanbruinessen/personal/publications/violent_fringe.htm (accessed July 29, 2004).

Vatikiotis, Michael. "Terrorism and the Problem of Binary Vision." *Asia Times Online*, August 29, 2006, http://www.atimes.com/atimes/Southeast_Asia/HH29Ae01.html (accessed March 15, 2008).

Wahid, Abdurrahman. "Best Way to Fight Islamic Extremism." *Sunday Times* (Singapore), April 14, 2002.

Wong, Chun Wai, and Lourdes Charles. "More than 100 Marriages Involve Key JI Members." *The Star Online* (Malaysia), September 7, 2004, http://thestar.com.my/news/archives/story.asp?ppath=%5C2004%5C9% (accessed September 11, 2004).

Woodward, Mark R. "President Gus Dur: Indonesia, Islam and *Reformasi*." N.d., http://web.archive.org/web/20030219093713/http://www.asu.edu/clas/asian/pubs/woodward.htm (accessed October 18, 2007).

"Wounded But Still Dangerous: Terrorism in Southeast Asia." *Economist* (US Edition), June 16, 2007.

Yusof, Zalman Mohamed, and Mohammad Ishak. "Inside a JI School." *New Paper on Sunday* (Singapore), January 4, 2004.

Zabriskie, Phil. "Did You Hear . . . ?" *Time (Asia),* March 10, 2003.

Published Official Reports

"ASEM "Bali Interfaith Dialogue." July 21–22, 2005, http://www.aseminfoboard.org/content/documents/050722_BaliDeclaration.pdf (accessed March 5, 2008).

Civil Paths to Peace: Report of the Commonwealth Commission on Respect and Understanding. London: Commonwealth Secretariat, 2007.

"Second Asia-Europe Youth Interfaith Dialogue 2008." Asia-Europe Foundation Web site, http://www.asef.org/index.php?option=com_project&task=view&id=1079 (accessed March 5, 2008).

Silber, Mitchell D., and Arvin Bhatt. *Radicalization in the West: The Homegrown Threat*. New York: New York Police Department Intelligence Division, 2007.

Singapore. Ministry of Home Affairs. *The Jemaah Islamiyah Arrests and the Threat of Terrorism*. Cmd. 2 of 2003. January 7, 2003.

United Nations Office of Drug and Crime (UNODC). "Definitions of Terrorism." N.d., http://www.unodc.org/unodc/terrorism_definitions.html (accessed August 16, 2007).

Wike, Richard, Pew Global Attitudes Project, and Brian J. Grim, Pew Forum on Religion and Public Life. "Widespread Negativity: Muslims Distrust Westerners More Than Vice Versa." October 30, 2007, http://pewresearch.org/pubs/625/widespread-negativity (accessed February 26, 2008).

UNPUBLISHED PAPERS, DISSERTATIONS, DOCUMENTS, AND PRESENTATIONS

Papers, Dissertations, and Presentations

Anza, Usmar. "Islamic Education: A Brief History of Madrassas with Comments on Curricula and Current Pedagogical Practices." Unpublished paper, March 2003.

Azra, Azyumardi. "The Megawati Presidency: The Challenge of Political Islam." Paper presented at the Joint Forum on the First 100 Days of the Megawati Presidency, organized by the Institute of Southeast Asian Studies (Singapore), and the Center for Strategic and International Studies (Jakarta), Singapore, November 1, 2001.

———. "The Transmission of Islamic Reformism to Indonesia: Networks of Middle Eastern and Malay-Indonesian Ulama in the 17th and 18th Centuries." PhD diss., Columbia University, 1992.

Fuller Collins, Elizabeth. "Dakwah and Democracy: The Significance of Partai Keadilan and Hizbut Tahrir." Paper presented at the International Seminar on Islamic Militant Movements in Southeast Asia, Jakarta, July 22–23, 2003.

Ismail, Noor Huda. Presentation on Pondok Pesantren Al-Mukmin, Institute of Defence and Strategic Studies (since Jan. 1, 2007, the S. Rajaratnam School of International Studies), Nanyang Technological University, Singapore, April 8, 2005.

Karnavian, M. Tito. "Rehabilitative Program of Terrorists in Indonesia." Workshop presentation, London, November 8, 2007.

Metcalf, Barbara D. "'Traditionalist Islamic Activism: Deoband, Tablighis, and Talibs." International Institute for the Study of Islam in the Modern World (ISIM) Annual Lecture, Leiden University, November 23, 2001.

Pastika, Made Mangku. "The Uncovering of the Bali Blast Case." Presentation, Jakarta, January 20, 2003.

Singh, Bilveer. "The Emergence of the Jemaah Islamiyah Threat in Southeast Asia: External Linkages and Influences." Paper presented at a workshop on International Terrorism in Southeast Asia and Likely Implications for South Asia, organized by the Observer Research Foundation, New Delhi, India, April 28–29, 2004.

Suprapto, Brig-General Bekto. "De-Radicalisation Strategy and Practices in Indonesia." Paper presented at a seminar in London, October 2007.

Van Bruinessen, Martin. "'Traditionalist' and 'Islamist' Pesantren in Contemporary Indonesia." Paper presented at the workshop on The Madrasa in Asia: Transnational Linkages and Alleged or Real Political Activities, organized by the International Institute for the Study of Islam in the Modern World (ISIM), Leiden, Netherlands, May 24–25, 2004.

Woodward, Mark R. "Introduction to Abdurrahman Wahid, Islam Pluralism and Democracy." Consortium for Strategic Communication, Arizona State University, April 19, 2007.

Yunanto, S. "Darul Islam (DI) and Jemaah Islamiyah (JI): The Dynamics of Militant Islamic Movements in Indonesia." Paper presented at the International Seminar on Religion and Conflict, organized by Parahyangan Catholic University, Indonesia Conflict Study Network and Asia Links, Bandung, January 10-11, 2005.

Yunanto, S. "The Rise of Radical Islamist Groups in Indonesia and the Political and Security Consequences of the Political Activities." Paper presented at the International Conference on Democratization and the Issue of Terrorism in Indonesia, organized by the Department of International Relations, Parahyangan Catholic University and Konrad Adenauer Stiftung, Jakarta Office, Bandung, April 13, 2005.

Official Indonesian Documents (English Translations)

Amrozi bin Nurhasyim

Transcript of "Official Report of Further Interrogation." Balinese Police Force, Detective Directorate, November 14, 2002.

Transcript of "Official Report of Confrontation." Balinese Police Force, Detective Directorate, November 15, 2002 (witnessed by Silvester Tendean, Gubeng, Surabaya).

"Results of Psychological Investigation." November 15, 2002.

Transcript of "Official Report of Further Interrogation." Balinese Police Force, Detective Directorate, November 23, 2002.

Transcript of "Official Report of Interrogation." Balinese Police Force, Detective Directorate, November 27, 2002.

Transcript of "Official Report of Further Interrogation." Balinese Police Force, Detective Directorate, November 28, 2002.

Transcript of "Official Report of Further Interrogation." Balinese Police Force, Detective Directorate, December 13, 2002.

Transcript of "Official Report of Further Interrogation." Balinese Police Force, Detective Directorate, December 14, 2002.

Imam Samudra

Transcript of Police Interview, November 29, 2002.
Transcript of Police Interview, December 16, 2002.
Transcript of Police Interview, January 12, 2003.

Ali Ghufron bin Nurhasyim, @ Mukhlas

"Police Statement." Bali Region Police Detective Directorate, December 13, 2002.
"Police Statement." Bali Region Police Detective Directorate, December 14, 2002.
"Police Statement, Additional." Bali Region Police Detective Directorate, December 16, 2002.
"Police Statement, Additional." Bali Region Police Detective Directorate, December 30, 2002.
"Police Statement, Additional." Bali Region Police Detective Directorate, January 6, 2003.

DOCUMENTARIES

Bombali, television documentary, written by Phil Craig and Steve Westh. Produced by Electric Pictures Productions and Brook Lapping Productions, FilmFinance Four, Australia, 2006.

AUTHOR INTERVIEWS

Al Chaidar, January 8, 2006.
Col. M. Tito Karnavian, November 9, 2007.

Index